The J.C. Nichols Chronicle

J.C. Nichols died on February 16, 1950, just before his 70th birthday. This portrait, which hangs in Miller's office, is said to be an excellent likeness, catching his intensity, purposefulness, and vision.

The
J.C. Nichols Chronicle

The Authorized Story
of the Man, His Company,
and His Legacy,
1880–1994

by
Robert Pearson
and
Brad Pearson

Published by the
Country Club Plaza Press

Distributed by
the University Press of Kansas

Distributed by the University Press of Kansas
2501 West 15th Street
Lawrence, Kansas 66049

Pearson, Robert, 1917–
    The J.C. Nichols chronicle: the authorized story of the man and
his company / by Robert Pearson and Brad Pearson.
      p.   cm.
    Includes bibliographical references and index.
    ISBN 0-7006-0685-8 (alk. paper : cloth)
    1. Nichols, Jesse Clyde.   2. City planners—Missouri—Kansas City—
Biography.   3. Real estate developers—Missouri—Kansas City—
Biography.   I. Pearson, Brad.   II. Title.
HT168.K2P43   1994
307.1′216′092—dc20
[B]   94-12824

British Library Cataloguing in Publication Data is available.

Printed in the United States of America

10 9 8 7 6 5 4 3 2 1

The paper used in this publication meets the minimum
requirements of the American National Standard for Permanence of Paper for Printed Library Materials Z39.48-1984.

Contents

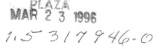

List of Illustrations

Chapter 9   **1978 - 1994**

Introduction

The name of city planner and developer Jesse Clyde Nichols is still known to Kansas Citians if only through such place-names as the J.C. Nichols Parkway, the J.C. Nichols fountain, and J.C. Nichols School. Residents also take great pride in the nationally known Country Club Plaza, one of the showplaces of the city, which they correctly associate with the J.C. Nichols Company—one of the oldest real estate firms in the United States. However, Nichols died in 1950, and few Kansas Citians today are aware of his dominant influence in and driving force behind the Liberty Memorial, the Nelson-Atkins Museum of Art, the Kansas City Art Institute, and the Midwest Research Institute.

J.C. Nichols' seminal contribution to his city and his country, however, was his planning for permanence in the residential developments he built. Before he became active in real estate, the concepts of city planning, zoning, and protection of residential property through deed restrictions were virtually unknown. But through his perseverance in developing these concepts, Nichols' Country Club District, comprising roughly the southwestern quadrant of the city in his time, became a model area of gracious and beautiful homes that have continued to increase in desirability and value for nearly a century. And Nichols, through his active leadership in national real estate organizations, was able to carry his gospel to the industry, nationwide.

Nichols devoted most of the last third of his life to public service. Among other activities, he was a member of the National Capital Planning Commission for 22 years; a division head of the National Defense Advisory Council just prior to World War II, which enabled him to bring industry to the plains states; and a leader of a long but eventually successful campaign to make the Missouri River navigable.

In 1987, Jesse Clyde Nichols' sons, Miller and Clyde, Jr., then in their seventies, decided that their father's remarkable life and legacy deserved to be chronicled in book form. They engaged Dr. James Olson, the recently retired president of the University of Missouri at Kansas City, to study the feasibility of such a project and to determine sources of research. On the basis of Dr. Olson's favorable report, the Nichols family and the J.C. Nichols Company commissioned the authors to write this book.

We are neither scholars nor historians, so this is not a scholarly history. We are a father-and-son team of professional writers with experience and credentials in this genre. We were given access to the J.C. Nichols Company records and received the cooperation of family members, company associates, civic leaders in Kansas City, and others for interviews, which were taped and transcribed. We are also indebted to the Miller Nichols Library and the Western Historical Manuscript Collection at the University of Missouri at Kansas City (which houses the Nichols papers), the Liberty Memorial archives, the Nelson-Atkins Museum of Art, the *Kansas City Star* morgue, the Kansas City Board of Park Commissioners, and the Missouri Valley Room of the Kansas City Public Library. Our research also took us to Washington, D.C., to the National Archives and the archives of the Urban Land Institute; to the Chicago archives of the National Association of Realtors; and by telephone to sources in Colorado and California.

From the beginning, it was evident that understanding J.C. Nichols and his work would be impossible without understanding the city he influenced so profoundly, the times in which he worked, the history of real estate development before his time, and the story of his company both during his life and afterward.

Although we cannot mention all the individuals to whom we are indebted, we wish especially to acknowledge Jeannette (Mrs. Miller) Nichols, once a research associate at *Fortune* magazine, who took a keen interest in the project and was of immense help; Lee Fowler, retired vice president of the J.C. Nichols Company, who was our ever-available contact there; Conger Beasley, Jr., for his editing and Betsy Beasley for her photo editing; and Fred Woodward, director of the University Press of Kansas, for his interest and encouragement.

Robert Pearson
Brad Pearson

Prologue

Jesse Clyde Nichols, Jr., recalls his father's arrival at the end of the day at their palatial home at 1214 West 55th Street in Kansas City, Missouri. Hardly inside the door, he would collapse onto the sofa, still in his business suit, moaning, "Oh, Lord, I'm tired!" He would lie with his eyes closed—entering occasionally nonetheless into the family conversation going on around him—until he was called to dinner. More often than not, at the sound of the doorbell, J.C. would jump up from the sofa or dinner table, saying: "That's so-and-so. We have to go to such-and-such meeting." And out the door he would dash.

Jesse Clyde Nichols in the Incredible 1920s

This scene was perhaps most typical of the decade of the 1920s, when J.C. Nichols was in his forties, soaring like a rocket across the local and national sky. The kaleidoscope of activity and leadership that characterized his life was best exemplified in this ten-year era, coming as it did 15 years after he built his first house in the Country Club District and before the Great Depression, World War II, and the postwar recovery years that preceded his death.

He had been mostly bald since his early twenties, having only a fringe of hair around the back of his head. He liked to banter with his barber, claiming that he should get a discount for a haircut. Rather large, brown eyes gazed intently from behind rimless spectacles, and his other features were strong and even. His round face was smooth, without lines or wrinkles. Of medium height, he was portly but not heavyset. Although his well-cut suits and other clothing indicated his position as a business executive and leading citizen of the city, he was notoriously indifferent to his sartorial appearance. A chain smoker—which eventually led to his death—he was too preoccupied to use an ashtray consistently and often let the cigarette ashes fall onto his coat and vest.

Ernest Holt, the Nichols chauffeur, recalls that J.C. would jump out of the car and tramp through a field or muddy building site in his polished leather shoes. Ernest carried a spare pair of shoes for himself in the car in case he had to follow, but his employer never did. Evelyn Fisher, a maid at the Nichols house, was able to keep J.C. in clean shirts by simply grabbing soiled shirts from his room and throwing them down the clothes chute. But keeping him in presentable suits was a bigger challenge because he refused to spend money for dry cleaning. If a suit were spotted or soiled, he would say to Evelyn, "Just use a wet washcloth on that."

Finally Mrs. Nichols (Jessie) and clothier Jack Henry devised their own conspiracy. When Jessie decided it was time for J.C. to buy a new suit, she would call Jack Henry and tell him to take a selection of suitings over to her husband's office. After J.C. had made his choice and later had it fitted by a tailor in the office, Jack would make up *two* identical suits. One would be delivered to J.C.'s closet and the other sequestered in another closet at the far end of the house. When one suit became soiled, Evelyn would replace it with an identical clean suit and send the soiled one to the cleaner. J.C. was so intent on more important matters that he never caught on. One day, however, he happened to look in the storage closet and asked Clyde, Jr., who was passing nearby, "What are all these suits doing in here?" Clyde answered quickly, "Oh, those are just some of Miller's clothes he put in there." It was a close call, says Clyde.

It is small wonder that Jesse Clyde Nichols was near exhaustion at the end of a day, for his activities and involvements during this single decade were legion. His Country Club District was already recognized nationally and internationally as the country's finest residential community. The basic land had been assembled, over 4,000 acres, and the area composed the world's largest contiguous development of quality single-family homes under single management.

The J.C. Nichols Company had embarked on building homes, not simply selling building lots. Restrictions, filed with the plat and self-perpetuating, applied to each of the subdivisions, assuring that the value of the homes would be preserved. Landscape planning, architectural control, and the placement of statuary and art objects throughout the Country Club District had made it an example of beauty. Homes associations were formed for each new subdivision, and not only was J.C. personally involved with their organization and elected officers, but he always seemed to find time to attend their field days, flower shows, beautification projects, and annual dinners.

The J.C. Nichols Company grew and changed dramatically during the twenties. It had begun with such basic functions as land acquisition, engineering, the grading and paving of streets, the laying of sewers and water mains, and sales. It operated its own machine shop, planing mill, and cabinet shop, and a loan department arranged financing for home buyers.

During the 1920s the company organized a department to develop business and apartment properties. It started its own nursery under famed horticulturist Stanley McLane, and the nursery became one of the largest in the nation, with as many as 125,000 shrubs and trees under cultivation at any one time for the beautification of the district. A farm department was organized to handle properties, not only in the Kansas City area, but in the Southwest and West. J.C. kept his officers and department managers stirred up and motivated with a constant barrage of questions, memos, and personal meetings; he also knew most of the company's employees by name.

Conceived and planned over several years, construction of the Country Club Plaza, the nation's first shopping center, began in 1922, and its development, improvement, and beautification have not ceased since. During the 1920s, J.C. met continually with architects, purchased attractive art objects, counted customers' cars in the parking lots, and literally noted any flyspecks on the storekeepers' show windows.

Nichols' influence also spread rapidly outside Kansas City. In 1920, the National Association of Real Estate Boards held its annual convention in Kansas City. The association's national secretary, Tom Ingersoll, declared: "The Country Club District . . . is the national model of high-class [residential] development. . . . It has elevated the entire real estate profession and is vitally affecting many of our larger cities." City planners from other sections of the United States and from other countries came to observe, admire, and learn from J.C. Nichols. After one such visit, William K. Midgley reported in the *London News* how the Country Club District's homes associations "provided community services and maintained community spirit." British city planner Charles Read commented after several trips that "not another such spot in the world nor another man have done so much to bring beauty and comfort into everyday life."

Fellow Kansas Citian, lumber baron, and philanthropist Robert A. Long called upon his friend J.C. Nichols in the 1920s to plan and advise in laying out the city of Longview, Washington. After J.C. had made a number of trips and devoted considerable time and energy to the task, he had pretty well decided on $25,000 as his fee. But Long got one up on him by saying, in effect, "J.C., I realize you wouldn't really want to be paid for this project, so I'm honoring you by naming the main street of Longview Nichols Boulevard." Nonplussed, J.C. was speechless for one of the few times in his life, and Nichols Boulevard is there today.

On another occasion, J.C. was asked to consult with three visitors concerned with planning Oklahoma City. He was offered $1,000 a day, a huge fee in those days. Nichols, who was noted for wearing out

younger men who tried to follow him for even a single day, apparently wanted to give his visitors their money's worth. They hardly paused for breath during five days, after which one of the visitors was taken to the hospital with nervous exhaustion; another, upon his return home, took a week off to rest.

Nichols was the nation's most outspoken proponent of city planning and zoning during the teens and 1920s. Traveling throughout the country, he made talks on these subjects before local civic-planning associations, at conferences, and especially at real estate conventions. Some of the talks were published and distributed in pamphlet form. By 1919, several cities had formed planning commissions, including St. Louis, Minneapolis, and Denver, with Cleveland in the process.

Ironically, Nichols' early efforts in his own city met with considerable resistance, even though he was chairman of the city-planning committees of both the Chamber of Commerce and the Real Estate Board. In the early 1920s, his efforts did result in the adoption of a much-needed planning ordinance for Kansas City. J.C. Nichols was a pioneer in the development of zoning regulations, and in 1923 Kansas City became one of the first cities to establish zoning to protect property values. He continued his efforts at the state level until both Missouri and Kansas enacted planning and zoning legislation.

As chairman of the National Council of Real Estate Subdividers, he vigorously spread his "city beautiful" gospel. As vice-president of the American Civic Association, he attended an international housing conference in Rome. He represented the National Planning Conference in the United States at a town planning conference in London, England, after which he toured England and Spain, gathering ideas and looking for art objects to beautify the Country Club District and the Country Club Plaza. President Calvin Coolidge appointed him as one of nine outstanding developers to represent the United States at the Fourth International Conference of the Building Industry in Paris. At home, the American City Plan Conference named him one of the nation's outstanding community builders.

Widening fame led to what he regarded as "one of the most gratifying achievements of my life" when President Coolidge invited him to serve on the National Capital Park and Planning Commission upon its establishment in 1926. This proved to be one of his most time-consuming responsibilities. He journeyed to Washington, D.C., for the commission's weekend meetings every month for the next 22 years; each meeting took at least two full days plus travel time. This small body of prominent citizens literally shaped the design and appearance of the nation's capital.

Meanwhile, in his home city, he was a leader throughout the decade in planning and bringing about construction of the Liberty Memorial. Vice chairman of the overall committee (chaired by R. A. Long), Nichols served as chairman of the Committee on Location. An immense responsibility in itself, the memorial, under J.C.'s guidance, became part of two of his other pet objectives: the beautification of the unsightly view of shanties, billboards, and raw bluffs that greeted visitors as they stepped from the handsome new Union Station and the creation of a civic and cultural center that would be the pride of every Kansas Citian.[1] As one of the three trustees of the William Rockhill Nelson trust, and subsequently one of three university trustees for the gallery, J.C. took on the task of assembling the art collec-

tion for and later the operation of the Nelson Gallery of Art and Mary Atkins Museum. In the 1920s he also served as president of the Kansas City Art Institute, as a director on the board of the Kansas City Little Symphony, and as treasurer of the Conservatory of Music.

Education was one of his consuming interests. In the first half of the 1920s, he was active on the Kansas City school board. He was a leader in establishing two private schools within his district: the Sunset Hill School for girls, of which he was acting chairman of the board at one time, and the Country Day School for boys to which he gave both time and money. Also in the 1920s, he was part of a drive led by William Volker, another Nelson estate trustee, to establish the University of Kansas City.

For eight years he led a campaign to get a new Kansas City water plant and system built for the growing city. Chairman of the "Committee of 25," he worked with the state legislature and struggled mightily to rouse the lethargic business community to support the project. Finally, in 1921, he "beat the streets" personally to raise funds to ensure the passage of an $11-million bond issue; the resulting plant still serves the city.

Throughout the decade, J.C. Nichols led a herculean effort to make the Missouri River navigable—an accomplishment that he felt would be of tremendous value to Kansas City and the region. To this end, he organized a ten-state association and made talks up and down the length of the river to drum up enthusiasm and support. He made numerous trips to Washington, D.C., to testify before congressional committees and to lobby for the project. The battle was finally won when Congress appropriated $100 million, followed by other funds, to dredge a channel the length of the river. By the mid-1930s, barges were carrying grain from the farms of the Midwest to New Orleans and the Gulf, and railroads were forced to reduce their freight rates to a competitive level, thus benefiting the economy of the whole region.

Simultaneously, he campaigned vigorously for better roads, making frequent trips to Topeka and Jefferson City leading delegations to lobby Kansas and Missouri legislatures for this cause. And in talks before farm groups and business organizations, he urged support for road improvement.

During this period, he also served energetically as a director of the Commerce Trust Company, the Kansas City Title and Trust Company, the Business Men's Assurance Company, the Kansas City Fire and Insurance Company, and the Mission Hills Country Club. Not incidentally, he had family obligations as husband to his supportive and strong-minded wife, Jessie, and father to his growing children, daughter Eleanor and sons Miller and Clyde, Jr.

The man's seemingly inexhaustible energy and diversity of efforts led historians of the time to state: "The greatest impact on Kansas City came from a young man, J.C. Nichols, whose activities touched virtually every phase of civic activity. During this period, the story of J.C. Nichols was a large part of the story of Kansas City." They might have added, "and of the Midwest region and even of the nation."[2]

Chapter 1

Before 1880

Jesse Clyde Nichols has sometimes been characterized by journalists as a kind of Horatio Alger hero who pulled himself up from humble beginnings by his bootstraps. This impression may have arisen from the fact that young Clyde, while still a boy, worked for neighbors to make money and because as a youth, with an abundance of energy and intensity, he had several money-making enterprises. The impression is wrong.

Family Heritage

Like his wife, Jessie Eleanor Miller, Nichols came from strong pioneering stock. His father was a distinguished citizen of Olathe, Kansas, not rich but comfortably prosperous. His mother, a strong and resourceful woman, led a life straight out of a historical novel. Jessie Eleanor Miller's father was one of the most successful and wealthy men in Johnson County, Kansas, and her mother's family went back to the beginnings of the nation.

Nichols' paternal grandparents, Thomas T. Nichols and Elizabeth Hoge Nichols, lived near St. Clairsville, Ohio. The Hoges were of Scottish ancestry and Quakers by birthright and training. One of Thomas and Elizabeth's eight children, Jesse Thomas Nichols, born in 1847, enlisted as a private in the Ohio National Guard in the Civil War—as did two other brothers, despite their Quaker upbringing. After the war, in 1869, the family headed west, ending up in Johnson County, Kansas. They spent the first winter in Kansas City, Missouri, and then settled on a 220-acre farm northwest of Olathe.

Kansas, named after the Kanza tribe of Indians, had been Indian territory until it became the 34th state in 1861. Johnson County got its name from the Rev. Thomas Johnson, who organized a mission for the Shawnee Indians in 1829. Wagon trains bound west were outfitted in Westport, on the Kansas-Missouri state line, before setting out through Johnson County. Olathe, incorporated in 1856, was the county's largest and most important town.

Jesse Clyde's maternal grandmother, Fannie Oslin, was born in Newton County, Georgia, in 1835. The first Oslin in America had settled in Virginia in the late 1600s. Fannie recalled that in her early childhood her parents were well-to-do, but that later they met with financial reverses and moved in 1843 to Cobb County, Georgia, "a wild, new country." Their log home was near Stone Mountain, on a hill overlooking a river. As no free schools existed in the South at that time, Fannie attended simple country schools supported by the childrens' parents until age 13, when she was sent to a boarding school in Atlanta for one year.

She had known Zachariah Nathaniel

"Zach" Jackson from childhood. His parents were neighbors, so Fannie and Zach had been together at school, Sunday school, and parties. As they matured, the childhood playmates fell in love; they married on December 24, 1850, when Fannie was 15. Four of their six children were born in Georgia: Horace, the eldest; then Joanna, called "Josie"; Emma; and finally, Joe Brown, who died of smallpox at a young age.[3] As frontier farmers, the Jacksons suffered hardships and sickness.

Although reared in Georgia, Fannie and Zach had strong antislavery feelings. In the early 1860s, talk of secession heated up. Zach was against it, as were many others in northern Georgia. After South Carolina seceded in 1861, almost every able-bodied male was pressed into service. Zach reluctantly enlisted in the 8th Georgia Battalion, hoping for local duty; but the unit was conscripted into the Confederate Army, where he was made a captain.

Fannie was left to labor in the fields and care for her young children without help. The Union blockade of southern seaports caused severe shortages that made life even harder. Then, on May 8, 1864, General Sherman's Union Army drove the retreating Confederate forces through Snake Creek Gap. Northern units bivouacked at the Jackson farm, taking cows, sheep, hogs, and chickens, as well as the garden crops and meal.

Five days after the Union occupation, Lt. Col. LeDuc, attached to Maj. Gen. Joseph Hooker's corps, was asleep in his tent nearby when he heard what he thought was a baby's cry. He rose and traced the sound to the Jackson cabin. Peering in, he saw the floor covered with wounded and sick Union soldiers. Nursing them before an open fire was Fannie Jackson. She explained to LeDuc that the cry he heard was the bleating of her children's hidden pet lamb. Touched by her courage and compassion, the officer had his orderlies care for the lamb and gave Mrs. Jackson two sacks of corn and some pork. He also wrote her a letter of commendation. A few weeks later, sending her son Horace to stay with neighbors but taking nine-year-old Joanna and her younger sister, Emma, with her, she joined the general field hospital of the Army of the Cumberland and continued nursing the Union Army wounded.

During the months that followed, Fannie wrote letters regularly to her husband but received no reply. She even prevailed on a soldier to search for him among the Confederate prisoners, without result. Then one day during the occupation of Atlanta, Colonel LeDuc happened to hear the provost marshal arguing with a surgeon about a claim made by a recently captured prisoner that his wife was a nurse under the surgeon's command. The provost marshal demanded to know what a Rebel woman was doing nursing in a Union hospital. The surgeon produced a copy of the letter written by LeDuc at Snake Creek. Together, with the help of others who knew of Fannie's work, they obtained Zach's release. Fannie and her Confederate husband had a joyous reunion.

When Sherman resumed his march to the sea, the Jacksons were sent to Lookout Mountain, Tennessee, where Fannie nursed at a federal hospital and Zach worked for the U.S. government in the military construction corps. At the conclusion of the war, neighbors in Georgia raised a fund to help the Jacksons go north to Iowa, where they settled for about two years. Fannie found the weather inclement, however, so they purchased a team and covered wagon and set out for Kansas with their children. Reaching Johnson County, they homesteaded 80 acres of land ten miles northwest of Olathe and settled down to farm.

When Joanna, or "Josie," Jackson was 15 years old, she taught school in a one-room schoolhouse in Johnson County, three miles away from the family farm, riding there and back by horseback every day. Part of the teacher's job was to build her own fires and care for the school building. Her salary was paid by the parents of the children she taught. For her first four months' term, she received the monthly salary of $12.50—which she used to put plaster on the walls of her parents' crude home. The following year, she used the salary to enter Baker University.

Joanna developed into a gracious, cultured young lady. She took a leading part in the Ladies Literary Society of Olathe, the Methodist church, and many other social and educational activities. In 1873, Jesse Thomas Nichols and Joanna Jackson were married and went to live with Jesse's parents on their farm, which was only two miles from the Jackson's.[4] Soon after they were married, Jesse T. became manager of the Grange store in Olathe, and five years later they moved to town.

Today, it is hard to imagine the central role of the Farmers' Grange in rural and small-town life in the latter part of the nineteenth century. There were hundreds of Granges throughout the United States, constituting the nation's largest retail business. At first selling farm produce and other groceries, they grew to include dry

This sturdy house, built of native limestone and located on a 220-acre farm near Olathe, Kansas, was the home of J.C.'s grandparents, Thomas T. and Elizabeth Hoge Nichols. They had pioneered westward from Ohio and settled here in 1870. It was to this house that their son, Jesse T., brought his bride, Josie Jackson, in 1873; five years later the young couple moved into town.

J.C.'s father, Jesse T. Nichols, was a prominent and respected citizen of Olathe.

Joanna (Jackson) Nichols, mother of J.C. Nichols, came west from Georgia with her parents following the Civil War.

goods, clothing, boots and shoes, hardware, tools, and farm implements. More importantly, the Grange was a fraternal organization devoted to "building character, developing leadership, encouraging education, promoting community betterment and instilling high ideals" in its membership. Interestingly, although it called itself a fraternity, the Grange admitted women to full membership, with equal voice and vote with the men. All family members over 14 were eligible to join.

Essentially a cooperative in both its commercial business and its idealism, it became a significant influence in both local and national politics. Local Grange leaders were often community leaders. Nationally, it is credited with placing the Department of Agriculture in the cabinet, with instituting rural free delivery of mail, and with encouraging the establishment of agricultural colleges and the conservation of natural resources. While intensely patriotic, the Grange deplored the militaristic spirit, opposed peacetime conscription, and advocated arbitration instead of resorting to arms.

Jesse T. Nichols was not only manager of the Olathe Grange store for 30 years, but he also held various offices in the Grange organization, including that of president. His starting salary as manager was about $80 a month. Joanna clerked in the store and took in boarders to improve the family finances. William E. Connelly, in *A Standard History of Kansas and Kansans*, published in 1918, says: "His honesty was proverbial and he was distinguished by strength of character and intellect. He gave his influence to the cause of Prohibition." Jesse T. was an ardent Populist. When the Populist party dissolved, he became a Democrat. His reputation in the area was demonstrated in 1910 when he was elected Johnson County treasurer by the biggest majority ever polled up to that time by any candidate for public office in the county.

With F.O. Ostranger, he organized Ostranger & Nichols company, later the Olathe Packing Company, whose hams and sausages were known throughout the area. He also helped establish the Patrons Bank of Olathe, of which he was stockholder. Jesse T. Nichols died in 1916; Joanna in 1947.

Jessie Eleanor Miller, who was later to become Mrs. Jesse Clyde Nichols, was also from Olathe. Jessie's maternal grandfather, David Phenicie, was born in 1797 in Washington County, Maryland, and was reared in Bedford County, Pennsylvania. Her maternal grandmother, Mary Jenkins, was born in 1803 in Hagerstown, Maryland. In 1832, David and Mary moved west to Ohio and then to Indiana, near the Michigan line, where, in 1844, they had a daughter, Mary Ellen. She married Manuel George Miller in 1867.

Jessie's paternal grandfather, David Miller, was born in 1816 on a farm in what is now West Virginia; her maternal grandmother, Sarah (called Sally) Heimbach, was born in 1818 near Gettysburg. They were married in Branch County, Michigan. Son Manuel George was born on December 3, 1843.

Manuel served in the Union Army in the Civil War; after the war, he, like many other young veterans, did not return home, but set out on his own. He went west to St. Marys, Kansas, where he became construction foreman for the Union Pacific Railroad and later construction superintendent. After he had been in Kansas two years, he returned to Michigan in 1867 to marry Mary Ellen Phenicie and bring her back to St. Marys.

In 1869, they moved to Olathe, where Manuel started a general grocery store and bakery. He later organized the Bank of Olathe, one of the first banks in Johnson County. With partners, he built and later bought the local grain elevator and flour mill. From the time he arrived in Olathe, Manuel Miller began acquiring farm land, eventually owning several thousand acres. He is believed to have been the largest-ever land owner in Johnson County. He later told J.C. that when he first came to Kansas he could have bought a large part of the west bottoms of Kansas City including the site of the old Union Station for only $800, but that he never regretted going on to Olathe.

Throughout his lifetime, Manuel George Miller maintained a deep interest in the development of better methods of farming and livestock raising; he also bred fine trotting horses. He became the owner of the Olathe Citizens Telephone Company, which had lines out into rural Johnson County. Naturally, the Millers were among the first families to have electric lights and a telephone in their home, which also boasted the first bathroom and furnace installed in Olathe.

Although he had only a country school education, Manuel Miller was an avid reader. He was well informed on a wide range of subjects, with special interest in science and health. A forward thinker of considerable daring and vision, his progressive ideas and assertive personality made him many enemies, but he always fought for the betterment of his adopted town of Olathe and of the county. For example, over great opposition, he successfully promoted the first paved streets in town. Manuel used his business sense and considerable wealth to help deserving young people. He started many of them in business, losing a good deal of money when some of them failed and defaulted on their loans.

The Millers had two daughters: Jessie Eleanor, born in 1879, and Mona Louise, born two years later. Mrs. Miller, who suffered from asthma, worsened to the point that she found it necessary to live during the winter months in San Diego, California. The two daughters lived with her, Mr. Miller making frequent trips west to be with them. After attending school in California and three years at Vail-Deane School in New Jersey, both Jessie and Louise Miller were graduated from Vassar College, an unusual achievement for midwestern girls at the time.

In the summer of 1909, the family vacationed at Stead's ranch in Estes Park, Colorado. On August 25, after lunch, Manuel George Miller, then 66, declared his intention to climb nearby Eagle Mountain. Over protests from some of the others, he set out. When he did not return, many hours later, friends walked up to look for him. They found him lying beside the trail, dead of heart failure. Across his left arm was his coat, which he had removed, and his glasses lay a foot from his head where they had fallen.

The Birth of Subdivisions

The dream of owning land was what drew most of our forefathers to America. The early settlers built homes in the forests or on the plains, where they began to farm. Towns and cities grew up around seaports, river junctions, and other natural

Manuel George and Mary Ellen Phenicie Miller were the parents of Jessie Eleanor Miller, J.C. Nichols' wife. Manuel Miller came with his bride from Indiana to Kansas after the Civil War. He established several successful businesses and became the largest-ever landowner in Johnson County. They raised two daughters in Olathe.

crossroads of travel. By the mid-nine-teenth century, land ownership began to focus on city and suburban development.

In the forefront of city growth was the subdivider. His role was to purchase acre-age of raw land, plat it (i.e., lay out streets and subdivide the resulting residential blocks into building lots), and aggressively market the individual homesites. The last half of the nineteenth century was a pe-riod of phenomenal urban and suburban growth, punctuated by frequent boom and bust cycles. Many subdivisions lacking in necessary improvements such as roads and sidewalks, water lines, and sewer systems were sold in the speculative heat of the boom cycles. The majority of residential development in that era was done with little concern for aesthetics; the houses, personal statements by individual owners and builders, were often at odds with the styles of neighboring dwellings.

There were several reasons for the hap-hazard nature of the subdivisions that sprang up in this era. First, American and European financiers alike were reluctant to invest large sums in residential develop-ments that could generally make a profit only over the long term, if at all. The track record of planned communities as investments was not good. This limited availability of capital resulted in the real estate developer, property owner, and builder each pursuing his own short-term interests without any continuing feeling of responsibility. City planning was unheard of, and the concept of ensuring continued value in the home and the neighborhood was unknown. Home buyers cherished the notion of self determination and resisted interference from any quarter. The con-cern and interest they expressed in the details of the construction of their own homes did not extend to the neighbor-hood. Finally, this situation was exacerbated by the assumption that resi-dential districts would ultimately become retail or commercial—that's what usually happened. One reason land owners and real estate entrepreneurs preferred the rec-tilinear grid design for their plats was that home buyers could be promised maximum appreciation on their investment when business interests subsequently moved in. The crowding that resulted from lot front-ages as small as 25 feet was tolerated because the footage corresponded to the future needs of store fronts.

During the mid-1800s the wealthy and influential leaders of most cities and towns built their own homes either in the center of town or in the outskirts, often clustered together—"the big houses on the hill"—but otherwise uncoordinated. And in those days, the value of almost all homes, including those of the rich, began to de-cline from the moment they were built. The reason was that it was taken for granted that commercial interests would intrude. As homes grew older, they were sure to become boarding houses or "light housekeeping" apartments, funeral par-lors, veterinarian hospitals, or the like. In fact, banks of the day customarily limited mortgages to 50 percent or less of the cost of the home and to no more than 15 years' duration—because the value of the col-lateral for the loan was constantly de-clining.

This was the process that J.C. Nichols later set out to reverse. His enduring vi-sion was to build *permanence* into his residential communities, where home val-ues would be retained and would even increase over generations, and most of his remarkable innovations were toward this end. He changed the face of real estate development, not only in Kansas City but in the nation, with a vision that produced gratifying profits as well.

J.C. Nichols did not invent the planned subdivision. There had been quality developments in other parts of the country for a half century that were the unique exceptions. Certainly J.C. learned from these.

The first, chronologically, was Llewellyn Park (named for its developer, Llewellyn Haskell), a planned subdivision designed in 1853 near Orange and West Orange, New Jersey. Llewellyn Park was the first to utilize restrictive covenants (dictating one-acre homesites and specific building standards) within its 350 contiguous acres. This subdivision's use of landscape gardener Eugene A. Baumann for planting and topographical considerations and architect Andrew Jackson Davis for the design of homes, the creation of a homeowners association, and the development of community spirit within the subdivision made Llewellyn Park a portent of things to come.

It failed to become as influential as several subsequent communities, however, because of the 1857 panic. Funding for a needed sewage system dried up when Haskell went bankrupt. Residents of the community, who were also feeling the financial pinch, could not contribute sufficient funds to maintain the common grounds properly; some contributed nothing at all due to a loophole in the legal covenants. Nevertheless, Llewellyn Park's woodsy ambience, highlighted by a meandering walkway (referred to as the Ramble) along a rustic ravine, made it a unique endeavor.

Immediately following the 1857 panic, another planned residential community similar to Llewellyn Park began to take form in Lake Forest, Illinois. The founders of this project were the trustees of Lake Forest College who envisioned it as a residence area for professors. They hoped it might also attract wealthy Chicagoans who would take an interest in the college 28 miles away. The trustees approached the eminent landscape architect Frederick Law Olmsted to lay out the plan, who declined because he was doing Central Park in New York City but recommended Jed Hotchkiss of Chicago. The exclusive character of the community was ensured by selling lots in acre increments rather than by front footage. One innovation at Lake Forest was to be adopted not only by J.C. Nichols but by countless other developers since: a 200-acre golf course and country club created as the community's focal point. The Onwentsia Club eventually included not only a golf course but also a polo field, tennis courts, croquet courts, and bowling alleys. Among the residents of Lake Forest were the A.B. Dick family, the Armour family, and other Chicago business leaders.

Also in the Chicago area was Riverside, a subdivision planned in the late 1860s under the auspices of Emery E. Childs. Again, Frederick Law Olmsted was sought as the landscape architect, and this time he was able to accept. Central to his plan for Riverside was a landscaped "long common" along the Des Plaines River, which meandered through the property. Other features of his plan included curvilinear streets to de-emphasize the site's flat terrain, designated open park space, planting of additional trees (not in rows), restrictive covenants attached to the deeds, owner maintenance of trees, and a prohibition on front yard fences. All these features were later included in Nichols' Country Club District.

While Llewellyn Park and Lake Forest had targeted their lots primarily for wealthy buyers, Riverside was the first community to embrace planning criteria for predominantly upper-middle-class home buyers.

Kansas City

Kansas City, Missouri, was one of the cities in the vast American interior that grew up because of its location at the confluence of two important rivers. What are now the states of Missouri and Kansas were part of the Louisiana Purchase of 1803. When President Jefferson sent Lewis and Clark to explore the newly acquired territory, they established one of their early camps on a high bluff overlooking the confluence of the Missouri and Kansas rivers (the latter also known, then as now, as the Kaw). In 1821, Missouri became a state; six years later, a fur trader from St. Louis named Francois Chouteau founded a French trading village on what was to become the town site. In the 1820s, Santa Fe Trail traffic shifted from Independence to the village of Westport, a few miles south of Chouteau's trading post. Cargo bound for western settlements was brought upriver by boat and unloaded at Westport Landing. The cargo was then transferred to wagons pulled by straining oxen that carried it across the grassy plains to Santa Fe, Oregon, and California. A town began to grow around this spot.

In 1838, 14 of the early settlers at Westport Landing decided to organize the "Kansas Town Company" and purchase Gabriel Prudhomme's farm, which bordered the river. According to legend, a meeting was held about a decade later to officially name their town. It was chaired by a whiskey dealer called One-Eyed Ellis. One of the citizens, Abraham Fonda, suggested the town be named Port Fonda. Other nominations were Chouteau, French Town, and Possum Trot. For-

tunately, One-Eyed Ellis exercised his prerogative as chairman. "It is agreed that we shall name our place "The Town of Kansas," he declared. The name stuck as the town continued to grow, until, in 1853, it was incorporated by the state as the "City of Kansas."

The following year, the Territory of Kansas was officially designated, and five years later, in 1858, the City of Wyandotte was incorporated directly across the river from the City of Kansas. Its first mayor, Col. James R. Rensselaer Parr, was the great-grandfather of Jeannette Terrell Nichols (Mrs. Miller Nichols). He had brought the lumber for his home from Pennsylvania, down the Ohio and Mississippi rivers and up the Missouri River. The two towns grew side by side for a quarter century. But in the 1880s, the City of Wyandotte changed its name to Kansas City, Kansas, and the City of Kansas changed its name to Kansas City, Missouri. This was the origin of a confusion that has continued in the minds of the rest of the nation for more than a century.

Meanwhile, to the south of the City of Kansas, other developments were taking place that would be significant to J.C. Nichols' Country Club District. Encouraged by the federal government to settle the recently acquired Louisiana Purchase land, Dr. David Waldo had purchased one thousand acres in 1828; the property was on both sides of what is now Wornall Road, extending from 63rd Street to 75th Street. Dr. Waldo maintained a farm on part of the land, and he and his brothers also planted a large walnut grove in the 1840s around 63rd and Walnut. As the land was largely treeless in those days except along the streams, the walnut grove was a well-known landmark. In addition to being a practicing physician, Dr. Waldo engaged in a number of business enterprises, including a flourishing trade over the Santa Fe Trail. With several partners, he operated a stage line which had a contract with the government to carry mail to Santa Fe. Because of this activity, the town of Waldo grew up at the southern edge of Dr. Waldo's land. In the 1860s, a rail line was built between Westport and Dodson to the south, with Waldo as a main stop. In the late 1880s, the community developed a somewhat raffish reputation, with a race track and later an assortment of bars, dance halls, and honky-tonks.[5]

In 1844, John B. Wornall came from Kentucky and bought 494 acres of land adjacent to Dr. Waldo's for $2,500. He built a four-room log house near what is now 61st Street Terrace and Wornall Road. In 1858, the Wornall family built a substantial brick mansion some 200 feet north of the original cabin. The family still owned most of the original land when J.C. Nichols bought it for the Country Club District in 1908. (The Wornall home is today designated as a Historic Landmark and is maintained as a museum by the Jackson County Historical Society.)

During the Civil War, the Battle of Westport was fought, October 21–23, 1864, on what is now the Country Club Plaza, Loose Park, and early parts of J.C. Nichols' Country Club District to the south. Confederate soldiers used the bluffs south of Brush Creek as a vantage point for bombarding the town of Westport. Union soldiers fought their way up from Brush Creek through a breach in the defenses where Summit Street is now located. A major portion of the battle took place on the present site of Loose Park. The Wornall home was used as a hospital during and after the battle. Many years later, bullets, cannon balls, and pieces of rifles were still being found there by golfers at the Kansas City Country Club, original tenant of the Loose Park site.

In 1854, the land area of Kansas City (or the City of Kansas, as it was then called) comprised just 440 acres on the banks of the Missouri River just below its junction with the Kansas River; its population was less than 450. Six years later, in 1860, the land area had increased sevenfold and the population tenfold, primarily because of the settling of the Kansas Territory to the west. During these years of blossoming growth, plats for 42 new subdivisions and two resurveys were filed.

Kersey Coates, one of the earliest subdividers, developed Coates' Addition and Peery Place, both in 1857, and Lucas Place in 1860. Active in the abolition cause, Coates donated land in Peery Place for a black church and black school and placed no building restrictions in that subdivision. As a result, although Peery Place was not intended by design to be segregated, it came to have the second largest concentration of black families in the city.

By contrast, though Coates' two other developments had only one restriction, namely, that the houses had to be constructed of brick, the cost of brick construction effectively excluded the working class. Wealthy newcomers to the city, particularly those of abolitionist persuasion, bought in Coates' Addition and Lucas Place and built fine brick and stone townhouses. By the 1880s, the two developments together were known as "Quality Hill," today the west side of downtown.

In recent times "block-busting" integration of predominantly white neighborhoods by black residents is well known. Interestingly, the opposite of this phenomenon occurred in Peery Place in the

1860s. Wealthy white neighborhoods grew up around the predominantly black community, raising land prices and ultimately forcing rents in Peery Place to a level that most blacks could not afford. Gradually, whites began buying up the vacated properties until the subdivision was essentially white. The city's black population moved east of downtown, and Troost became the line of racial demarkation. The black area south of 12th Street and along Vine became celebrated as the birthplace of Kansas City jazz.

The decision by local Kansas City citizens in the mid-1860s to contribute money for construction of the Hannibal railroad bridge spanning the Missouri River, thus giving the Burlington Railroad a direct link to Chicago, precipitated a real estate boom that proved to be a heady time for land developers. Both Kansas City and St. Joseph, Missouri, approximately the same size, were being considered for a bridge over the river. However, when Kansas Citians offered to build the bridge at no expense to the railroad, Burlington Railroad management diverted most of its tracks to Kansas City. From that time on, St. Joseph stagnated while Kansas City grew.

In the five years following the Civil

This memorial to the Civil War Battle of Westport stands in the Jacob L. Loose Memorial Park, a battle site. (Courtesy of the Civil War Round Table of Kansas City)

War, another 42 new subdivisions were platted. Fueled in part by the arrival of the big Armour and Plankington meatpacking plants, the city's population surged eight-fold to more than 32,000 before the panic and depression of 1873 put a temporary lid on growth.

As economic conditions improved in 1876, land development began gathering steam, reaching its zenith in 1880 when 27 plats were filed. Better transportation in the form of newly added mule line routes helped the new boom.

Chapter 2

1880 - 1905

Jesse Clyde Nichols was born August 23, 1880, in Olathe, Kansas. Throughout his life, he seemed to have endless energy and a superabundance of ideas, the vision of a dreamer joined with the determination to reach his goals. He was described variously as "intense," "tightly wound," and "perpetually on the go." Competitive, ambitious, and extremely hardworking, he stated in his memoirs, "The only reason I worked so diligently was because I enjoyed work, and liked the feeling of independence that I got from earning my own money." These characteristics were in evidence from early childhood on; even after his successes and achievements had brought him national fame and innumerable honors, he remained particularly proud of the enterprises of his childhood and youth. He loved to spin stories about them to his own children—as well as to interviewers from the press.

Childhood, Youth, and Education

Clyde (the initials J.C. were adopted in his mid-twenties to give him an air of dignity beyond his years) wasted little time on the normal distractions of childhood. At the age of six, he walked a mile on a dirt road to and from the schoolhouse each day. By his eighth birthday, he was holding down three jobs.

One of his home chores was to milk the family cow and herd it out to pasture in the morning and back to the barn at night. He was permitted to sell any excess milk to neighbors, delivering it himself.

Most of the other farmers in the area also kept one or two milk cows, so young Clyde, mounted on Old Fan, the family buggy horse, ran his own cowherding operation. He was paid 50 cents per cow per month. One summer his herd grew to 43 cows.

On Saturdays, "from seven in the morning until ten at night," he clerked in his father's Grange store. As a youngster, he started out at 25 cents per day, but when he began leading in sales, he received a raise to a dollar a day. On the days he worked at the store, he had to subcontract the cattle-driving business out to a friend.

Clyde learned at a young age that success can breed envy. In his memoirs, written in 1949, he said: "At that time there was a tough 'East End Gang' of kids in Olathe, headed by a boy nicknamed 'Bulldog,' who used to let my cows out to stray every place, making it necessary for me to do considerable extra work to gather them up. Finally I got so mad at this that I organized a 'West End Gang' and we licked hell out of the 'East End Gang' (which resulted in a broken leg for one of the boys), but thereafter they let my cows alone!"

Employees of the Grange store followed

in Bulldog's mischievous footsteps. Clyde's memoirs offer several stories: "The older clerks amused themselves by playing all kinds of tricks on me. For instance, they would rib up a customer to ask for such crazy things as 'white lamp black,' 'left handed monkey wrenches,' 'jugs open at both ends,' etc., and I, unwilling to seem uninformed, would search diligently for these impossible things."

As a result of another Grange store prank, Clyde carried the unflattering moniker "Swiney" all through high school. "Once they had a customer ask me for some 'nice swiney canute,'" he wrote. "I very politely told the customer we had it in stock and started to look for it. All the other clerks stood around and watched my diligent search, and for years thereafter they called me 'Swiney.'"

He recalls struggling to load his hand truck with boxes that "those damn 'friendly' clerks" had nailed to the floor. On another occasion, his co-workers spread a layer of sticky molasses on the floor in front of the sorghum barrel, disguised it under a light film of sawdust, and had a good belly laugh when "Swiney" knelt down to fill a customer's order.

In addition to carrying a full courseload at school, Clyde spent the spare time of his 13th year working a number of jobs. He washed dishes in a restaurant, clerked in both a hardware and a clothing/dry-goods store, and, lest he appear slothful, spent one of his vacations rising well before dawn and working nine-hour days for a bakery making bread and pastries and then selling them from a wagon.

In the summers when he was 13 and 14, Clyde worked as a farmhand, earning 50 cents a day plus board; the following year, he was awarded a 25-cent-a-day raise. He was the brunt of another round

of pranks as well. To initiate the young town boy, the other hands "rigged up an arrangement by which they pulled a rope while we slept in the haymow so that it sounded like an intruder walking below," recalled the venerable J.C. Nichols many years after the incident. "They told me it was robbers, and then disappeared leaving me alone, quaking with fear."

Another anecdote from the memoirs suggests that his nervous system barely survived his summers as a farmhand: "After eating our noonday meal out in the field, we used to lie down under the wagon for a nap while the horses finished eating. The other farmhands had killed a large rattlesnake, which they coiled up so that it looked alive and placed near where I was asleep. Suddenly they all yelled, 'Rattlesnake!' I turned over to look and there was the snake about two feet from my face. I jumped to my feet and ran across eighty acres of farmland before I stopped! This story became a legend in that part of the county."

On more than one occasion, Clyde's co-workers stole his clothes while he took an after-dinner dip in a neighboring pond, forcing him to walk the mile back to the hayloft stark naked. Young Clyde might well have asked himself, "With friends like these, who needs enemies?" Nichols later recalled that in 1894, only thirty years after the abolition of slavery, the one farm hand who treated him as a true friend was a young black man named George Washington. George's efforts to shield Clyde from the unkind pranks of the others were never forgotten by the town boy from Olathe.

An August 1945 *Saturday Evening Post* article by George Sessions Perry stated that the eminently successful J.C. Nichols had once been a "peddler." According to Nichols, the more accurate word is "huckster"—highly gainful employment during high school vacations. The entrepreneurial Clyde "bought an old team, one big horse (which was blind) and one little fellow, and a second-hand wagon, and organized a route to buy up chickens, butter, eggs, apples, potatoes, etc., from farmers. I hauled them to Kansas City, Missouri (twenty-five miles from Olathe), where I sold them to grocery stores and restaurants. Then in Kansas City I bought oranges, lemons, bananas, etc., at wholesale and sold them on my return trip to stores throughout the country." He also took orders from farmers' wives, purchased the produce in the city, and delivered it on his return. "My huckster route," he related, "covered about eighty-five miles [at a pace of two to four miles per hour, depending on road conditions], including nine small towns, and I tried to cover it twice a week, sometimes sleeping on the ground under my wagon and cooking my meals over a campfire."

One night he was awakened by hoof-beats; looking out from under the wagon, he saw three men on horseback conversing together about 100 yards away. A few moments later, they dismounted and walked toward him. From under his pillow he removed his father's Colt revolver, which he had along because of the cash he carried, and waited in fear and trembling.

The men stopped about 50 yards away and again entered into a discussion that seemed to take an eternity. Then they abruptly disappeared into the roadside underbrush, taking their horses with them. Shortly, in the distance, Nichols heard splashing and laughing. The three men were swimming in a nearby creek and didn't reappear.

Nichols' early job experiences proved significant a number of years later when he needed capital to go into the real estate business. To purchase land for development, J.C. persuaded the neighbors whose cows he had tended and some of the customers on his huckster route to invest with him in the purchase of the land. He wrote that he "repaid all of these backers within two years—with a 100 percent profit on their initial investment."

The first day of his new huckster route, Nichols proudly arrived at the Grange store in Olathe, parked his motley team in the back alley, and went inside to pick up his cargo. When he returned to the team his old clerking buddies had hung signs on his wagon: "low prices for rotten eggs," "foul smelling butter at low prices," and "scrawny chickens at bargain prices."

J.C. admitted that the teasing on that score was not always unfounded. On one occasion he bought twenty bunches of overripe bananas in Kansas City at a bargain price, figuring to sell them at a Fourth of July celebration in the town of DeSoto. The weather did not cooperate, and virtually no one showed up for the festivities. He was forced to unload his black bananas for hog feed.

On another occasion, a fire engine in Kansas City spooked his team, which bolted and upset his loaded wagon. Nichols spent the rest of the day salvaging his scattered produce from the dusty street, and later selling it at a loss in the north end of town. These disappointments might have soured any other young person, but, as Nichols explained in his memoirs, "My parents [were] comparatively prosperous, so there was no real need for me to work so hard; but from my earliest childhood I had been deeply impressed by the manner in which my parents and grandparents worked hard, and I was fired by the keen desire to do my full part at all times."

Doing his "full part at all times" was not an empty phrase for Clyde Nichols. While utilizing a good deal of his spare hours in money-making endeavors, he still found time to court his high school sweetheart Jessie Eleanor Miller and to graduate valedictorian of his class with a 99.2 average, the highest recorded up to that time at Olathe High School. He admits it didn't come easy: "Two older farm boys, Bartlett and Hall, were in my class. They did not run a 'cow route,' did not work in stores on Saturdays, [did not teach Presbyterian Sunday School,] did not spoon at night with girls. . . . They did nothing but study. I knew my competition and by

Jesse Clyde Nichols, age 18, upon graduation from Olathe High School in 1897. He was valedictorian with a grade point average of 99.2, organized the school's first debating team, and made up its first school yell.

God, it damned near killed me to lick their grades!" He later wondered "where that other eight tenths of a percent got away from me."

Nichols also organized Olathe High's first debating team and first football team—and made up its first school yell. In his valedictory oration in 1897, "Is Peace a Dream?" in the overblown language of the day, he asked, "Lo! As we scan the pages of history, what so boldly stares us in the face? . . . War! . . . War to the death." Drawing on the Civil War, he eloquently decried "brothers struggling in deadly conflict, in frenzy, with the madness of ferocious beasts—wounds, agony, despair. . . . Hatred and vengeance overcome love and mercy. . . . Reason is forgotten, justice shunned. . . . Shuddering, we ask in amazement, *why?*" Several minutes later he dared to predict that better communication and transportation between nations would effect change. "When governments shall determine differences by arbitration and international congresses, when nations shall universally disarm and better employ the billions lavished on war systems, then will the human family be reunited in perpetual peace. Then will the nations be United Nations."

J.C. remembered later, "While I was in the midst of this ringing peroration on the stage of the packed Olathe Opera House, all the lights went out and I had to continue my speech in the dark. . . . Perhaps the lighting company knew how crazy my predictions were! My Olathe friends still remind me of this, and considering that since that time we have been through the Spanish American War and two world conflicts, they may have some basis for their remarks!"

Clyde's frenetic pace in high school took an understandable toll on his body, and his health suffered as a result of his constant activity. Perhaps this was a contributing factor, along with the desire to pay his own way to college, in his decision to work for a year before attending the University of Kansas.

And work he did. Nichols established a wholesale meat market at 1611 Grand Avenue in Kansas City. The rent was $35.00 a month for a space 40 x 125 feet. He slept behind a canvas curtain strung across one corner of the shop. He said he got to know the back entrance of every important restaurant and hotel in the city, and "when I finally added Fred Harvey's [restaurant] to my list of customers I felt I had reached the top in the meat selling business."

He met the 6:00 P.M. train from Olathe every evening at the old Union Station in the west bottoms. After hauling the meat to 1611 Grand, he worked until ten or eleven putting up orders for early morning delivery the next day. He garnered sufficient income during the year to begin college in the fall of 1898.

When J.C. looked back on his active youth and young adulthood, he admitted to being surprisingly timid—more introverted than extroverted. He recalled hoping secretly that prospective meat customers would be absent from their premises so he could avoid confronting them with his sales pitch. Those who knew Nichols in his later years conducting motivational sales meetings at his company, a master of interpersonal communications and a prime mover in many civic endeavors—find it difficult to believe that J.C. occasionally felt the vulnerability and insecurity of most young men.

It took courage to overcome his fears and persevere in his enterprises. At a banquet in his honor many years later, J.C. stated:

I regard this [work] experience as the finest training I could possibly have received; for I learned from it the value of courage. Initiative is necessary; vision is fine; but without the courage to carry on in spite of every obstacle a man will not go far.

Sometimes the produce in my wagon would rot before I sold it. Sometimes the market would drop and for several trips I would lose money. It took courage to dig into my pocket time after time to pay for produce, and to go ahead in spite of losses.

Jesse Clyde Nichols entered the University of Kansas at Lawrence in 1898 at the age of 18. Although his parents were able and willing to send him through college and did give him some assistance, he elected to pay most of his bills by having a variety of jobs.

The success of Nichols' wholesale meat route in Kansas City encouraged him to set up a similar operation in Lawrence his freshman year at KU. He bought meat at the Kansas City meat market and sold it to butcher shops, restaurants, fraternities, and sororities. He later recalled having had only one disgruntled customer, a Lawrence butcher. One day the butcher complained that one of the hams was spoiled. To prove it, he jabbed a probe deep into the ham and withdrawing it, ran it under Clyde's nose. The young man sniffed it, looked thoughtful, and finally said, "Sweet as a nut."

Clyde also worked as a correspondent or "stringer" for the *Kansas City Star* and as steward for his fraternity, Beta Theta Pi, for which he received free board. Although the Betas ate very well with only a modest house bill, some of the brothers grumbled that during the four years of

Clyde's frugality, the Betas on campus could always be recognized because they were so lean. But at the end of those four years, he had managed to pay off the mortgage on the chapter house.

He also managed the university's debt-laden athletic association and was able to return it to fiscal health. Baseball was his first love. (He played third base one year, "always hoping the ball would never come my way!") He arranged it so that many of the players became Betas and thus lived at the fraternity house, where they paid their house bills by working as waiters. That meant less food for the paying brothers, as well as cries of "favoritism" from the other fraternities. However, said Clyde, "we all wanted a winning team, and we won games. In the long run, that's what everybody wanted, so everybody was happy."

When the baseball team went on its first long road trip, all the way to Chicago, manager Nichols economized by buying one less ticket than the number of players. When the conductor came through, Nichols kept his boys dodging around through the train to confuse him. ("The toilet came in mighty handy," he recalls. "I am a little ashamed to admit all this.") KU won six games out of ten on the trip.

Disgusted with the unethical recruiting practices of rival schools, Clyde called a meeting to discuss the problem. Representatives from the attending institutions denied paying players, signed a written agreement condemning the practice, and, in Nichols' words, "proceeded to violate the agreement." As an example of their "rotten practices," he cites an incident in which KU was forced to bench a great pitcher, "Amy" Morgan, because Baker University had filed a protest. KU lost the game. Morgan left school shortly afterward, only to show up on Baker's baseball roster. In spite of these problems, under

Clyde's managerial leadership KU fielded an undefeated football team, baseball teams that won a large majority of their games, and a high-ranking track team.

Perhaps Clyde's greatest contribution to the University of Kansas was the organization of a successful statewide letter-writing campaign to pressure an economy-minded state legislature to grant more funds to the institution. As a state university, KU was dependent on legislative appropriations. At the turn of the century, most of the legislators came from farm areas and took a jaundiced view of spending money on higher education; the school was in woeful need of money. Nichols, participating in almost every campus activity, was well aware of the need; and in his senior year, he determined to do something about it.

In his room at the Beta house, night after night, he wrote letters to influential alumni all over the state, urging them to bring pressure on the legislature. Not a county was overlooked, and the lawmakers couldn't help but realize that their constituents were interested in more appropriations for higher education. When the legislature convened in Topeka, Clyde Nichols, representing the student body, appeared before the committee on appropriations, emphasizing his points with an extended finger. An increased appropriation was won.[6]

Through the letter-writing campaign, Nichols became acquainted with Frank Grant Crowell of Atchison, Kansas, later of Kansas City, a partner in the country's largest grain export firm. Crowell was sufficiently impressed with Clyde to invest with him after Clyde began his home development in Kansas City.

Meanwhile, during the summers of his college years, Clyde continued to hold many jobs. Between his freshman and sophomore years, he loaded potatoes into railroad cars for $1.50 per carload. He quickly devised a method of using a hand-cart to handle the heavy sacks and was soon making $10 a day. The growers temporarily struck to protest Nichols' high pay, but they backed down, and Clyde made enough to pay his tuition for the following year.

He held two jobs the following summer. For the first two months he made good money selling large McCauley world and U.S. maps in Utah and Wyoming. To cut expenses, he often slept in barns and hay-stacks or any other handy shelter. He shared one anecdote that reveals a growing understanding of human psychology: "One day in Cass River Valley, between Salt Lake City and Ogden, I sold my five-by-seven-foot maps to seventeen wives of one Mormon, all living on separate farms. All I had to do was to say that the other wives were buying them." On another night, in a saloon in Wyoming, he jumped up on a whiskey keg and sold 19 maps in 20 minutes.

By claiming to be 21 years old (a year older than his actual age), Clyde spent the final month of that summer vacation wearing the badge of deputy United States marshal. He went in pursuit of a ring of Japanese criminals who were allegedly importing prostitutes into America. Nichols recounts: "I took a train trip into Nevada where I hired four mule teams and drove fifty-five miles to a mining camp and handcuffed a [Japanese man] while he was still asleep. . . . Thank God he was asleep. I drove back with my prisoner and flagged a through transcontinental train, showed my United States Marshal badge (got hell from the conductor) but got my prisoner to Salt Lake City three days before the expected time."

If Clyde was still suffering from shyness, he did a good job of masking it. He de-scribes one memorable trip: "I took a desperate [Japanese prisoner] to Seattle, all handcuffed and docile. But when the train stopped at a small wayside station, the local Japanese tried to take him away from me. Somehow my nerve came to my rescue (or perhaps it was my fear), and at the point of my two revolvers I put the raiders off the train and finally turned my prisoner over to the Washington State Penitentiary."

The summer between Nichols' junior and senior years marked the first break in his nonstop work schedule in over a decade but would prove to be the most important summer experience in terms of his later career. He was accompanied in this adventure by a college friend, Wilkie Clock. The boys first worked their way to Boston herding four cars of cattle on a freight train. They then hired out on a cattle boat bound for Europe. They slept on bales of hay in the hold and ate with the rest of the workers out of large common pans sitting on the deck. Wilkie was forced to handle most of Clyde's cattle-feeding duties as the latter was seasick for almost the entire voyage.

The two young men had brought bicycles from Boston, for which they had paid $15 each. But after riding them to London, they lost them in a fluke fire that destroyed the repair shop in which they were parked. The owner of the shop graciously agreed to replace the charred bikes with new (and better) models. After biking through Belgium and Holland and into Germany, the young men sold the bicycles in Cologne for $60.

They went up the Rhine by boat and hiked through Switzerland. Limiting themselves to a dollar a day, they eked out extra money when Wilkie sang on street corners while Clyde took up a collection.

They employed a native guide while touring Switzerland. After climbing Mt. Rigi, they claimed to be expert guides themselves and made good money for a few days leading other parties up the mountain. They ended up seeing the risqué sights of Paris (which J.C. admits he enjoyed much more than Wilkie) and then returned home via Montreal in steerage class, which was full of immigrants.

After purchasing his train ticket from Montreal to Kansas City, Clyde had 85 cents in his pocket. Subsisting on apples and ginger snaps, he was down to six cents upon his arrival in Kansas City. Running into an acquaintance in Union Station who was headed for Montana to harvest wheat, "without a warm sweater," Clyde was able to sell the young man the old, worn-out sweater off his back for just enough to give him the necessary fare for the remaining train ride home to Olathe.

Clyde then sold the story of his trip to the *Olathe Mirror* for $25. In the article, his appreciation of England's countryside and its subsequent influence on his Country Club District was evident:

> Everywhere we turn, we see grand and interesting things, here an age-worn castle or its ruins, there a beautiful range of hills and a shaded valley. . . . Every home is surrounded by parks or beautiful lawns and flower gardens. . . . There are few hills and always grand scenery. Whenever possible, a road runs around a hill instead of over it. . . . We stop on every knoll to drink in the exhilarating breezes from the fields of daisies, buttercups and poppies, then ride down a beautifully shaded road, bordered by hawthorne hedges artistically trimmed, and dash by the

sculptured gates opening into handsome parks surrounding magnificent manors.

He found Paris a city of "wide streets, clean and straight" and explains in his memoirs the significant impact on the rest of his life made by the 1901 summer in Europe: "This three month's trip made a lasting impression on me. I was struck most forcibly with the imposing plans and permanent character of the cities and buildings. *I believe it was then that the spark was struck that ultimately brought the Country Club District into being*" (emphasis added). He added that European cities, although built by "many, many generations of builders," retained visual variety with a cohesive style. America's stereotyped cities, on the other hand, lacked aesthetic planning and often applied the "checkerboard scheme to streets and roadways."

Returning from a European tour in 1922, he recorded the features he most admired and the tremendous influence the experience had on his own planning and development:

> European cities taught me never to apologize for beauty in city planning. Beauty pays, like commerce; it is a hold on the people—beauty born in orderly lines, in stretches of uniform cornices, in artistic shop fronts, in the play and sparkle of fountains, in parks and free spaces, in vistas and in public buildings enhanced by proper placing . . . add cultural advantages—museums and art galleries, splendid music halls and municipal operas. And for further entertainment of the people, parks, water courses and sports stadiums, with a liberal sprinkling of playhouses and cafes. . . . Practically every city of

any size in Europe has its own university. They realize its value to a city. . . . It is realized that if cities are not built broad and open enough, there will be unfavorable situations later. . . . In Europe they appreciate the importance of roads connecting centers of industry. . . . All European cities are built to last. The buildings are not flimsy. . . . High class shops today are situated just where shops of that type were started 300 or 400 years ago. . . . European cities do not place an important building in an inadequate setting without an impressive approach, as is frequently done in American cities.

Perhaps most significantly, he noted:

One of the greatest lessons I learned from European cities is that the life of a city is not measured by a day or a year. [In America] we have been thoughtless, carefree opportunists, outgrowing our cities [and] the houses of our fathers. Either we tear it down and rebuild or we move away from the old centers. . . . This is not "progress," but an enormous destruction of property values.

Back at KU for his senior year in the fall of 1901, Nichols was elected class president—the beginning and end of his career as a politician. He graduated in 1902 with a grade-point average unsurpassed in the school's history to that date and was subsequently inducted into the scholastic honor societies Phi Beta Kappa and Beta Gamma Sigma. His remarkable record also won him a scholarship to Harvard University for the following fall.

That summer, Clyde earned the money he thought he would need at Harvard by selling stock in a gold mine near Mead-ows, Idaho, owned by the Thunder Mountain Gold Reef Mining and Development Corporation—an enterprise founded by his future business partner Franklin E. Reed. Clyde proved to be one of the most successful salesmen, garnering $500 in three months; but, much to his chagrin, the mine subsequently failed.

Upon arriving at Harvard with the rather nebulous intention of studying law, Nichols was struck with a malaise that was to affect him at intervals throughout his life.

Upon graduation from the University of Kansas in 1902, Phi Beta Kappa with the highest grade point average to that date, Clyde (as he was then known) won a scholarship to Harvard. While at the University of Kansas, he managed the athletic association, organized a statewide letterwriting campaign to pressure the legislature to grant more funds to the university, and toured Europe on a bicycle following his junior year.

The writer of a 1929 *Kansas City Star* article on J.C. Nichols' life (a piece presumably based on personal interviews) speculates that the cause of this malaise was that J.C. compulsively took on more challenges and causes than his physical strength would allow. Whenever he saw anything that needed to be done "to better conditions," even though "he knew he was undertaking too much, he could do nothing but put his ideas into effect."

For whatever reason, Clyde decided to forego the rigorous law curriculum in favor of general graduate studies. This fortuitous decision proved to be a turning point in his life. He enrolled in an economics course taught by a young, charismatic professor, Dr. Oliver Mitchell Wentworth Sprague, later an internationally respected economist, an adviser to the Bank of England and to the U.S. Treasury under President Franklin Roosevelt. Professor Sprague's course dwelt on the broad ramifications of shifting economic centers in the country, and especially the effect on land values. According to Sprague, the East was overdeveloped for its natural resources, which suggested that the West would soon experience phenomenal industrial growth and a resultant shift in demographics.

This theory was enthusiastically embraced by Nichols, who wrote his term thesis at Harvard on the increase in value of raw land through development. These new ideas led him to perhaps the only unsuccessful venture of his life, one that nearly derailed his career. But the ideas also enabled him thereafter to transform Kansas City from a cowtown to a midwestern hub of culture, education, business, and transportation, to revolutionize residential real estate development in the United States, and to create lasting land values through community planning.

Early Real Estate Ventures

Fired up with the theory that the value of raw land in the West would increase dramatically through development as population moved in that direction, Clyde set out for Texas, New Mexico, and Mexico to look for marginal land that could be purchased cheaply. Since he was promoting future traffic for them, he persuaded the presidents of the railroads to let him ride free.

Back in Olathe, he then sought financial backing from friends of his father, affluent farmers in the area. Although a few consented to accompany him on an inspection trip, he was largely unsuccessful in selling them on his plans. To them, the Southwest seemed unfertile, barren, and inhospitable. "Johnson County has much better farms than these," they told him. He even came dangerously close to alienating his prospective father-in-law, Olathe banker Manuel G. Miller, who was one of those who took the trip with him. Mr. Miller told his daughter Jessie that he thought Nichols was "getting carried away" with his project.

Ironically, young Clyde Nichols' vision was basically right—just 80 years ahead of its time. Some of the Texas land he was considering became immensely valuable because of oil and gas, and migration to sun-belt states after World War II eventually caused the price of residential property to soar. In 1903, however, "the whole scheme was a flop," Nichols wrote in his memoirs. "One day I was sitting in a Ft. Worth hotel, somewhat discouraged. I flipped a coin to see whether I should give up and return home: heads, I'd go home; tails, I'd stay and keep hitting the ball. It came up *tails*—[but] I came home anyway! I was completely broke; in fact, pretty heavily in debt. I felt licked financially and almost mentally, as well. In Olathe, I kept to side streets because I was embarrassed to see my friends. I was convinced I was a complete failure and there was no future for me whatever."

Fortunately for Kansas City and the real estate business nationwide, Nichols decided to try his ideas closer to home. At Harvard, he had discussed with Sprague the growth potential of Kansas City. At the turn of the century, the city had a population of over 150,000, having grown 50 percent in a little more than ten years. It ranked second in the United States in livestock shipping, meat-packing, and milling and was the largest winter wheat market in the world. It was one of the most important railroad centers in the country, with 12 trunk lines and 50,000 miles of rails reaching out in all directions.

In 1904, with renewed courage, Clyde turned to Kansas City. His first contact was with two friends from the Beta Theta Pi house at KU, Franklin Everett Reed and W.T. Reed, brothers who were practicing law in Kansas City, Kansas. After Clyde explained his ideas to them, they told him of a tract of land on the Kansas side that had to be sold for cash in a bankruptcy proceeding. They thought it would be a practical site on which to build small homes.

"I knew nothing whatever about building houses of any kind," Nichols confessed later, "but it presented a challenge to me." Back in Olathe, he organized a syndicate under the name Reed Brothers & Nichols to buy the property. He turned again to his farmer friends, and this time, with a down-to-earth proposition having promise of more immediate returns, he obtained their backing. One of his backers, to his satisfaction, was his future father-in-law. The land, near 13th and Lathrop, was purchased for $22,500 and platted into lots from 25 to 33 feet wide. On these he began to build small frame homes, with outhouses and no street improvements, offering them for sale from $800 to $1,000 each.

The year before, in 1903, the industrial district of the west bottoms of Kansas City had been hit with the worst flood in fifty years. The stockyards, meatpacking plants, and other industries had been all but wiped out. Although they were able to rebuild, thousands of blue-collar workers and their families had been driven from their homes, which had been destroyed in the flood waters. The property loss was estimated at more than $15 million, but an even greater tragedy was the number of workers who needed to find houses that were inexpensive and accessible to their jobs.

The Reed-Nichols district, named California Heights to suggest safety from flooding, proved to be the answer. Clyde had circulars printed, setting forth the wonderful advantages of his houses, which he handed out to the destitute workers as they left their places of work at night— not the best environment for real estate sales, he decided. Nevertheless, the houses sold rapidly, helped no doubt by terms of $10 down and $10 a month (vacant lots sold for $1 down and $1 a week). Purchase of homes on an installment plan was a real innovation at that time.

In 1905, Reed Brothers & Nichols bought a second property in Kansas City, Kansas, at 33rd and Georgia—which they named the Highlands—and developed it in the same way. In all, Clyde Nichols built some 100 houses in Kansas City, Kansas, and within two years was able to return to his farmer friends their original investment and eventually a 65 percent profit. J.C. always said he felt "a little ashamed" by profiting from selling houses to families who had lost everything in the flood of 1903.

During the first year of this venture, Nichols worked harder than he ever had before in his life, determined to prove himself. "I was ridden by the obsession of another failure," he said. "I was so determined that would not happen that I wouldn't stop work even for meals, sleep or pleasure." To save money, he slept on the sofa—or often, on the floor—of his head carpenter's home. Rising at 5:30 A.M. to look after his horse, he was on the building job at 7:00, working all day with the construction crews. When they quit at 6:00 P.M. Clyde became a salesman, selling houses until 10:00 P.M. Evenings were the best time to catch his working prospects at home. He rented space for a desk at $5 a month in back of the prescription counter of a drugstore at 13th and the Chelsea Park streetcar line. After a good deal of close figuring, he decided he could afford an extra $1 a month for the use of the druggist's phone. He even managed to sell a lot to this druggist in exchange for rent! Encouraged by this ploy, he traded a lot to the livery stable operator for use of a horse and buggy.

Early in 1905, the Reed brothers moved their law firm to the New York Life Building at 9th Street and Baltimore Avenue in downtown Kansas City, Missouri; J.C. Nichols also moved his desk to this office. The real estate firm was now called Reed, Nichols & Co. It was there, on April 10, 1905, that John Cyrus Taylor applied to Clyde for a job. "A keen-eyed, alert young man of 19 who appeared to be unusually bright and willing, with a good personality," was the way Nichols described him.

The Reeds were less sanguine, feeling the job-hunter was seriously lacking in experience. Taylor had grown up in Emporia, Kansas, where he was senior class president and manager of the football team in high school, after which he attended the College of Emporia for one year. His only business experience consisted of a summer job selling a one-volume encyclopedia door-to-door and clerking in the local bookstore.

John Taylor had come to Kansas City from Emporia that spring seeking a better job than clerking. He contacted Luther Thomas, a high school friend who had a junior position in the real estate department of the Pioneer Trust Company. Thomas was able to introduce him to the heads of several of the established real estate firms: Crutcher & Welsh and B.T. Whipple—but they had no openings. Frank Luther then suggested that he try a new subdivider named Clyde Nichols. "He and my brother were at KU together, in the Beta chapter," said Luther. "He is new to the game, but he might be able to get you started."

There was "a quality of eagerness and friendliness" about John Taylor that appealed to Clyde Nichols and he was hired. "It was one of the luckiest breaks I ever had!" Nichols declared later. It was the beginning of a lifelong friendship and business association between the two men. Nichols was the driving genius, with creative, daring, and visionary ideas. Taylor was the profoundly competent administrator, quiet and friendly with his feet on the ground. From the 1920s until the end of his life, J.C. Nichols was almost constantly involved in huge, demanding public service undertakings that took at least half of his time. In a sense, this was possible only because John Taylor was at the J.C. Nichols Company looking after business; he became president in 1940 and chairman of the board after J.C.'s death in 1950. He filled that position with great distinction until his retirement in 1963— after 57 years of service!

Taylor's starting salary as a salesman for young Clyde Nichols was $50 a month. He built his first house in the Highlands and sold it for $1,100. He was pulling his weight ably, looking forward to helping develop another tract of land in Kansas City, Kansas—a five-acre piece to be called California Park. Suddenly, Reed and Nichols had a chance to sell the whole tract at a good profit, and they did. Taylor was dismayed, certain that it would mean the end of his new job.

Almost immediately, however, to Taylor's great relief, Reed and Nichols bought a ten-acre tract (for $800 an acre), not in Kansas City, Kansas, this time, but from 49th Street to 51st Street between Main and Grand Avenue, just beyond the south city limits of Kansas City, Missouri. They called the first subdivision in the tract Bismark Place, an inauspicious beginning for what was to become the Country Club District.

The City Grows Up

As Jesse Clyde Nichols had grown and matured, so had Kansas City. Its strategic location—together with the rise of railroads as the dominant economic factor in the nation—enabled Kansas City to become, truly, the "gateway to the West." The central states had become the breadbasket of the nation. Kansas, which had achieved statehood in 1861, had become a major wheat-growing and cattle-raising state. As a result, Kansas City, Missouri,

was first in the world as a wheat marketplace and second in the world as a cattle market. It was the shipper of many other crops as well. At one time, every potato grown in the West was brokered through Kansas City on its way to the tables in the East.

In the process, the city became a financial center as well, with the Kansas City Board of Trade, the Kansas City Livestock Exchange, numerous banks, headquarters of the Tenth Federal Reserve Bank District, and the home office of major insurance companies, including Business Men's Assurance and Kansas City Life.

The city leaders in this era—grain merchants, meat packers, bankers, insurance executives, and other businessmen—valued the quality of life in the city in which they lived and worked. They strove not only to improve its appearance and ambience but to bring to it the advantages of art, music, and theater. At the turn of the century, there were 21 legitimate theaters in Kansas City. Touring singing stars and concert orchestras traveling by rail stopped here to perform. Interest in art by the civic leaders was exemplified later, when a bronze statue, the "Indian Scout," executed by the eminent sculptor Cyrus E. Dallin for the Panama-Pacific Exposition in San Francisco, was on temporary exhibition in Kansas City. The civic leaders were so impressed with the statue and its appropriateness to the "gateway to the West" that they hurriedly raised money to purchase it and donate it to the city. To this day, the "Scout" is a beloved landmark, standing on a bluff in Penn Valley Park, gazing northward.

Civic-minded business leaders were to be of vital importance to J.C. Nichols. His earliest financial backers were grain merchants, and the banks and insurance companies became sources of capital for his real estate development. The moneyed business people of the city also became the buyers of homes in his Country Club District.

The rebuilding of Convention Hall in 1900 epitomizes the kind of spirit that characterized the city at the turn of the century. In the late 1890s, spurred by William Rockhill Nelson's *Kansas City Star* and spearheaded by business leaders, the city set out to build a convention hall. Funds came largely from public subscription—from single dollars from schoolchildren to large contributions from wealthy boosters—totalling $250,000. As the structure rose downtown, T. W. Johnston, managing editor of the *Star,* waxed eloquent in an editorial: "A community that can build Kansas City's Convention Hall can do anything. That great building is a majestic symbol of energy, wealth, wisdom, confidence, and best of all, unity of purpose." He apparently did not exaggerate, for Kansas City, then with a population of 165,000, was chosen by the Democratic party as the site of its 1900 nominating convention over intense competition from larger and more prestigious cities. Then, on April 4, 1900, three months to the day before the Democratic Convention was to open, the 18-month-old Convention Hall burned to the ground.

Almost before the ashes were cold, community leaders made plans to rebuild the hall—in time to meet the July 4 deadline. They went back to the public for more donations, they leaned on suppliers to rush materials, and they contacted railroad officials to personally expedite deliveries. They offered a bonus to an eastern steel mill to fabricate the beams and trusses on special order and then fur-

nished armed guards to ride with the order all the way to the job site. Hundreds of workers toiled in multiple shifts through April, May, and June. On July 4, the Democratic delegates flooded into the rebuilt Convention Hall, and the gavel was sounded to begin the session on schedule. The convention nominated William Jennings Bryan and adjourned the following day.

At the end of that year, as the nineteenth century ticked away and the twentieth century began, Kansas City threw the biggest party in its history, as a kind of public inauguration of the rebuilt Convention Hall. Thousands of people crowded into its great space to dance and celebrate and cheer as electric lights in a huge hourglass simulating the sands of time ran out for the 1800s.

At the same time, the city was undergoing a transformation that was to affect J.C. Nichols' career and in which he was to become personally involved, namely, the Parks and Boulevard Movement. It is safe to say that no other city has seen anything quite like it, before or since. In the late 1870s, the growing city had only one park, originally a cemetery and only about two acres in size. Farsighted citizens began calling for more parks, which prompted William Rockhill Nelson to take up the cause in the editorial pages of his *Kansas City Star.* When August R. Meyer moved to the city in 1891, the parks movement found a crusading leader.

Born in St. Louis, August Meyer had helped found Leadville, Colorado, where he was in the mining business. In Kansas City, he built a smelting and refining company into one of the city's major industries. As president of the Municipal Improvement Association, he was passionately committed to making the city more pleasant and attractive. In an 1892 speech to rally the Commerce Club (predecessor of the Chamber of Commerce), he delineated his platform:

> City building is a science and a business, not an accident. Cities need parks, also whatever else is needed to maintain the health and comfort of the people and to permit their full development and the enjoyment of all human faculties—as well as providing for material well being. . . . Those cities will grow in population, power and wealth that offer the greatest advantages, and that most quickly and fully meet the demands of the times and of civilization.

A permanent planning and administrative body, the Board of Park Commissioners, was established in 1892, led by Meyer, with landscape architect George Kessler as its paid secretary (and unpaid engineer). Kessler had already worked with his teacher and mentor, Frederick Law Olmsted, on Central Park in New York City and was familiar with Olmsted's ideas for the City Beautiful theme at the Chicago World's Fair of 1893. With Kessler's arrival, broad boulevards and scenic drives were incorporated into the plans for the beautification of Kansas City, along with parks. By 1893, Kessler had surveyed the city and laid out a system of parks connected by boulevards.

It was Kessler's belief that such a road network, a connected boulevard system, would control and direct urban expansion and act as a stabilizing force on property values. His aim was to end the spread of blight and the growth of small villages around the city's perimeter. He believed that the ease of boulevard accessibility would attract residents to these new areas and, in turn, attract needed shops and services suitable to the style and character of the residential sections. The wide streets planned with four or more lanes as major arterials extending well beyond the developed urban area would dictate the pattern of urban growth and easily meet traffic needs of the future. Thus the City Beautiful Movement in Kansas City became defined by parks and their connecting boulevards, which have remained.

The movement was not without stiff opposition from some who, while favoring beautification of the city, objected to the method of paying for it. August Meyer and his organization were against relying on outside capital; said Meyer: "No city can succeed that has not within itself—in its institutions and in its citizens—the force

George E. Kessler, the landscape architect who designed Kansas City's parks and boulevard system, was hired by J.C. Nichols to design his new Sunset Hill subdivision, which quickly attracted prominent Kansas Citians.

that compels success and the qualities that attract population and capital. Capital from without will not deliberately undertake to build a city. The force [must come] from the city."

This meant higher taxes, which were assessed most heavily against the residents of the city who would most benefit from the proposed projects. George Kessler, even before J.C. Nichols, deplored the deterioration of residential neighborhoods by the incursion of commercial uses. He quite frankly intended his boulevard system to "give a *permanent* residence character to certain sections of the city, and determine and fix for a long time to come, if not permanently, the best and most valuable residence property" (emphasis added). In fact, Kansas City's Parks and Boulevard Movement has been called an example of city planning before such a concept existed, an effort at zoning 25 years before the first zoning law, and a type of urban renewal 60 years ahead of its time.

By 1900, opposition to parks and boulevards had lost its steam, largely because of a series of court decisions. Meyer was appointed head of the Park Board; Kessler, park engineer. By 1905, when J.C. Nichols came to Kansas City, 26 miles of boulevards and drives had been laid out, 15 miles of which were completed; and the city's parks had grown to more than 2,000 acres—all at a cost of $6.5 million, an astronomical expenditure in 1905 dollars. Cliff Drive in the northeast section of the city, where large homes already existed, was one of the first completed. South Boulevard, projected to run east and west at what would have been 35th Street, followed. After it was built and lined with lovely trees, it attracted fine homes, some of them built by the Armour meatpacking family. S.B. Armour was a

member of the Park Board, and after his death in 1899, South Boulevard was renamed Armour Boulevard and remained a symbol of elegance until the migration of wealthy families continued southward to Rockhill Place and the Country Club District.

August Meyer died on December 2, 1905. His name is commemorated in Meyer Boulevard, which was built to run through the middle of the Country Club District between 63rd and 64th Streets. Young J.C. Nichols immediately joined the city's progressive leaders in seeking to carry on Meyer's work to beautify the city and preserve real estate values.

Meanwhile, technological advances in transportation continued to spur Kansas City's growth in the early 1880s. A central power station, driven by a steam generator, not only powered the city's first electric arc street lights in 1882, but also provided the power for the 9th Street Line, the city's first cable car line, which ran through a tunnel from the west bottoms to downtown Kansas City. Other traction companies built lines south through Quality Hill to Westport and east along Independence Boulevard. One company built a line south on Troost Avenue to the edge of an affluent neighborhood near Hyde Park. Dummy lines—trains with the steam engine "hidden" to avoid frightening passing horses—provided access to the city's hinterlands.

As the best streetcar service went east from the center of the city, the most active residential growth was in that direction. McKinney Heights, an eight-block subdivision located due east of R.A. Long's bluff-top mansion, became one of Kansas City's most prestigious addresses. This was due in part to its extensive use of deed restrictions that prohibited cesspools, excluded businesses, delineated mandatory

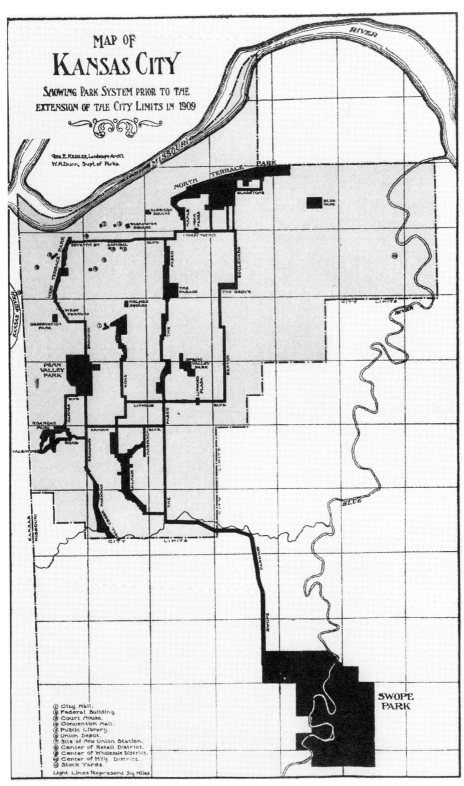

Map of Kansas City's park and boulevard system prior to the extension of the city limits in 1909. (Courtesy of the Kansas City Parks Department)

set-backs from the street, and established a minimum housing cost. McKinney Heights lacked essential elements that would later characterize Nichols' Country Club District; most importantly, it did not control enough bordering property to protect the subdivision from the influence of surrounding developments. The other direction of movement of wealthy and influential Kansas City families in the 1880s was south to Hyde Park and Kenwood, new subdivisions around 36th Street.

In 1887, the publisher of the *Kansas City Star*, William Rockhill Nelson, began construction of his huge, rambling stone home, Oak Hall, still farther south on an estate that covered six city blocks between 44th and 47th Streets, from Oak to Cherry. Beginning in the 1880s, Nelson had slowly acquired additional adjoining land until by 1905 he had 275 acres. On this acreage he had set out to establish "a residential district of high class." The roads curving through the Rockhill District were lined with elm and oak trees. Along the sidewalks, miles of stone walls were covered with rambling roses and honeysuckle. The homes, ranging from relatively modest rental houses to impressive and sturdy stone dwellings, were individually designed (often by Nelson himself) and luxuriantly landscaped with trees and shrubs. Nelson was assisted by George Kessler, whom J.C Nichols later employed.

Southmoreland, a section of estate tracts in the western part of the Rockhill District, was designed to attract the city's most successful and wealthy leaders. One of these was none other than August Meyer, whose mansion and property were later to become the campus of the Kansas City Art Institute. Other Southmoreland landowners included members of the Armour and Cudahay meatpacking families, a nephew of John Deere, and some well-known grain merchants and lawyers. Many of these families had formerly lived adjacent to downtown on Quality Hill, which had begun to decline in the 1880s. But Nelson protected the new properties in the Rockhill District through the use of restrictions to keep out commercial business—an example not lost on young J.C. Nichols.

Nelson had also privately built Rockhill Road, a tree-lined boulevard that wound from north of Oak Hall over a stone bridge spanning Brush Creek, to 52nd and Oak, where an extension went straight west for ten blocks to Wornall Road, giving Rockhill residents a convenient route to the Kansas City Country Club, which lay just south and west of Nichols' Bismark Place.

During this time, William Rockhill Nelson and Mary McAfee Atkins were both affected by two trends that culminated decades later in the Nelson-Atkins Museum of Art, which was to become one of J.C. Nichols' principal responsibilities. The first of these trends was the above-mentioned City Beautiful Movement, which had its origin at the Chicago World's Fair of 1893. The fair featured "The White City," a prototype that dramatized the possibilities for urban and suburban beauty. Designed by noted Chicago architect Daniel Burnham, with landscape architecture by the renowned Frederick Law Olmsted, "The White City" brought together the talents of many of the nation's other sculptors, engineers, and architects. The two principal thrusts of the City Beautiful Movement were the parks and boulevards and making art accessible to ordinary people.

A second trend was a growing interest

in European art. Prominent citizens and civic leaders visiting Europe and touring its art museums in the late nineteenth and early twentieth centuries came to realize that the United States lagged far behind the Old World in the arts. The result was the opening of art museums in several major U.S. cities.

Nelson visited the Chicago Fair, became a champion of the City Beautiful Movement, and spoke out through editorials in the *Star* on the need for an art museum in Kansas City. He also visited European art galleries in 1896, after which he personally undertook to bring art masterpieces to the schoolchildren of Kansas City. Eschewing originals because of their prohibitive cost, he bought instead 19 quality reproductions which he donated to the school system. His personal art collection, however, eventually contained original paintings by Corot, Reynolds, Troyon, Monet, Constable, Gainsborough, and Ribera.

Mary McAfee Atkins, the other prime benefactor, at the age of 34 had married an old friend, James Atkins, who had made a fortune in real estate speculation. He died only eight years later, leaving his widow grief-stricken and for a time in virtual seclusion. In 1893, however, she traveled to the Chicago World's Fair where she was enthralled with the exposition's "White City" and immediately became an enthusiast of the City Beautiful Movement. She also visited relatives in Europe seven successive summers, during which she saw the Louvre, London's National Gallery, the Dresden Gallery, the Luxembourg Museum, and other museums.

Music was also becoming an important part of the city's cultural life in this era. As early as the mid-nineteenth century, there had been brass bands, singing so-cieties, and piano recitals. Around 1878 a group of music enthusiasts began bringing touring orchestras and soloists to present concerts of classical music at the Coates Opera House. At the same time, several theater orchestras offered employment to professional musicians. It was these musicians who formed the core of Kansas City's first real symphony orchestra under the leadership of John Behr. Behr, a violinist who had played in the Boston Symphony, had come to Kansas City in the early 1890s as director of music at the Grand Opera House. His wife was a brilliant pianist. The Behr orchestra performed regularly until it disbanded in 1905.

In the early 1900s perhaps the most celebrated musician in the history of Kansas City appeared on the scene. Carl Busch (later Sir Carl, after he was knighted by the king of his native Denmark), only 25 years old when he arrived, was a handsome, courtly gentleman; in addition to playing the viola, he was a fine teacher, a popular conductor, and finally a composer whose works have endured. He formed the Kansas City Symphony, which performed until the outbreak of World War I.

Roland Park

While Kansas City was growing up, the most important precursor to the Country Club District, Roland Park, was taking shape near Baltimore, Maryland. Interestingly, several of the principals in the development of Roland Park had previously been involved in Kansas City real estate.

In the Kansas City land boom of the 1880s, one of the successful speculators was the publisher of the *Kansas City Times*, Dr. Morrison Mumford. The editor of the *Times*, Charles Grasty, having been encouraged by his employer to dabble in real estate himself, also made some money at it. Grasty was to become the connection between Kansas City and the Roland Park project. For funds, Grasty used mortgage bankers Samuel Jarvis and C.C. Conklin, whose firm was, in turn, a conduit for money from English investors seeking profits in growing American cities. In the late years of the 1880s, the Kansas City land boom cooled off and, coincidentally, Charles Grasty accepted an offer to become editor of the *Baltimore Evening News*.

When he moved in 1890, Grasty took with him his interest in real estate speculation. He soon met William H. Edmunds, president of a trade paper, who wanted to develop 100 acres he owned north of Baltimore. Grasty knew that Jarvis and Conklin's English friends were looking for a more active investment market than Kansas City, so he contacted them. He also got in touch with a young Kansas Citian named Edward H. Bouton, who had helped build a number of houses in developments financed by Jarvis and Conklin between downtown Kansas City and Nelson's Rockhill subdivision to the south. In the spring of 1891, Jarvis, Conklin, and Bouton journeyed from Kansas City for a meeting at the site of Edmunds' land with Albert Fryer from London and Charles Grasty. The men ended up buying not only the 100 acres but also an adjoining 396 acres and forming the Roland Park Company to develop the tract.[7] Edward Bouton, who was manager of the project from the beginning, contacted landscape architect George Kessler in Kansas City, where they had worked together.

Bouton hired Kessler to design the first plat, with instructions to preserve existing trees and add additional plantings. Olmsted's firm was brought in to plat the opening of subsequent acreage, which resulted in larger lots and the addition of curvilinear streets. Roland Park differed from other subdivisions of its day in the amount of preparation that preceded its' offering lots to the public. For one year following approval of the plat, $115,000 was spent on improvements—streets, sidewalks, storm drains, and gutters. Several of the principals built houses to give the development an appearance of ongoing progress and a sense of completion. In spite of initial transportation difficulties (poor roads and no commuter railroad), the first house was sold to a noninvestor in 1893.

The relatively complete deed restrictions employed by Bouton and company set an important precedent for Nichols' later developments. Roland Park limited business zoning to a specific block, set a minimum construction cost for its houses, required set-backs of 30 to 40 feet from the road, prohibited privies and "other nuisances, noxious or dangerous to health," prohibited hog raising within the district, and mandated architectural review of new building plans (a rule referred to by Bouton as "one of the most troublesome and, from my standpoint, the most necessary of all restrictions we have"), the purpose of which was to help ensure consistency and lasting property values.

These restrictions, originally established for perpetuity, were later reduced to a 25-year period, and finally were made renewable by a majority vote of the homeowners. (Nichols, who maintained close personal contact with Bouton beginning in 1912, was to face similar problems settling on an acceptable time period for deed restrictions; he solved the dilemma in an ingenious manner by making their restrictions self-perpetuating at the end of each 25-year period, unless overturned by vote of homeowners representing a majority of the front footage of the subdivision.)

It should be emphasized that the isolated nineteenth-century planned residential communities were not typical subdivisions of the period. In far too many cases, especially during boom times, platted areas were sold to speculators and were never improved at all. The subdivider took his money and ran. However, Edward H. Bouton was a worthy predecessor to J.C. Nichols, sharing the latter's aim of creating a beautiful place to live where property values would endure indefinitely and even increase. Their friendship and mutual respect most certainly exerted a strong influence on J.C. Nichols and his Country Club District.

Chapter 3

1905 - 1920

Reed and Nichols had made about $18,000 from their first two ventures in Kansas City, Kansas. This money, bolstered by additional backing from J.C.'s father, J.T. Nichols, and another Olathe farmer-friend, John Schrader, made it possible for them to turn to the larger metropolis on the Missouri side. In the early spring of 1905, they purchased a ten-acre tract just south of Brush Creek, between 49th and 51st Streets, from Main to Grand. They called the little development Bismark Place.

It did not seem like an opportune location at the time. As we have seen, the residential growth of the city was toward the east along Cliff Drive, though some prosperous citizens were moving southward to such small, private enclaves as Janssen Place, Kenwood, and Hyde Park (between 30th and 36th Streets). Conventional wisdom for realtors of that day dictated that their developments follow streetcar lines. The nearest streetcar line to Bismark Place terminated at 47th and Troost, a good mile away. "Inasmuch as we were beyond the city limits," says J.C. in his memoirs, "there were no streets except those we built ourselves, no city water, [no sewers,] no gas, no telephones, electricity or transportation. Even the stores would not deliver goods to our area."

Growth of Family, Company, and Country Club District

The greatest asset of the new development was that northward and slightly eastward it overlooked W.R. Nelson's Rockhill District. J.C. Nichols was not above gaining a little prestige—and added land value—through association. His first advertisements mentioned the proximity of the Rockhill District. Within a few months, the newspaper ads said that his subdivision "overlooked Rockhill Boulevard to the east and the Kansas City Country Club grounds [now Loose Park] to the west." It was a short leap from this to referring to his entire development as the Country Club District. The term began appearing in his advertising around 1908.

While the embryonic Bismark Place was hardly comparable to Nelson's Rockhill District, J.C. and his new associate, John Taylor, set out to make it a quality area. He later recalled, "Hitting the same stride [as in the Kansas City, Kansas, subdivisions] with long hours and no leisure, John and I worked from early morning building sidewalks, piling rock, cutting brush and grading [using mule-drawn drag buckets and scrapers] what we hoped might one day be streets." Peter Larson, Nelson's supervisor of construction, later loaned them equipment with which to pave the streets and even build curbings, which were practically unknown at that time in the city's outlying subdivisions. Someone gave them an old barn at 26th and Grand on the condition that they raze it and haul away the lumber. J.C. and John tore it down with their own hands and with the boards built two-and-a-half-foot wide sidewalks. The trouble was that the old barn had been built of rock-hard walnut, so the two young men nearly wore themselves out hand-sawing and attempting to pound nails through it. They were eventually forced to drill guide holes for the nails.

After heavy manual labor all day long, Nichols and Taylor would put on their suits and ties, harness up their horse-and-buggies, and greet prospects at the end of the carline a mile away. They worked at selling homes every evening and all day Sundays. "Almost from the start our sale of lots was good," J.C. recalled later. "It was quite a surprise to us when people bought lots even with no assurance as to when utilities or street improvements might be provided."

Apparently J.C. found time during those early years to go to Olathe frequently enough to continue the courtship of his childhood sweetheart, Jessie Eleanor Miller, whom he had known since second grade. Jessie's father, Manuel George Miller, was the wealthiest and most prominent citizen of Johnson County. J.C. said later that when the Millers and their two beautiful daughters rode to church on Sunday in a fancy carriage drawn by a pair of handsome horses from the Miller stables and driven by John McDonald, lifelong family retainer, people along the route gathered on their front porches or peered

from curtained windows to admire the sight.

Jessie had attended boarding school at Vail-Deane Prep School in Elizabeth, New Jersey, where she graduated in 1898. Enrolling in Vassar College, she graduated in 1902 and then returned to Olathe where she was active in the intellectual and social affairs of her town.

Jesse Clyde Nichols and Jessie Eleanor Miller were married on June 28, 1905. The wedding, linking two of the leading families of Olathe, was described in the local paper as "one of the notable social events of the history of the town. All of

Jessie Eleanor Miller, shown in an eighth-grade graduation picture, attended Vail-Deane Preparatory School and later Vassar College, graduating in 1902.

local society was represented as well as friends of the [two families] in university circles and social life."

Though Jessie obviously encouraged young Nichols' attentions, she once told him she would consent to marry him only on the condition that she would not have to live in Kansas City! Nevertheless, Kansas City was where J.C. brought his bride immediately following their marriage. They moved into their first home at 5030 Walnut, in Nichols' Bismark Place subdivision. (The house is still standing, in excellent condition, but has had several additions.) Actually, this house was the third that Nichols had built. Upon his completing the first, which he had intended as his own, a purchaser came along; J.C. couldn't resist the sale. The same thing happened with his second house.

The young couple lived at 5030 Walnut for three years, and during that time, having no city water, they had to carry water from a spring about a quarter of a mile away. They soon managed to obtain a telephone (essential to J.C.'s business), but a year passed before they had gas, water, city sewers, or electricity. Even the streets and sidewalks were not completed. J.C. wrote

The Nichols family gathered in 1908 at the Olathe home of Jesse T. and Joanna (Josie), front row left. In the center of the front row are Josie's parents, Zachariah and Fannie Oslin Jackson; J.C. and Jessie Nichols are in the top row, left; the young boy in the front is Ansel Mitchell.

in his memoirs, "Mrs. Nichols' beautiful trousseau shoes were soon ruined by the mud, but her wonderful sense of humor came to her rescue, and she continued to carry on cheerfully and willingly."

As Bismark Place was adjoined by an open field on the east (presently traversed by Brookside Boulevard and Oak Street), the Nichols kept a cow. But when the boy who was supposed to milk her failed to show up, which happened frequently, J.C. had to perform his childhood chore once again. They had horses and buggies, but these had to be stabled at 47th and Troost, over a mile's walk away. All in all, J.C. characterized that period as "hectic" but added that even his bride's banker father concluded he wasn't going to have to support them.

John Taylor, who could barely sustain a bachelor's lifestyle on his beginning earnings, waited until 1911 to marry Clara Emilie Ruhl. The couple set up housekeeping at 6010 Brookside, in the company's developing Wornall Homestead subdivision.[8]

One of the first lots sold in Bismark Place, right next door to the youthful Clyde and Jessie, was bought by an Olathe friend Albert I. Beach, who completed a house on it and moved in within six months. Beach and his wife soon had a baby girl, Eleanor (later Mrs. Wood Arnold), the first child born in the Country Club District. Beach, an attorney just setting up a law practice in Kansas City, later became mayor of Kansas City for two terms in the 1920s.

Soon, Mr. and Mrs. William Thomas Grant became neighbors. W.T., a college friend of J.C.'s, was already organizing the Business Men's Assurance Company. Starting with $5,000 in capital, BMA, headquartered in Kansas City, grew to be one of the larger life insurance companies

in the United States, with Nichols serving on its board of directors. W.T. and J.C. remained close, lifelong friends, working together in a multitude of civic organizations and volunteer committees for the cultural and business betterment of the city.[9]

During these early years, the young real estate developer attracted the attention of a number of moneyed and influential men who would become his backers. Several were in the grain business. These affluent businessmen with money to invest were ripe prospects for large, attractive homes in an area where home values would be maintained.

When Nichols was a student at the University of Kansas, Frank G. Crowell, from Atchison, Kansas, was on the Board of Regents. He was greatly impressed by the young man's successful letter-writing campaign to pressure the state legislature into increasing appropriations for the school. Crowell had come to Kansas City and organized the Hall-Baker grain company, which became the largest exporter of wheat in the country. He had confidence in J.C. Nichols as an individual and believed in what he was trying to do. Consequently, he became one of Nichols' principal backers.[10]

Other significant early backers were Herbert F. Hall, Crowell's partner in the grain business, and Edwin W. Shields, another grainman whom Nichols met through the first two. "These three men were to have a great influence in my life," J.C. wrote later. "Mr. Hall lived in northeast Kansas City and Mr. Shields near 31st and Forest in Hyde Park. Both neighborhoods were on the downgrade, and these two men were desirous of building fine new homes on large tracts of ground. Together they purchased about fifty acres of land lying between 51st and 55th

Streets, Oak to Holmes," land that adjoined Nichols' property to the east. Hall reserved 11 acres and Shields 10 acres for themselves, "upon which they built two of the finest and most beautiful homes ever built in Kansas City."[11]

The remainder of the tract was turned over to J.C. Nichols to develop as part of his district. The two backers paid for such improvements as curving streets, trees, and landscaping, and in return received one-half of all profits over and above cost. The subdivision was called Southwood Park and remains today a lovely area of fine homes with rolling lawns, adjoining the campus of the University of Missouri at Kansas City.

Still another influential supporter of young Nichols, though not financially, was William R. Nelson. In his newspaper, he carried on ceaseless campaigns for parks and boulevards, good roads and clean streets, tree-planting, and other causes to make the city better, more beautiful, and livable. Attracted by what he saw developing just south and west of his own district, he encouraged Nichols and carried favorable stories in the *Kansas City Star* about the Country Club District over the years.

J.C.'s ability to inspire the confidence of prominent business leaders and to attract them as major financial backers was an enormously important factor in his early success. E.W. Shields was one of these.

H.F. Hall was another financial backer of J.C. Nichols. Both Hall and Shields built imposing mansions in the Country Club District.

Their relationship got off to a rocky start, however. Nichols' second subdivision, platted in 1907, was located just to the south of Bismark Place. The land overlooked Nelson's prestigious Rockhill Gardens residential development, so J.C. called it Rockhill Park. One day Nelson's secretary called to request that J.C. come over to the editor's palatial Oak Hall home to talk to him. Nichols, who had never met Nelson personally, was surprised and not a little impressed at the invitation. So he dressed up in his best suit and arrived at the appointed time. When he was ushered into the study, the big man proceeded to blast him, saying, "You young whipper-snapper, who do you think you are, using my middle name for your new subdivision?" Nichols, taken aback, stammered out, "Sir, I don't understand." He explained later that Nelson was always called by his initials, "W.R."; his full name was never heard. "I had a hard time convincing him that I really had not known that Rockhill was his middle name and not just a name chosen for his beautiful residential district."

Several months later J.C. decided that he and Jessie should pay a proper Sunday afternoon call on the Nelsons. The butler graciously showed them into the foyer of Oak Hall and took Nichols' card, only to return shortly to report that Mr. Nelson had declined the visit. Young J.C. took Jessie firmly by the arm, pressed past the butler, and headed directly to Nelson's library, where he spent the next hour and a half getting properly acquainted.[12]

As soon as J.C. Nichols began selling lots in Bismark Place, he recognized that he had to overcome the disadvantage of the undesirable neighboring properties to the west. The area adjacent to the city limits at 49th Street was occupied by a foul-smelling hogfeeding lot; where the Board of Trade building now stands were a smoky and odorous brick kiln and squatters' shacks. To make his property attractive, Nichols had to buy this adjoining land and get rid of the nuisances. He went back to his Olathe friends and organized a syndicate to purchase the 25 acres, "which proved a profitable venture for them," J.C. noted laconically in his memoirs. Nichols learned a valuable lesson; namely, that to protect the high quality of his residential subdivisions, it was necessary to buy adjoining land to keep out undesirable commercial incursions and create buffer zones, a policy he continued to develop and promote all his life.

In so doing, J.C. Nichols saved the

In spite of an inauspicious beginning to the relationship, William Rockhill Nelson, the powerful and influential publisher of the Kansas City Star, *became an important supporter of young J.C. Nichols and the Country Club District.*

southwest part of Kansas City from the intrusion of industrial development. In the early 1880s, a railroad line had been built from Westport south about eight miles to the small community of Dodson, Missouri. (Originally, an announcement had been made that it would extend on south to the Gulf of Mexico, but it never got beyond Dodson.) The trains were little more than a few freight cars with one or two open passenger cars hooked on behind, the hybrid drawn by a smoky steam engine, which was partially disguised in consideration of the residential section through which the northern part of the tracks ran. Hence it was known as a "dummy line." Southbound passengers from downtown could take a streetcar to

Westport Road and transfer to the Dodson Line. As it made only two irregular trips a day, it was little used by passengers.

Its existence as a freight line, however, was a potential magnet for industry. By 1905, there was active interest in erecting lumber yards, coal yards, warehouses, and factories along Mill Creek (now J.C. Nichols Parkway) and even worse, between Oak and the railroad line, 50th to 52nd, adjoining Nichols' newly acquired residential property on the east. Alarmed, Hall, Shields, and Nichols went together and acquired 27 acres along this part of the route, so that instead of becoming industrial, it became the entrance to the Country Club District.

From Nichols' viewpoint, however, it

In 1887, William Rockhill Nelson began construction of his mansion, Oak Hall. Shown is the library where J.C. and Jessie became properly acquainted with the Nelsons. The surrounding development, which Nelson named Rockhill, featured curved streets lined with elm and oak trees, stone walls covered with roses and honeysuckle, and attractive stone homes protected by deed restrictions.

was equally essential that public transportation be provided to his new district. So he and John Taylor—with financing from Crowell, Hall, Shields, and others—organized the Westport and South Side Improvement Association, which in turn raised $15,000 to buy the old Dodson Line and turn it over to the Metropolitan Street Railway Company. They also offered a $50,000 bonus if the company would electrify the right-of-way as far as 51st Street and provide streetcar service to be called the Country Club Carline. A further stipulation of the bonus was that the company would never haul freight on the line. In March 1907, the company began providing the service, but, unwilling to agree to the freight provision, never claimed the bonus. As soon as the new Country Club Carline was completed, Nichols featured it in his advertising and set up a small sales office at its termination point at 51st Street.

Meanwhile, when Bismark Place sold out, Herbert Hall advanced Nichols money to buy another 20-acre tract immediately to the south and extending to 53rd Street, which he called Rockhill Place and Rockhill Park. These were the first subdivisions in which Nichols applied restrictions—effective for ten years at the time, which the developer soon learned was much too short a period.

With the success of Bismark Place and the adjacent Nichols subdivisions, it was evident that the young developer's ventures would be profitable. The 10-acre Bismark Place tract had been bought for $800 an acre. Each acre was subdivided into at least seven 50-foot-by-125-foot building lots. Even though these lots sold for only $6 a front foot, or $300 per lot, the gross income was $2,100 per acre.

As the Country Club District expanded, the average cost of the un-improved and unplatted land was $1,000 per acre and the price of lots was from $8 to $15 per front foot. This meant that the Nichols Company would realize a gross income of $2,800 to $5,520 per acre. Thus as early as 1907 it became possible to employ a landscape architect to lay out handsome curving streets, to provide a lavish planting of trees, shrubs, and other landscaping, and to build first-class paved streets with curbs and concrete sidewalks—all of which attracted more sales from Kansas City's business and social upper crust. Small wonder that investors sought out J.C Nichols without much effort on his part.

In 1908, after five years of partnership between J.C. Nichols and his fraternity brothers, Franklin and W.T. Reed, the three agreed to a friendly parting of the ways. The Reeds were lawyers who didn't want to become deeply involved in landholding. (Both Nichols and John Taylor continued all their lives to give credit to the invaluable help and sound advice of the Reed brothers in the critical early days of Reed, Nichols & Co.)

J.C. Nichols now set up his own company in a separate downtown office location at 911 Commerce Trust Building. To accomplish this, he received help from W.T. Kemper, president of the Commerce Trust Company. Kemper, a Kansan, had already taken notice of the young developer and apparently admired what he was trying to accomplish. Frank Crowell and Herbert Hall, directors of the bank, helped arrange the deal, in which the Commerce Trust provided financing and office space.

In 1908, at age 28, J.C. became a director of the bank. In that era, when bank directors tended to be gray-haired with mutton-chop whiskers, Nichols was at least ten years younger than any other bank director in the city. He wrote in his memoirs, "Some of the other [Commerce Trust Company] directors were indignant at Mr. Kemper's putting a young, green boy from the country, with so little means, on the board of this great bank. I cannot help but recall that some of those who protested later became financially involved with our company."[13]

A fellow Commerce Trust director, Hugh Ward, a young lawyer whose family estate of some 400 acres was situated west and south of Nichols' property, proved to be another important friend and business contact. Hugh Ward was the son of Seth Ward, a former trapper and army sutler at Fort Laramie, who had purchased the land from William Bent in 1871. Bent had been an early fur trader and scout who had married the daughter of a Cheyenne Indian chief. He had settled the property in 1853 and had built a brick farm house, known today as the old Ward family home at 1032 West 55th Street.

Just before the turn of the century, Hugh Ward had leased a large pasture west of Wornall Road, 51st to 55th Streets to the Kansas City Country Club. In 1906, Hugh Ward approached J.C. Nichols about developing the remainder of his estate. He left all the platting of streets, blocks, building lots, street improvements, and restrictions to Nichols. The Wards bore all of the expense, which came to more than $100,000; Nichols supervised the work and received in return 15 percent of all sales.

For this project and other subdivisions

The lovely and historic Bent/Ward homestead on 55th Street is still admired. Known for its underground passageway through which slaves escaped into Kansas during Civil War days, it was later the home to the Ward family on whose farm property J.C. Nichols built his handsome Sunset Hill District and Country Club Plaza. The adjacent parkway boulevard, which leads south through several handsome neighborhoods, was named for the Ward family.

being developed at the same time, Nichols employed George E. Kessler, who designed the Ward property to take advantage of the hilly terrain, saving the large, native trees where possible. He made the blocks longer in the east-west direction than in the north-south and provided winding streets wherever possible. Many of the lots were oversized, some with 200-foot frontages.

By the time the new subdivision was announced publicly and opened for sale in 1908, Nichols realized that long-term restrictions, strictly enforced, were a key to preserving property values. These became a part of every purchase contract and every deed of title. The new development was named Sunset Hill and very quickly attracted a number of the wealthiest Kansas Citians.

Part of Nichols' planning for Sunset Hill was to provide adequate transportation. The Wards agreed to pay $60,000 as an inducement to the Metropolitan Street Railway Company to extend a streetcar line from 47th Street southwest to 56th Street. The new system, which commenced service in 1910, was called the Sunset Hill Carline.

At the same time, unique among real estate developers of the day, Nichols foresaw the coming importance of the automobile. Impressed with Kansas City's boulevard system, he and Taylor used the Westport and Southside Improvement Association, organized earlier, to lobby the Park Board to approve a boulevard that would run south from Westport down through the Mill Creek Valley to Brush Creek. (Initially called Mill Creek Parkway, it was later renamed J.C. Nichols Parkway.) Simultaneously, with the help of George Kessler, who was a consultant to the Park Board, they proposed a broad divided boulevard to go southwest from 49th

and Wornall Road, curving up and south at the western edge of the Ward land.[14]

In anticipation, the J.C. Nichols Investment Company and Hugh Ward had acquired the necessary additional land from 48th Street to 51st Street, which they combined with Ward land to form a 90-acre parcel. This land was given outright to the city as a right-of-way for the new boulevard. The Park Board approved naming the boulevard after Hugh Ward (who had died in 1909). Ranging in width from 225 to 500 feet, the double roadway with a landscaped median quickly became the most prestigious boulevard in Kansas City and remains so. Lined with beautiful trees and planted with shrubbery and blooming flowers initially paid for by the Ward Investment Company and the J.C. Nichols Company, it became the site of some of the most impressive mansions in the city. (In 1930, Ward Parkway won national recognition as one of the best examples of landscape architecture in the country.)

Adjacent to the Ward land and contiguous with the Bismark Place and Rockhill tracts was the 105-acre Old Simpson Homestead, which reached from 53rd Street south to 57th Street between Main and Wornall Road. After many conferences, the owners, Mr. and Mrs. Edwin S. Yeomans, turned it over to Nichols to develop. As with the Ward estate, the agreement gave Nichols complete say over the platting and supervision of street improvements, which were paid for by the Yeomans family, who also contributed ten cents per front foot sold toward advertising; Nichols received 15 percent of gross sales, out of which he had to pay the rest of the advertising and sales expense. The new addition was called Countryside. Nichols stepped up the frontage of its lots from 75 to 100 feet.

The first J.C. Nichols shops were built at 51st Street, east of Brookside Boulevard. Earliest among these was the Country Club Grocery Company and Meat Market.

Pictured here circa 1919, the area now known as Crestwood (east of Brookside Boulevard and south of 55th Street) housed shanties and showed little prospect for upscale retail development.

As part of the Yeomans arrangement, Nichols set aside a 20-acre tract, between 55th and 57th Streets, Wyandotte to Main, for the relocation of St. Theresa's Academy from 39th Street in Westport to the new Countryside addition. Wealthy Catholics and Protestants alike sent their daughters to this old and prestigious school for girls, so its presence in the Country Club District lent a bit of class. As St. Theresa's trustees were willing to pay $40,000 cash for the site, it made the whole contract more attractive to Edwin and Kate Yeomans.

When work was begun grading Main Street in Countryside, the workmen uncovered some graves, mainly of Union soldiers who had perished in the Battle of Westport fought on the site in 1864. The Nichols Company purchased some lots in the Union Cemetery on Union Hill south of downtown, to which the remains were removed by horse and wagon.

In April 1908, Nichols and his backers purchased the first portion of the Armour farm. The Armour family, from Chicago, was extremely successful in meatpacking and banking. In the 1890s Kirk Armour had begun assembling farm land that finally totaled 1,000 acres to raise registered Hereford cattle. The land lay directly to the west of the Ward estate, extending south from Brush Creek in a widening triangle to 63rd Street. J.C. organized a syndicate with Crowell, Hall, and J.J. Simonds to buy from Kirk Armour's heir, Charles W. Armour, 229 acres of the farm that lay *west* of State Line and south of 55th Street. The price was $75,000, roughly $300 per acre for what was to become, four years later, Mission Hills. This was J.C. Nichols' first venture across the state line and into Johnson County, Kansas. (Later, in several successive purchases made after World War I and in the

early 1920s, Nichols acquired the remainder of the 1,000-acre Armour farm.)

In 1909, Nichols again pushed south on the Missouri side, purchasing 25 acres from 57th to 58th Streets, Brookside to Wornall. The name Brookside referred to a creek that ran from 63rd Street down through a valley to 47th Street, where it joined Brush Creek. Brookside Boulevard now runs alongside the former stream bed, and the waters of the creek are carried in a large underground storm sewer. Again, a hogfeeding lot and a cider mill had to be disposed of before the acreage could be developed into what was named Rockhill Heights. East of Rockhill Heights, Nichols acquired a partially developed tract from Nannie Davis Shelby that became a part of Crestwood.

Indicative of the success that J.C. Nichols had already achieved by 1908 was the second home that he built for his family, this one at 48 East 52nd Street. The large, Midwest-style house was built entirely of native stone on a five-acre site overlooking the creek (later Brookside Boulevard); over the trees to the north could be glimpsed the rooftop of W.R. Nelson's Oak Hall. Nichols employed as architects Wight and Wight, who designed the new St. Theresa's Academy and later, the Liberty Memorial and the Nelson Gallery. The many large windows were framed on the exterior with white stone. Inside, the 30-foot living room was finished in English oak, with a stone fireplace large enough to take four-foot logs. The dining room and upstairs bedrooms, off a large center hall, were finished in mahogany trim with white enamel walls. Each bedroom had a mahogany fireplace; there were four baths. The walls of the house were so thick that the 18-inch deep windowsills provided a handy place for the hired girls to change and dress babies. In this house, the Nichols' daughter, Eleanor, was born on July 1, 1909, and their older son, Miller, on July 24, 1911. (The home, beautifully preserved, was designated a Kansas City Historic Landmark in 1981.)

The Nichols family moved seven years later, in 1915, to a home at 225 West 53rd Street, where their younger son, Jesse Clyde, Jr., was born on September 20. "The people from the Nichols Company pitched in to hurry up the move," says Clyde, "as it was a race with the stork." Miller remembers the home as a tall, three-story house just west of Wornall Road and facing a large pond on the Kansas City Country Club golf course (later, Loose Park). According to Miller, the pond flooded one spring, closing Wornall Road and causing excitement among the neighborhood children as ducks swam al-

most in their front yard. A summer pastime was wading in the pond and retrieving golf balls from the mud with their toes.

In 1909, the year after the Nichols moved into the stone house on 52nd Street, the *Kansas City Star* published an interview with J.C., expressing some amazement that the young developer, at age 29, had 1,000 acres under his management and a $1.5-million operation (in 1909 dollars!). The article added, "Where he got his insight into the development of real estate is somewhat of a mystery. Nichols said it is simply a matter of hustle and watching carefully the growth of the city. However that may be, he became a real estate operator with $1,500,000 behind him to spend in the development of 1,000 acres of land in the same length of time that would take the average young man to

This impressive home of native limestone, built for the Nichols family in 1908 at 48 East 52nd Street, was indicative of J.C.'s success by age 28. Here his first two children were born. It was designated a Kansas City Historical Landmark in 1981.

reach the position of clerk in a rental agency."

Nichols is quoted in the same article, explaining and defending his meteoric rise:

> It isn't my ambition to get all the land out there. . . . but after I would get the management of one tract, I would have to get the next tract to protect it. . . . It is difficult to improve an extended area. . . . We were fortunate to be able to secure, by purchase or cooperation of owners, a sufficiently large area to make it practical to carry out the improvements and develop a high class residential district with regard to the general good of the whole district. . . . We take as much ground each year as the growth of the city justifies and put in paved streets, parkways, broad boulevards and complete a residential section that under the [usual] method would not only take years and far greater expense to develop, but generations could not fit it all together into a large, uniform, protected district.

Just two years later, in 1911, the *Star* reported in another story how Nichols was carrying out his stated policy. He held at that time 1,250 contiguous acres in the Country Club District. He "owned half of it personally" (with financing from his backers, as we have seen), and the rest was "land of other owners that he combined into his proposition so that his general scheme of beautification could be carried on . . . over the whole area." His payroll had reached $1,500 a day, and more than $2 million had been expended in street improvements alone.

After Nichols parted from the Reeds and after he had obtained financing from W. T. Kemper at the Commerce Bank, he set up two corporate entities—namely, the J.C. Nichols Realty Company and the J.C. Nichols Land Company. In the former, Frank Crowell and Herbert Hall held one-quarter interest each (for which they invested $50,000 apiece). J.C., together with his family, John Taylor, and other working associates, held the other one-half interest and exercised control. In the land company, Shields and Simonds were investors, but again J.C. held the controlling interest.

There was a relatively long period of time between 1905 and the late teens before Nichols' ventures began to show substantial profit. In the beginning, when he was situated outside the city limits and without services, some of his competitors wisecracked that his lots were "like cemetery lots: people might buy them, but wouldn't want to use them." As Nichols went on to add large areas of land, imposing rigid restrictions of indefinite length, he had to pay taxes and other carrying charges and then had to add expensive streets, sidewalks, trees, and other improvements. Further expenditures were necessary to bring public transportation to the subdivisions. So for many years, profits were deferred; investors had to be patient and have great faith in what the developer was trying to do.

Throughout this period, J.C. never lost sight of his vision; in fact, it assumed vastly larger and more exciting dimensions. As a result, J.C. Nichols' Country Club District was not only in the path of the city's growth as it turned southward, but the district's distinctive and enduring values exerted a significant pull on the city's more affluent and influential population.

By 1920, it was recognized as a model to be studied by city planners and developers, an example for builders and realtors all over the United States and in many foreign countries. For example, the president of the U.S. Chamber of Commerce, R.F. Grant, a resident of Cleveland, Ohio, said to the press following a visit to the Country Club District, "It can be truthfully said it is the most beautiful residence section in America. . . . There is nothing to compare with it in all the world." The *Ladies' Home Journal* said, "There is a lesson for all cities in the way the Country Club District in Kansas City was laid out and built up with an eye to beauty and harmony and the preservation of the natural charms of the site." And in *World's Work* magazine the same year, Henry Haskell, editor of the *Kansas City Star*, wrote, "J.C. Nichols has made a district of homes, protected by restrictions in the deeds against business invasion, giving the residents a new sense of security and creating a community atmosphere. . . . The Country Club District has become almost as distinctive a feature of the city as the boulevard system. Its contributions to the science of city planning are recognized throughout the country."

Unique among real estate developers, J.C. was obsessed with a determination to build, not just for this generation, but for their children and grandchildren. He sounded this theme many times in advertisements and speeches. As early as 1910, a newspaper advertisement asked, "Wouldn't you and yours enjoy and take pride in a home built in The Country Club District . . . where your children will get the benefit of an exclusive environment and the most desirable associations?" In an attempt to draw buyers from older deteriorating neighborhoods, where houses were crowded onto small lots, he wrote in another ad the same year, "Children's lives are af-

fected by the atmosphere in which they are reared. Build a home in the beautiful Country Club District and insure a healthy growth for your boys and girls— give them the advantages of out-of-doors living, pure fresh air, desirable associations and beautiful surroundings."

So avidly did J.C. believe in the family values he was building into his communities and his city that he took it as a personal affront if anyone moved away! When he learned that any resident of the Country Club District was putting his house on the market, J.C. would call on him and try to convince him to stay—for the sake of his children. At the First Conference of Developers of High Class Residence Property, which he helped organize in 1916, he said in a speech that, "it is a deplorable thing, especially in our western towns, that any man will offer his home for sale" in order to make a profit. This, he said, was a shameful attitude because of the effect on children. "It is an awful thing to raise children and have them think, 'Daddy doesn't own anything; he is here today and there tomorrow.' They have no playmates with any lasting feeling in life, they will have no chums of their youth."

Nichols told the developers that his company had sent postcards to both prospective and current residents with a picture of a quiet residential street with a caption noting it was "where children could take their naps in the afternoon."

He stated his philosophy clearly in a 1920 article in the *National Real Estate Journal*:

> It is the belief of the founders [of the Country Club District] that there is no safer way of bringing about a constant increase in value in its remaining holdings than the creation of an

enthusiastic belief and assurance among the residents of the District that they and their children may continue to live safely and comfortably in their same house and same location in this rapidly growing city for a long term of years.

As noted earlier, one of J.C.'s first innovations was the use of curvilinear streets that conformed to the topography of his subdivisions. Prior to the turn of the century, rectangular platting of blocks was almost universal, as it had been from the time of Egyptian civilization, through the Roman Empire, and in the layout of all American cities. And (with the notable exception of Manhattan Island in New York City) the blocks typically were longer north-south than east-west. Kansas City was laid out in the typical grid pattern, with the blocks nearly square in the downtown business section, but longer in the north-south direction in the residential sections. Some relief was provided by the city's Park and Boulevard system.

In the early Sunset Hill subdivision on the Ward property (the land between Wornall Road and State Line), the streets conform to the topography of the land and, for the first time, the blocks are longer in the east-west direction than north-south—a feature of all Nichols' developments thereafter. J.C.'s reasoning was that this gave the houses better protection from the prevailing winds and a more pleasant orientation to the sun. Clyde, Jr., recalls from his drives around the district with his father that J.C. was fond of pointing out that "the ever changing vista of a curving street is more pleasing to the eye."

Nichols' attention to the streets in his Country Club District went far beyond their vistas. He was committed to providing high quality paved streets. Most subdividers simply staked out the streets according to their plat and graded them. If the lots were to be premium-priced, the developer might lay down gravel or crushed rock. But W.R. Nelson had paved the streets in his Rockhill District, and J.C. decided to follow suit. By 1908, Nichols specified that an eight-inch base of crushed stone was to be laid down and then covered with two inches of heavy macadam (i.e., asphalt) paving. The streets were crowned to drain properly and bordered with two-foot-wide cement curb and gutters. Four-foot-wide "granitoid" sidewalks were added on both sides of the street.

In planning his Country Club District, including the construction of its streets, J.C. shrewdly and correctly foresaw the coming of the automobile. Incredibly, less than 400 cars and trucks were registered in all of Kansas City in 1908; six years later, the number had shot up to 9,774, and this figure doubled in the four years that followed. A high percentage of the cars that accounted for this astounding increase belonged to purchasers of homes in J.C. Nichols' developments, because they were literally engineered for the automobile. By 1917, the increased traffic and heavier weight of motor vehicles caused Nichols to specify a 12-inch base under the macadam asphalt topping of his streets. This far exceeded the standards of street construction in Kansas City (or any other city) and was a powerful attraction to car-owning prospects. The construction of high quality streets prior to the sale of building lots was made possible only by J.C.'s collateral-free line of credit with the Commerce Trust Company. [15]

When George Kessler moved away from Kansas City to St. Louis in 1911, the J.C.

Nichols Company began working with a Kansas City landscape architect, Sid J. Hare, who had trained under Kessler in designing and building the city's Park and Boulevard system. Hare was keenly aware of the coming impact of the automobile upon residential developments and landscaped them accordingly. His son, Herbert, attended the Harvard School of Planning, the first in the U.S., where one of his professors was Frederick Law Olmsted, Jr. After graduation, young Hare helped Olmsted plan Roland Park in Baltimore. Upon Herb's return home, father and son formed a partnership, Hare & Hare, which handled the landscape architecture of all the Nichols Company's developments until the Great Depression of the 1930s.

The Hares' first landscaping assignment was Hampstead Gardens (east from Ward Parkway to Summit, 59th to 63rd) in 1913, where, besides continuing to use curving streets and long blocks in the east-west direction, they introduced small triangular parks at intersections. J.C. delighted in overseeing the landscaping and decorating of these parks with statuary and other art objects. The same year, they began designing Mission Hills, laying out the first "superblocks" that provided oversized homesites for palatial mansions. [16] On Hare's trips abroad he carried letters of credit from Nichols, authorizing him to buy art objects for placement outdoors to beautify the Country Club District.

Another important sales feature of the district from 1911 on was the provision of all utilities: water, sewers, electricity, and gas without special "benefit-district" taxes. As noted earlier, when Nichols started building outside the city limits in 1905, none of these services was available. Therefore, in his early subdivisions such as Bismark Place, Rockhill Place and Rock-

hill Park, Southwood, Countryside, and others, houses were built with septic tanks. Septic tanks work satisfactorily if soil conditions are favorable and if there is room for a good-sized effluent drainage field. Septic tanks on 50-foot frontage lots are marginal. In Sunset Hill, where Nichols was aiming at a "high-class" clientele and where the price of lots was higher, he built his own sewers and sewage disposal system. With the extension of the city limits in 1911 and accompanying annexation of Nichols' properties, city sewers were provided.

Even before annexation, the city ran water lines to supply Nichols' subdivisions, for a nominal up-front cost to the Nichols Company, on the theory that it encouraged growth which would eventually translate into higher tax revenues. The electric and gas utilities followed a similar policy. Thus Nichols was able to advertise his "Country Club District, 1000 Acres Restricted" with "all improvements included" in the price of the lot.

With Kessler's vision of the City Beautiful for inspiration, J.C. Nichols visualized his whole Country Club District as a park-like area, with manicured lawns, trees and shrubs, flowers, parkways, parklets adorned with statuary and art objects, and golf courses to provide large, green, open spaces. In one of his well-known talks, delivered in 1923, he said: "A park is simply one of the fine arts, just as much so as music and fine painting. [Greenswards with trees and gardens] have the power to preach . . . a sermon, to give . . . inspiration to those who come to enjoy. Every people in the history of the world that has accomplished anything worthwhile has done so as a direct result of inspiration. No inspiration ever came from a city of ugliness."

Trees were of special importance to J.C. He may have gotten some of this feeling from his father, Jesse T. Nichols, who, on the very day after his marriage to Josie Jackson, planted a grove of trees on their farm. The grove grew up to be a spot known throughout Johnson County for its shade and beauty, giving shelter to songbirds and animal life. Jesse T. loved its peace and quiet. Also, from his bicycle trip as a youth, J.C. carried with him the impressions of tree-shaded villages in Europe.

In planning his district, he studied the land contours with an eye to saving good native trees wherever possible; and elsewhere he planted tens of thousands of trees from nursery stock. He insisted that the trees lining the streets be pruned carefully upward "to create a nice arching effect." He and his landscape architects approved ten-foot-wide parking areas between the curbing and the sidewalk to give the trees ample space for strong roots. And he specified high curbings to keep cars off this grassy area.

In a very real sense, the golf courses in the Country Club District have served as parks, and also are barriers protecting the district from commercial intrusion or undesirable development beyond its borders. The first of these, the Kansas City Country Club, pre-dated Nichols' first subdivision and, as we have seen, gave the district its name. The club had begun in 1895 as a nine-hole golf course in the exclusive Hyde Park District. When a fire destroyed the club house the following year, the members decided to move farther south. Hugh Ward, one of the club's officers, offered to lease the club about 100 acres of his land from 51st to 55th Streets west of Wornall Road, where the club remained for 30 years.

In 1913, J.C. organized the Mission Hills Country Club, guaranteeing the dues for the first 100 members. Adjoining his subdivision of the same name, it provided an alternative for residents of his district who were not members of the older, exclusive Kansas City Country Club. The 18-hole course, lying west of State Line and south of 53rd Street, was designed by Tom Bendelow, a nationally known golf course architect of the day. The club formed a natural buffer protecting the Mission Hills District on its north border and included stands of stately trees, planted over the years at Nichols' insistence.

The one drawback to the location of the new Mission Hills Country Club was that Kansas had statewide prohibition long before the 18th amendment was passed nationally. J.C.'s solution was to locate the clubhouse just across State Line Road on the Missouri side at about 54th Street, on a small piece of land purchased from the Hugh Ward estate. There, alcoholic beverages could be served.[17]

From the time the Mission Hills Country Club opened in 1915, J.C. Nichols was on its board of directors, serving for many years as treasurer. Under his influence— and on the not unreasonable theory that anyone who could afford a home in his development would probably be acceptable—membership was open initially to all Country Club District residents. Dues were $30 a year plus $5 for each added family member using the club.

As the Country Club District grew, so did the pressure on the two country clubs. In 1918, J.C. organized a Community Golf Club; five years later he added the Armour Fields Golf Club. These provided the Nichols Company with a way to hold onto land prior to its development while accommodating residents and buffering their neighborhoods. (When the Kansas City Country Club was displaced by the formation of the Jacob L. Loose Memorial Park in 1926, it in turn displaced the Community Golf Club. J.C. helped the members of the latter club reorganize themselves into the Indian Hills Country Club, with a large golf course tract east of Mission Road and south of 69th Street.)

Prior to J.C. Nichols developments, almost all residential and business blocks had alleys running lengthwise down the middle. Alleys provided a right-of-way for utility lines; they were used for deliveries, for trash pick-up and sometimes for access to garages—as well as a place for kids to play and cats to caterwaul in the night. J.C. thought them unsightly and unnecessary, and he eliminated them when he laid out the Country Club District. Though utility companies wanted to retain the alleys, they were persuaded to run their poles and wires along the back property line of the homes, where they were given easements to enable them to come in from the street in front to repair or maintain the lines. Garages in Nichols neighborhoods were designed as part of the houses and reached by driveways from the street.

J.C. also thought fences could detract from the beauty of his residential developments. His restrictions prohibited fences in front of the front building line of the house; if fences were added on the sides or rear, their height was limited.

Builders prior to Nichols usually placed corner houses close to the side street in order to get one extra home site per block. Not only did this give the corner houses less yard, but J.C. objected to the practice on aesthetic grounds. In his district, he gave up two lots per block in order to set corner houses back, away from both streets. The result is a more open, gracious look at intersections.

One of J.C.'s more radical departures from traditional home design was the elimination of the front porch and reorientation of the house toward the back garden. When he was growing up in Olathe, houses all had front porches where people sat and watched the carriages and pedestrians go by. But since automobiles went by fast with their passengers enclosed, J.C. argued that the front porch was obsolete. He thought the square footage could be better used to provide a screened porch or a semi-enclosed room at the rear of the house, an extra living room opening out onto the garden that the whole family could enjoy. Not infrequently, he even went so far as to locate the kitchen on the front of the house and the living room at the back, a plan which was not always as popular as he thought it would be.

Perhaps the most distinguishing feature of the Country Club District was the placement of outdoor statuary, fountains, and other art objects as part of the landscaping of parklets, grassy triangles at street intersections, the median strip of Ward Parkway, and any other spot where they might be pleasing to the eye. Most of the art was gathered by J.C. himself on his trips abroad, but other Nichols Company executives and associates also helped, at J.C.'s request, purchasing more than $500,000 worth.

Although J.C. was initially optimistic that the ornaments would be "as safe as they would be on a private lawn," vandals have periodically damaged the statues, knocking off heads and arms and senselessly wrecking other pieces. With its 85 years of experience, the company methodically, skillfully, and promptly repairs the damage and restores the objects, as do the neighborhood homes associations. J.C. introduced educational films and lectures to teach students in the district schools to appreciate and preserve the beauty of their surroundings, while attempting to convey that such beauty belongs to everyone.

The appearance and quality of the homes built in the Country Club District, were, of course, a principal selling point. J.C. realized early on that to achieve his dream of permanence, he had to maintain architectural control of the houses. Architects of the day generally spurned residential design, especially residences built in quantity in subdivisions, preferring to work on public buildings and office structures. As a result, builders usually had the say in house design, working from mail order plans or from plan books sold over the counter. Architect Frank Lloyd Wright did much to break out of this mold in the early part of the century by designing exciting houses in the Chicago suburbs and throughout the Midwest that received national recognition.

While initially Nichols sold lots on which "builders' houses" were erected, as early as 1909 in Southwood and Rockhill Park he began working with the local architectural firm of Wilder & Wight, who designed substantial and impressive homes for clients. From that time forward, Nichols and the J.C. Nichols Company took a direct, lively interest in the architecture of all homes built in the district.

The primary means of architectural control was deed restrictions on the minimum cost of construction. This varied with the character of the subdivision, from an early $2,350 in Rockhill Place (a figure which, astonishingly, limited building such a home to fewer than 6 percent of the wage earners of that era) to $50,000 in Mission Hills. By 1917, sales contracts for lots in the district required that building plans be filed with and approved by the J.C. Nichols Company before construction could begin. Furthermore,

review and approval was not by some outside architectural board, as in some wealthy subdivisions elsewhere, but either by J.C. or John Taylor personally or by another designated company person.

The J.C. Nichols Company organized its own building department in 1909, which was reorganized in 1915 under John Taylor. By the end of July of that year, the company had completed or was working on 65 homes; by the end of August, that number had increased to 98, placing J.C. Nichols among the largest home building companies in the nation. The Pembroke Lane, Greenway Terrace, and Wornall Manor subdivisions and large homes in the Meyer Circle neighborhood were among the many residential areas developed under Taylor's direction. In September 1918, the company announced that nearly 1,500 houses had been built in the Country Club District.

Although America's entry into World War I brought home building almost to a halt, the J.C. Nichols Company resumed with a boom after the Armistice. In 1919, it was at work on 157 homes; ten months later, it had for the first time over $1-million-worth of homes under construction. One of these homes was the A.R. Jones mansion. Jones was an oilman who was moving from Independence, Kansas, and had chosen a five-acre plot in Mission Hills on which he planned to build a $100,000 house. The Nichols Company building department was given the job of designing and building the mansion, the largest single contract they had ever received. J.C. was immensely and justifiably proud of the breakthrough. Subsequently, they built a comparably large residence for A.R.'s brother, Frank Jones.

Mansions built earlier in the Country Club District were an important influence in creating prestige for new developments and for J.C. Nichols. They established and protected the property values in their neighborhoods and attracted other wealthy and influential people. They helped J.C. advance toward his goal of permanence for the Country Club District.

As noted earlier, grainman E.W. Shields, one of Nichols' financial backers, started the trend in 1909 when he built a large, imposing home on the Missouri side at 52nd and Cherry Streets, east of the streetcar line. (Later a part of the Barstow School, it is today the handsomely enlarged site of the Henry R. Bloch School of Business at UMKC.) The same year, Bertrand Rockwell, also a grain merchant, built a huge, 8,600-square-foot home to the west in Sunset Hill, at 52nd Street and Belleview. The first floor featured a 26-by-30-foot reception hall; the second floor had seven bedrooms and four baths plus a large sleeping porch. The Rockwell home was especially notable because it was designed by Mary Rockwell, daughter of the owner and the first female architect to practice in Kansas City. (Mary subsequently designed other adjacent homes for family members along what was named Rockwell Lane.)

In 1910, H.F. Hall, another of J.C.'s major backers, built a 14-room Tudor-style home across the street from the Shields mansion. (This magnificent home was eventually given to a family foundation for the establishment of the Linda Hall Library of Science and Technology.) In 1912, W.S. Dickey, a manufacturer of clay pipe, moved to Kansas City and began construction of a massive $700,000 residence just east of the H.F. Hall residence. (It eventually was given to the University of Kansas City and became the administration building.) Oilman J.R. Battenfeld erected an imposing home nearby.

By far the largest of the mansions on the east side of the Country Club District was the baronial castle of U.S. (Uriah Spray) Epperson, a meatpacking executive and insurance underwriter known for his support of the Conservatory of Music and the Art Institute. Located at 53rd and Cherry Streets, it was begun in 1919 and completed three years later, requiring more than a hundred workmen, many of them European craftsmen. (The residence was later converted into a men's dormitory for the university.)

To the west and south of the Sunset Hill subdivision, other spectacular mansions graced the Country Club District, especially along Ward Parkway. One of the earliest of these was built by Joseph J. Heim, president of the Kansas City Brewing Company, who had been urged by J.C. for over a decade to build a fine home. The architect, E.D. Curtiss, followed Frank Lloyd Wright's Prairie School style, with a low, massive look. Unfortunately, Heim died before the project was completed. Clyde, Jr., remembers, "Dad used Heim's tardy decision and death as a vital sales point with procrastinating buyers from that time on, arguing that each year's delay reduced the *return* available to a buyer." The Heim house, located on the northwest corner of 55th Street and Ward Parkway, was purchased by Bernard Corrigan (head of the city's streetcar system), who lived there for six years before selling it in the 1920s to the Robert Sutherland family.

Adjacent on the west, C.S. Keith, whose fortune came from coal, built a Mediterranean-style, 18-room mansion on a sweeping, four-acre expanse of lawn and gardens. The address was 1214 Santa Fe Road (later renamed 55th Street). The Keiths placed the house on the market in 1919, found a buyer, and signed a contract consummating the cash sale. However, the buyer died shortly after the papers were signed, leaving his widow with a large financial obligation and less need for a large home. She approached J.C. Nichols to see if he could help her find another purchaser for the property. Sensing a unique opportunity, J.C. offered to assume the purchase if the Keiths would agree to an installment sale with very little cash up front. The deal went through, and in 1920 the Nichols family moved into what would be their family home for the next 30 years.

Entered either through the formal door or the porte-cochere entry on the east, the first floor featured a large drawing room, an oak-paneled dining room that seated 18, and a big sun room with French doors that led out onto a paved veranda. These spaces proved ideally suited to the kind of entertaining that J.C. and Jessie felt obligated to do as J.C. assumed leadership of innumerable civic organizations. The second floor had three bedrooms, two sleeping porches, and three baths; the third floor, two bedrooms and a bath, plus three servants' rooms with a bath. The guest bedroom suite was often occupied by prominent figures from Washington, New York, Chicago, and other parts of the country or from abroad. A separate out-building had space for three cars and a stable area with two horse stalls and a tack room; a four-room chauffeur's apartment occupied the second floor. To the west of

The J.C. Nichols family home for 30 years was this 18-room mansion atop a sweeping four-acre expanse of lawn and gardens at 1214 West 55th Street. The first floor, with a large drawing room, an oak-paneled dining room seating 18, and a spacious sunroom, was ideal for entertaining. Upstairs were five bedrooms and a sleeping porch plus servants' quarters. The house, built by coal magnate C.S. Keith, was purchased by Nichols in 1920.

the house stood a lovely columned pergola with a formal ornamental rose garden and a cutting garden.

In the Mission Hills subdivision, J.C. brought the best of his experience to his vision of what a premier residential area should be. It was and is the showcase of the Country Club District and J.C. Nichols' masterpiece, although it came amazingly early in his career. Full-scale development began in 1913/14; however, the first lot was sold in 1909 to A.C. Jobes, a Kansas City banker who was also on the board of two corporations that required him to be a Kansas resident. The lot he bought was on the northwest corner of 59th Street and State Line Road.

Up to that time, prominent Kansas Citians had been snobbish about living in Kansas City, Missouri; they wouldn't have considered living on the "Kansas side." So J.C.'s plan to develop his most prestigious and exclusive subdivision entirely in Kansas was a bold and risky move. He chose to make its location an asset in his advertising: "Mission Hills offers the first opportunity ever given to persons who may wish to reside in a restricted residence section in Kansas, yet share in the convenience and social environment of Kansas City proper."

Because the new section was over the state line, beyond city jurisdiction, all services had to be provided—first by the J.C. Nichols Company and later by the incorporated homeowners association. These included sewers (connected by contract with the Kansas City sewage system), electricity, gas, maintenance of streets and common areas, police and fire protection, and bus service. To furnish water to Mission Hills residents, the Nichols Company established its own water company, buying water from Kansas City, Missouri.[18]

Mission Hills was the first automobile suburb in the Kansas City area—that is, it was not served directly by a streetcar line, the only form of public transportation, and hence was a radical departure for the times. Advertisements assured prospects that "it is possible to cover the distance from Mission Hills to Twelfth Street and Grand Avenue downtown in only eighteen minutes by automobile." In order to sell Jobes his lot, Nichols had to guarantee to build a paved road connecting the home site with what was to become Ward Parkway, Jobes being one of the first residents of the Country Club District to commute to work by car.

In Mission Hills, J.C. Nichols and George Kessler dared to lengthen the blocks even more in the east-west direction. Virtually *all* streets were curvilinear, with the exception of the traffic-bearing arteries, 63rd Street and 59th Street leading into Colonial Court.[19] "Superblocks" were platted with oversized lots with up to 175 feet of frontage, some even larger; one, an entire 30-acre square block, was the site of a single magnificent home.[20]

As stated in a 1913 brochure, the principal aim of the Nichols Company was "to so maintain this property that it will permanently remain Kansas City's best residential district . . . assuring buyers of home-sites that the high standards established will be forever jealously guarded and protected against all undesirable conditions or any civic neglect."

Residential Restrictions

J.C. stated in his memoirs:

> Mr. Taylor and I and others of our staff began to travel over the country to study the history and record of other high-class subdivisions. We were disturbed that many of them

eventually proved financial failures, even though in many cases they had been developed by the heirs of the original owners of the land. . . . It was obvious to us that it was wise to look ahead and study carefully the many influences which would maintain permanency of good neighborhoods, all of which led to the study of self-perpetuating restrictions and setting up of homes associations.

They were able to begin their research without leaving Kansas City. The northeast area of the city along Gladstone and Benton boulevards, originally an elegant neighborhood for well-to-do Kansas Citians, had been gradually encroached upon by apartments and commercial structures. Without zoning, or restrictions on setbacks and height, the new structures had been built at the front edge of the lots, thereby eclipsing nearby homes from both light and air. The wealthy neighborhood of Hyde Park had been controlled by rudimentary 15-year restrictive covenants; but when these expired, allowing businesses to move into the residential area, property values dropped.

Nichols and Taylor's research into the premature demise of tasteful subdivisions took them to Philadelphia, Boston, San Francisco (to inspect St. Francis Wood), the Cleveland environs (to study Shaker Heights), Los Angeles (to analyze Palos Verdes Estates), and to Hugh Potter's Houston subdivision, River Oaks. Europe, where artistic residential areas had shown remarkable longevity, also fell under their scrutiny. Research convinced them that restrictive covenants and responsible homes associations were the keys to preserving a well-planned residential community.[21]

They observed that in the communities that had failed, no provision had been made for schools, churches, parks, shopping centers, or playgrounds. Streets were often not connected with major trafficways, making it difficult to travel to the central business district or to places of employment. In many cases unsightly fringe areas had sprung up, with filling stations, drive-ins, and miscellaneous shops. Billboards, projecting signs, and hodge-podge building design detracted from the appearance of the commercial properties.

The most productive source for information about restrictive covenants was the innovative Roland Park project near Baltimore, developed by Edward H. Bouton. J.C. notes in his memoirs that "meticulous attention [had been] given to every detail . . . [in an effort] to protect the original standards of the property. . . . [We] marveled at the multitude of details to which careful study was given." Restrictions controlled the set-back distance of the houses, forbade stables, swine, and other "general nuisances," established a minimum construction cost for houses, outlawed coal smoke, and, not uncommon for that era, prohibited blacks from living in the neighborhood, except as servants. Additionally, the Roland Park Company provided for a tax levy, not to exceed twenty-five cents per front foot of property width, to pay for street maintenance, sewers, and street lighting, a practice that the J.C. Nichols Company would institute to fund subsequent homes associations in the Country Club District. The first plat of Roland Park carried restrictions "in perpetuity," but Bouton later established a 25-year duration, reasoning that no planner could claim to be "wise enough for eternity."

Nichols differed with Bouton's Roland

Park in the means by which architectural plans for houses were approved. Bouton had used an outside panel of architects to ensure design compatibility of neighboring houses, while J.C. chose to use capable J.C. Nichols Company architects, whom he felt were "better able to interpret the character of the neighborhood and pass on the type of home desirable, rather than placing reliance on outside judgement." Nichols' belief that his company should basically "leave individuality and a spirit of independence to the home owners," prevented his in-house jury from becoming too arbitrary in enforcing design. As a result, less than a dozen sales were "kiboshed" in the first ten years that the company demanded prior approval of plans.

J.C. Nichols initially had some difficulty in overcoming the fears of others about restrictions. His early partners, the Reed brothers, and his financial backers from Olathe were convinced that restrictions would prevent sales, and so the restrictions attached to deeds in Bismark Place called only for strictly residential use, a minimum cost of home construction, and a ten-year duration on the restrictions.

The Country Side Extension, platted in late 1908, was the first Nichols subdivision for which restrictions were filed for the entire project with the initial plat. Although the restrictive covenants carried a 20-year life span, no provision was made for renewal. The basic Country Side restrictions mandated only single-family homes with a minimum construction cost; certain houses on unique lots were obliged to face a specific direction; and blacks were excluded from owning or occupying houses in the community. As J.C. continued to plan and build, he made additions and alterations to earlier restrictions.

Many years later, in 1959, John Taylor remembered: "It is surprising how few residential areas up to that time were protected with restrictions. Our first restrictions were all contained in one paragraph. Later, with the addition of homes association agreements, these covenants covered several pages."

Proper duration of the binding agreements continued to be a nagging problem. J.C. found that a 25-year span was preferable to a 10-year term in certain respects, but that the longer time period made it difficult for the Nichols Company to locate the various owners in order to obtain their legal consent on subsequent renewal efforts. Ownership of some property had passed into estates. Banks and other loaning institutions couldn't be bothered by restriction renewals in a small Kansas City suburb. Some owners, recognizing the profit potential in selling their property to commercial interests once the restrictions had expired, refused to sign new agreements, thus forcing the J.C. Nichols Company to spend thousands of dollars to buy back the land at artificially inflated prices.

J.C.'s first successful effort to solve the dilemma of proper duration for restrictions was in the Southwood Park and Southwood Extension subdivisions. Deeds there included a clause that allowed for renewal of the restrictions if passed by the owners of a majority of the front footage of the subdivision five years prior to the expiration date of the existing agreement. This was a step in the right direction but still proved to be time consuming for J.C. and his associates when the time came to rally support for the vote to renew.

Then, in 1914, J.C. hit upon a method of extending restrictions and allowing for necessary changes without the laborious renewal process. As with many creative notions, his was a very simple strategy, one that reversed the existing procedure. In three subdivisions, South Country Side (55th to 57th Streets, Wornall to Wyandotte), Country Club Ridge, and Mission Hills, he instituted a system that automatically extended restrictions unless the owners of a majority of the front footage of the lots voted to do away with them five years before the expiration date. J.C. commented, "For the first time in the United States, as far as we know, a plan was evolved by which restrictions automatically extended themselves at the end of the original period . . . unless a majority . . . signed, acknowledged and recorded an agreement canceling all or part of said restrictions." Up to the present time, there has been no instance in which the restrictions have been canceled or changed in the Country Club District.

Thus, restrictive covenants became J.C.'s prime instrument of choice to ensure preservation of value in the Country Club District. And J.C. took personal delight in inspecting the district for signs of lax compliance. Later, he made sure his salesmen and "grounds man" patrolled the district for the same purpose. J.C. always carried his small, black leather pocket notebook in which he jotted memos—a garage door left open, a trash can left in front, a street sign obscured by shrubbery. Both Miller and Clyde, Jr., have vivid memories of Sunday drives with the family spent "touring the district," with J.C. making notes of improvements needed or changes to be made. John Taylor once commented jokingly, "J.C. didn't build the Country Club District—it was built by a little black book!"

As the J.C. Nichols Company grew, adding subdivision after subdivision, it became impractical to use company employees to police residential areas in search of unsightly infractions. J.C.'s answer was to convert the existing voluntary neighborhood associations into mandatory homeowners associations, whose first priority was to diligently enforce the legal restrictions. J.C. later declared, "Next to restrictions themselves, [homes associations] are the most important feature in the development of residential property."

The inaugural meeting of the Country Club District Improvement Association, a volunteer group established to represent all Nichols Company developments, was held in Morton's Hall on the corner of Westport Avenue and Main Street in December 1909. Cement company executive Howard McCutcheon was elected the first president and, with his fellow officers, assumed the task of collecting funds and overseeing expenditures throughout the Country Club District. J.C. gave the group a large financial boost by committing his company to pay the fee for all vacant lots in the district.

It was after the large central Improvement Association proved unwieldy that J.C. Nichols proposed flexible, individually organized, state-chartered homes associations as better able to represent the particular needs of each unique subdivision. Mission Hills can rightly claim that its Mission Hills Home Company was the first homes association created by the J.C. Nichols Company. Attorney Edwin C. Meservey wrote the original Homes Association Agreement, which, beginning in 1914, was filed as part of each home site deed. It made membership in the Home Company mandatory and stipulated that the association was not legally permitted to operate with its budget in the red. The agreement further outlined numerous responsibilities: enforcing deed restrictions, maintaining vacant property, constructing and maintaining common sewers, providing electric street lighting, supervising plumbers' requests for cuts in the streets, maintaining streets and removing snow, caring for shrubs and trees and all aspects of the public areas, removing garbage, providing fire protection, maintaining street signs, paying taxes on streets and parks, and furnishing water, gas, and electricity.

Annual dinner meetings of the individual associations allowed homeowners to approve the annual levy, hear reports from committees headed by the directors, and elect new officers. Expenses for the evening were split equally. J.C. also considered the meetings important as social events; they helped promote community spirit and established friendships between neighbors. Casual dinners, bridge tournaments, and an annual Halloween get-together were some of the events sponsored by the homes associations.

The J.C. Nichols Company helped the individual neighborhoods recognize that certain services could be provided more efficiently by cooperation among all the associations. These included fire and police protection, planting and spraying of trees, district-wide park and playground maintenance, care of ornamental statuary and fountains, and the joint purchase of garbage trucks and snow removal equipment.

As early as 1910, when the Country Club District was still outside the city limits, J.C. had solicited homeowners for voluntary contributions toward the provision of fire and police protection, utilities, and public transportation. He discovered, however, that a number of homeowners who stood to benefit from the services did not contribute their fair share. His solution was to include a general maintenance agreement in all sales contracts, making it mandatory for all owners "to pay an assessment not to exceed ten cents per front foot per annum on the first day of July each year for the general maintenance and beautifying of said addition."

In the early stages of a new development, the J.C. Nichols Company, in accordance with a legal agreement filed with the plat, assumed the functions of the homes association until the subdivision had between 25 and 50 property owners. The company scrapbooks note that harsh weather in the winter of 1915 kept company crews busy plowing sidewalks and streets with mule- or horse-drawn plows. The company often continued to provide a variety of services, but at the expense of the new homes association.

The Sunset Hill subdivision was the only one of Nichols' 30 residential areas in which he never succeeded in creating a homes association. Ironically, it also happened to be the location of the Nichols family residence from 1920 on.

Another feature critically important to the Country Club District was the presence of the best public and private schools available in the city. When J.C. laid out the district, he projected the number of children who were expected to live in each section and set aside strategically located land for public schools. In effect, he subsidized them by selling the sites to the board of education at a discount. According to Clyde, Jr., prospects shopping for lots would sometimes say, "This one's very nice, but how about that spot at the top of the hill in the next block?" And the salesman would have to reply, "I'm sorry, but that is set aside for a school." Even if the prospect were willing to pay a higher price, J.C. would not budge; the sites for future schools were inviolate. The E.C.

White School was placed at 51st and Oak, and later moved to 49th and Main; the Bryant School at 57th and Wornall Road; Border Star School at 64th and Wornall; and the J.C. Nichols School at 69th and Oak.

In the same way he planned for schools, J.C. set aside land for churches. Although he usually sold these sites at full price, he customarily made a substantial contribution to the building fund of the churches that moved to the district. The first of these was the Second Presbyterian Church. Its experience is a dramatic affirmation of Nichols' success in creating permanence in his neighborhoods. Second Presbyterian had been one of the dominant churches on Quality Hill. Destroyed by fire in 1900, the church was rebuilt at the same location, 15th and Broadway, where most of its sizeable congregation lived within walking distance. But in just ten years, the neighborhood had declined so alarmingly that only five families in its membership remained there. One elder explained, "Quality Hill has become a district of boarding houses" whose wealthy and influential residents have "moved south." And so it was decided in 1912 that the church "should follow its members and keep them together," which meant following them to the Nichols Company's Country Club District. After a building fund campaign, Second Presbyterian opened its doors in 1915 at 55th and Oak, in a splendid and imposing stone structure that within seven years had 800 members and is still a prominent church today.

In 1916, Visitation Catholic Church and parochial school was built at 51st Terrace and Main; within three years, an addition was needed for the school. At about the same time, St. Andrews Episcopal Church bought land at Wornall Road and Meyer Boulevard, after moving from the northeast section of the city where its once elite parish had deteriorated.

In 1920, J.C. Nichols himself, reared a Presbyterian but not a regular churchgoer, joined with 11 other millionaires to found the Country Club Christian Church. Members first met in the community hall of the Brookside Shopping Center, while planning and then erecting a cathedral-like stone church building with a Sunday school on a large Ward Parkway site at Huntington Road (i.e., 61st Street). Dr. George Hamilton Combs accepted the call to be its first minister. Highly literate and intelligent, a compelling speaker and leader, Dr. Combs served for more than 30 years a large congregation that probably included more influential and socially prominent individuals than any other church in the city.

The year 1920 also saw the beginning of the Wornall Road Baptist Church, the Country Club Methodist Church, the Country Club Congregational Church, and the Sixth Church of Christ Scientist—all within the Country Club District and all an important part of J.C.'s commitment to creating a lasting community where families would live for generations.

Contributing to this aim was J.C.'s continuing effort to build what he broadly termed "community spirit." At this, he was a past master. In the beginning, he relied mainly on his genius for interpersonal communication. He sent notes and letters to the residents of his subdivisions in the same way that he kept in touch with *everyone* important to him. He sent letters to them on job promotions, births of children, personal achievements, and letters of condolence. As mentioned earlier, if district residents failed to mow their lawns or left their garage doors open, they would receive a friendly reminder; but if their grounds looked especially attractive, this, too, would be recognized with a letter from J.C.

The J.C. Nichols Company sponsored, beginning in 1912, an annual "beautiful lawn contest" with cash prizes for the winners. Judges rated the Country Club District lawns according to a complicated formula that took into consideration size of property, landscaping, blooming flowers, and condition of the grass, with additional points for well-kept rear yards and parking areas next to the street. The residents loved it and competed with zest. [22]

Although the company took the initiative in organizing and running most "community spirit" activities, J.C. personally organized a Women's Community Council in 1919. Its chairman was Mrs. A.I. Beach, wife of the mayor of Kansas City. To support the council's work, the company hired a young woman as community secretary and commenced publication of the Country Club District Bulletin—itself a community spirit builder. The women at first concerned themselves with such matters as the speed and noise of automobiles on district streets, the fire danger of candlelit Christmas trees, and the "servant problem." With the arrival of women's suffrage, they put on citizenship classes. For the children they organized clubs for bicycling, horseback riding, nature-study and bird-watching, a summer baseball league for boys, and a weekly story hour for younger kids. They ran a huge outdoor children's pageant in June with more than a thousand participants and a full orchestra.

Perhaps no other "community spirit" activity so well exemplifies the essence of J.C. Nichols as his bird campaign. He was convinced that an abundance of songbirds in his developments would add immeasurably to the pleasing environment and the enjoyment of the residents. He also realized shrewdly that birds would be a God-given tool for effective public relations (decades before that term was invented) to impress potential buyers that the beauties of nature awaited them in the Country Club District. To start, he hung homemade birdhouses in his own back yard and found which species of songbirds they attracted. He then found a supplier of birdhouses in quantity and ordered hundreds at a time, which he sold to residents at cost. Also at cost he provided trees, bushes, shrubs, vines, and grasses that were identified by his nurserymen as desirable nesting sites for the birds.

J.C. found out through his congressman that the government issued a pamphlet describing birds and their habits. The company in turn purchased literally thousands of these, which were distributed not only to the residents but also to prospects, teachers, ministers, and others. Company salesmen put the pamphlets in doctors' and dentists' waiting rooms. Every copy was stamped "Compliments of the J.C. Nichols Company, Developers of the Country Club District."

The next step in his campaign was to mail 15,000 postcards to a mailing list of people in Kansas City and the surrounding area outside the district, enthusiastically praising the value of birds. This was followed up shortly afterward with a second postcard to the same people that acted as a return coupon, inviting them to request a free booklet on the Country Club District. J.C. received 5,700 replies. Each name was checked in the city directory by a salesman to find out the respondent's job status and what kind of a neighborhood he lived in. If he appeared to be financially able to purchase a home in the Country Club District, he was mailed a copy of the booklet.

Nichols brought an ornithologist from Harvard University to deliver a lecture on birds in the Kansas City area. He offered prizes to schoolchildren for the best designed homemade birdhouses. Encouraged by the response, he also awarded cash prizes to children for the first spottings of different kinds of birds on their arrival in the spring. He also asked residents to report to him personally any instances of boys shooting at birds with air rifles.

Was J.C.'s bird campaign successful? He had a census taken in 1914 that showed over 1,000 birdhouses in the Country Club District and 50 different species of birds.

Unmowed, weedy vacant lots were an anathema to J.C.; he was almost fanatical about keeping unsold lots mowed. But he actually ordered the spring mowing of vacant lots delayed in order to protect nesting meadowlarks until the babies could fly. A J.C. Nichols Company salesman who thought that giving such an order was carrying the protection of birds a little too far told of a woman getting up at a 1921 homeowners association meeting to complain about the unsightly tall grass in a vacant lot. She was informed that it had to remain in that condition one more week to protect the baby meadowlarks. The salesman went up to the woman afterward and expressed his own disparaging opinion about the importance of birds. But within that very week, a couple entered his office and said, "We have decided we want a house in the Country Club District where we can hear the birds singing around us all summer." Not long afterward, that same salesman was showing a house to a husband and wife who seemed to be losing interest until she stepped outside and heard the song of a brown thrush from a treetop in the yard. Suddenly she clasped her hands and exclaimed to her husband, "I think I shall like this place, dear. Let's buy it!"

Early Company Leaders

When in 1908 J.C. Nichols dissolved his business association with the Reeds and set up his own company, two corporate entities were established—the J.C. Nichols Realty Company and the J.C. Nichols Land Company. In the former, Frank Crowell and Herbert Hall held one-

A Bryant Elementary School student proudly displays his birdhouses.

quarter interest each, for which they invested $50,000 apiece. J.C., together with his family plus John Taylor and other working associates, held the other one-half interest and exercised control. In the Land Company, Shields and Simonds were investors, but again J.C. held the controlling interest.

In his memoirs, J.C. Nichols stated:

> Through the years, many [individuals] have become part of the organization and have remained to build a great company and a great residential district. I am inordinately proud of the long association of these men, and wish to give them every possible credit for the splendid part they played in the final building of the Country Club District and all that it means to Kansas City. Without their loyal cooperation, hard work, and heartfelt interest and belief in the ultimate goal toward which we strove, it could never have been done.

It was a source of pride to J.C. that no member of the early organization was hired because of an ability to supply needed capital. All the company's vast acreage was acquired through outside backers coupled with good internal management. The early employees, most of whom began in sales, grew into key management positions that they held with distinction for decades. Because J.C. Nichols was such a dominant figure, the critics of the company sometimes accused it of being a "one-man band." In 1939, the *National Real Estate Journal* addressed this criticism directly: "As to the 'one-man' organization [theory], the best answer is that one of Nichols' best achievements was the development of a large and loyal organization that is one of

the most stable real estate groups in the country."

"Stable" was an understatement. Frank Weldon, who joined the company in 1917, spoke for many when he said: "The J.C. Nichols Company really never was a 'company'; it is more like a big family, all working together, making a living and a life. It always was so and always will be, I am sure." (At a 1951 dinner for 31 veterans of the Nichols Company, they collectively accounted for 860 years of service to the company—an average of 28 years apiece! According to Bob O'Keefe, who served over 50 years himself, "If you weren't there over 25 years, you were a newcomer.")

The first and most important man to join Nichols, as has been noted, was John Taylor, whose contributions to the company cannot be overstated. J.C. once commented to Helen Harvey, Taylor's longtime personal secretary, "I never could have made it without John." The *National Real Estate Journal* observed of Taylor: "His sane judgement and rare quality of being able to analyze a project quickly, and put his finger immediately on hidden flaws, has served as a balance wheel to Mr. Nichols' enthusiasm and optimism. J.C.'s career of far-reaching impact was possible because John Taylor was on the job looking after the business of the fast-growing J.C. Nichols Company." Faye Littleton summarized the thoughts of many other employees and associates thus: "Mr. Taylor's intense devotion to the organization and his considered thoughtfulness to every employee, regardless of position, were his trademarks." He was to serve as president of the company for ten years beginning in 1940. Upon J.C.'s death in 1950, Taylor was elected chairman of the board, from which position he worked closely with the new company president, Miller Nichols.[23]

Early Shopping Centers

As J.C. Nichols successfully prevented commercial incursion into his residential neighborhoods, he also recognized the need to set aside specific areas for shops and services. He was one of the first real estate developers in America to realize that money was to be made from building and managing these "shopping centers," as they came to be called.

As early as 1907, he had erected a small pharmacy and grocery/meat market at the end of the streetcar line at 51st Street and Brookside Boulevard, for the convenience of the early shoppers in the Country Club District. Between 1914 and 1917, he had invested $60,000 in the construction of four aesthetically designed service stations at a time when automobiles were still a curiosity. These stations may have been the beginning of the percentage-lease concept, which the company—first under J.C. and later under Miller Nichols' leadership—made famous on the Plaza. When the station leases yielded a 60 percent profit, J.C. was prompted to say to his fellow developers at a 1919 meeting in Birmingham, Alabama: "I may be mistaken, but I don't think there is anything we have discussed that is more vital [than leasing shop and filling station properties on a percentage of sales basis]. I will tell you why. Before this year is over, I will earn $100,000 more [using this type of lease]— double the rent I was getting on a flat rate."

J.C. frequently talked about what had motivated him to develop the percentage lease. When he started to build shopping centers, he recruited merchants from Independence, Liberty, and other nearby towns. These early merchants agreed to put in a store, but often couldn't pay their full rent. So, Nichols worked out the unique concept of a lease based on a percentage of sales. Once the idea was put into practice, it had the immediate advantage of putting the J.C. Nichols Company and its tenants in partnership to ensure that the businesses were as successful and as profitable as possible.

In 1915, Nichols enlisted the help of noted city planner John Nolen to design the Brookside Shops at 63rd Street and Brookside Boulevard. This cluster of businesses and services was planned as a neighborhood center, which included a

"I could not have done without him," J.C. said of lifelong friend and business associate John Taylor, shown here in the 1920s. J.C. was the driving genius, creative and visionary; Taylor, the practical, competent administrator. Starting out with Nichols in the early 1900s, Taylor became president of the company in 1940 and chairman of the board after J.C.'s death in 1950.

combination police and fire station, the site having been sold to the city for that purpose. The attractive buildings were English Tudor in style with half-timbered stucco exteriors. They obviously reflected the appearance of villages J.C. had observed in England and the Roland Park Shops near Baltimore.

An important Nichols innovation was the designation of second-story space at Brookside for doctors' offices. The idea of professional offices above retail shops was an immediate success; seven doctors, lured by the center's proximity to residential concentrations (house calls were still the order of the day), relocated to Brookside within a year. In accordance with J.C.'s original intention to create a community center, the Nichols Company constructed a large second-story meeting room. The space was made available for music and dance lessons (J.C. realizing their importance to suburban parents), for meetings of the Masonic and Eastern Star chapters, and later for the district's flower shows sponsored by the J.C. Nichols Company.

In 1919, as construction began in earnest on the Brookside Shops, the company also expanded the area of the little shops at 51st and Brookside, reconstructing the buildings in the Colonial style of architecture and renaming them the Colonial Shops. At the same time, homes were being built in the upscale Crestwood subdivision, so the first phase of another shopping center was started at 55th and Oak Streets. A Colonial motif was again chosen to help integrate the new shopping center with the existing Colonial Shops only four blocks north.

Merchants associations became key components in the success of Nichols' smaller shopping centers (as they were later to be on the Plaza). Their primary function was to organize activities and promotional campaigns that would help

The Brookside Shopping Center at 63rd Street and Brookside Boulevard opened in 1920. Attractive English Tudor–style buildings housed a drugstore, grocery store, and other shops and services as well as a combination police and fire station. The second floor of this building was designated for doctors' offices and a large community meeting hall.

attract the public. They also were an indispensable link between the Nichols Company and individual merchants, emphasizing that with percentage leases the interests of both are served.

The City Grows in Beauty and Culture

Just as J.C. was dedicated to quality of life in the Country Club District, he enthusiastically joined his fellow civic leaders in creating quality of life for the city as a whole.

Carl Busch had formed the Kansas City Orchestra, which presented concerts until interrupted by the country's entrance into World War I. After the war, Nazareno De Robertis organized the Kansas City Little Symphony. Among its directors and principal fund-raisers were J.C. Nichols, Sigmund Harzfeld, and Cliff Jones, Sr. De Robertis's group of about 30 musicians remained active until 1927 and are credited with building an audience base that appreciated classical music, thus preparing the way for a full-sized philharmonic orchestra.

It was during this era that the musical education of Kansas Citians was first furthered through the Conservatory of Music. In the late nineteenth century, the only music training had been at the Charles F. Horner School, affiliated with the music store of the same name. The conservatory was established September 10, 1906, with familiar names on the roster of original sponsors: W.T. Kemper, Irwin Kirkwood, W.T. Grant, R.A. Long, Herbert Hall, and J.C. Nichols. After a board was organized, J.C. was elected to it and served six years as its treasurer, improving the conservatory's financial condition and helping to raise additional funds for its support.

The Kansas City Art Institute, founded in 1885, was housed in a downtown building on McGee Street. Besides offering instruction in drawing and painting, it provided a gallery for exhibiting the work of local artists at shows held periodically. The fledgling institute ran consistently in the red, however, and was floundering when J.C. Nichols was elected its president in 1920.

Kansas City celebrated the completion of the magnificent new Union Station in 1913, described at the time as "an outstanding architectural contribution to the City Beautiful Movement." Twelve railroads joined in building it at a cost of $6 million. While the building was still in the planning stage, the architect, Jarvis Hunt, proposed that a civic center "in a suitably landscaped park" be built opposite the structure. He was understandably concerned because the station fronted on ugly, massive clay bluffs covered with shanties, signboards, and weeds. Kansas City civic leaders agreed with Chicago architect Louis Sullivan that their city "should insist on proper approaches and a proper environment for the new station . . . set a pace for the entire west . . . [and ensure that the] station has a setting befitting its dignity."

Accordingly, in 1914, the Commercial Club (precursor to the Chamber of Commerce) formed a committee to study plans for station beautification, consisting of, among others, R.A. Long, Walter S. Dickey, William Volker, banker J.W. Perry, and J.C. Nichols. The group proposed an ambitious plan not only to beautify the bluffs but also to build a station park and civic center. When the necessary bond program was brought to the voters the following year, it was rejected.

Mary Katherine Goldsmith in her excellent unpublished thesis, "J.C. Nichols—City Builder," writes: "The general failure of the civic center idea was owing first of all to the tremendous cost involved. Beyond that, the dedicated and experienced leaders of the early park and boulevard movement were missing. August Meyer was dead; Nelson died in April 1915; Kessler was now living in St. Louis; Haff, president of the Park Board, showed little enthusiasm for the civic center idea. The newer civic leaders were hardly organized, and lacked experience to take on such an enormous project."

Even before his appointment to the Commercial Club Committee, J.C. was determined to bring about beautification of the Union Station site, feeling that the first impression that visitors received when arriving by train was important to Kansas City's image and that what was good for Kansas City was good for the J.C. Nichols Company, and vice versa. From this time on, part of his vision was to provide an art and cultural center, originally as part of the civic center, but later separate.

It seemed for a time that his great opportunity would come as a result of his 1919 appointment to the Liberty Memorial Association. As vice-chairman, later chairman, and especially as chairman of the committee for site selection, he influenced the location of the Memorial on the hill to the south of Union Station. Beautification of the bluffs and a plan for an art and cultural center along a landscaped mall were included in the master plan, but were again postponed because of cost. Nichols continued to push for the complex for several years, until another opportunity came for him to envision a major cultural-educational-scientific center almost adjacent to his Country Club District and Country Club Plaza.

City and National Impact

The *National Real Estate Journal* wrote of J.C. Nichols: "In building his homes district, his emphasis on quality and the maintenance of high standards of beauty through control of design; his desire to make every piece of property more valuable, and to provide for retention of value through the years by self-perpetuating restrictions and organizations of property owners to enforce these restrictions; his staying on in a district even after the property had been sold and paid for—these achievements made him an outstanding community builder."

If J.C. Nichols were known only for his creation of the Country Club District and the Plaza, he would still be honored as a pioneer in quality real estate development. Yet his own vision was much broader. His intention was not only to create a better residential community and a better shopping center, but to make the city better, make his peers better professionals, and make the face of the nation better. He spent a great amount of time and energy throughout his career trying to accomplish these goals. J.C. was a crusader for city planning and zoning and an evangelist in raising the sights and standards of his fellow realtors and developers.

As exhausting as it is to contemplate, he was a member and leader (usually on the board of directors) of the National Association of Real Estate Boards (NAREB), National Council of Real Estate Subdividers, National Association of Home Builders, American Civic Association, and, above all, the Urban Land Institute, among others. It is safe to say that most businessmen join such professional organizations to benefit and improve themselves. Not Nichols. He joined to benefit and improve his fellow members.

Before the 17th annual convention of the NAREB in 1925, he said:

> Cities are hand made. Whether they are physically bad or physically good is the responsibility of the Realtor. We cannot claim that our business is a profession unless we constantly endeavor to improve the product of our hands. . . . Unless the Realtor will devote his time to the actual creation and stabilization of property values, the improvement of living conditions, the making of his city more efficient, economical and practical, better planned, more beautiful, cultural, orderly, we fail to rise to the standards of our profession and to our responsibility and opportunity in the building of cities.

After giving his audience scores upon scores of "for-instances," he sounded one of his favorite themes:

> Are real estate values stable in your city, or do they shift almost with each decade? Have you blighted residential areas or abandoned business sections? [There is] gigantic economic loss . . . from unproper encroachment of enterprises of undesirable and conflicting character. The permanence of location, permanent durable construction, stability of real estate investment through the centuries in Europe afford a striking comparison with the constantly shifting locations and character of various sections of American cities, creating a condition causing loan [institutions] to refuse to

lend more than 50 percent of the value of the property. The Realtor can and should stabilize property values, not only as a national economic saving, insuring permanency of investment, but to justify the collateral for larger loans.

And later on, another of his familiar dicta:

> Are you creating the proper standards for developing the best child life in your community—for the future citizens of your city? Are you teaching them to be observant of the beauties and joys of life, appreciative not only of [their] home, but of the . . . right order of things in neighborhood and civic development? The Realtor may be largely responsible for good or bad public taste, resulting from architecture and design, particularly of public structures throughout his city.

Then he challenged them that

> in Kansas City, the Realtors have been the ones who first demanded city planning and zoning for our city. . . . What municipal board should exist without a Realtor as one of its most influential members? In Kansas City, we have several Realtors members of our City Council; president of the Board of Park Commissioners; a chairman of the City Plan and Zoning Commission with four other Realtors on his Board; a Realtor is a member of the Board of Education; a Realtor on the Water Board Commission. . . . a Realtor is president of our Art Institute, vice-president of the Symphony Orchestra Association, and Liberty Memorial Association, and so on. . . . In every study of the city's transportation or

traffic system; in every housing, sanitation, or building code commission; in every industrial survey, population density study, or investigation of freight rates affecting the city; yes, in every educational, cultural, and recreational activity, the Realtor should lead. He is, by profession, best adapted to forecast the city's future needs. Will your city soon outgrow its water supply? What man in your city is in as close touch with its future growth and population needs as the Realtor? Realtors should not be only concerned with those things affecting their subdivisions, but they above all other citizens should be city-wide, suburb-wide and trade-territory-wide in their grasp of future needs.

All very true, but the delicious thing about these exhortations was that the realtor he was talking about, with few exceptions, was J.C. Nichols himself.

His rhapsodic conclusion indicates how passionately he felt about his subject:

The City Practical, the City Orderly, the City of Economy, the City of Efficiency, the City of Health, the City of Wise Plan—yes, the City of Culture and Beauty . . . is one that will stand the competition of time, is the one that will win its race for commercial supremacy, and hand down to future generations a heritage of unconquerable spirit, of imperishable human values, of undying influence for better life among its citizenry [in the future]. . . . The position of America throughout the civilized world is becoming more and more dominated . . . by the success and achievement of American cities. . . . And in the building of cities, no other group of men, no

other profession, has so great a responsibility as the Real Estate Boards of America. . . . [So] make no little plans for your City. They die and are soon forgotten. Make big plans, to stir men's blood and grapple the souls of future generations. . . . May each man in this Convention go home to his own Board, thrilled, inspired, and driven by a desire to assume the responsibility and opportunity that is ours, and so plan and build our cities for the future as to make them the glory and achievement of modern times, and the greatest contribution to civilization our world has ever known.

City Planning

Almost from the beginning of his career, J.C. pushed for city-wide planning to deal with the problems he foresaw: population growth and pressure, traffic congestion, shifting neighborhoods, and ugliness. He began by talking to local groups, later using his national real estate associations and organizations as platforms to carry his message. In 1914, he wrote to George Kessler, who had moved away by then, about his concerns for planning in Kansas City. Kessler suggested that there should be a strong, nonpolitical body to be in charge of the planning function.

Nichols was not alone in his alarm over run-down business districts and urban decay. Like-minded men in other cities, usually realtors or developers, were also talking about the need for city planning. In 1916, the American Civic Association appointed a city planning committee, with J.C. a founding member. A National City Plan Conference was organized in 1917, which J.C. succeeded in bringing to Kansas City for its annual meeting. He contributed $4,000 out of his own pocket to accomplish this, in the hope that it would generate interest among local business and civic leaders. He was disappointed when only three local leaders showed up. Two years later, he wrote in a local article his own specific thoughts and arguments for city planning:

Efficient city planning involves vitally every industry and every individual. It [involves] the use of reason, fairness and foresight in the organic construction of a city—on exactly the same principles as govern any commercial undertaking. . . . An *intelligent* city plan thinks impartially for all parts of the city at the same time, and does not forget the greater needs of tomorrow in the press of today. It recognizes the economy of preventive measures over corrective costs. It is simply good, practical hard sense. . . . A *scientific* city plan should be prepared after a most comprehensive survey, under a well-balanced, continuing commission of realtors, merchants and experts in all phases of civic life.

Nichols had rallied the Chamber of Commerce and the Real Estate Board to support the city-planning concept. Both formed city-planning committees, with J.C. as chairman. (By that time, of course, the Country Club District was the city's prime example of planning.) St. Louis, Minneapolis, and Denver already had planning commissions and Cleveland was working on one. Kansas City's mayor, James Cowgill, himself a believer in planning, called a meeting and began a study. With the help of J.C. and others, a proposed city-planning ordinance was drawn up. It passed the upper house of the city council in May 1919 but was held up in

the lower house. Nichols testified before them, "I am interested more from an industrial and commercial viewpoint than from the point of beautifying the city. We must solve our traffic problem or the value of downtown business property is going to . . . drop." He also felt the proposed ordinance was too weak because the commission was purely advisory and without authority.

As the weeks went by, J.C. told the lower house that each day's delay was costing the city another $100,000. He pointed out that, without a plan, the school board (of which he was a member) was unsure where to build new schools or enlarge old ones. The public works and water departments were unsure where to lay mains. "Every day Kansas City delays city planning," he declared, "is putting money into the pockets of my particular business. The lack of [a plan] in the older parts of the city is driving people to the new districts where there has been planning and where there are restrictions."

Under Nichols' goading, the lower house passed a strengthened ordinance on December 8, 1919. Mayor Cowgill tried for two weeks to twist J.C.'s arm to accept the chairmanship of the new city-planning commission. Nichols, realizing he was in a conflict-of-interest situation, finally declined. A blue-ribbon commission was appointed, four from each political party.

At the same time he was fighting the planning battle in the city, J.C. was also urging state planning. This was necessary in order to give the city commissions the power he thought they should have. In March 1919, he led 160 members of the Kansas City Chamber of Commerce to Jefferson City, where they were guests of the governor at a joint session of the Missouri legislature, called for the purpose of hearing Nichols address them on planning. He was also active in the formation of a Metropolitan Area Planning Committee (representing Jackson and Clay counties in Missouri and Wyandotte and Johnson counties in Kansas) primarily to lay out plans for highways in the area.

Goldsmith declares in her thesis: "During the late teens and early twenties Nichols was probably the leading exponent for city planning and zoning in the real estate business—traveling throughout the country to make talks before civic and planning associations, conferences, and real estate conventions. Some of the talks were published and distributed in pamphlet form. In them he urged fellow developers to 'cooperate at all times with your city planning commission and fit the planning of your property with the general plan of the city.'" And she quotes Herbert Hoover: "The enormous losses in human happiness and money which have resulted from lack of city plans . . . need little proof. The lack of adequate open spaces, playgrounds and parks, the congestion of streets, the misery of tenements . . . are an untold charge against our American lives. . . . The moral and social issues can only be solved by . . . city planning."

Nichols' first talk on planning to a national audience had been made at a National Association of Real Estate Boards (NAREB) convention in Louisville in 1912. He told them, "The growth of your town is largely affected by the foresight of the man who subdivides the land." An efficient plan, he continued, "gives the greatest value and security to every purchaser and adds the greatest amount of value and beauty to the city as a whole."

As will be seen in the chapters that follow, J.C. expended great time and energy the rest of his life to implement these beliefs on a national basis.

Education

J.C. Nichols, from childhood a scholastic overachiever and a Phi Beta Kappa, was keenly interested in education throughout his life. He contributed time, energy, ideas, and money to a number of educational institutions in which he took a leadership role.

In the Country Club District, it all began with two prominent Kansas City matrons concerned with providing "progressive education" for their children and with J.C. Nichols' awareness of the value of having fine private schools within his new Country Club District.

The first of the two women, Vassie James, was born in 1875. Her father, J.C. James, a graduate of Brown University, was a china merchant and served as president of the Kansas City school board. Her mother was in the second graduating class of Vassar College in 1874, which Vassie also attended. She married Hugh Ward, son of Seth Ward and graduate of William Jewell College and Harvard Law School. Hugh Ward died in 1909, leaving Vassie with four young children.

The second woman was Ruth Carr, born in North Carolina, who married William Patton, a Kansas City lawyer and real estate man. He died in 1911, leaving Ruth with one young daughter.

The two women were friends and both had become intrigued with a new trend in education above and beyond that offered by public schools. Based on theories of John Dewey, this "progressive" education stressed knowledge from experience rather than rote-learning and emphasized the "whole person" rather than just the mind. Vassie and Ruth traveled together to Chicago and New York to see the new progressive schools at first hand. Returning, they decided in 1910 to launch a "country day school," favoring this concept over the eastern boarding schools or prep schools. In addition to classes, the full school day included study periods, athletics, and extracurricular activities.

The new Country Day School opened September 28, 1910, in the old Wornall home, at 61st Street and Wornall Road. There were 17 students and three faculty including the headmaster, Ralph Hoffman, who had been hired from the Brown & Nichols School in Cambridge, Massachusetts. The school grew rapidly, to 45 students the second year and 52 the third year. Then the Wornall heirs repurchased the family homestead, and the school moved to a building at 420 West 57th Street. In January 1913, a temporary board of trustees was formed to begin considering the purchase of land for a new and larger campus.

The board settled on 22 acres at 51st Street between Ward Parkway and State Line, part of the Ward property for which J.C. Nichols Company was the agent. The price was too high, so the board began looking much farther south. It was then that J.C. recognized that the construction of a fine private school adjacent to his Sunset Hill properties in the Country Club District would be advantageous. So he countered with better terms for the purchase of the site and an agreement was reached. The first permanent board for Country Day School was established June 30, 1914. Enrollment that fall was 74.

The first location of the Country Day School was the Wornall homestead at 61st Terrace facing Wornall Road.

In 1913, Vassie Ward and Ruth Patton had decided to start a private day school for girls, aided financially by Mrs. Justin Bowersock. Part of their motivation was to lift Kansas City out of its image as a "cow town." A thriving metropolis, they felt, should offer private education comparable to that in other cities. Emphasis was primarily on academics with secondary attention being given to sports, music, and nutrition. The latter subject was of special interest to Mrs. Patton—60 years ahead of her time. Mrs. Ward stressed academics.

They named the school Sunset Hill after an area on the Vassar campus, not the Country Club District subdivision by the same name. The first class was held in September 1913 in Mrs. Ward's stately home at 800 West 52nd Street. The streetcar line stopped at 47th Street; cars were few, so transportation for students was by horsedrawn bus. The school moved the following year to 420 West 57th Street

when that building was vacated by Country Day School. There, the popular extracurricular offerings included theatrical productions, pets, and a May Day celebration patterned after those at Vassar College.

As Sunset Hill expanded, an association was formed to purchase a large stone house at 51st Street and Wornall Road. Membership included J.C. Nichols, who was a generous helper and leader. When a permanent board of trustees was formed in 1919, J.C. was one of them, along with other community leaders who had students at Sunset Hill. His daughter, Eleanor, was in the first class and continued there until twelfth grade when, like her mother, she attended and graduated from Emma Willard, a boarding school in the East. Both Miller and Clyde, Jr., also attended Sunset Hill, as the school accepted male students through the third grade.

J.C.'s interest was not limited to private education. In 1918, as a Democrat, he

The Sunset Hill School was first located in the home of Mrs. Hugh C. Ward at 800 West 52nd Street.

was elected to the Kansas City Board of Education, a bipartisan body with three members from each major political party. It was the only elective public office he ever held. With William Volker, he served on a committee to supervise repairs and improvements of school buildings. This involved spending several weeks each summer inspecting the buildings and determining what needed to be done.

When $5 million in bonds was voted for additional school buildings and renovations, Nichols had an opportunity to make a significant contribution through his experience as a builder. Instead of accepting architects' plans and turning them over to construction contractors to implement, he worked out a procedure calling for conferences between architects and contractors to go over plans and work out their differences, with the primary goal of effecting economies where possible. J.C. estimated that this practice resulted in savings of $500,000.[24]

Family

The Nichols household was a lively one during the decade of the teens. J.C. was increasingly occupied with his company, the development of the Country Club District, and civic affairs. Jessie was a strong mother figure. Eleanor was already exhibiting the stubbornness and rebelliousness that characterized her adolescent years. Miller was active and mischievous, dominating his younger brother, Clyde, Jr.

In the last year of her life, in a newspaper interview, Jessie Nichols expressed

J.C. Nichols, shown here in 1915, was increasingly occupied with the development of the Country Club District and civic affairs.

Jessie Nichols, shown here in 1916, was a busy wife and involved mother.

the two sons' situation succinctly and accurately: "When Miller was born, we wanted him to grow up to take his father's place. When Clyde came along, I knew he would be the last child we would have, so we just let him grow up in his own way."

When Jessie's third child was born, she had wanted him to be named after his father; however, J.C. insisted that the baby should be named Herbert Hall Nichols, after his financial backer. The decision was a standoff for more than a week, when the attending physician took matters into his own hands and inked in "Jesse Clyde Nichols, Jr." on the birth certificate. Jessie recalled later than when J.C. actually saw the certificate, he beamed from ear to ear.

The decision was appropriate, for each son grew up as if their genes followed their names. Miller is tall and lean, like his maternal forebears. Clyde, Jr., on the other hand, matured to bear an uncanny

Eleanor, Miller, and Clyde (on the horse) at the Kane family ranch in southwestern Kansas in 1920.

resemblance to his father. (He joked later, "I got the name and the looks, but Miller got the Company!")

J.C. and Jessie decided they could get away for a trip to Europe in 1914, J.C.'s first trip abroad since his college years. They embarked on a ship of the Hungarian line at the end of July. In mid-ocean, heading toward Europe, they retired to their cabin one night; when they awoke, they discovered the liner was headed west. During the night, World War I had broken out, forcing the ship back to port.

During the war years, J.C. traversed the country from coast to coast spearheading Liberty Bond drives. He was called to Washington, D.C., to map out a national campaign for the American Red Cross. According to the *Kansas City Star*, Nichols was chairman or vice chairman of every Liberty Bond and Red Cross drive held in Kansas City, except for one when he was in Washington.

Miller remembers his mother in her Red Cross uniform. She was very active in the organization through the war years. During World War I a virulent flu epidemic swept the United States, killing thousands of people. J.C. and all three children were seriously ill, but the hospitals were full to capacity and doctors were literally overwhelmed by the number of house calls. So the rest of the family had to be nursed through the siege by Jessie.

In 1921, the entire Nichols family embarked on another trip to Europe. Miller says:

Dad had two business purposes: he was interested in acquiring sculpture and other garden art for his subdivisions, but primarily he was interested in studying Spanish art and architecture and in acquiring artifacts for the premier shopping center he envisioned, the Country Club Plaza.

Because traveling conditions were primitive in some parts of Spain, we three children were put in school in Switzerland, near Lucerne. My principal recollection is of the food. It was German, with lots of noodles and sauerbraten and red cabbage every meal. After three days of this, I rose and addressed our schoolmaster, announcing that "American boys don't eat purple cabbage!"

Chapter 4

1920 - 1929

Of America's many monuments and memorials to World War I dead, none is more impressive than the Liberty Memorial in Kansas City, Missouri. Sometimes ridiculed by its critics as resembling a huge silo or oversized smokestack, it is nonetheless deeply moving in its immensity and simplicity as the visitor approaches it down a long, grassy mall in Penn Valley Park. Situated on a bluff facing Union Station and flanking Crown Center, it dominates the landscape and provides appealing views of the downtown skyline. To strangers approaching the city from the international airport and by trafficway around downtown, it is still the first scenic landmark to greet them.

Though J.C. Nichols is remembered and respected in connection with the fine homes of the Country Club District and with the Country Club Plaza, not many persons associate him with the Liberty Memorial. Yet it was he who, perhaps more than any other individual, was responsible for it.

The Liberty Memorial

In 1919, less than a year after the Armistice that ended World War I, a Committee of One Hundred had been selected to erect a suitable memorial to the sons of Kansas City who had perished in the conflict. Millionaire lumberman R.A. Long

was chairman. J.C. Nichols was first-vice-chairman. At that meeting, J.C. cautioned about the importance of choosing the right name for the project: It should not be a monument to the dead but rather to Liberty.

The first task of the group was to raise the necessary money. It was decided that the base of support should be as broad as possible, with everyone in the city given the opportunity to contribute, even schoolchildren, who might only give a dollar. Incredibly, during a single ten-day drive in November 1919, over 100,000 people contributed $2,517,000. To celebrate, a meeting was held at the Hotel Baltimore before a packed crowd of Liberty Memorial Fund campaign workers. A Nichols Company employee who was present wrote this account:

> Mr. R.A. Long, addressing the crowd, said, "You don't know the value of this man [J.C.] to Kansas City. I have been associated with many big men in my time, but never with one so untiring and so unselfish when the interest of Kansas City was at stake. To no man in Kansas City do we owe as much as Clyde Nichols for his work in this campaign."
>
> The crowd lost control of itself here. The cheer that greeted Mr. Nichols was the longest of the campaign. It was hard to subdue the

workers. Mr. Nichols was visibly moved by this reception which greeted him. He finally spoke, and it could be seen he spoke from the heart. "I love this city. I love the people who are so willing to leave their offices and homes and work as unselfishly as they have worked in this campaign. It is a wonderful thing to live in a town with people such as these," he said, waving his hand over the audience. His voice failed him from emotion. He returned to his seat, and the crowd climbed up on chairs and roared and stamped out a testimonial of approval.

J.C. was appointed chairman of the Committee on Location, which included landscape architect George E. Kessler. In his report to the rest of the trustees on January 24, 1920, J.C. said that his sub-committee had surveyed every possible location in the city, and after a process of elimination, their unanimous choice was an eight-and-a-half acre site on the clay bluff between Union Station and Penn Valley Park. He pointed out that Union Station was a "fixed location which will always surpass any other in Kansas City." It was, he continued, near the heart of the city and the heart of the population. No cost would be involved in improving the site; it was elevated, prominent, and strategically located in an existing 41-acre park. While all these points were indisputably true, J.C. Nichols could hardly be said to be unbiased as chairman. As we noted earlier, he had been determined for years to bring about beautification of the unsightly shanty-littered bluff opposite Union Station.

The committee as a whole accepted the recommended location but did not an-nounce its decision immediately. The high estimated cost of a previously planned beautification program across from Union Station had been due in part to land speculation on the property. The committee decided that this time they would try to move anonymously. Nichols and others formed the "Mazda Realty Company," and realtor H.F. McElroy (later city manager) was put in charge of acquiring 3,600 front feet of property. To avoid any association with the Liberty Memorial project, the men put up their personal money to make the purchases, which took about three months. The Mazda Company then turned over the property to the city at cost, $329,000. This land was about 40 percent of the total needed, but its purchase price established the condemnation price for the remaining 60 percent. It is believed that this tactic saved about $2 million, which proved to be the difference between the ultimate success or failure of the project.

The Liberty Memorial site was dedicated on Armistice Day, November 11, 1921, with an impressive ceremony preceded by a grand parade up Main Street. Sixty-thousand war veterans marched, members of the American Legion, which was holding its annual convention in Kansas City. A crowd of 100,000 cheered from the sidewalks and gathered around the station hill. Miller Nichols recalls watching this colorful occasion from a balcony on the south side of Union Station. Vice-president Calvin Coolidge delivered the dedication speech. Seated on the speakers' stand were the military leaders of World War I, rarely all assembled: Gen. John J. Pershing, Commander of the American Forces and a native Missourian; Marshal Ferdinand Foch of France, Allied Supreme Commander; Admiral of the British Fleet David Early Beatty; Gen. Ar-

Five of the major Allied military leaders of World War I were present at the dedication of the Liberty Memorial site, Armistice Day, November 11, 1921: (left to right) Gen. Baron Jacques of Belgium, Gen. Armando Diaz of Italy, Marshal Ferdinand Foch of France, Commander of the American Forces Gen. John J. Pershing, and Admiral of the British Fleet David Early Beatty.

A second dedication of the Liberty Memorial, celebrating the completion of the central column, was held on Memorial Day, 1926. A crowd of 150,000 gathered on the hill to hear President Calvin Coolidge dedicate the monument. Among other notables in attendance was Queen Marie of Rumania.

mando Diaz of Italy; and Lt. Gen. Baron Jacques of Belgium.

H. Van Buren Magonigle was appointed architect for the project. The unrealistically ambitious plans for the Memorial included the single tall column or spire, "a pillar of cloud by day, a pillar of fire by night," in the grandiose words of the Bible. (Steam was to be generated for the cloud effect, and a gas flame for the fire. The steam idea was later dropped, but the "perpetually lighted torch of Liberty" idea persisted.) The plans also included reshaping, landscaping, and beautifying the bluff and developing the overall cultural/civic center concept espoused by Nichols that had failed earlier. When the cost estimates came in, the plan had to be drastically cut, but the trustees decided to proceed with the Memorial itself, the towering 217-foot column flanked by two small marble buildings housing a modest war museum and exhibits, with the administrative offices and remarkably complete archives housed below the west building.

Completion of the column took five years, marked by a gala dedication ceremony on Memorial Day 1926, preceded by a parade. On hand were representatives of most of the city's civic, professional, service, and military organizations. A crowd of about 150,000 gathered at the hill to hear President Calvin Coolidge dedicate the memorial. Queen Marie of Rumania, on tour of the country, was also present.[25]

New Waterworks for the City

By 1920 Kansas City was experiencing the post–World War I boom. Population had reached 325,000—an increase of over 30 percent in a single decade. Demand for housing far exceeded the supply. The J.C. Nichols Company was sharing in the prosperity, with a record number of houses

under construction. But the waterworks system was outdated and inadequate to meet future needs.

J.C. had become concerned as far back as 1913. Partly at his urging and because of his growing Country Club District, the southern city limits had been extended in 1909, adding about 34 square miles to the city area. J.C. had estimated that as many as 50,000 people would one day live in his subdivisions. And other parts of the city were growing rapidly as well.

The source of city water was the Missouri River and its tributaries. The water system consisted of three pumping stations with intake, followed by filtration and chlorination, and pumps to push the purified water through the city mains. They were located in the east bottoms, the west bottoms (called the Turkey Creek station),

Millionaire lumberman Robert A. Long, shown here at the 1921 dedication of the Liberty Memorial site, served as chairman of the project.

81

and Quindaro, on the Kansas side. Engineers estimated that the city would soon need a huge new facility consisting of settling basins, mixing tanks, filtering and chlorinating plants, a chemical testing building, and primary and secondary pumping stations. The new facility, which would occupy 150 acres, would require six or seven years to build and would cost $11 million. To raise this sum, the city would have to issue water bonds that would have to be authorized by a public referendum.

As the existing system seemed to function satisfactorily—i.e., when faucets were turned on, clean water gushed out—the public wasn't too concerned about providing for *future* needs, especially at such an enormous cost. Nichols could see that a lot of preparation was required and that an effective selling campaign would have to be conducted if the bond issue were to pass.

He started with the Chamber of Commerce and the Real Estate Board, on which he was active. These bodies gave critical support throughout the campaign. The Committee of Twenty-Five was formed, headed by Nichols, to plan and work for passage of the $11-million issue. Nichols spent days at a time away from his office, calling on businessmen, trying to organize them and obtain financial backing for the committee's efforts. To his dismay, he found many of them lukewarm to the project.

Nichols also traveled to and from Topeka to lobby the Kansas legislature to permit Kansas City to acquire tax-exempt land on the Kansas side for the new plant. He finally succeeded in getting an enabling act passed, only to have the engineers and politicians select an alternate site in Clay County, Missouri.

During 1921, as the voting day grew nearer, J.C. literally "beat the streets" (as

he described it) to drum up support for the waterworks bonds. In November, the voters passed it. When the facility was completed, it had a capacity of 100 million gallons of water per day—three times the total consumption when the bond issue passed. Foresight of the engineers, the Committee of Twenty-Five, and of Nichols himself is indicated by the fact that the plant still serves Kansas City today.

Rivers, Railroads, and Highways

In a speech before the Kansas Association of Realty Boards in October 1925, J.C. Nichols said, "Every real estate man should be interested, not exclusively in his own city, but in the whole trade territory—as it is only through the general prosperity of the whole territory that any city can hope to build permanent prosperity."

Nowhere did Nichols better exemplify that philosophy than in his herculean efforts, both regionally and before congressional committees and government agencies in Washington, to have the Missouri River made navigable. Under his leadership, a lobbying drive resulted in an expenditure of $100 million by the federal government to dredge a six-to-nine-foot channel that permitted barge service from Kansas City to New Orleans and the Gulf of Mexico. River transportation of farmers' crops and industries' products helped break the railroads' discriminatory freight rates and thus proved a boon to the regional economy. It enabled the central states to compete with the East and West coasts and the Great Lakes states, which had the advantage of shipping routes through the Panama Canal.

Historically, the Missouri River had provided the first access to the region, as the French-Canadian fur traders came by canoe in the late 1700s to trade knives and hatchets, red cloth and beads, and whiskey to the Plains Indians in return for pelts.

As the size of the cargoes increased, canoes had given way to pirogues and pirogues to keel-boats. The laborious keel-boats had been eventually replaced by steamboats. As trading posts along the river mushroomed into small settlements, which eventually became towns like Atchison, Leavenworth, and St. Joseph, keel-boats were inadequate to service the growing population and freight business. The first steamboat churned its way up the river in 1819; the golden era of steamboating on the Missouri was from 1840 to 1860. These steamboats were beamy and shallow-drafted, averaging 250 feet long, with accommodations for 300 to 400 passengers and room in the hold for 60 tons of freight. Over 700 steamboats traveled the Missouri during their heyday. Many brought westbound settlers to Independence, Westport Landing, and Wyandotte, where they were outfitted with covered wagons to continue their trek westward.

The riverboats, in turn, were replaced by the railroads. With the completion of the Hannibal bridge in 1873, the convenience and almost limitless capacity of the railroads gave them an advantage in all types of shipping to and from the Midwest. The advantage became a monopoly as steamboat lines, unable to compete, went out of business. The rail companies, seizing upon the lack of competition, levied steep freight rates on producers from the seven-state region. An effort to reintroduce larger and more efficient steamboats in the late 1880s met with failure because they could not navigate the river's shallows.

Prominent Kansas Citians tried unsuc-

cessfully to bring about river improvements that would restore competitive shipping on the Missouri. These men included *Kansas City Star* founder William Rockhill Nelson, lumberman Robert A. Long, congressional representative E.C. Ellis, merchant Lawrence M. Jones, and others.

Their efforts culminated in the early 1900s in a campaign by Walter S. Dickey, head of a clay pipe manufacturing firm, to reinstate shipping on the Missouri. Dickey organized the "Kansas City, Missouri, River Navigation Company," with a capitalization of over $1 million from 4,200 stockholders. Fifteen vessels, including twelve barges, were purchased and prepared to haul freight for 20 percent less than the railroad charged. Dickey also invested a large amount in the construction of a wharf, warehouse, and railroad spur to receive the freight at St. Louis. When the United States entered World War I in 1917, the federal government requisitioned the company's boats and barges for use on the Ohio and Missouri rivers.

After the war, Dickey stepped down, saying he was "worn out with the fight." He then approached the Kansas City Real Estate Board, asking them to take over the leadership. J.C. Nichols accepted the challenge. He had no business motive, but was convinced of the importance of agricultural and industrial strength to the health of the regional economy and understood that the reintroduction of water transport would break the railroad's stranglehold on the area.

J.C. states in his memoirs:

> I agreed to accept this responsibility because it seemed to me it was of tremendous value to Kansas City and this part of the country. I organized the Missouri River Navigation Association, raised a considerable fund of

money in contributions, and employed a capable full-time [Executive] Secretary, the late George J. Miller.

For several years I traveled up and down the river, from St. Louis to Yankton, South Dakota, visiting cities and making speeches before public officials of the cities and states. To prevent it from being regarded as too much of a Kansas City affair, Arthur J. Weaver of Falls City, Nebraska, was selected as President of the Association, and he did an excellent job. (Mr. Weaver later became Governor of Nebraska.)

I expended some $42,000 of my own money to carry on that fight, and was successful in developing strong support in a majority of the states . . . along the river. I made many trips to Washington to appear before proper departments of the government and Congressional committees.

An example of the kind of argument J.C. used appeared in a speech before the Waterways Congress in December 1925. He stated: "River transportation would put five cents a bushel more in the pockets of Kansas wheat farmers and mean an additional $7 million annually in farm purchasing power, benefiting every town and village in the region. Statistics show that Kansas farmers would save enough in three years on the two items of wheat and hay export alone to pay for the Missouri River development project."

Nichols' efforts finally carried the day. A nine-foot channel was dredged from St. Louis to Kansas City, and a six-foot channel on up to Sioux City, Iowa. The Missouri was now navigable.[26] The *Star* gave credit where credit was due when it reported: "The simple truth is that, had it

not been for the foresight, the resourcefulness, the energy and the unselfish public spirit of J.C. Nichols, the channel of the Missouri would still be only a dream."

As he was striving to render the Missouri River navigable, J.C. was simultaneously campaigning for better highway transportation, again with the economic betterment of the region as his motive. This was a logical outgrowth of his earlier recognition of the importance of the automobile. In a 1925 speech to the Real Estate Board, he predicted flatly that roads, motor trucks, and cars would become "more potent factors in changing the status of cities and relative population density than were the country's first railroads." He emphasized that roads and autos would change the economic laws as they applied to cities and that "new highways would bring about a vast suburban population, [increased] spending power and more intensive agriculture."

But all this depended on adequate roads and highways, and in the early 1920s roads were abominable. So, throughout the decade of the 1920s, J.C. used his river transportation crusade to campaign for better roads as well. He also made many special trips to Topeka and Jefferson City to lobby the Kansas and Missouri legislatures to improve existing roads and to build new highways that would bring farmers closer to their markets and to extend Kansas City's trade territory. Furthermore, he viewed greater and more efficient truck transportation as still another club, along with river transportation, to force the railroads to reduce freight rates.

The Company

Despite myriad other activities in the service of the city, the region, and the nation, J.C. Nichols' primary focus was on the company during the decade of the twenties. And the J.C. Nichols Company flourished. With nearly 15 years of phenomenal but solid growth behind it, the company was now adding subdivisions to the Country Club District at the rate of almost one a year. By 1920 it was recognized as the preeminent planned residential community in the United States and perhaps in the world. And having added shopping centers as population flowed south, it was now poised to build the Country Club Plaza.

We have seen how J.C. had striven to make the district a parklike area with manicured lawns, shrubs, flowers, and an abundance of beautiful trees. To implement this program, the Nichols Company in 1920 started its own nursery, probably the first developer anywhere to take such a step. The following year Stanley R. McLane, a University of Missouri graduate and member of its faculty, was hired to head the landscaping and nursery department. Horticulturist, entomologist, landscape architect, and contractor, Stanley McLane proved to be a man for all seasons in the Nichols Company.

The nursery, which was first located at 64th and State Line, was later moved to an 85-acre site at 67th and Monticello. There, 150,000 trees and shrubs were under cultivation at any one time, yielding 10,000 plantings annually. By the 1930s, under McLane's management, the company had grown and planted an estimated 600,000 deciduous trees, evergreens, and shrubs to beautify the district streets, shopping centers, and even individual home sites at no cost to the buyer.

Because of the ongoing program, thousands of trees were planted in areas owned by Nichols long before the subdivisions were platted and sold. Although these included many large elms, McLane made a point of diversifying with maples, oaks, honey locusts, lindens, sycamores, and sweet gums. Not only did these provide a profusion of color in the fall, but they were not affected by the Dutch elm disease that later devastated stately elm trees along many streets and boulevards.

Stanley McLane was the author of two books, *Garden Guide by Month for the Midwest* and *The Garden Manual for the Country Club District,* the latter published and distributed by the district's homeowners associations. Among professional horticulturists, an annual national competition was held of identifying and correctly naming a vast variety of plants. Miller Nichols recalls, "McLane won first place

Stanley McLane (left), horticulturist, entomologist, and landscape architect, headed the J.C. Nichols Company's landscaping and nursery department. The nursery, probably the first to be operated by a developer anywhere, produced no fewer than 600,000 trees and shrubs that were planted to beautify the Country Club District.

so consistently that the real competition was to see who was going to get second." Some of McLane's techniques were imaginative, if not innovative. In 1923, Mac used 2,000 head of sheep to "mow" the grass along Indian Lane and along properties adjoining Tomahawk Road, from State Line Road to Mission Road.

The company's planting and maintenance of the district's many street trees won national acclaim for excellence. The landscaping department was responsible for the prompt repair of injured trees, watering, annual trimming, banding, spraying, and other forms of pest control. Timely annual care accounted for the less than 1 percent mortality rate, even in drought years.

J.C. Nichols felt that it was extremely important to begin landscaping immediately following the construction phase. He accomplished this by sending each new homeowner a letter announcing the company's intention to give them "a gift of two deciduous trees, one flowering tree and some shrubs." This program, which promoted and encouraged the homeowner's responsibility for the appearance of the immediate environment, continued through the development of subsequent Nichols subdivisions until the company ceased building homes in 1958.

The Nichols Company added a farm department in 1920, bringing in Ray D. Jones to head it. A graduate of the University of Missouri's College of Agriculture, Jones had worked as a farmer prior to going to work for the company. He and his sales representatives were initially engaged in farm and ranch brokerage in the Midwest, but partly because of Jones' ability and reputation, the department's scope expanded to handling large farming concerns throughout the United States and Canada. In addition to brokering properties,

the department offered a farm management and appraisal service.

One of the key executives who became a part of the company in the 1920s was J.C.'s nephew Ansel Mitchell. He had begun his long involvement with the Nichols Company in 1913 when at age ten he stood on street corners counting traffic on frigid winter afternoons and hauling water to crews during the broiling summer months. Two or three years later he moved up to office boy.

After graduating Phi Beta Kappa in engineering from KU in 1925, Mitchell began his ascent up the corporate ladder by putting his education to use, often doing manual labor in field construction as well. He rose, in time, to be vice-president in charge of the land development department, and later joined the company's board of directors.

The function of the land development department is to convert open land into fully improved, platted property. Under Mitchell's direction, streets, curbs, and sewers were built, utilities installed, art objects situated, parks and playgrounds, golf courses, and parking lots constructed. In short, he was responsible for everything pertaining to the physical layout of the property. Where the Country Club District extended over into Kansas and was not in an incorporated municipality, the land development department functioned almost as a public works department for a town. It was responsible for fire protection, street maintenance and cleaning, and rubbish and garbage disposal as well.

During the 1920s, J.C. continued to expand the building of golf courses to serve both as parks and as barriers that would protect the district from commercial intrusion or undesirable adjacent development. The first of these, the Kansas City

Country Club, predated Nichols' first subdivision and, as we have seen, gave the district its name. The club had begun in 1895 as a nine-hole golf course in the exclusive Hyde Park district. When a fire destroyed the clubhouse the following year, the members decided to move farther south. Hugh Ward, who was one of the club's officers, offered to lease the club about 100 acres of his land south of 51st and west of Wornall Road, where the club remained for 30 years.

Hugh Ward died in 1909 and his widow remarried in 1921 to A. Ross Hill. Not long afterward, the couple became interested in developing the Country Club site. Accordingly, they gave notice that the club would have to move when its lease ran out in 1926. J.C. was concerned about the potential loss of this large open green space in the midst of his subdivisions. His concern increased when the real estate boom of the twenties faded, leaving little demand for high-priced residential lots. So J.C. approached Mrs. Jacob Loose, widow of the founder of Sunshine Biscuits, now a part of Nabisco. He convinced her to buy most of the golf course property and donate it to the city as a public park to be named after her late husband. Thus, the Jacob L. Loose Memorial Park came into being. Its rolling meadows, lovely lake with tame wildfowl, and its handsome rose garden continue as an attractive and popular recreational spot today.

Eager to keep the Kansas City Country Club a part of his district, J.C. then called on Phillip Rheinhardt, a German wagonmaker who had sold valuable downtown property in 1873 and bought large acreages south and west of the city. By 1926, Nichols' Mission Hills subdivision bordered the Rheinhardt land, which lay across the state line, north of 63rd Street and west of Brush Creek (where the creek

runs north and south along Indian Lane). The two men agreed on conditions of sale, and Rheinhardt's son said later, "It is a tribute to my father and Mr. Nichols that the lease and option as signed didn't vary a particle from the verbal but conditional agreement they outlined in their very first interview." The Kansas City Country Club has enjoyed this site ever since.

In 1925 J.C. Nichols made a gift to the city in keeping with the City Beautiful/ Parks and Boulevard ideas initiated by George Kessler. At the intersection of Meyer Boulevard and Ward Parkway, J.C. envisioned a landmark that would epitomize residential beautification—the Sea Horse Fountain set in a 100-foot circular park centered on an 80-foot pool. The Carrara marble figures purchased by J.C. on his 1921 trip to Europe had stood in a Venetian square for 300 years. Now they would adorn Meyer Circle where 28 sprays of water would focus attention on the fountain site.

It was at this time that the Park Board created an art commission to advise in the selection of statues and monuments proposed for boulevards and parks. Quoting from the *Kansas City Star*, "The move comes simultaneously with a generous gift to Kansas City by J. C. Nichols. . . . The Art Commission will begin its work by considering Mr. Nichols' offer."

J.C.'s zeal to provide schools and churches for the home buyers in the district did not diminish. He had set aside a 15-acre site on Wornall Road, between 65th and 66th Streets, and this was purchased by the school board in 1922 for Southwest High School, which began holding classes in 1926. Southwest soon became recognized as one of the outstanding secondary schools in the United States, cited in the national evaluations of 1930 and 1936. In

The Sea Horse Fountain (top), brought from a Venetian square, was given to the city by Nichols in 1925 and placed at the intersection of Meyer Boulevard and Ward Parkway. The graceful pink marble columns (bottom) were imported by J.C. Nichols from Verona, Italy, to grace his Mission Hills subdivision. Together, the fountain and columns represent J.C.'s focus on residential beautification.

the late 1920s and during the 1930s, the children of many Mission Hills, Kansas, families attended either the private day schools (Country Day, Sunset Hill, and Barstow) or Bryant, Border Star, or Southwest High, all on the Missouri side.

During this busy decade, J.C. somehow found the time to personally promote community spirit. William Worley, in his book *J.C. Nichols and the Shaping of Kansas City*, describes what he terms

> possibly the most successful activity of this sort, a series of games sponsored by Nichols each spring for the students of schools in the District . . . called "Community Field Days." Company personnel did the planning in conjunction with a committee consisting of a representative from each participating school.
>
> Nichols attended each Field Day to personally award prizes and to congratulate the winners and runners-up. The first Field Day was on May 12,

1921, with six schools participating. The youngsters engaged in races and relays that included three-legged races, sack races, potato races, handicap races, dashes, pole vaulting, kiddie car races for preschoolers, broad jumps and tug-of-wars. There was a winding of the Maypole.

. . . In only three years the event grew from small beginnings to an involvement of over 3,000 youngsters from eleven public and private schools. The J.C. Nichols Company continued the event until well into the 1930s.

Another popular and colorful annual event during these years was the model-boat regatta, held at the pond in the median of Ward Parkway just north of Meyer Circle until 1927, and after that at Lake Hiwassee.

On Christmas Eve, 1919, J.C. organized a caroling party, going through the district by mule-drawn hayrack wagons.

Community Field Days sponsored by the J.C. Nichols Company involved children from several schools in the Country Club District and their families.

Both the mules and the carolers were from the company. Everyone had so much fun that the custom continued through the following decade. Within two years, the Christmas Eve program included a Christmas Nativity pageant held under a decorated tree at 54th and Brookside. The wagons then took the carolers through the district, where they left a lighted candle at each home they caroled, ending at a coffee shop for hot coffee and doughnuts.

The field days and other annual company events were well publicized in the *Kansas City Star,* where they reflected the warm family atmosphere of the Country Club District and not only engendered community spirit and loyalty to the district, but provided a long-term sales tool. In fact, the Christmas caroling event was coordinated by the Nichols Company sales department.

J.C. Nichols was a consummate communicator, not only verbally and through letters and memos, but through the many postcards he sent home from almost every out-of-town trip. He dashed them off daily not only to his mother, other family members, friends, and associates in his many enterprises, but also to a whole spectrum of government officials, civic leaders, Plaza merchants, and others. He usually took along a Kansas City telephone directory and a city directory for addresses. Clyde, Jr., who patronized his father's barber on the Plaza, remembers once when the barber couldn't wait to show him a postcard he had received from J.C. in Europe. "Mr. Nichols took time to write to me," he kept saying wonderingly.

By 1921, homeowners associations were being formed, and they gradually took over neighborhood activities. An annual dinner for homeowners association directors was begun in 1926 to promote friend-

ships among members of the various associations and to familiarize them with problems being faced by groups in Nichols Company neighborhoods. Acknowledging the need for ongoing civic education, J.C. often arranged for business executives from utility or transportation companies, as well as city and county government officials, to be guest speakers at the gatherings.

Early in the development of the Country Club District, J.C. Nichols and John Taylor realized that protecting it for posterity would necessitate the exertion of some indirect influence on surrounding properties. They felt that the more general use of restrictive covenants, such as they had in the district, would discourage unaesthetic, haphazard building practices in other city neighborhoods. In their view, the establishment of city-planning and zoning commissions, endowed with the power to enact city-wide ordinances, was the only long-term way to prevent an encroachment of unsightly filling stations, hot dog stands, and drive-ins on the perimeters of well-designed residential areas. Zoning regulations, they believed, should attempt to group stores into shopping centers within close proximity of area residents. Not only that, the design of such shopping centers should be harmonious with the surrounding neighborhood.

Nichols and Taylor also perceived that zoning commissions should all use similar criteria when allocating space for churches, schools, golf clubs, and parks. Accordingly, J.C. worked persistently to bring a planning and zoning commission to Kansas City. Later he stumped the rest of the country to accomplish the same thing in other cities—the most prominent community planner to do so.

John Taylor, on his retirement, recalled:

In the early days there was, of course, no such thing as zoning. Today, the first question asked about a property is, how is it zoned? In spite of the complaints that some of us may have from time to time concerning zoning on a piece of property, there is no question but that zoning has been very beneficial to our city. I can recall when there were men who made a business of buying ground on one of our boulevards or better streets and, with the threat of building either an apartment building or a store on some corner immediately adjacent to a nice residence, would sell this vacant property to the neighbors at a substantial profit. Under such conditions, the public gradually became sold on restrictions and zoning.

The first zoning ordinance in Kansas City was passed June 4, 1923. With the passage of this ordinance, a use map was prepared showing the use to which any piece of property in Kansas City might be put. Quite naturally, there were many complaints but actually it was surprising that such a radical move could be made without more serious objection. You had men say, "I bought and paid for that property and nobody is going to tell me how I can use it," but the law was upheld and the rights and benefits of the many over the individual have now become well established.

Within the district, the nature and duration of restrictive covenants were being formulated and applied. By the time the Nichols Company filed its plat for the Armour Hills subdivision in 1922, J.C. had decided to standardize previous subdivisions up to the same level of pro-

tection. Nichols' legal consultants determined that the binding agreements should provide for single family residential use, set minimum home construction costs, ban blacks from residency, dictate the placement of any outbuildings, establish requirements for yard space and setbacks from the street, set maximum house widths, determine the placement and alignment of houses on their lots, and limit the distance structural features could protrude from a house. All these restrictions were self-perpetuating and enforceable by the J.C. Nichols Company, or by the legally established homes associations.

As early as October 1911, one of the J.C. Nichols Company advertisements had read, "Permanence—That's the Spirit upon which the Country Club District was conceived and upon which every detail of it has been developed, established and protected." By 1929, J.C. had achieved this aim. He had also set out to attract the wealthy and influential people of the city to the district, and he had accomplished this goal as well. Of the eleven millionaires living in the state of Kansas (according to the 1930 census), the Nichols Company had built homes for seven of them in Mission Hills and Indian Hills during the 1920s. In 1930, the Century of Leadership Project, a sociological study, identified about 1,300 names as composing upper class society in Kansas City. More than 55 percent of them lived in Nichols subdivisions. This was an era of realized dreams for J.C. Nichols. [27]

The Country Club Plaza

Sometime in 1912, J.C. had stood atop the hills overlooking the marshy, weed-infested oxbow of Brush Creek valley and envisioned the glistening magnificence of a beautifully designed commercial business district laid out below him. It would be still another application of the axiom that had been central to J.C.'s Harvard studies and was the creed of the Nichols Company: In any successful land development, you must create permanent value.

His Country Club District was growing; J.C. estimated that some day 50,000 people would live there, who needed more than neighborhood shops and services. Yet uncontrolled commercial development adjacent to his residential neighborhoods was an anathema to him. Instead, the business district he envisioned would provide needed shops and services in a controlled environment, a Spanish marketplace magically transported to suburban Kansas City. It would be, simultaneously, a gateway to his residential area and an all-important buffer to protect his subdivisions from the encroachment of an expanding city.

The realization of J.C.'s vision, the multimillion-dollar Country Club Plaza, has taken its place in real estate history alongside his residential development. Kenneth Jackson, in his 1985 book *Crabgrass Frontier: The Suburbanization of the United States,* called it the first modern shopping center in the world. "Nichols created the idea of the planned regional shopping center," he declares. It was also the first shopping center planned specifically for the private automobile.

The seeds for the idea of the Country Club Plaza had been planted during Nichols' European trips. Before construction got under way in October 1922 on the first Plaza building, J.C. and Jessie had visited Italy to study hillside villas, Spain for architectural style, France for the uniform building heights of Paris, Germany for streets planned in relation to building density and the most efficient traffic movement, and England for its thoroughly planned "new towns."

This mansion, commissioned by millionaire oilman Frank E. Jones, was the first completed after the J.C. Nichols Company began the construction of homes. It later was the home of Mrs. Russell Stover and presently of the Barnett Helzbergs. By 1930, the company had built homes in Mission Hills and Indian Hills for seven of the eleven millionaires living in the state of Kansas.

J.C. was especially intrigued by the colorful Spanish markets with their ornate towers, open plazas, balconied buildings, fountains, and generous display of tile and ornamental iron. An article by Richard Longstreth in the *Harvard Architectural Review*, offers this explanation for Nichols' choice of a Spanish theme for the Plaza:

> The fact that European towns had sparked his concern for building as a long-term investment made them a logical source of inspiration. The specific choice of the Spanish colonial motifs for the center stemmed from several factors. . . . The Spanish had once had colonial control of the region where Kansas City lay; Spanish explorers had earlier penetrated into parts of eastern Kansas; and the metropolitan area had been an important departure point for the Southwest since the mid-19th century. Nichols' love of Hispanic architecture was also reinforced by a trip to the Iberian peninsula in 1922.
>
> Spanish motifs were viewed as being ideal for generating a festive, slightly exotic atmosphere that could enhance merchandising efforts. Spanish classical architecture offered a rich source for the design of towers, yet one that for most Americans would carry less overt religious or institutional overtones than would counterparts in, say, England or France. Stucco wall surface and plaster ornament were handsome and relatively enduring [in] the region's climate, while they were less expensive than . . . brick or stone. Glazed tiles and ornamental ironwork offered further flourish that could be concentrated in a few areas and required little maintenance.

> Spanish motifs may also have been chosen because they offered a new image, especially in the Midwest. During the 1920s work of the genre was for the most part concentrated in the West Coast and Florida. The mode, now generally known as the Spanish Colonial Revival, had gained considerable recognition and popularity at the 1915 Panama-California Exposition in San Diego and was fast becoming a symbol of elegant suburban and resort developments in other regions.

J.C.'s vision of the Country Club Plaza was based on his belief in the future of the automobile, which, as we have seen, had already influenced his residential development. His travel experience, starting with his Liberty Bond drive tours across the country during World War I, had confirmed his conviction that the automobile was catching on and would change the face of cities. He foresaw that retail trade would move outward from downtown centers, where it had always been concentrated. Downtown retail centers had not been designed to accommodate the automobile. Cities in the 1920s were compact and depended on the streetcar. But the American people had chosen the car not only as their primary mode of transportation, but also as an economic and social status symbol. Nichols reasoned that if people could not or would not drive downtown to shop, they would drive somewhere else rather than take a streetcar.

Accordingly, in planning the Country Club Plaza, he devoted 46 percent of the land to wide streets and landscaped parking lots that sometimes occupied whole city blocks. And he emphasized in his publicity that people would drive there to shop. However, it was not his intention to harm the downtown shopping area. J.C. stated his position in a talk at a convention of the National Association of Real Estate Boards: "Every realtor should have his first interest in the perpetuation of the downtown business center. On the other hand, we should all be alert to avoid the mistakes of the past . . . when . . . laying out and developing suburban shopping centers. . . . Future traffic congestion will but multiply the problems of our cities."

In fact, as soon as J.C. realized the impact that the automobile would have on the downtown retail business, he tried to interest downtown landowners and merchants in providing offstreet parking, but they would not listen. At his retirement, John C. Taylor shed some insight into the causes of some of this shortsightedness: "One of the handicaps frequently encountered in central areas is that much land in these areas is owned by a second and third generation, and often absentee, owners. In many cases, these owners are unable or unwilling to spend money on improvements, are unwilling to sell, and [are] content to sit and milk the property of the greatest possible income. That means that if a major improvement in the area is being considered, one or two owners can prevent the improvement from being made."[28]

Brush Creek valley, which J.C. Nichols had chosen as the site for his prestigious residential shopping center, was not promising in 1912. It was largely a marsh and covered with dense underbrush. Against the hill to the south was the old Lyle Rock Company yard whose smokestack belched black smoke over the valley. Nearby was a hog farm whose odor was overpowering when the wind was right. Just west of what is now Wornall Road was an un-

sightly dump. Gradually, the Nichols Company had to purchase and eliminate these eyesores.

The site did have several advantages, however. It was on level ground, which would minimize building and maintenance costs. And J.C. was determined to buy enough land to provide a large buffer zone. Brush Creek itself would become permanent park space, leaving the Plaza open to the prevailing breezes. At the east end of the proposed site, a small stream called Mill Creek ran down a valley south from Westport and joined Brush Creek. Nichols thought this an ideal location for a roadway to provide automobile access to the Plaza and to his residential developments to the south. Although city officials turned down the roadway, claiming, "It would never have any use," the Nichols Company obtained permission and built and paved a new 16-foot-wide road, named Mill Creek Parkway.[29]

From the time that J.C. first visualized his shopping plaza in Brush Creek valley, it took nine years to acquire the site. The acreage was part of a defunct residential subdivision platted during the real estate boom of the 1870s by a young Scotsman named George Law. He had sold the subdivision lots mainly through mail-order solicitations to early land speculators, many of whom had subsequently scattered across the United States and beyond—one owner was eventually located in India. A number had died in the intervening years, transferring ownership of the land through their estates. Hence, the daunting task of locating the appropriate persons, then negotiating for the purchase of the property, and finally filling in all the gaps, took J.C. Nichols, John Taylor, and commercial properties manager George Tourtellot nearly a decade. One of the largest properties was obtained from a New York jeweler, who had owned the land for 36 years without ever having seen it.

In the Plaza land acquisition process, the Nichols Company bought and demolished a total of 26 small houses and some ramshackle stores that had been built on the site. George Tourtellot arranged for the Chandler Floral Company, owner of one of Law's original lots, to build a steam-heated greenhouse and florist shop on its land at the east edge of the Plaza where Mark Shale now stands, and its tall chimney became a well-known Plaza landmark.

Needless to say, J.C. was shrewd enough to avoid announcing his intended use of Brush Creek valley during this phase. Nevertheless, it is a good bet that the various owners profited from their investment in spite of the carrying charges; Nichols spent over $1 million in 1921 dollars to acquire the 40 acres.

During this period, Tourtellot and Taylor wanted an aerial view of the Brush Creek valley and other Nichols Company properties. One afternoon they visited a rustic air strip between 67th and 71st Streets in Indian Hills, which was leased from the company by pilot Tex LaGrone, one of Kansas City's aviation pioneers. LaGrone was glad to take the men up, but after taking a look at the flimsy old biplane with its fabric covered wings, Tourtellot asked casually, "What happens if the engine stalls while we're up in the air?" LaGrone smiled knowingly and replied, "Well, I just go into a dive and the air rushing through the propeller restarts the engine."

Apparently satisfied, Taylor and Tourtellot squeezed into the front seat and LaGrone lifted off. After sight-seeing for a while, LaGrone intentionally shut off the engine, yelled to his startled passengers, "Don't worry, I'm going to show you what

Lyle rock yard, later the site of the Board of Trade, belched black smoke over the future location of the Plaza.

Aerial view of the Plaza before development. The Chandler greenhouses are in the foreground.

Architect Edward B. Delk's original 1922 plan for the Plaza.

I was talking about," and pointed the plane into a steep dive. As the aircraft screamed toward terra firma, his wide-eyed, white-knuckled passengers waited for the engine to catch. It never did. LaGrone pulled the biplane out of its dive at the last instant and managed to negotiate a rough landing in a muddy corn field.[30]

The initial architectural plan for the Plaza was the work of architect Edward B. Delk. Young Delk had been recruited from Philadelphia by John Taylor, by promising him enough Nichols Company work to support him while he built up a private clientele in Kansas City. The first step was to send Delk on trips to Spain, Mexico, and South America to draw inspiration for the Spanish/Mexican architectural style. At the same time, Nichols, Taylor, and Tourtellot were studying land use, traffic, and architecture in other cities in the United States and in Germany, France, and England. They analyzed Kansas City's future growth pattern, projected purchasing power, shopping and service needs of district residents, the traffic flow, and parking needs. The ground plan landscaping for the proposed Country Club Plaza was entrusted to George Kessler and Herbert Hare.

The resulting plan for the Country Club Plaza was therefore a joint effort. Delk's final three-dimensional architectural rendering depicted a shopping center such as no one had ever seen before, a marvel of architectural unity and harmony, with wide streets, landscaped parking areas, and no building over three stories high. Although the proposed drawing was made well before any construction began and the Plaza is considerably larger today than envisioned in 1922, the architectural design, landscaping, and general layout of the streets is remarkably similar to Delk's original rendering.

Longstreth, however, in his *Harvard Architectural Review* article, offers this additional perspective:

> The basic idea behind the Plaza was developed during its inceptive phase, yet some aspects took longer to reach full resolution. As had long been the practice in Nichols' residential tracts, development proceeded incrementally, encumbering no outside capital but financed through returns on work already completed. This policy also gave the J.C. Nichols Company time to test assumptions on a modest scale, making any necessary modifications before a large investment was made. Furthermore, Nichols seems to have understood early in his career that long-term comprehensive planning should not be bound to an intransigent physical form.
>
> The initial design, prepared by consulting architect Edward Delk in association with landscape architect George Kessler, was perhaps created to publicize the idea as much as it was to provide a growth [model]. Virtually all of its features were altered in execution, beginning with the development of the first two blocks that same year. Furthermore, this was the only occasion that the company commissioned a formal master plan. As executed, the Plaza was more pragmatically arranged, reflecting the concerns of its clients and the inclinations of the staff architect, Edward Tanner, who designed most of the buildings.

In April 1922, J.C. Nichols finally announced his plan to build a $5-million, 30-acre shopping center to serve all of the residential neighborhoods to the south of downtown. He showed drawings of one-

and two-story buildings in Spanish style with red- and apricot-colored tile roofs and beautiful intricate towers adorned with wrought-iron grille work. The initial announcement was met with a wall of skepticism. Says Longstreth:

> The proposal was at once branded "Nichols' folly." Critics insisted that the site, some . . . [five] miles south of downtown was too remote. The nearby population was growing, in large part because of the network of residential tracts Nichols himself had been developing for more than a decade. Yet his envisioned . . . complex was considered much too large for an outlying area. Plenty of stores already existed along streetcar lines connecting this precinct with the city center. The Plaza would be close to a car line, but customers would have to walk several blocks out of their way along curving streets. Nichols anticipated many people would actually drive there to shop. Skeptics were certain that the venture was a colossal mistake.

However, the writer of an editorial in the *Kansas City Star,* while guarded, proved to be a better prophet:

> J.C. Nichols is applying to a new business district the principles of advance planning that have gained him at least national recognition in his residential developments. It is essential the new district be not only attractive to the eye, affording also a maximum of convenience, but that it be made commercially profitable. . . . The new Kansas City development may set a new standard for outlying business districts all over the coun-

> try. . . . It is certain to be watched closely by architects and realtors in [other] large cities.

Prior to the Plaza, developers of commercial properties considered parking a nuisance and relegated cars to vacant dirt lots that happened to be nearby. J.C., on the other hand, considered parking to be a merchandising asset; he incorporated vast, landscaped and paved, off-street parking areas in his overall plan. These areas on the Plaza were beautified with fountains, marble statues, and attractive urns, a policy unheard of for parking lots at that time and seldom seen since. These were enclosed with parapet walls about four feet high, and the pedestrian entrances through the walls were adorned with antique wrought-iron gates.

The first Plaza parking areas were a full square block in size. The parking surfaces were deliberately lowered several feet below the surrounding sidewalk and street level so that people in cars or strolling on the sidewalk around the perimeter could see the shops beyond with an unobstructed view. Nichols spent $26,000 on decorative fencing, landscaping, and artistic embellishment for two lots that were built in 1929. To help ensure dry feet for the shoppers, he built in a drainage system under the pavement throughout the parking lots, and maintained the aesthetic quality by burying the electric lines to the lights.

A rule at all J.C. Nichols shopping centers was that merchants and their employees had to park in designated employee parking areas, always the least convenient locations, freeing the convenient spots for customers. Clyde, Jr., recalls the rebellion of one cantankerous merchant: "John S. Watkins, a long-time owner of the drug store at the corner of Central and Ward Parkway, insisted on parking his own car in the curbside parking stall closest to the front door of his store. The Nichols Company wrote a number of reminder letters to him, without effect. John was finally broken of this habit only by receiving formal notice that his lease was to be canceled. Even this had to be done several times before John reformed. He had to be stopped from taking up a stall that would otherwise be used by at least 10 to 15 of his customers on any given day!"

November 1922 was a momentous month in the history of the Country Club Plaza. Delk completed plans for the two-story Suydam Building (today, the Mill Creek Building, west of the J.C. Nichols Memorial Fountain). Construction could begin on the Plaza's first structure. The *Star* described the building, named for the Suydam Decorating Company, as "truly Spanish, forecasting the colorful warmth and Old-World charm . . . that will one day provide a unique and imposing entrance way to the Country Club District."

The first tenant to occupy the new building was Mary B. McGavran, who in March 1923 moved into the unfinished building to commence operation of the Marinello Beauty Shop. McGavran's salon was later the first to introduce the permanent wave to Kansas City women. Other early tenants were portrait photographer E. Blanche Reineke and Mrs. M.C. Chisholm's "smart millinery and sportswear shop."

Ironically, homeowners from nearby residential districts expressed the most concern about the proposed Plaza shopping center. J.C. had to muster his best salesmanship to convince them that preplanning and restrictions (mandating similar architecture, harmonious color schemes, and controlled appearance of the sides and rears of buildings) would ensure

an artistic setting, capable of enhancing the value of their homes rather than detracting. He vowed that Plaza stores would avoid "screaming advertising placards, hideous combinations of color, great scrawling, flaming advertising lettering across an otherwise pleasing storefront or plate glass window." Automated sprinkler systems for fire prevention, the prohibition of smoky, coal-fired furnaces, height limits, and other architectural considerations would, in his words, make the Country Club Plaza "America's paramount suburban business development! Through it, downtown shopping facilities will be brought to the very door of every Country Club District home."

Development continued apace for several years after the completion of the Suydam Building. By 1925, the Triangle Building (in the next block to the west along 47th) included among its tenants the Piggly Wiggly grocery, a pioneer in self-service and mass food retailing and hence an acknowledged forerunner of the supermarket. The Tower Building (just around the corner from the Suydam Building facing 47th Street) with its ornate 70-foot tower and the Balcony Building (which stretched along the north side of 47th Street west to Broadway) were completed next.

Wolferman's grocery store, a Kansas City institution with headquarters downtown, catered to different clientele than did Piggly Wiggly, offering the ultimate in elite personal service. Many of the Country Club District housewives simply phoned in their orders, which were promptly filled and delivered by one of Wolferman's shining panel trucks. If they chose to come into the elegant store personally, they were greeted by a clerk who called their grocery list over an in-house telephone system to one of the stock boys.

The first building on the Plaza was the Suydam Building, into which five tenants moved in 1923: Suydam Decorating Company, featuring European antiques; Hunter Brothers Drug Store; Mrs. M.C. Chisholm's Millinery Shop; Miss Reineke Photography; and Lu-Frances Baby Shop.

The interior of the Suydam Decorating Company in August 1923.

The Hunter Brothers Drug Store, one of the new tenants of the Suydam Building.

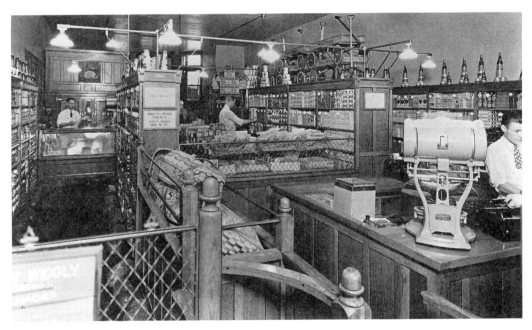

This Piggly Wiggly grocery on the Plaza in the late 1920s was the first self-service, check-out type market in Kansas City.

The order was brought to the counter where the bill was written up, and the boxes of groceries were then either carried to their cars or delivered to their homes. If a customer wished, the clerk would select her items from a bakery display case or glass-front cooler of sausages and meats, which were, of course, cut to order by Wolferman's butchers. In a day before mass marketing of food resulted in a proliferation of brands, Wolferman's featured its own top-quality private brand of canned goods, bottled goods, and baked goods.[31]

The first structure to be erected on the south side of 47th Street was the Knabe Building, named for the Knabe Music Studios (presently home to Bruce Watkins drugs and the Overland Sheepskin Company on the north at 47th Street). In a 1928 addition, the second story contained a large community meeting room similar to the successful prototype located above the Brookside Shops. This later gained renown as the site of Martha Belle Aikens ballroom dancing classes for boys and girls. Also completed that summer was a car dealership (which in 1953 became the Ward Parkway Garage), facing Brush Creek.

The second downtown store to locate on the Plaza was Robinson Shoes. It hoped to attract women shoppers by providing a children's play area as well as a location for a children's barber. Robinson's thrived on the Plaza for over 65 years.

Edward Tanner, Nichols Company architect, received accolades for his superb design of the Plaza Theater, which was also designed for use as a legitimate theater. A unique achievement with its ornate tower and carefully selected interior decor featuring art works imported from Spain, the theater became a showplace that won an award from the Architectural League for "the best architectural design completed in Kansas City in 1928."

Entering the inner lobby of the Plaza Theater, the large, iron-work gate to the left was an antique hand-chiseled one from Seville. A balcony overlooking the entrance to the foyer had iron grilles from seventeenth-century Ronda on either side. Two inset wood capital carvings on supporting columns were from Cadiz; the rosette plaques over the foyer doors, from Granada. The lobby with its red-tiled floor was a Spanish patio with a fountain and glazed tile benches from Seville, and the tile coat-of-arms on the north wall was made especially for the theater by Sevillian craftsmen. The interior of the theater itself was decorated in similar motif. Jessie Nichols assisted her husband and John Taylor in the selection of much of the theater's artwork during a visit to Spain and Portugal while the building was under construction.

During excavation of the theater site, a two-and-three-quarter-pound prehistoric mastodon tooth, five-inches-wide with roots over four inches, was found intact at the depth of 24 feet. According to a University of Kansas paleontologist, it is believed to have been deposited there by a glacier in the Third Ice Age, approximately 35,000 years ago.

Country Club Plaza construction during the busy decade of the twenties was climaxed with the completion and grand opening of the Plaza Theater on October 9, 1928. Miller Nichols, then a teenager, recalls: "I was wearing my first tuxedo for the gala opening reception and was feeling pretty important as I stood beside my father greeting guests as they passed through the lobby. When they were all seated, Dad turned to me and said, 'Grab a broom, Son, and sweep out the lobby. It's got to be clean when these people come out for intermission.'" The motion picture that graced the screen on opening night was "a synchronized sound Movietone production" entitled *Street Angel*, starring Janet Gaynor and Charles Farrell.

Just as J.C. had augmented the beauty and charm of the Country Club District with outdoor art objects and statuary, he now helped foster the Old World ambience of the Plaza in the same way. In the late twenties, he approved the purchase of the "Pool of Four Fauns" by Brandisi and Romanelli's bronze and Verona marble fountain entitled "Boy and Frog." Both pieces were discovered in Florence by John Taylor during a trip to Italy and were bought to grace the new shopping center.

Planners in the late twenties, taking their cue from the Plaza, began to locate shopping districts close to quality planned residential communities: in Dallas's Highland Park, in Houston's River Oaks (J.C. was called in to consult on the planning for these), and Shaker Heights outside of Cleveland. The automobile was here to stay, and, led by Nichols, farsighted developers began to take advantage of the new

The decor of the Plaza Theater lobby was supervised by J.C. Nichols personally, employing antique art objects and architectural detailing that he, Jessie, and John Taylor had selected on trips to Spain.

The Plaza Theater opened on October 9, 1928, to great excitement. It was a triumph for Nichols and architect Edward Tanner, and its billing as the "show place of Mid-America" was not overblown. The opening attraction was Street Angel, starring Janet Gaynor and Charles Farrell at the peak of their careers. The film was "a synchronized sound Movietone production," which was also a marvel of its time. (Courtesy of John H. Herbst)

trend. None, however, has equaled the beauty, charm, elegance, or even the size of the Country Club Plaza in Kansas City.

Recognizing that increased population density around the perimeter of his proposed business district would provide important walk-in traffic for the merchants, Nichols planned almost from the beginning for residential apartments. His first step was to urge the city to zone the areas bordering the Plaza for apartment complexes. Construction began in 1926 with Charles E. Phillips' development of garden apartments that could house several hundred families on the western rim of the Plaza. Phillips had over 15 years of experience in the construction of Kansas City hotels and apartment buildings. For the Plaza project he hired Kansas City architect James F. Lauck. Among their buildings is the so-called author group: the Washington Irving, Thomas Carlyle, Mark Twain, Eugene Fields, Robert Louis Stevenson, and James Russell Lowell.

The J.C. Nichols Company began its direct involvement in apartment construction in 1927, hiring the firm of Hare & Hare to landscape the abandoned quarries of the Lyle Rock Company just across Brush Creek to the south. Nichols envisioned the entire 15-acre parcel filled with a high-rise apartment complex. In an effort to simultaneously arouse public interest and secure excellent design, the company sponsored an architectural competition. Fifteen local firms competed for the opportunity to design plans for a row of apartments that would house up to one thousand families, providing a light and airy ambience with a good view of the Plaza. The firm of Hertz, Wilkinson, and Crans was awarded the job by a jury comprising a landscape architect, an architect, and several Nichols Company executives.

These apartments along Brush Creek were built by the G.H. McCanles Company (beginning in late 1927) and marked a new development in urban living. The soundproof and fireproof units constructed of steel and concrete were given a brick and/or terra cotta exterior to match the Plaza's architectural style. They were among the first apartments in the nation to be located near an outlying suburban shopping and recreation district and to depend primarily on automobile transportation. J.C. later admitted he had erred in not providing parking for them. He had failed to realize that apartment dwellers, too, would have cars. The 64-unit Casa Loma, the Locarno (with rental rates ranging from $115 to $185 per month), and the 124-unit Villa Serena (with rates ranging from $95 to $235 per month) were the first three structures built by McCanles. The other three in the McCanles development were the Casa Loma West, the Biarritz, and the Riviera (today the Raphael Hotel), all completed by 1930.

Although J.C. sold the land and promoted the construction of the apartments, the Nichols Company did not own or operate them. Clyde, Jr., tells of company efforts to keep the apartments fully occupied, however: "Each new apartment building had a manager. Nichols employees were given the job of wooing those apartment managers, showing them that they were considered important, and throwing parties for them so that they would encourage their residents to shop on the Plaza. Maximum occupancy of the apartments was considered so important for Plaza business that the company set up an apartment-rental office in the heart of the shopping area.

Bob O'Keefe, who was with the Nichols Company for over 50 years and with the commercial properties department much of that time, says, "J.C. took a *deep* interest in the merchants" (in all the Company's shopping centers, but especially on the Plaza). O'Keefe remembers that in the beginning commercial leases were for only one year so that the company could go back every year and raise the rent, if necessary.

However, he points out, J.C. had the concept that longer leases could be made fairly if they were made on the basis of a percentage of sales. At first, the merchants were suspicious and had to be sold, but then they liked the idea and came to prefer it. (A toy store, for example, was allowed to pay a minimum rent through the slack months and then catch up in the heavy sales periods.) And under this concept, the tenant was assured that the J.C. Nichols Company would have a continuing interest in his success. "The landlord is in business with you," Bob told them. At the end of the year an audit was taken of all the businesses and the amount

owed either way on the lease was paid accordingly. O'Keefe says that the company would almost always refund more than it collected. Fellow developers who had turned a deaf ear to Nichols' exhortations a few years previously about the benefits of percentage leasing now began to visit the Plaza and learn more about the concept by seeing it in action.[32]

December of 1925 marked the beginning of a cherished and long-standing Yuletide tradition in Kansas City. After Plaza merchants voted to decorate their sidewalks with miniature Christmas trees, Charles "Pete" Pitrat, head of maintenance operations for the Nichols Company, joined in the spirit of the season by hanging several strings of colored lights over the doorway of the Mill Creek Building. The idea caught on and Pitrat gradually established the elaborate Plaza Christmas lights program. This has become one of the nation's most spectacular outdoor lighting displays, with every Plaza building and tower out-

Christmas carolers on Christmas eve, 1919.

lined in lights.[33] Annually, Thanksgiving night is the occasion for throwing the switch that lights the Plaza's Christmas spectacular. Not only is it carried on television and pictured in the newspapers and magazines, but as many as a hundred thousand people pour into the area to see the event in person. Traffic is bumper-to-bumper, busloads of visitors come in from outlying areas, and there is much festive bustle as families stroll the Plaza streets. The cost of the decorations, which now runs over $100,000 a year, is paid by the Plaza Merchants Association. Miller states, "One year we tried to turn the lights on a week early and caught hell! People saw it as a break with Thanksgiving tradition."

Historically, it is believed that the first Christmas lights on the Plaza were responsible for the nationwide custom of outdoor lighting at Christmastime. Before 1925, there were no outdoor Christmas bulbs to be had. Pitrat used indoor Christmas tree lights for his first rudimentary display. Inspired by what they saw, two or three residents of the Country Club District followed suit by stringing a few strands of lights over their own doorways. The custom was encouraged by the homeowners associations and spread rapidly not only through the district, but to other parts of the city and other parts of the country. Sometime in these early years, the manufacturers of Christmas lights rushed to fill the perceived need by designing larger, safer, and more weatherproof outdoor bulbs. Many creative home displays of Christmas lights now complement the Plaza's annual show.

Stringing the Plaza Christmas lights, 1920s.

In the twenties, the Nichols Company offices were located in the Commerce Trust Company building downtown. But in the spring of 1929, the final year of boom times, construction began on a two-and-one-half-story building on Ward Parkway, part of which would house the main offices of the Nichols Company. In typical J.C. fashion, he insisted that the majority of company office space be located on the second floor to free the ground floor for merchants. Miller remembers working as a carpenter helping to lay the oak floors in his dad's office (now the company board room) just before he went off to college. Then in October of 1929, the stock market crash and the depression that followed brought company construction to a resounding halt, along with real estate development nationally. The Nichols Company offices at 310 Ward Parkway were largely completed in November, but J.C. felt he had been much too extravagant and foresaw dire times ahead for the real estate industry.

The Nelson-Atkins Museum

As related previously, Kansas City had been blessed since the late nineteenth century with civic leaders who were devoted to improving the city's quality of life, as expressed in culture and the arts. When J.C. Nichols achieved eminence as a community planner and developer, he had moved, as noted, into civic leadership as well. Today, the magnificent, columned Nelson-Atkins Museum of Art, housing superb collections and exhibitions, owes much to his accomplishments as a facilitator for culture and art.

When William Rockhill Nelson died in 1915, he left no provision in his will for a facility to house the artwork that would be purchased with his bequest. Upon the death of his wife (and co-executor), Ida, who had always supported his interest in an art collection, a $2-million trust fund was established for the Nelsons' daughter, Laura Kirkwood, and her husband, Irwin, during their respective lifetimes. Upon Irwin Kirkwood's death, this fund, plus an additional $750,000 left by Ida and Laura, became available to purchase a site and construct a building. Frank Rozelle, friend of Nelson and family attorney, left an additional $150,000 for the same purpose. (The central courtyard of the present museum is named Rozelle Court.)

In accordance with the terms of William Rockhill Nelson's will, three "university trustees" were appointed on March 3, 1926. Nelson had specified they were to be "only such men as having superior taste and good business ability, who will carefully and conservatively manage the trust estate for the best interests of all concerned." Appointed as president was William Volker, 67, owner of a prosperous business of picture frames, window shades, and other household furnishings. A millionaire by 1900, he was shy and reserved, avoiding publicity. He was reported to have spent $10 million of his own money in philanthropy during his 36 years in Kansas City. He believed "a rich man is merely the custodian of his money. . . . The real reason he has it is so he may use it for the benefit of others."

Another trustee appointed was Herbert V. Jones, 48, a pioneer in commercial real estate and a civic leader—chairman of the City Planning Commission, president of the University Club and the Kansas City Country Club, and a director of the Chamber of Commerce. Most important, Jones was a trustee of both the Atkins and Nelson estates.

The third member and vice-president of the trustees was J.C. Nichols, at 46 the youngest. Kristie Wolferman, in her excellent thesis, "The Creation of the Nelson-Atkins Museum of Art, 1911– 1933," states that from the beginning, Nichols was the "dominant trustee." Like Volker, he believed that his gifts and talents were to be used for the benefit of his community.

Before her death, Laura Kirkwood had made it clear to Irwin that she wished to see the gallery located at Oak Hall, site of the Nelson family home. Less than a year after his wife's death, Kirkwood waived his life interest in Oak Hall and offered the 20-acre site to the city as a location. Ironically, Nichols and the trustees had to contend with initial resistance from a Country Club District homes association, but J.C. succeeded in winning their endorsement. In July 1927, parties representing the Atkins and Nelson estates agreed it would be in the public interest to situate both art museums at the Oak Hall location in Nelson's Rockhill neighborhood.

When the university trustees held their first meeting on March 4, 1926, the first order of business (per the will) was to sell Nelson's two newspapers—the *Kansas City Star* and *Times*—in order to obtain funds to purchase works of fine art. Whereas the other two trustees would have been content to wait for bids to come in for the purchase of the papers, Nichols set out to seek the expertise and advice of other major newspaper publishers to determine the maximum price that should be sought. He called on the *Chicago Daily News*, *Baltimore Sun*, and the *New York Times*.

When the sale was announced, there were 11 prospective buyers. Bids were opened on July 9, 1926, in room 914 of the Muehlebach Hotel. The papers were sold to a company that had been formed by Nelson's former associates and employees under Irwin Kirkwood, his son-in-law, for a near-record $11 million (the *Chicago Daily News* had sold the year before for $13.5 million)—$2.5 million down with a mortgage for the balance. In spite of the staggering price, the purchase proved to be a sound investment; thirteen years later the entire mortgage was paid off.

Walter S. Dickey, publisher of the *Kansas City Journal* and *Post*, although only a minor competitor of Nelson's, made himself a thorn in the side of the university trustees. Maintaining he had submitted the highest bid for Nelson's newspapers, Dickey sued the trustees all the way to the Supreme Court. His suit was repeatedly deemed unfounded, but he managed to tie up the sale to Kirkwood & Associates for three years. The three-year delay proved fortuitous; the trustees used the time to educate themselves, thus avoiding some

A 1920s aerial view of Oak Hall, future site of the Nelson-Atkins Museum of Art.

OAK HALL

SOUTHMORELAND PARK

OAK STREET

LOOKING NORTHEAST FROM ROOF OF SOPHIAN PLAZA

hasty, uninformed art purchases. Wolferman says: "J.C. Nichols took a special interest in investigating other museums and trying to receive as much gratuitous advice as possible. On his trips east and to Europe, he interviewed such learned men as Henri Verne, director of the Louvre, and Sir Frederic Kenyon, director of the British Museum. Nichols also reported studying museum methods at the Metropolitan Museum of Art and consulted with the directors of the new Philadelphia Museum and the Fogg Museum at Harvard."

Kansas City Art Institute

From 1920 to 1927, J.C. Nichols served as president of the Kansas City Art Institute. When he assumed leadership, the Institute was $25,000 in debt; when he stepped down, it had substantial assets. His dynamism served well in other areas than financial. Speaking before a Rotary luncheon in 1925, he pointed out that in a little over four years, enrollment had grown from 100 to 700 and visitors to the shows in the Institute's galleries from 500 a year to more than 50,000. He also succeeded in moving the Art Institute from downtown on McGee Street to a rented house on Armour Boulevard and finally to its present quarters on a 10-acre campus at 45th and Warwick.

As a university trustee of the Nelson-Atkins Gallery, J.C. Nichols recognized the desirability of locating the Art Institute in the same Oak Hall neighborhood. In the fall of 1927, Howard Vanderslice proposed a plan to purchase the August Meyer estate adjacent to the gallery site. J.C., used to working with neighborhood groups, understood the concern of the Rockhill Homes Association that this eight-acre plot might be developed into apartments and their strong preference for the Art Institute, and he worked with them toward this end. The Vanderslice plan called for his gift to be supplemented by donations from the Institute trustees and a gift from the Rockhill neighbors to refurbish the Meyer home as a school. The Rockhill Homes Association pledged $20,000 and the purchase was completed by December.

In September 1928 the *Kansas City Star* reported the dedication of the new Kansas City Art Institute campus: "Seated in the shade of graceful shade trees on the lawn of one of the city's finest homes, an audience of several hundred persons listened to . . . J.C. Nichols summarize the accomplishments of Kansas City in the realm of art and describe the needs and possibilities still ahead." J.C. then turned to express the community's appreciation of Howard Vanderslice's generosity in making the new campus possible.

Nichols later solicited a gift from Mrs. U.S. Epperson to add a wing to the Meyer residence. Epperson Hall, dedicated in February 1930, became a cultural center for the community, the venue for numerous civic gatherings related to the arts. J.C. rejoined the Institute board in 1932 and remained for the rest of his life.

Perhaps Nichols' greatest long-term contribution was to relate the Art Institute to Kansas City business by establishing a department of industrial design. He worked to convince "hard-headed businessmen" that "art had a definite place in building a better city [as well as] bringing more manufacturing here." As part of this effort, the name was changed to the Kansas City Art Institute and School of Industrial Design. As the Institute continued to grow in enrollment, in distinguished faculty, and in prestige, it included among its notable students Walt

Disney, Jackson Pollock, Robert Rauschenberg, and Robert Morris; Thomas Hart Benton also taught there.

Kansas City Little Symphony

Meanwhile, J.C. participated in the next phase of the move to a full-sized philharmonic orchestra for the city. After World War I, a musician and conductor named Nazareno De Robertis organized the Kansas City Little Symphony. Among its directors and principal fund-raisers were J.C. Nichols, Sigmund Harzfeld, and Cliff Jones, Sr. De Robertis's chamber orchestra of about 30 musicians presented concerts until 1927, touring as far as British Columbia. The Kansas City Little Symphony is credited with identifying an audience base that appreciated classical music, thus preparing the way for a major orchestra.

The Shawnee Methodist Indian Mission

J.C. Nichols was interested not only in fostering cultural institutions, but also in the preservation of the city's cultural history. During the 1920s, he and other civic leaders joined with historical societies to preserve the oldest Indian mission still standing in Kansas, the Shawnee Methodist Indian Mission (the inspiration for Nichols' newest and most impressive development, Mission Hills). The old Mission had great historical significance for the state of Kansas. Established in 1829, it had housed the first territorial legislature and the state's first printing press. Founded by Rev. Thomas Johnson, after whom Johnson County was named, it originally contained 16 buildings. Three substantial brick buildings remained, dating back to 1838 and all in need of major repair.

When the owners refused to sell, citizens of Johnson County lobbied the state legislature for the passage of a bill permitting purchase by condemnation of properties with unusual historical significance. Kansas' lawmaking body was quick to pass the statute in 1921 but was slow to appropriate the funds needed to accomplish the condemnation/purchase process. Nichols and other civic leaders, joined by a number of patriotic and historical societies, continued to put pressure on the legislators. Eventually, on the last night of its 1927 session, the legislature appropriated $48,000 to acquire and restore the historical buildings and to make the 12-acre site into a state park. The Mission was restored and opened to the public.

Leadership in Education

During the incredibly busy twenties, J.C. and Jessie Nichols were actively involved with two private schools in the Country Club District. J.C. served as an original trustee on the board of the Sunset Hill School for Girls (1919–1927); Jessie Nichols was a trustee for eight years (1925–1933) of the Country Day School for Boys.

In May 1920, the Sunset Hill trustees purchased from the J.C. Nichols Company 95 feet of property to the west of the school's 51st Street site and erected a new building containing classrooms and a dining room with a stage. For a time, J.C. served as acting chairman of the board, never pressing for money owed on the property. When the board could not afford to keep the school's grass cut in the summer months, the company mowed it, rationalizing that it was a front entrance to the Country Club District. In winter he ordered the coal and saw that the furnaces were in working order. Vassie Hill later recalled that J.C. was an invaluable help during these years in guiding her through a maze of school-related real estate negotiations and other business arrangements.

Nichols also took an active role in establishing a university for Kansas City. Early in the development of the Country Club District, J.C. concluded that Kansas City suffered from the lack of comprehensive higher education; the city did have a junior college, the Jesuit Rockhurst College, a dental college, and schools of law and pharmacy. But J.C. was concerned that young people had to leave home to attend a university or even go east for higher education, often not returning to benefit and enrich their city.

In July 1922 the Chamber of Commerce appointed a committee to study the need for a university. Although the *Star* did not support this effort, the June 1925 committee had stimulated enough interest for the chamber to appoint a special university committee under A. Ross Hill, former president of the University of Missouri. The committee was charged to present a detailed university plan and make recommendations.

At about the same time another university opportunity occurred. In the spring of

Nichols and other civic leaders joined with historical societies in the 1920s to preserve the Shawnee Methodist Indian Mission, shown here before restoration. The oldest Indian mission still standing in Kansas, a century before the building had housed the first territorial legislature. The mission was founded by Rev. Thomas Johnson, after whom Johnson County was named, and it was an inspiration for Mission Hills.

1925, Kate W. Hewitt, widow of a former president of the Kansas City Dental College, offered the Methodist Episcopal Church 147 acres of land on the Kansas side of State Line at 75th Street for a university, one that would "establish and maintain an institution of higher learning . . . devoted to Christian education . . . constructing educational buildings of not less than $500,000." The Methodists got busy, recording their conviction that a university under Christian auspices should be established and that the Chamber of Commerce should have representation on its board of trustees.

An organization committee proceeded rapidly in the hope of opening in the fall of 1926. A charter was developed with the proposed name of Lincoln and Lee University. By the end of the year a board of 75 trustees had been elected; J.C. Nichols was one of these. In January the board met and adopted by-laws, established eleven standing committees, designated the tract of land as the Hewitt Campus, and announced a campaign to raise $5 million.

But early in 1928 the Lincoln and Lee movement began to fade. The campaign for $5 million had yielded only $800,000 and doubt arose among community leaders that sufficient support would be forthcoming for a sectarian university. Dissatisfaction had also developed over the lack of public transportation that made the 75th and State Line campus site inaccessible to most students.

During the summer of 1928 a new university committee of the Chamber of Commerce initiated efforts to establish a nonsectarian university. In the fall, 124 citizens signed, as "sponsors and incorporators," an "essentials of agreement" that delineated "fundamental policies representing a consensus of the views of Kansas City civic leaders, policies which likewise had proven universally successful in the history and experience of leading American universities."

A charter for this University of Kansas City was drawn up in the spring of 1929 and granted on June 10. Thus there were, at this point, two distinct university movements. Fortunately, there was enough intelligent, overlapping, and friendly leadership in the two movements to realize the futility of competition and dissipated effort. A joint committee of the two boards, on which J.C. Nichols served, entered into negotiations, and on November 28, 1930, the trustees of Lincoln and Lee agreed to merge with the University of Kansas City. On December 16, 1930, the first meeting of the board of trustees of Lincoln and Lee–University of Kansas City was held; at the third meeting, on February 4, 1931, it was voted to amend the charter to change the name to the University of Kansas City.

The university trustees of Nelson's estate agreed to sell the board 70 acres of the Nelson property, with the possibility of 75 acres more, for a campus. This site was purchased outright by Nelson trustee William Volker, who then gave it for a new university. The property, bounded by Cherry Street on the west and Rockhill Road to the northeast, included the home of Walter S. Dickey, publisher of the *Kansas City Journal-Post,* a massive stone mansion that would serve admirably as an administration building.

The proposed location was fortuitous from J.C.'s standpoint, lying just south of the Nelson-Atkins Museum of Art, the Art Institute, and the Conservatory of Music. Thus the University of Kansas City would become a contiguous extension of the cultural-scientific-educational center he now envisioned for the area to the east of the Country Club District.

On the National Scene

During the 1920s, J.C. Nichols served as chairman of the National Council of Real Estate Subdividers, to whom he repeatedly spread the gospel of the "City Beautiful." As vice-president of the American Civic Association, he attended an international housing conference in Rome. He also represented the National Planning Conference at a town planning conference in London, England. In addition, Calvin Coolidge appointed him as one of nine outstanding developers to the Fourth International Conference of the Building Industry in Paris. (At the last moment, he was unable to go.) The American City Plan Conference named him one of the outstanding community builders of the country.

But of all J.C. Nichols' work with national associations and organizations in the real estate field, the most significant and far-reaching was that with the Urban Land Institute (ULI), of which he was a founding member, as well as with its autonomous division, the Community Builders' Council (CBC), of which he was a founder and a chairman.

This involvement began in the 1920s with his active leadership on the board of trustees of the National Association of Real Estate Boards (NAREB). Another active member was Walter S. Schmidt, whose particular area of concern was the manifold problems posed by the steady decline of the central business district, not only in his native Cincinnati, but in many other American cities as well.

There was nothing new about urban blight; tenements and slum conditions had been condemned by writers and reformers since the 1880s. But the people who should be most concerned—downtown property owners, merchants, banks, mortgage companies, city governments—seemed unwilling or unable to do anything about the situation. Despite the enormity of the problem, not enough seemed to be known about the causes, the economic factors, or what courses of action might be taken to prevent it or correct it.

According to a history of the Urban Land Institute, published in 1959 and entitled *Of Land and Men,* Walter Schmidt "felt what was needed was an organization or institution which would devote itself to research and education in the field of real estate, urban blight, and the rebuilding of our central city districts so that people might enjoy the surroundings in which they lived and worked and shopped." Among the builders and developers in the NAREB, Schmidt found ready support— and more importantly, a forum for sharing much-needed information. In fact, the developers of high-quality planned residential communities (who catered to people wanting to escape urban blight) were well aware of each other's work. They corresponded, visited each other's projects, and met at each other's homes and at NAREB conventions to exchange experiences. These meetings started with J.C. Nichols visiting his friend, Edward H. Bouton, who had left Kansas City and founded Roland Park in Maryland. They came to include Hugh Potter, developer of River Oaks in Houston, Hugh Prather, who had developed Highland Park in Dallas, and a half dozen others. Over time these informal meetings were to lead to the organization of the Urban Land Institute.

Planning the Nation's Capital

President Calvin Coolidge appointed J.C. Nichols to serve on the National Capital Park and Planning Commission in 1926.

In outlining his qualifications, the president stated that he was "probably the leading exponent for city planning and zoning in the real estate business" and "father of city planning in the West." (President Herbert Hoover reappointed him to a six-year term, President Franklin Roosevelt named him to the same post, and Harry Truman was president when Nichols finally resigned in 1948.)

The nation's capital was unique among American cities in that it had started with a plan, that of Pierre L'Enfant, French engineer, Revolutionary War hero, and friend of George Washington. L'Enfant had envisioned and laid out a city of broad boulevards and classic buildings, with its streets in a grid pattern intersected by avenues that ran diagonally like spokes in a wheel. But with no provision made for carrying out the plan, the city grew in a haphazard, hit-and-miss fashion, with L'Enfant's vision more disregarded than followed. There was no zoning, so as the city grew after the Civil War, the beautiful, marble government buildings were often surrounded by squalid slums and decayed areas.

Congress, charged by law with overseeing the capital, made an attempt in 1901 to go back to the L'Enfant plan and to extend it, by authorizing the park commissioner to gather a committee that included New York architect Charles F. McKim, Daniel Burnham of City Beautiful fame at the 1893 Chicago World's Fair, sculptor Augustus Saint Gaudens, and the ubiquitous landscape architect Frederick Law Olmsted. Although the resulting "Park Commissioner's plan" ran afoul of congressional politics so that sufficient money was never authorized, some of its main proposals were followed piecemeal and were the foundation for the initial work of the National Capital Parks and Planning Commission when it was established in 1926.

The first move in that direction was made by the chairman of the Senate Committee on the District of Columbia, who happened to be Sen. Arthur Capper of Kansas. Knowing Nichols' reputation, Capper invited him to appear before the committee and describe how better city planning for Washington, D.C., might be accomplished. Nichols suggested that a commission be established as an advisory body to Congress in legislating for beautification of the capital. In addition to the necessary government officials and civil servants, the commission should include "four eminent citizens well qualified in traffic engineering, landscape architecture and city planning." When the commission was established, J.C. Nichols was the natural choice for the city-planning slot.

The Parks and Planning Commission was charged with the responsibility of planning for transportation and traffic, plats and subdivisions, highways, parks and parkways, playgrounds, sewage, water supply, housing, building, zoning, public and private buildings, bridges, waterfronts, and "other proper elements of city and regional planning." To exercise this awesome responsibility, the commission met monthly for two to three days over a weekend. One of the commission's principal duties was to serve as a zoning commission, since no such body existed. Another challenge was to bring together the surrounding towns and counties to work out a plan for the entire area. This included acquiring land outside the District of Columbia to construct a Fort-to-Fort Drive linking scenic and historic sites and providing a traffic artery that bypassed the congestion downtown.

The location, height, and design of all federal buildings and monuments had to come before the planning commission for approval—or, more often, for revision. This alone was a tremendous job, as the number of buildings swelled rapidly in the late 1920s, then climbed astronomically as "big government" took off in the days of the New Deal and exploded during World War II. Sometimes politics entered in, as Clyde, Jr., remembers his father relating at the family dinner table in Kansas City. A proposed Thomas Jefferson Memorial came before the commission for approval. The Republicans had the stately Lincoln Memorial at the head of the Mall, with its oversized statue of the seated, brooding Lincoln. Now the Democrats planned for their Jefferson Memorial to be just a little bigger and in an equally prominent location. Nichols (himself a Democrat) thought it a monstrosity. With Nichols in the forefront, the commission persuaded the sponsors to scale down their planned structure to more graceful proportions. As a result, the Jefferson Memorial is today considered one of the capital's gems.

In locating public buildings and monuments, Nichols pushed for wider dispersement in order to give them the most impressive settings possible, similar to those he admired in European cities. This also served to spread the load on street traffic and public transportation. Gen. Ulysses S. Grant III, chairman of the commission, gave credit to Nichols for helping keep down the costs of capital improvements and for planning on a practical, economic basis. Drawing on his Kansas City experience, Nichols got the commission to acquire land for parks and boulevards before other construction in the area pushed the price up. He tried to influence the growth of the city toward the northeast and southeast quadrants and away from the population trend toward the northwest section. In this, he ran into resistance from local builders as well as from other commission members.

Constantly urging the preservation of Rock Creek Park, which ran its wooded course through the valuable land in the northwest part of the city, he told the Senate Committee on D.C., "What you need in Washington is a man like the late George E. Kessler, who laid out Kansas City's park system . . . who knew how to make ugly spots beautiful. . . ." Then he proceeded to accomplish this himself.

J.C. played a significant role in the present layout of the Federal Triangle and in the assembling and purchase of the land for the National Airport. He also helped design the U.S. Capitol grounds and helped organize the Potomac Power Project.

Family Life

Social life in Kansas City in the 1920s revolved around the home. The principal form of entertainment was going to call on friends in the evening and on the weekends. In the Nichols family, the children were included, and they recall warmly the festive Christmas Eve visits to friends' homes, with an exchange of gifts. Social life also included musicales in the home or attending concerts by visiting orchestras. Theater evenings and book reviews were popular. In the afternoon, the ladies enjoyed bridge or mah-jongg, which was Jessie's preference. In the evening, couples would gather for dinner and often a game of poker. The children were intrigued with the various games of poker and were taught at a rather early age.

J.C. occasionally played high-stakes poker with W.T. Kemper, Herbert F. Hall, and other well-to-do friends. On his arrival home from these games, if Jessie inquired how he had done, he would reply, with poker face still in place, "Oh, all right, I guess." Jessie said that if she happened to confront one of the other players afterward, they would likely admit, "Boy, did J.C. clean us out the other night!"

The Nichols family moved into their permanent family home at 1214 Santa Fe Road (later 55th Street) as the decade began, and so the memories of the 1920s of Miller and Clyde, Jr., are centered there. According to Miller, the family's life was quite traditional, with a regular family dinner hour. However, if the Nichols had guests for dinner, the children ate in the breakfast room; after dinner they were always expected to study. The calendars for J.C. and Jessie were dotted with civic and business-related dinners and political occasions. As J.C. spent more and more time traveling around the country and participating on the national scene, an ever-increasing and interesting stream of guests were entertained, often as houseguests at the handsome Nichols home.

Eleanor (Ellie) Nichols was intrigued with some prominent guests invited to one of the dinner parties when she was about 12. So she and chum Beachy Arnold hid under the big dining room table to eavesdrop on the conversation. Trapped there undetected throughout the entire meal, they claimed afterward that they had heard some fascinating grown-up gossip and even some risqué stories.

Included among the prominent guests was the Secretary of Commerce, later President Herbert Hoover, who visited twice. For the first occasion, Jessie purchased a new table setting, which was ever afterward referred to as the "Hoover china." On Hoover's second visit, the family was giving a large dinner party in his honor out on the lawn. Jessie was busy overseeing the preparations when J.C.

realized that he couldn't locate the president. He sent Jessie searching and she located him sitting in the sun room in a large, overstuffed chair reserved for their airedale, Sandy. He was happily petting the dog, both of them looking quite content.

On occasion, J.C.'s frenetic pace took its toll. As soon as he came in the door in the evening, he would lie down on the davenport in the sun room. "God, I'm tired," he would sigh. But then, within a few minutes, he would call Miller into the room and say something like "son, call Dave Kennard and ask him if we can go see his prospect." Miller would go into the library where the phone was located, make his call, and return with the answer. But then his father might say, "No Miller, you didn't get that right; that can't be the answer. What did you say to him?" Although Miller bore the brunt of being his father's errand-boy, he realized later that he was also being groomed in the business and was gaining valuable experience.

One of the persons who influenced Miller's childhood most strongly was Ernest Holt, who came to work for the Nichols family as chauffeur the year Miller was born. Ernest drove the children to school and to after-school activities. Miller recalls, "I usually rode downtown with Ernest late in the day to pick up Dad, who was always on the phone or conferring with someone; so my first work for the Company was to seal and stamp the large batch of daily mail while we waited. Ernest taught me to hunt, to tinker with cars, and he shared with me the stories of his German heritage and his philosophy of life." (After 16 years with the family, Ernest married, and in 1926 he decided to move to California where he raised a family and named his first son Miller.)

J.C. did not have much time to spend

with his children except on Sundays and on family vacations. Even on Sundays, he often combined the family drive and social visits with business. He would say, "Let's go out and look at the property." With Ernest Holt at the wheel, the family would spend the next several hours cruising the streets of the district with J.C.'s little black notebook out, recording what needed to be tended to via a stream of memos on Monday morning.

One Sunday in 1922—the grand opening of Armour Hills, a new subdivision that extended from 65th to 71st Streets and from Holmes east to Oak—J.C. had Ernest drive the Packard touring car south along Holmes quite slowly, with all three children instructed to hang out of the sides pointing to a large billboard announcing the opening. J.C. figured that with all the passengers waving, passers-by would take note when Ernest turned into the subdivision, one of the first to feature modest-size homes on irregularly-shaped lots and curvilinear streets. They drove round and round, with the children having a grand time feigning irrepressible excitement for the new community.

This photo, circa 1920, of a Nichols family picnic in a sylvan setting on Indian Lane became famous because the occasion was fabricated and the participants posed—presumably for publicity purposes to show the quiet charm of Mission Hills. J.C. (far left) is gathering firewood and Jessie is seated at the far right. Standing in front of the stone grill is Ernest Holt, the family chauffeur. Miller is kneeling, Eleanor is seated on the ground, and Clyde, Jr., is perched atop the oven with the family dog, Sandy. The onlookers in the background are not identified.

"Incidentally," adds Clyde, "Armour Hills sold very well."

J.C. and Jessie trained their children to put away their belongings. If the kids' bicycles were found under the porte-cochere by the front door when the senior Nichols arrived home from an evening engagement, the offender would be rousted out of bed and asked to wheel his bike around to the garage. If Eleanor or the boys left clothes or toys on their bedroom floors, Evelyn, the upstairs maid, was instructed to dump the offending items down the laundry chute. Responsibility for personal belongings, needless to say, was learned in short order.

Clyde remembers how J.C. sought to prepare his children in the art of making a good first impression: "Dad trained all three of us how to shake hands. He had us practice! The procedure was to walk up to a person, put on a big smile, and stick out our hand while saying good and loud, 'Hello, my name is Clyde Nichols,' 'My name is Miller Nichols,' 'My name is Eleanor Nichols.' Dad always said, 'When you shake somebody's hand, do a good job of shaking it. I want to see a good, firm handshake.'" Miller adds, quoting J.C., "and look 'em in the eye!"

Family vacations by car were highlights for the children. The large trunk of the Packard touring car would be packed with suitcases, which also were strapped along the left running board. California curtains were on board in case of rain. Roads in those days were designed to allow farmers to haul their crops to market—farm to county seat. There were no signs to mark inter-city highways except colored stripes blazed on the telephone poles. The stretches of pavement were very short; the stretches of gravel or rutted dirt, very long.

Armour Hills tract billboard showing land between Wornall Road and Oak Street and 65th and 71st Streets under development by the J.C. Nichols Company.

Miller recalls the summer when J.C. announced to Jessie at breakfast one morning that he wanted to take the family on vacation in two days. "Where are we going?" she queried. "I haven't decided," J.C. replied; "just be ready to go by eleven o'clock." As they started down the driveway, Ernest asked in his German accent, "Vhich way, Mr. Nichols?" J.C. answered, "Let's go north." So off they headed and ended up going clear to Winnipeg. Clyde recounts, "Every morning as we climbed into the car and headed out again, Dad would study the maps before saying something like, 'I was thinking that maybe we could have lunch at such-and-such a town.' Of course, it was just a little too far to reach by lunchtime. We would eat lunch at about two o'clock, after which he would start plotting our destinations for the rest of the day. We'd argue with him every time, because, inevitably, he'd set an unrealistic goal. That was his nature. Get it out of the way; get as much done as possible, every day."

Chauffeur Ernest Holt later wrote that his memories of the Nichols family vacations were a treasured part of his life. He recalled traveling over roads that were less than perfect to such distant places as Hibbing, Minnesota; Montreal, Canada; Santa Fe, New Mexico; Mesa Verde, Colorado; and Magnolia, Mississippi. "Then came geography and history," wrote Holt, "and on these trips, college towns were prime destinations as well as state capitols." He told how the family sang cowboy songs as they rode along, with J.C. leading and Jessie joining in to keep everyone on key.

In 1927 Jessie suffered a near-fatal bout with blood poisoning. She had pricked her finger on a pin from a new dress tag and contracted a serious case of septicemia, so serious that the *Kansas City Star* prepared an obituary in anticipation of her death. It was long before the discovery of antibiotics. Her alarmed husband assembled a team of doctors to consult about her situation and prescribe treatment. He took complete charge, convening the medical team morning and evening; he led the discussion so that the doctors stayed in full communication with one another and were in agreement about treatment. He did not leave the house. When she finally did recover the doctors stated that if it hadn't been for J.C.'s constant vigilance and help in working with them, she probably wouldn't have made it.

Clyde recalls that one problem during her recovery, which was during Prohibition, was that Jessie wouldn't eat enough. A doctor suggested that Three Star Hennessey brandy would be good for her appetite and her system. J.C. asked the company secretary, Max Stone, to try to locate some Hennessey. Max used his connections and word got out to a number of bootleggers who responded with enthusiasm. The result was a surplus of Three Star Hennessey in the Nichols house for some years.

Ellie inherited her father's energy and her mother's spirit. Independent and headstrong, she is remembered as "a handful." An attractive teenager with a charming smile, she was "generous and fun to be around—as long as everything went her way," according to her brothers. Jessie not infrequently clashed with her daughter. Clyde, Jr., recalls that "Ellie sported a spit-curl when she was in her teens, and Mother didn't like it. Finally Mother paid her $100 to cut it off. Imagine! That would be comparable to paying your daughter $1,000 in today's money!"

Eleanor attended Sunset Hill, where

one of her friends was Mary McElroy, daughter of the city manager. At one point during their school years, Mary was kidnapped and held for ransom. Kidnappings were not uncommon in the twenties, before federal law made the crime a federal offense punishable by death. Mary's kidnappers demanded ransom in cash, but since the abduction happened on a weekend, McElroy couldn't get his hands on the funds. He enlisted the help of J.C., who managed to raise the necessary amount, and Mary was returned safely.

As the result of this incident, J.C. hired a bodyguard. The guard, posted in the Nichols' downstairs hall through the night, would report every morning that he had heard someone prowling around outside. After a few days, J.C. realized that the man was fabricating the reports to preserve his job and promptly fired him.

Eleanor, like her mother, went off to boarding school in the East and took her senior year at Emma Willard Academy in Troy, New York. She then entered Sarah Lawrence College where she became interested in acting. Clyde traveled east with his mother to attend one of the college theatrical productions, in which, since Sarah Lawrence was an all-women's college, Eleanor was given the role of a knight. "I'll never forget her striding onto the stage and delivering her lines in a low, powerful voice," says Clyde. "She certainly had presence."

Eleanor received positive reviews in several productions and appeared to have a bright future as an actress. Jessie, however, had strong objections; young women of social standing simply did not seek careers, and especially not in a "tainted" profession like acting. This proved to be a bitter pill for Ellie to swallow, but she followed her parents' wishes; after her graduation in June 1929, she returned to Kansas City.

Miller, like Eleanor, commenced his schooling at Sunset Hill, which in those days accepted boys through third grade. His only vivid recollection today is of the "T-Square & M Club" which he organized with a buddy named Dan James. The name stood for "Torture and Trouble Making" and their regular victim was Malcolm Brundret, who lived a couple of doors away. They regularly ordered him to go home and get his little red wagon to use in their principal activity, digging a secret cave across the street in what is now Loose Park. Miller attended nearby Bryant School for one year, in fourth grade, before transferring to Country Day from which he graduated in 1929.

His chum at 1214 Santa Fe Road (now 55th Street) was Herman Sutherland. The Sutherlands, who lived next door, had a garage with adjacent stable and paddock (like that of the Nichols), and this became the neighborhood clubhouse and headquarters for general mischief. One night, Miller and Herman got up at 3:00 A.M. to pilfer a little lumber from a neighboring construction site for a cave and treehouse they were building on a company-owned vacant lot just down the street.

Their favorite prank was to soap the Sunset Hill streetcar tracks at a midway stop on the Ward Parkway hill. When the motorman tried to start up, the wheels would spin and the car would slip backward. He would have to back down still farther to get enough momentum to make it up the hill to 55th Street. An even more provocative Halloween prank was to slip behind the car when it was stopped, pull down the trolley pole, and cut the rope that held it on the cable.

For three summers, starting at age ten,

Miller joined his Kane and Greenleaf cousins on the Kane ranch in southwestern Kansas near Greensburg. There the daily schedule began at 5:30 A.M. — getting up to bring in the horses and the milk cow, then saddling the horses for the day's work and milking the cow, followed by breakfast. By 7:00 or so the boys were off to do their morning work assignments: fixing fence, counting and/or moving cattle, cultivating with horse drawn equipment, and fix-it chores.

Midday dinner at 12:30 included everybody on the ranch, after which Aunt Kitty insisted that the boys take an hour's rest (which not infrequently ended up in pillow fights). In the afternoon the boys were free to do whatever they chose— most often they chose to race a half-mile on horseback to the swimming hole that was near the headwaters of the Medicine River.

Miller remembers they also enjoyed repairing and reclaiming farm buggies that had been abandoned along the road as motorized vehicles came into broader use. One time Miller and Bob Kane had taken one of the rebuilt wagons to the far end of the ranch when their horse decided to return to the barn at full speed. When Miller made a sharp turn, the wheels hit a boulder, sending Bob flying over the head of the horse and knocking him unconscious, while the horse became entangled in the sheaves. Miller says he was scared to death, but Bob soon regained consciousness, and the boys spent the rest of the afternoon repairing the wagon.

From age twelve on, Miller had a series of summer jobs for a month or so at the J.C. Nichols Company. The first of these was in the planing mill behind the old police station that faced 63rd Street. Here the company fabricated the window sashes and doors for homes it was building;

Miller's job was to sand and to sweep. Another summer he hauled bales of hay to the horse and mule barn where the company kept 90 head of mules used in all of their construction projects. He then had to stack it for winter feed. When he passed out from the heat one day, his worried mother objected strongly, but J.C. and Miller prevailed and next morning he was back on the job. Another summer he worked in the machine shop overhauling trucks and still another with the nursery gang planting and watering trees in the new Indian Hills subdivision.

But the job he remembers best was the summer he helped to build Jefferson Street, hauling rock from a quarry west of Main Street (present site of the Board of Trade). He helped lay the rock base for the street and break it up with a knapping hammer, after which the base was rolled and graveled and covered with asphalt. Hot summer work!

After a summer job Miller usually spent a month at Doc Foster's camp near Weekwetonsing, Michigan. Doc Foster, the Latin teacher at Country Day School, was a close family friend of the Nichols who frequently joined them at Christmas as well as at other family holidays. Miller recalls: "One summer when Dad came visiting camp, he noted that while the cabins were on a hill overlooking the lake, you couldn't see the lake because of the dense woods. So Dad devised a plan to provide vistas that would give the boys a view of the water from the camp, and immediately set them all to work cutting down trees to clear vistas. He was always thinking in terms of the aesthetics."

After Miller and Herman Sutherland were of driving age, they motored north to Doc Foster's camp on their own one summer, buying themselves a sailboat en route. That summer they had great fun learning to sail, while also filling duties as junior counselors. One August, the Kanes joined the Nichols family for a family lake vacation, as the Miller sisters never overlooked an opportunity to get their families together. The North woods with their many lakes were a popular summer choice for Kansas Citians in the 1920s.

But the prosperous decade of the 1920s ended on a note of anxiety for J.C. Nichols and his family, as for thousands of families across the country. The stock market crash of October 28, 1929, portended dire times ahead for the economy, and no one perceived more clearly than J.C. the disasters that lay ahead for the real estate industry.

Chapter 5

1930 · 1939

The Great Depression that gripped the country in the 1930s was perhaps more damaging to the real estate industry than to any other segment of American business. In a market that dwindled to nothing and unable to carry their debt loads, most of the largest and most successful builders and developers failed. J.C. Nichols was desperately worried about the fate of his company and anguished over the fate of his friends.

The Company, the District, and the Plaza

During the boom times of the 1920s, the J.C. Nichols Company was averaging nearly one new subdivision a year, the final one being Armour Hills Gardens in 1930. The company, at that time carrying a $7-million debt load, failed to start a single new development during the next seven years. In the worst year, the entire sales force sold a total of six inches of land—and that was to enable a home-owner to adjust an existing fence line.

Miller remembers how distraught his father felt watching all but three major full-line real estate development firms in the country go into bankruptcy. On Miller's 21st birthday in July 1932, his father wrote him a poignant letter in which he said, "I hope you never have to witness the tragedies, give up the things in life and make the sacrifices that I have had to."

In November 1929, a month after the stock market plummeted, the company completed the handsome building with company offices at 310 Ward Parkway. Miller recalls his father's feeling that he had made a grave mistake in spending so much money to construct offices for his company, and so, for many months, J.C. worked at home at the breakfast room table. Business conferences and even company board meetings were held at the Nichols house, seven days a week.

Miller recalls that the company had been on the verge of purchasing a substantial parcel of land just east of the Plaza when the stock market crashed. "It's a unique piece of land, and I wish we owned it today." He adds, however, that the interruption of the purchase was fortuitous, as the additional encumbrance surely would have bankrupted the J.C. Nichols Company in the lean years that followed.

J.C. and his management team devised a Depression survival strategy, consisting of renegotiation of company obligations, tight budgetary constraints, along with hard work and personal sacrifice on the part of all employees. Miller remembers his father's marching orders: "Try not to lose too much."

John Taylor's secretary, Helen Harvey, recalls that the office staff received across-the-board pay cuts during the Depression. "I had a son in college at the time," she states, "and really felt the pinch."

A confidential 1935 credit report on the company had this to say about J.C.'s ability to navigate the turbulent waters of the times:

> At the outset of the present depression, Mr. Nichols displayed rare business acumen by inaugurating a policy of "contraction" as opposed to "expansion" with respect to his residential construction and improvements, and began to devote his energies to disposal of his various properties and the development of his business and shopping center project, the Country Club Plaza. In this manner, he has been able to avoid the difficulties which have overcome many other realtors and builders. . . . All informants stress the remarkable energy of Mr. Nichols and he is credited with having unusual foresight. The latter was shown and is shown by the manner in which he has handled his companies during the past five years.

The Nichols Company's ownership of shopping centers was a significant factor in its survival. As home sales dwindled to nothing, commercial property rentals based on sales percentage leases were a source of urgently needed income. Filling-station leases were particularly helpful in keeping the company afloat. No matter how hard the times, people continued to

In November 1929, just a month after the stock market crash, the J.C. Nichols Company completed its handsome office building with a splendid Spanish art interior on the Plaza at 310 Ward Parkway.

drive their cars. Also, filling stations were the least likely to go broke due to their affiliation with financially sound national petroleum companies.

The timing of the development of the Country Club Plaza was particularly advantageous, as it was still adding tenants as the decade began. In early 1931, the Plaza Bank of Commerce, a branch of the downtown Commerce Trust Bank, opened for business at the corner of Alameda Road (now Nichols Road) and Central. This branch location proved convenient for both commercial and residential accounts. Lucy Drage, who would ultimately design the interiors of many Country Club District homes, opened her interior decorating shop in the Nichols Company building in August of that year. One year after Drage's opening, Jack Henry began selling men's hats and accessories on the Plaza from a tiny store only 20 feet deep and 11 feet wide on 47th Street in the Plaza Theater building. Schoenhards, Mindlins, John Watkins Drugs, and Martha Washington Candies followed.

J.C.'s go-get-'em style helped shape the aggressive marketing strategy employed by Plaza merchants during the lean Depression years. Although adversely affected by bank closures and diminished customer purchasing power, the Plaza stores fared

The Country Club Plaza continued to grow and prosper despite the lean years of the Depression. Prodded by J.C. himself, Plaza merchants mounted an aggressive "Buy on the Plaza" marketing campaign, featuring a variety of activities, major special events, and special focus on new residents of the apartment complexes surrounding the Plaza.

better than their counterparts elsewhere. People from the new apartment complexes that encircled the Plaza dramatically increased foot traffic at a time when every buyer counted. The Plaza Association, composed of merchants and professional doctors and dentists with offices there, instituted a "Buy on the Plaza" campaign, featuring style shows in the Plaza Theater, free weekly book reviews, bridge lessons, and a cooking school. A "plaza visitor" program, initiated by Eleanor Nichols, called on new residents in the area to give them a directory of Plaza merchants. And the Los Amigos club formed to welcome new residents, in time, putting out its own newsletter as well.

Bernice Nault became the executive secretary for the Plaza Merchants' Association housed at the Nichols Company, a position she held for more than 25 years. She organized the first Plaza Art Fair, assisted by Eleanor, in 1932. Located on a vacant lot at the southwest corner of Central and Nichols Road (currently the site of Eddie Bauer), it drew 95 artists displaying their creative works. It was also in 1932 that the Easter bunnies (still enjoyed today) were added to the celebration of major holidays, a drawing card for Plaza Merchants. Eleanor Nichols originated the Spanish Fiesta, which joined the other Plaza celebrations in 1936; company pictures in 1938 show festival decorations adorning the Balcony Building and handsome Señors John Watkins, Jack Henry, Bill Schoenhard, and Ed Chandler all wearing enormous sombreros grouped about the lovely Señora Eleanor Nichols Allen.

According to longtime residential salesman Randy Knight, the "Buy on the Plaza" campaign was implemented by J.C. personally among Nichols Company employees. "If Mr. Nichols saw one of us on the Plaza, he wouldn't hesitate to walk right up, open our sport jackets and examine the inside label. If he discovered that we hadn't purchased that coat from Jack Henry's or someone else on the Plaza, he would promptly straighten us out in no uncertain terms." Jessie Nichols once declared that J.C. made her shop every Plaza merchant every month.

J.C. prowled the Plaza, frequently at night, checking the shops. If a merchant had left trash on the sidewalk or there were dirty handprints on a doorjamb, out would come the notebook and a letter would follow the next day. On more than one occasion, he counted the dead flies on the inside sill of a shop-window and communicated his census to the tenant responsible. On the other hand, if a shop was especially spotless and attractively decorated, Nichols would send a note of praise and encouragement. When a store's sales were up compared to the year before, he often stopped by and congratulated the merchant personally—sometimes before the store owner had compared the numbers himself. J.C. checked the figures constantly, since the rent was based on sales. "Some of we family members might accompany Dad when he drove down to the Plaza on Thursday night," says Clyde. "He would count the parked cars to see how business was going. I remember one night he counted only fourteen cars and he darn near cried."

J.C.'s "unusual foresight" was never better illustrated than in his concern over the possible effect of the Depression on the restrictions that ensured the long-term well-being of the Country Club District. Nichols and his legal staff had recognized early on that the country's financial woes would ultimately cause an increase in local residential foreclosures. Fearful that restrictions could be rendered meaningless in any Nichols development in which the original property owner foreclosed on the Nichols Company, repossessing the underlying land, J.C. went to great lengths to convince the original landowners that by allowing the restrictions to be attached to unencumbered land, their property would retain greater value. Had he not prevailed, and if several large landowners had succeeded in foreclosing on the Nichols Company, it is conceivable that the caliber of the contiguous Nichols developments might have been blighted by areas suddenly left without quality control. J.C.'s foresight, however, rendered such a situation only hypothetical.

It was also fortunate that the responsibility for and cost of community services had been shifted from the company to the homeowners associations by the time the Depression came along. One of these services, of course, was fire protection. Clyde Nichols, Jr., tells of being at the maintenance shed of the Nichols Company, which doubled as the Mission Hills/Indian Hills fire department, when a fire alarm came in—a brush fire at the edge of the district. Asked if he would like to ride along, young Clyde jumped onto the truck next to several barrels of water for the ride to the site of the fire. Each firefighter, using a hoe handle fitted with a large wire loop over which a gunny sack had been drawn and tied, dipped the sack into the barrel and dragged it along the fire line. In this manner the "firemen" (including Clyde) extinguished the blaze within a few minutes, earning J.C.'s youngest son $3.35 for his efforts. The significant thing, says Clyde, was that the Nichols Company stopped paying employees who doubled as firefighters the minute they switched hats and headed for a blaze. The firefighting bill went to the appropriate homeowners association.

In February 1934, Miller Nichols graduated from the University of Kansas (having taken a semester out of college to work his way to Europe). His final responsibility as president of his Beta Theta Pi chapter had been to host a luncheon for the new chancellor of the university, Dean Mallot, who was also a Beta. As he drove his father back to the office after lunch, J.C. inquired, "What are you doing this afternoon?"

"Well, I thought I'd check with Mother and see if she had something she wanted me to do."

"Why don't you go buy a hat and come to work."

Miller jokingly refers to the "twenty

Among the earliest of the Plaza's seasonal celebrations were the Easter bunnies. Families come with children ready to climb and play and in their Easter finery for picture taking.

minutes I had to 'find myself' quite different than it is today."

And so he joined the sales department of the J.C. Nichols Company. Miller's first residential sale and his only sale during his first year with the company was a house at 70th Terrace and Valley Road to Bud Goetz, who subsequently bought two more homes from Miller over the years.

In 1935, the Depression was still holding residential development in a stranglehold. So company architect Ed Tanner took a leave of absence to accept a challenging opportunity offered by the federal government. He was given 90 days to design the entire town (streets, houses, shops, etc.) of Fort Peck, Montana, a development associated with the Army Corps of Engineers' Fort Peck Dam project. Sequestered away in a warehouse with a handpicked team of 100 architects, he accomplished the tremendous undertaking on schedule. For this, he received special congressional commendation and an Army-Navy "E" Award.

Ed Tanner was made a director of the Nichols Company in 1938 (and became a vice-president upon J.C.'s death in 1950). According to his widow, Katherine Tanner, he took special pride in his design for the Linda Hall Library (adjacent to the UMKC campus) and for the Danforth Chapel on the KU campus in Lawrence.

The 1938 Fiesta on the Plaza featured these handsome Señors: (left to right) merchants Bill Schoenhard, Ed Chandler, Jack Henry, O.D. Stewart, Whit Mulford, Ed Howe, and John Watkins.

In addition to his work ethic and dedication within the company, Tanner held many responsible positions in the community. He was one of the few men ever to serve two consecutive terms as president of the American Institute of Architects, a remarkable distinction considering the stigma attached by his peers to any close affiliation with a real estate development firm such as the J.C. Nichols Company.

Randy Knight, who has been in residential sales with the company for over 42 years, recalls J.C.'s personal involvement with his sales force:

Mr. Nichols came to many of the sales meetings [held twice a week] and gave very inspirational talks. He used to say, "Men, we're a partnership—you and us." He maintained personal contact with his salespeople by sending a personal note of congratulations and spurring the individual on to greater heights. He instructed us to take a different route to work each day, so that we could see what the competitors were up to.

Mr. Nichols insisted that all sales personnel attend Homes Association

Pictured at a J.C. Nichols Company sales meeting at 310 Ward Parkway about 1936 are (1) J.C. Nichols, (2) Herbert J. Snodgrass, (3) John "Jack" Frost, (4) Miller Nichols, (5) Clyde P. Buis, (6) M.E. "Monk" Baird, (7) Robert S. "Bob" O'Keefe, (8) Ray N. Eaton, (9) L.J. "Jack" O'Keefe, (10) James J. Meaney, (11) Clyde Nichols, Jr., (12) David M. Kennard, director of sales, (13) Walter G. Basinger, sales manager, (14) Lewis W. Keplinger, (15) Robert E. Kernodle, (16) unidentified, and (17) Ray D. Jones, farm department.

meetings. He would sidle up to one of us and ask the identity of a certain homeowner; then he would walk over to greet them by name.

In-house bulletins were issued to instruct the sales staff on existing company policies and inform them of any recent policy changes. During weekly sales meetings, Nichols shared sales techniques gleaned from his personal experience.

In a 1936 convention address on the subject, he shared many of the tips he offered to his staff over the years. Shortly thereafter the *National Real Estate Journal* published an article taken from Nichols' speech, entitled, "Lessons I Have Learned in Selling Real Estate." Following are excerpts:

> Enthusiasm is the best trademark of a Realtor. Be truthful in every deal, be interested, believe in your property, or get out of the business.
>
> Let's make the presentation of our merchandise an interesting, educational thing. Let's base our facts upon their proper relation to the business and the economic situation of the community and the nation.
>
> I would rather have a salesman with a good, sincere, friendly smile than one with a college degree.
>
> If you have a prospective buyer, first realize that you must know your property. It is a crime to offer property if you are unfamiliar with all its advantages and its disadvantages.
>
> It pays to boost your competitor. The favorable things you say about him will reach his ears. Reciprocity helps build business.
>
> Don't form the habit of knocking your government, your city, your own business or any other line of business.

> The world likes an optimist and shuns a pessimist.
>
> Never swear unless you're damned sure the other fellow likes to swear.
>
> When you meet and confer with people in a convention, don't spend all your time telling the other fellow what your views are, but try to get some ideas from him. There is not a man there who doesn't have some thoughts that are of value to you. Let's open our minds and our arms to one another and let us go home with some mighty fine ideas and thoughts of the other fellow's.
>
> Never stand or sit on the opposite side of the desk from your client.

J.C. practiced what he preached. When making a business call, he chose not to sit across the desk from the person he was calling on. Instead, he would pick up the visitor's chair and place it at his host's side, facing him. J.C. usually carried a plat, blueprint, or map of the Country Club District, which he would spread out on the desk on the pretext of pointing out something, and in the process, cover up any papers that might distract the other person.

He also trained the sales force in his own techniques for showing a real estate lot, based on decades of experience. "A lot is not very impressive in itself," he said, "just a piece of land with four corners." So as he stood looking at it with prospective buyers, he would say, "I think we ought to get a little better sense of the size of the home site. Mrs. Johnson, would you mind stepping over here and I'll show you where the corner is. There, would you mind standing right there a moment?" Then, "Mr. Johnson, let me find this other corner," and he would lead the man to the opposite corner. Finally, he would place his hat at the third corner (where it could hardly be seen) and would take his own place at the fourth corner. Practically shouting so his voice would reach them, he would say, "Now then, you can get a better idea of how big a piece of land this is. Look at how far apart we are!"

Even the Depression did not deter J.C. from continuing to beautify the Country Club District with outdoor statuary. In the spring of 1935 he purchased an imposing, one-ton bronze statue of an eagle with a 12-foot wing span, a Japanese piece that had stood for generations in the courtyard of a Shinto temple before being purchased by a New York art dealer. After buying the statue, J.C. had it placed on a base made of native stone in the median of Ward Parkway at 67th Street. He then persuaded the Armour Fields Homes Association to provide complimentary landscaping. Over the next few years, he placed a variety of garden statuary along the newly opened extension of Ward Parkway, Meyer Circle to Gregory. A 1935 company description of outdoor art noted wellheads, benches, statuary, urns, and fountains, pointing out that 200 works of art had been set out to adorn the Country Club District.

In 1936, residential building started to pick up. The Armour Hills Gardens subdivision, westward from Holmes south of Meyer Boulevard, was opened. In 1937, two more lovely upscale neighborhoods followed, Mission Woods, adjacent to Mission Hills golf course on the north, and Sagamore Hills just west of State Line and south of Tomahawk Road. But the strain of the Depression years was taking its toll on the health of J.C. Nichols.

Early in the winter of 1937/1938, J.C. became ill with the stress of his efforts to keep the company afloat and then to get it

This Japanese one-ton bronze eagle with a twelve-foot wingspan was placed in the median of Ward Parkway at 67th Street.

Exhausted from the strain of the Depression, doctors insisted in 1937 that J.C. take a three-month leave from the company; pictured here in Chile, he is riding with Miller and son-in-law Earl Allen (center).

going again and the heavy burden of civic commitments both locally and nationally. He was confined to his home for more than a month, and the doctors, concerned for his long-term health, insisted that he take some extended time away. The Nichols' first grandchild, Earl and Eleanor's infant daughter, was born in February but lived just a day. With Miller's help, Jessie planned a trip. The Nichols, the Allens, and Miller set sail down the west coast of South America, with the *Kansas City Star* announcing that Mr. Nichols was taking his first extended vacation in many years.

It was while they were on this trip that

W. T. Kemper, president of Commerce Trust Company, became worried about the financial health of Nichols' company and asked to see the books during J.C.'s absence in South America in 1938. This precipitated a legendary stand-off between the two men.

J.C. received an urgent call in Buenos Aires from John Taylor. Commerce Trust Company banker W.T. Kemper, a great friend of J.C.'s who had helped finance the Country Club District, worried about the financial health of the company, had sent Commerce Trust officer George Dillon to call at the offices of the J.C. Nichols Company with a request to go over the books. According to Miller, who was there when the call came through, J.C. commended John for declining to produce the financial records, using some colorful language to express how he felt about the banker's going behind his back and threatening to cut short his vacation. He said, "Tell them when I am returning and that I will be in to see Mr. Kemper."

Upon J.C.'s return to Kansas City, he strode into Kemper's office, his arms loaded with Nichols Company ledgers. "W.T.," he asked the startled banker brusquely, "have you ever considered going into the real estate business?"

"No, I never have," stammered Kemper.

"Well, give it some thought," said J.C., dropping the books onto the surprised banker's desk along with a big set of keys. "You're welcome to the J.C. Nichols Company if you think you can run it better than I can."

With that, he turned to leave. Kemper beat Nichols to the door. Overwhelmed at the thought of managing J.C.'s vast real estate holdings, the banker backed off and granted the Nichols Company additional time to make payments. Miller emphasizes, "We were faced with real bankruptcy. We couldn't pay all our bills, but we stayed in business because Dad convinced the bankers that they would be better off working with him by reducing the interest rate on outstanding loans. Also we successfully borrowed an awful lot of money from the Teacher's Life Insurance Company at 4 percent."

In 1938, the company opened the popular Fairway subdivision featuring charming smaller homes in a wooded setting, bounded on the east by Mission Hills Country Club and on the southeast by the Kansas City Country Club. Miller suggested that the district be named Fairway, noting that it was bounded by two golf course fairways, and this was accepted, although Frank Grant criticized the name as foolish.

The J.C. Nichols Company was up and going again, still building in Indian Hills while adding more lovely new neighborhoods. In 1939, the *National Real Estate Journal* honored the Nichols Company by devoting an entire issue to its accomplishments. This overview said:

> The firm represents a fitting ideal, whose methods and practices in all departments of the real estate business are worthy of close study and emulation.
>
> [The company] began with little or no capital, and no natural advantages. Then, the standards of its founder, Jesse Clyde Nichols, seemed far too idealistic. Now it is regarded as the foremost residential development in the country, and is studied as a model by the best subdividers and city planners. Its progressive ideas of land use, of restrictions, of expensive beautification, of cultivation and scrupulous maintenance of natural beauty, of scientific planning in every phase of building and development, of group planning of shopping centers and store buildings—all . . . have been proved not just idealistic but definitely good business.

The Nelson-Atkins Museum of Art

For J.C. Nichols the cloud over the real estate business that was cast by the Great Depression was not without its silver lining, for it permitted him to direct even more of his attention and energy to his public service projects. In Kansas City, the largest of these was his leadership position in the William Rockhill Nelson Gallery of Art.

As recounted in the previous chapter, J.C. was one of the three university trustees appointed in accordance with Nelson's will. When William Volker stepped down as chairman in December 1929, the post was assumed by Nichols, who had already begun traveling to visit and study museums and their collections as he sought the advice of museum curators and art historians.

J.C. Nichols and Herbert V. Jones took on the responsibility for assembling the museum collection and for determining just what kinds of art would be included. Arthur Hyde, who succeeded Volker, had been appointed Secretary of Agriculture in 1929 and spent most of his time in Washington, D.C. The university trustees had originally agreed with Nelson that artful copies of Old Master paintings would be the most cost-effective means of building an art collection. Nichols' research indicated, however, that times had changed; with the exception of Harvard's Fogg Museum, which collected both, all major American art institutions had turned away from reproductions in favor of original art. The Nelson trustees followed suit. Lacking the expertise to select original works, the trustees first sought the advice of R.A. Holland, director of the Kansas City Art Institute.

Soon, however, they appointed

Harvard-educated art historian Harold Parsons as an adviser for the gallery. His specialty was European art. Parsons continually tried to steer the trustees toward a generally representative historical collection, based on aesthetically unique masterpieces and carefully selected western art. A trip to New York City with Parsons in January 1931 provided Nichols and Herb Jones with an opportunity to make several satisfactory purchases and to make the acquaintance of some eminent art dealers as well. One of these was the Chinese dealer Dr. C.T. Loo with whom J.C. Nichols developed a personal friendship that continued for many years.

J.C. Nichols took pride in talking dealers down to prices much lower than Parsons estimated as the bottom limit. In one instance recalled by Miller, Lord Joseph Duveen, a formidable art dealer in the English field, arranged a private showing in New York of a Gainsborough he was offering to the trustees, one that Harold Parsons was eager to have. J.C., Parsons, and Herbert Jones were ushered into the viewing room and seated in big plush chairs on a raised platform. Attendants in knee pants wearing patent leather pumps with silver buckles offered them cigarettes and drinks. Velvet curtains were drawn back dramatically to reveal the painting. The room was darkened; the only light was on the Gainsborough. For quite some time, Lord Duveen stood beside the painting and waxed eloquent about the famous artist and what a treasure this picture would be in any gallery.

The south facade of the Nelson-Atkins Museum of Art in the 1930s.

The purpose of the elaborate presentation wasn't lost on J.C., who realized that his chances of buying the painting at a bargain price were rapidly disappearing. In the middle of the presentation, he got up, walked to the painting, put his arm around Lord Duveen's shoulder and said, "Joe, when are we going to talk turkey?"

With that the scene broke up, and once outside, the utterly humiliated Parsons said, "You did a terrible thing in there, Mr. Nichols. You have destroyed the reputation of the Nelson Gallery in the art world forever." But the upshot was that the trustees bought the Gainsborough at a good price. It hangs in the museum today. And J.C. and Lord Duveen became good personal friends.

Accepting the suggestions of friends and art experts alike that they branch into art areas less competitive than Europe's Old Masters, the trustees sought advice from Dr. Nicholas Pickard, who was retiring from the University of Missouri art and archaeology department. And in early 1932, they hired Paul Gardner as a resident assistant, at a salary of $3,600 per year. The next year they added Charles O. Cornelius as their adviser on American decorative art. A practicing New York architect and former associate curator of American art at the Metropolitan, Cornelius satisfactorily undertook the design,

Herbert V. Jones, one of the three "university trustees" appointed in accordance with William Rockhill Nelson's will to establish the Nelson-Atkins Museum of Art. (Courtesy of Nelson-Atkins Museum archives)

William Volker, the second of the three "university trustees." The third was J.C. Nichols.

furnishing, and installation of the Nelson-Atkins American wing.

It is not known what prompted Nichols to focus on Far Eastern art and most particularly on Chinese art. Perhaps it was advice from the art scholars and museum curators he visited. But Dr. Nicholas Pickard says that "J.C. Nichols wanted to collect a civilization. Cost made it prohibitive to try and do this with Egypt, or Greece, or Rome. He believed that national recognition would come with the establishment of a definitive collection representative of a civilization. Also," adds Dr. Pickard, "Chinese art in the Depression could be

bought very reasonably, which was always an important consideration for Mr. Nichols."

However the decision was reached, J.C. Nichols then went to talk with William Milliken, director of the Cleveland Art Museum and a connoisseur of Chinese art. Milliken put him in touch with Langdon Warner, who headed the department of Oriental Studies at Harvard. Warner recommended that a young Harvard graduate fellow named Laurence Sickman studying Chinese art in Peking at the time be hired to search out and purchase Chinese art for the new gallery and that he be put on a 10 percent commission. J.C. persuaded his fellow trustees to agree to the arrangement and to authorize

Art authority Paul Gardner was hired by the trustees in 1932 to advise them on the direction the new museum's collection would take. The following year, Gardner became the museum's first director. (Courtesy of Nelson-Atkins Museum archives)

Laurence Sickman, a Harvard Fellow in Peking, was hired by the trustees to purchase Chinese art for the new museum. (Courtesy of Nelson-Atkins Museum archives)

the purchase of $30,000 worth of Chinese art for the new museum through Langdon Warner and Laurence Sickman. Young Sickman had a fine eye for the unique and had established contacts in Peking that enabled Warner to make some advantageous purchases.

Kristie Wolferman states: "Sickman would send Warner photographs of objects he thought the new museum might want. Warner would then advise the trustees; and if the trustees wanted to buy, they wired Sickman the money. Because this system was slow, Sickman often used his own money or borrowed money from his mother rather than risk the loss of pieces he thought the museum should have."

The dealer C.T. Loo was also instrumental in locating works of Oriental art. J.C. particularly enjoyed bargaining with Loo on his visits to New York. C.T. would show him a variety of objects that he could make available to the new gallery, whereupon J.C. would proceed to bargain for the lot rather than purchasing the individual pieces.

Pickard spoke enthusiastically of the museum's Oriental art collection: "I'm oversimplifying it somewhat, but in the museum field, when you speak about Kansas City, you mean Oriental art. Among people who travel, we are known for our wonderful Oriental collection. It makes so much sense and reflects on J.C.'s foresight. He realized that concentrating in one field of art like that, and doing it well, would ultimately benefit the Kansas City cultural community. And besides, it was a field that enabled us to avoid competing with the Metropolitan and [other] institutions for popular European works by the great Masters."

Nevertheless, the museum collection does, in fact, include many notable European works of art. In April 1933, the

Kansas City Star reported: "More than 200 men and women assembled last night in Epperson Hall at the Kansas City Art Institute to honor an ideal bequeathed to them and to his city by William Rockhill Nelson when he left all he possessed to found a gallery of art." On this occasion, J.C. Nichols reminded the merchants present of the thousands of persons who would be attracted to Kansas City by the museum. He painted an attractive word picture of the hoped-for extension of the grounds. With that, he introduced Harold Parsons as the most reliable of art buyers.

The *Star* continues: "On the stage of Epperson Hall the largest canvas in the Nelson collection had been on view through the evening. Parsons turned to it with pardonable pride and introduced it as 'as great a Veronese as ever crossed the Atlantic.' It was Christ and the Centurion. The big canvas was removed and a Titian portrait was placed in the light, as Parsons described its beauty and rarity. El Greco's Penitent Magdalen came next, and then Rubens' Old Parr. As a Rembrandt portrait was placed on the easel, there was a round of spontaneous applause." In closing the meeting, Nichols urged those present to attend the ceremony of laying the museum cornerstone the following afternoon.

Meanwhile, the three university trustees, along with the Atkins trustees and those for Ida Nelson, Laura Kirkwood, and Irwin Kirkwood, had the responsibility for building a suitable museum edifice on the Oak Hall site that had been agreed upon. They chose the architectural firm Wight and Wight, known for its design of buildings in the neo-classical style, the style of choice for the majority of eminent museums in America. The firm borrowed extensively from the impressive Cleveland Museum of Art in its design for Kansas

City's new gallery. The east wing would house the Nelson Gallery of Art and the Atkins Museum would occupy the west wing. It was a sign of the times that the Long Construction Company, which contracted in 1930 to build the monumental six-story limestone structure, had such an established reputation locally that no other bids were sought; the $2.6-million deal was consummated with a simple one-page contract. Two years later, the shell of the building was completed; an additional year was required to finish the interior. The local landscape architecture firm of Hare & Hare was hired to create aesthetically appropriate grounds.

Lindsay Hughes Cooper relates that when the Long Construction Company was about to turn the museum over to the trustees, they were faced with manning the operation, something new to them. Nichols called George Herrick, one of the J.C. Nichols Company foremen and explained the situation:

> "We have a man who knows about art and a secretary who can keep track of the art as it comes in, but we need a man for the pipes, the boilers, the engine room and the toilets. George, you're a good man, but we don't have enough work for you right now. I want you to see Paul Gardner at the museum, but first we'll get an okay from Herb Jones. . . ." So George was the first man on the pipes—but he also raced upstairs every few minutes to unpack incoming art. From the first, Paul regarded him as an ideal teammate. If I tell you that for ten years there were only two keys to the museum's storage—one on P.G.'s belt and one on George's—you will know in what esteem he was held.

After a month of pipe and collec-

tion juggling, even Mr. Nichols could see there were two jobs involved. You can't be in the boiler room and receiving at the west door at the same time. So J.C. advised giving the job of engineer and maintenance to Clarence Simpson, who had been the Long Company's superintendent of construction during the first phase of building. And for some 40 years Clarence maintained the museum in the immaculate fashion that Mr. Gardner demanded. And George, who had fallen in love with handling art, unpacked and installed paints, pottery, tapestries, glass and sculpture.

The trustees temporarily used Nelson funds to provide for upkeep of the newly completed facility, but J.C. eventually prevailed upon the city fathers to maintain the museum with public funds, recognizing that the building is situated on property given to the city.

The trustees had begun to hire personnel to help with collection, display, and education. Paul Gardner was named director of the gallery in 1933; Phillip Beam became Gardner's assistant. R.A. Holland of the Kansas City Art Institute was named curator of collections.

The William Rockhill Nelson Gallery of Art and Atkins Museum of Fine Arts opened its doors to 2,500 invited guests on December 10, 1933. When it was opened to the public the following day, 7,500 people visited.

The weeks leading up to the grand opening were hectic for the trustees as well as for the staff. Nichols and Jones spent three weeks of 14-hour days at the building. Looking back at those times many years later, Paul Gardner remembers with fondness "the old days when we loved to work seven days a week plus four or five nights. None of us had a secretary. We all *worked* and were able to make it a *great gallery*. It was our memorial to hard, devoted work. Thank God for J.C. and Herb Jones."

Kristie Wolferman states that the invitation process was a headache for J.C., demanding all his tact: "In spite of the care that went into making the invitation lists, J.C. Nichols reported that 'many unpleasant circumstances arose, caused by people becoming disgruntled because they were not invited,' and for two weeks prior to opening a great deal of diplomacy was required to handle such complaints. The trustees felt that as a whole the invitation list was well and accurately handled, and that it brought all the appropriate people to the gallery."

Lindsay Hughes Cooper, in a talk entitled, "A Night of Remembrances," reminisces about the opening: "Mr. Gardner and Mr. Sickman were being lionized; Kansas City society was giving parties like mad. And now it was December 10th! A special car came from New York filled with the world's most prestigious art dealers. Britisher Lord [Joseph] Duveen accompanied by a personal valet came and stayed with the Nichols and infuriated Mrs. Nichols by bringing his own silk sheets. . . . My memory of the opening night is of white ties and tails, mustaches and goatees. . . . " After the gala reception, the gallery was opened to the general public.

The *Museum Journal* had high praise for the new Kansas City museum: "The collection of Old Masters which has been acquired is a most remarkable one and probably no such public collection has been brought together in so short a time." J.C. ended his talk at the dedication by saying, "May these halls become a rallying place for high ideas and aspirations, may they crystalize a greater love of beauty, a fresh enthusiasm for living; may they be a happy, democratic meeting place for all groups, all needs, all creeds, all men who call the middle west their home."

The Kansas City Philharmonic

At the very height of the demands on his time by the museum, J.C. was also helping organize a philharmonic orchestra for the city. The Chamber of Commerce, in which J.C. was extremely active, supported the move. Karl Krueger, a native of Atchison, Kansas, and a graduate of the University of Kansas, came to Kansas City in the summer of 1933 from a position as conductor of the Seattle Symphony. With the chamber's help, Krueger organized the Kansas City Philharmonic Society whose initial nine-man board included J.C. Nichols, Cliff C. Jones, W.T. Grant, and Fred Harvey. At an early meeting to plan a campaign for funds, J.C. announced, "It is going to be necessary to tell the businessman, no matter how hard-headed he is, that he must support the symphony orchestra."

The gala grand opening of the Nelson-Atkins Museum was the occasion of the fledgling Philharmonic Orchestra's first public appearance. It is remarkable that these two great Kansas City cultural institutions were born in the very depths of the Depression, when orchestras in other cities were being disbanded. However, the economic times were reflected in the fact that none of the musicians, even conductor Karl Krueger, had a set salary for the first season; concert revenues were divided among the members of the orchestra. The orchestra performed regular concerts in the old Convention Hall, where the acoustics were poor, until 1936 when it moved to the Music Hall of the new Municipal Auditorium. Krueger conducted the Philharmonic for ten outstandingly successful years, during which its subscription audience grew to be one of the largest in the country.

Pembroke–Country Day and the University of Kansas City

In 1932/33, the Country Day School and the Pembroke School *together* had a paying enrollment of 176. Both boys' schools realized that neither could survive unless they merged. This was accomplished for 1933/34, and Pembroke moved to the original Country Day campus. The new school was named Pembroke–Country Day, with a combined enrollment of 206. Both Miller and Clyde Nichols, Jr., are graduates of Country Day—Miller in 1929, Clyde in 1932.

Meanwhile, the University of Kansas City had applied for a state charter on May 28, 1929. It was legally cleared on December 2, 1930, and like the Nelson Gallery, opened its doors in 1933. Nichols was elected to the advisory council of UKC's board of trustees in 1939 and continued to serve in that capacity the rest of his life.

City Planning

Nichols continued to push the Liberty Memorial project—prodding the city administration and especially the Park Department, raising private funds, and finding ways to keep the work going. In 1932, in the depths of the Depression and with his real estate business in the doldrums, J.C. assumed the chairmanship of a committee to complete the Liberty Memorial plan, which was now minus the cultural center but included the beautification of its grounds with the building of walkways and steps and the planting of maple trees, shrubs, flower gardens, and lawns. The landscape architectural firm of Hare & Hare had taken over for George Kessler. In this instance, hard times proved to be a benefit as the federal Civil Works Administration (CWA) spent $84,485 and employed 6,700 unemployed men to do the work. Approximately 15,000 cubic yards of earth were moved in the process.

Concurrently, Nichols continued to push for a civic center in the same vicinity. Again, the Depression and the need to alleviate disastrous unemployment gave the needed impetus to bring a civic center plan to realization. An ambitious ten-year plan was put together, incorporating a number of needed public buildings and urban reconstruction projects that had failed in previous bond issues. Although the price of the new package came to $32 million, the bond issue had the backing of business, labor, the general public, and, most important of all, the Pendergast political machine, and it was passed May 26, 1931.

J.C. Nichols was appointed chairman of the public buildings committee, which was responsible for the location of the proposed civic center. Members of his committee were W. Laurence Dickey, R. Bryson Jones, H.N. Langworthy, George B. Longan (of the *Kansas City Star*), and R. Emmett O'Malley. The committee, which met 18 times in all, began with a study of civic center sites in other cities. It then made a list of 20 possible sites in Kansas City and visited each. Nichols' committee also worked with a corresponding committee of the city plan commission. The two groups finally issued a joint report that analyzed city growth, convenience, and other factors and recommended two locations—one on 9th Street, downtown, the other farther east on 15th Street.

The downtown merchants held a mass meeting to urge the 9th Street location, and the final choice was a compromise. It fell between McGee and Oak Streets, from 11th to 13th Streets. A magnificent new city hall and a fine courthouse were allocated $4 million each. Other buildings included a large new public library, school administration building, police headquarters, and jail.

Thus, in addition to his own business, Nichols was involved simultaneously in three major civic building projects: the Liberty Memorial and beautification of the bluffs facing the Union Station, the Civic Center downtown, and the Nelson-Atkins Art Museum to the east of the Country Club Plaza.

The Family

Jessie Miller Nichols also took an active part in civic affairs during the 1930s, including a campaign to enact a clean milk ordinance. In the twenties and thirties, milk was not customarily sold through grocery stores, but was delivered house-to-house by milkmen who worked directly for the dairies. Most dairies collected raw milk from farmers in large galvanized steel cans and processed it to produce cream, butter, and cottage cheese. The raw milk was subject to contamination from flies and careless handling as well as spoilage due to lack of refrigeration.

Jessie and some of her friends decided that Kansas City's milk wasn't safe and that the city needed to adopt a clean milk ordinance. One night at the dinner table she was expressing frustration because the group couldn't get to first base with the proposal. J.C. said, "Well, Dearie [his pet name for his wife], go talk to Tom Pendergast."

Pendergast didn't have an official position in city government; he was just a ward-heeler in one of the worst districts in Kansas City. But behind the scenes, he was probably the most notorious, powerful political boss in the country. He controlled the entire city administration and had tremendous clout all the way to Washington.[34]

So Mrs. Nichols, who had an impressive presence in her own right, sallied down to Pendergast's headquarters near 18th and McGee and went right in. Tom Pendergast was a good friend of J.C.'s and respected him but had never met Jessie. She proceeded to charm the city boss and impress him with her arguments. As she left he told her, "You're right, you're absolutely right. Leave it to me." At the next city council meeting the new ordinance was passed. Such was Pendergast's influence—council members either did as Tom directed or they didn't bother running for reelection.

J.C. also liked to tell about the time Pendergast had contracted with the J.C. Nichols Company to build him a mansion on Ward Parkway. After they had agreed on the plans and the price, J.C. took the contract down to Pendergast's office. The politician signed without even reading it. J.C. said, "Tom, it's customary in real estate contracts for the owner to put up what we call 'earnest money.'"

"How much?" asked Pendergast.

"Five thousand dollars."

"Sure," said Tom, and taking a roll of bills from his pocket, he began counting, "one, two, three, four. . . ."

J.C. interrupted, "Tom, I don't want to go out of here carrying $5,000 in my pocket. Can't you give me a check?"

"Oh yeah, sure," Tom said absently, "I can do that for you."

In addition to her efforts on behalf of cleaner milk for Kansas City, Jessie volunteered time at juvenile court. It was there that she met a young man named Richard White, who was in trouble with the authorities. Jessie, an avid garden enthusiast, offered him the opportunity of helping with gardening around the Nichols house, a formidable task considering the surrounding four acres of lawn, shrubs, and flower beds. She agreed to look after Richard for the court and ended up having a profound influence on the young man's life. They kept in touch over the years, and he retired from a career in the U.S. Army as a full colonel.

In the mid-1930s, J.C. and Jessie decided to build a country retreat on a family farm southwest of Stanley, Kansas. They employed the services of a local barn-builder, with all family members pitching in. The plans, drawn up by company architects Ed Tanner and Earl Allen, called for a 40-foot continuous span of double-hung windows alternating with picture windows along the west wall of the house. J.C., Miller, and Clyde were working together on the west wall one day, under the direction of the local barn-builder, when Clyde looked at the plans and noticed that the three of them were inadvertently installing the boxing across the upright studs, where the windows were to be. J.C. showed the mistake to the local builder, who shifted his tobacco cud, spit casually, and said, "No problem, we'll just cut them windows out later." It was far from a state-of-the art building technique,

The home of "boss" Tom Pendergast, who ruled Kansas City politics in the 1920s and 1930s, was built for Pendergast by the J.C. Nichols Company.

but that was the accepted method for making barn windows.

Next, without consulting his architect son-in-law Earl Allen, J.C. decided that running roof shingles in a straight line resulted in a dull and uninteresting roof. He had Miller and Clyde vary the amount of exposed shingle, thus creating a unique and picturesque roof design. But he ignored the fact that shingles are leak-proof only if there is a shingle squarely under the joint of the two shingles directly above it. So the randomly shingled roof design leaked like a sieve; the shingles had to be removed and reapplied by a skilled roofer.

The chimney was another blunder. The plans called for an inside fireplace plus a barbecue grille on the porch, both served by one chimney structure. J.C. apparently didn't know that separate flues were required in order for both fireplace and barbecue to draw properly. The Stanley house chimney was built with a single flue and consequently never worked properly. The family learned to stuff newspaper in the opening of the outside barbecue before building a fire in the inside fireplace, and vice versa.

While the masonry work was in progress, Jessie helped by doing one of the heaviest jobs—mixing the cement by hand in a mixing trough. She would first pull the new batch of cement all one way, using a hoe, then she would pull it all the other way. (She must have gotten warm at her task because she took off her blouse and was working in only her skirt and slip—a picture that is still treasured by the family.)

J.C.'s coup de grace on the Stanley project was his decision *not* to install an $8,000 sprinkler system for fire prevention. He stated with assurance, "Houses in the country, built when no one had ever heard of sprinkler systems, have regularly stood for 150 years or more." The Nichols family's retreat stood for one year, after which it caught fire and burned to the ground. The replacement, a rambling ranch house adorned in Mexican style, was equipped with a sprinkler system and, incidentally, was built by a professional contractor from Kansas City.

The Nichols children came into adulthood in the decade of the 1930s. Eleanor, who had graduated from Sarah Lawrence, a women's two-year college, in June 1929, had returned to Kansas City where she joined the Junior League and took its volunteer training. Dashing about in her Packard touring car, Ellie enjoyed the "Roaring Twenties" lifestyle. Marty Nichols remembers that Ellie's crowd frequented speakeasies and smoked in public, "very Great Gatsby era." In the summer of 1929, she began dating Oliver Dean Green, a young man of good family but remembered as rather a playboy at the time. On October 4, 1930, they were married at the Country Club Christian Church, and a lavish wedding reception followed in the Nichols garden, which had been wired for the event for hanging lights and Japanese lanterns. The setting was lovely indeed, and Eleanor was a beautiful bride. Clyde recalls that the brothers were duly impressed with the number of wedding gifts the couple received. Miller remembers that Eleanor and Dean built a home on Romany Road that reflected Eleanor's verve with its bright-red front door.

It was during the late summer of 1930 that the J.C. Nichols Company staff finally moved into their handsome new Plaza office building, with the Country Club Homes Association and the Plaza Association both accommodated on the first floor. It was here, in the newly formed

Plaza Association, that Eleanor found her niche at the J.C. Nichols Company. She worked with Bernice Nault, executive secretary of the association, whose husband, Cliff Nault, taught French at the Country Day School. Bernice and Eleanor made a dynamic team, dreaming up programs that would draw people to the Plaza through the Depression years.

Eleanor organized the Plaza Visitor Program, and as its first goodwill ambassador she visited newcomers to the area to explain the amenities of the Plaza and to present them with a listing of the merchants and services. Working with Bernice Nault, she helped put together the first Plaza Art Fair in 1932. Another of her projects was the Plaza's glassed-in Christmas creche. She was full of suggestions for elaborate holiday decorations at Easter, Halloween, Thanksgiving, and Christmas.

One of the projects, an outgrowth of the Plaza Visitor Program, was "Los Amigos." A 1933 article described how Eleanor talked her father into allowing the group to hold their meetings in the large Plaza Community Hall above Barnard's Camera Shop. New residents were invited to join the group and to attend monthly luncheons for a period of two years as they got acquainted with neighbors and the seasonal Plaza activities. A newsletter was published, and its mailing list continued to grow as Plaza news was sought even by those who had moved away.

Younger brother Clyde regarded Ellie's personality as quite dictatorial: "What she said was right, always right, and shouldn't be questioned. She would have made an excellent company manager. She had many of the right qualities but was a bit before her time."

When the J.C. Nichols Company dedicated its handsome new offices in October 1930, a large pictorial map of the Country Club District dominated the lobby's west wall, as it still does today. Earl Wilson Allen, a young company architect, managed to complete it by Labor Day so that reproductions could be printed and handed out at the opening dedication. Allen also designed some of the finest homes in Mission Hills and Indian Hills during the late 1920s, 1930s, and again after World War II. (Miller's favorite house in all of the Nichols Company's districts was designed by Earl and built for John Horn in Indian Hills at about this time. Home to the H.O. Peet family for over 40 years and French country manor in style, the house is entered through a large stone-walled courtyard and features beautifully designed detail inside and out.) In May 1935 Ed Tanner sent out a company memo in which he announced that the four senior men in his department were to be designated as architects. First among these he named Earl Allen, who was to become the company's chief designer and head of architectural research.

Eleanor Nichols (Nickie to her friends) had taken back her maiden name when she was divorced in 1933. She and Earl became friends at the Nichols Company; they were married in Lawrence at his family home on December 11, 1936.

The Allen's first daughter was born in 1938 but lived just a day. After the birth of a second daughter, Suzanne Eleanor ("Suzie"), on June 30, 1939, Eleanor turned her energies to home and motherhood. (Mary Louise "Mollie" Allen joined the family in April 1941.)

The dawning of the 1930s found Miller Nichols a freshman at the University of Kansas where, like his father, he had joined Beta Theta Pi. A Kansas City lawyer, Lyman Field, has a fond yet "painful" memory of his year as a Beta pledge under Miller Nichols' exacting eye:

This was 1932. Miller was President of the chapter, and Clyde and I were both pledges. In those days one of the requirements was that freshmen had to keep the upperclassmen's rooms in apple-pie order, and I was assigned to do Miller's room. Of course, we had to perform all kinds of other duties for them as well.

Miller was already quite a driver, and many times he would get kind of irked because I hadn't performed my duties precisely the way he wanted them done, and when he wanted them done. One day he'd had enough and sat me down and said he would put in writing what he expected of me. What he wrote was, "Do what you are told to do, when you are told to do it, and as you are told to do it."

Recalling his father's summer trip to Europe in 1900 when he worked his way over on a freighter and enjoyed a summer of adventure, Miller planned a trip with fraternity classmates Monk Baird and Dick Peck that envisioned even wider touring. He had bought a Model A Ford touring car for $100 and wanted to take the spring semester as well as the summer off to embark on a European adventure.

J.C. Nichols did not agree with a plan that included a semester out of college. So at the semester break in January of 1932, Miller dogged his father everywhere he went, arguing his case for a seven-month trip to Europe. He drove him to work, followed him to lunch, waited outside each meeting J.C. attended, making his sales pitch in every free moment on his dad's calendar.

After three days, J.C. came up with a singular proposition. "I will let you go on one condition. You go and talk with Chancellor Lindley, and if he says that you're right, you can make the trip."

Miller responded, "I will take you up on that with one condition—that I go alone to talk to Chancellor Lindley." By the time this agreement was reached, it was 8:00 in the evening; but Miller rushed to the phone and called the KU chancellor at his home, saying that he needed to talk to him just as soon as possible. The chancellor said, "Come ahead." So Miller hopped into the car and drove to Lawrence to present his case. For better than two hours the chancellor asked him question after question. Finally he concluded: "Miller, you are right and your father is wrong." Dashing back to the Beta house, Miller informed his two cohorts that he had permission, which, of course, they reported to their families. Overnight the plans were set.

The night before the boys left Kansas City, the Nichols invited Maxwell Blake, the U.S. diplomatic agent for North Africa, to dinner. Blake invited Miller to call him if he got down to Gibraltar. Departure had been delayed a bit because Miller's face was terribly swollen from extracted wisdom teeth, and his mother insisted that he wait until the next day. He agreed, but at 12:01 A.M. the boys waved goodbye.

The three boys worked their passage over by chipping and painting along the decks of a cargo ship. Touring south through France and Spain, their budget allowed $1 per day per person for bed and breakfast; sometimes they had to check out several accommodations before meeting this. Arriving in Gilbraltar, Miller called Max Blake in Tangier, Morocco. He urged them to take the ferry and come on over. They booked passage, in steerage of course, and rode below deck. So they were unaware that when the ship dropped anchor a handsome yacht flying the American flag had pulled alongside. Shortly a voice called down into the hold, "Is there a Miller Nichols aboard?"

The yacht, it turned out, had been sent by Max Blake, J.C.'s friend, who insisted on installing them at the American legation. After the disreputable-looking trio of American boys had bathed and cleaned up for dinner, they were invited to stay on and ended up spending 23 days enjoying Max Blake's hospitality in a garden oasis setting, with delicious food, lots of parties, and young people.

When they finally departed, Blake arranged for one of his sons-in-law to accompany them on a grand tour of North Africa, where they stayed in the homes of wealthy Moors. Ferrying from Tunis over to the toe of Italy, they motored north through Europe, arriving in England in July in time for Miller's 21st birthday. Jessie, Eleanor, and Clyde joined Miller for the occasion, but J.C., feeling he could not leave the business for any length of time, wrote a poignant letter that reflected the sadness he felt at not being with the family.

The entire seven-month adventure had cost Miller $700, almost the exact amount he earned writing articles about the experience for the *Kansas City Star*.

Miller's bachelor and young married friends spent a good deal of time gathering at the Nichols' house during the 1930s. Eleanor had her own home; Clyde was at first in college, then married and off to

Miller in Europe in 1932 with classmates Richard Peck and Morris E. "Monk" Baird.

New York; J.C. was spending an increasing amount of time in Washington, as well as giving talks to various real estate and other civic groups across the country. Jessie was delighted to have their company for dinner and a game of cards in the evenings. Young people's conversation was stimulating to her, and they, in turn, enjoyed her vision and understanding of what was happening in the world around them. Jessie also liked to exchange a good story with them—she was known for her keen sense of humor.

Like his older brother, Clyde worked for the company from the time he was old enough to hold a job. He recalls:

> The first job I had was sweeping up the new Plaza offices (then under construction) as a thirteen-year-old. I suppose there were child labor laws then, but Dad ignored them in our case. As a matter of fact, I don't remember any paychecks that first year!
>
> I particularly remember the nursery gang. We went around and cultivated all the flower beds and shrubbery in the District's parks and parklets. We took care of some of the vacant lots and fertilized new trees. Chiggers were our worst problem.
>
> I also worked one summer in the planing mill, but they got me out of there pretty quick for fear that I would cut off a hand or arm or something. I was transferred to the ditch-digging crew, where the other laborers gave me a lot of good-natured grief.
>
> I worked with the street repair gang as well. In those days, the Nichols Company owned a hot asphalt truck with a fire up under the bed.

> Our job was to patch cracks in the asphalt with the hot mix, then shovel sand over the patch.

Following in his father and brother's footsteps, Clyde attended the University of Kansas, where he was a member of Beta Theta Pi. While there, he met and fell in love with Martha Dodge. Marty was a Kappa Kappa Gamma, whose house was only a hundred yards from the Beta house. Pretty, vivacious, and popular, Marty was the second daughter of Wayne and Della Dodge, a prominent family in Salina, Kansas. But when Clyde told his parents of his serious intentions toward Marty, Jessie opposed the union—partly because of the couple's youth. The upshot was that Clyde and Martha eloped the fall after they graduated, in October 1936, and settled in New York City, where Clyde got a job in an advertising agency. They set up housekeeping in an apartment in Jackson Heights, a section of Queens.

It should be remembered that J.C.'s principal aim as a developer was to create residential communities where the children of the owners would want to live. In his efforts to attract more industry to Kansas City and in his work on behalf of education and the Nelson-Atkins Museum of Art, his oft-declared purpose was to keep the city's sons and daughters from moving away. How galling it must have been to him when his own younger son went to work back East!

Characteristically, J.C. embarked on a determined, subtle, and eventually successful campaign to persuade Clyde of the error of his rebellious ways and to lure the couple back to Kansas City. His hurt as well as his underlying affection for Clyde are revealed in a letter sent in December of 1936: "I hope you will always live in Kansas City and that we can always be

The KU chapter of Beta Theta Pi fraternity played an important part in the life of all three Nichols men. Miller (left) and Clyde (right) were both living at the Beta house when this photo was taken in 1932.

near one another as long as we live. Your constant thoughtfulness of me is appreciated, probably more than you realize." After a year, Clyde and Marty returned to Kansas City to accept his father's offer of a job on the sales force at the Nichols Company, where Miller was already working.

From the beginning, it was not a comfortable situation for Clyde. By way of illustration, he says: "When we were kids, Miller and I had a line drawn down the middle of our shared bedroom. I wasn't suppose to cross over, and if I did, I got pounded on. Being four years younger, I had always been a big fat nuisance of a baby brother as far as Miller was concerned. His friends called me meatball.

One day, soon after I went to work in sales, Miller stopped me in the office hallway and said, 'Clyde, home salesmen wear hats. Get yourself a hat.'

I said, 'Miller, I never wear a hat.'

He said, 'You've got to wear a hat. People who sell homes for the J.C. Nichols Company all wear hats and you're *going* to wear a hat!' That was our relationship." It was also the first business instruction that J.C. had given to Miller.

Clyde also remembers getting crosswise with his father on a couple of occasions. "I was heading downtown one afternoon and had to rush into the company's Plaza headquarters for a second. I was in such a hurry that I parked my car on the street in front of the building. This was a serious violation of Dad's rules. I ran into him inside and, sure enough, he asked me to give him a ride downtown. I started to sweat bullets and told him, 'Great, I'll go get the car. You can wait here.'

He said, 'No, I'll walk out with you.' He did, and when he saw the car, brother, did he chew me out! That was almost 50 years ago and I still can't bring myself to park anywhere but the parking lots when I visit the Plaza. You just don't get over those things easily.

On another occasion, when I was giving Dad a lift in the car, I happened to make a disparaging remark about the downtown region. He just lit into me, laced me up one side and down the other. 'Boy, don't you *ever* say anything bad about any part of Kansas City. It makes no difference that our residential properties and the Plaza lie to the south. The town depends on the downtown area. We have to work hard for its improvement. It's got to be a credit to the city.'"

Back in Kansas City, Marty enjoyed spending time with Jessie Nichols, and the two became close friends. Clyde and Martha's first child, son Jay, was born in the summer of 1939, just a few weeks after Suzie Allen.

The Urban Land Institute

On the national scene, J.C. Nichols was still extremely active on the board of trustees of the National Association of Real Estate Boards (NARB) when, in 1936, that organization sponsored the formation of the National Real Estate Foundation for Practical Research and Education, which in 1939 was renamed the Urban Land Institute. The National Association of Home Builders, in which J.C. was also active, engaged the new ULI as its technical consultant on land development.

From its inception, the Urban Land Institute's approach was to make available to urban communities the practical and realistic application of sound principles as developed through the actual experience of outstanding men in the urban development field. The Urban Land Institute 1959 publication *Of Land and Men* states: "Some of the results of the Institute's work may be seen in hundreds of residential communities and shopping centers built since World War II in the United States and Canada, and in the changing faces of such cities as Philadelphia, Detroit, Flint, Wichita, Raleigh, and Peoria, among others." Those words were written over 30 years ago, and the list would be vastly longer today.

As for J.C. Nichols, in helping form the ULI he succeeded in creating the ideal vehicle for conveying his ideas and influencing those in the country concerned with real estate. Preventing the deterioration of neighborhoods and the decline of real estate values was an obsession with him, and ULI was an organization dedicated to this very cause.

Industrial Expansion

Always a booster for Kansas City, J.C. Nichols became increasingly uneasy during the 1930s with the economic decline, quite apart from the Depression, that he perceived to be occurring in Kansas City. By 1938, as his uneasiness turned to alarm, he began studying population trends in the central plains states. He checked school enrollment figures over a ten-year period, new telephone connections, new customers for light and power, retail and mail order sales from the area, the number of insurance policies being written, and the size of grain crops produced and livestock shipped, among other data.

He discovered the frightening fact that the great middle part of the United States was losing population rapidly. Further, it was not older people who were moving, but the young people who were leaving home in large numbers to seek economic opportunity elsewhere. If this trend were allowed to continue, the result would be ghost towns, Nichols repeatedly declared.

The root of the problem was that the agricultural area, historically the chief source of Kansas City's prosperity, had suffered a decade of depressed farm prices and a catastrophic drought that turned it into the infamous "dust bowl." And as money dried up and population declined, it became a less attractive market center for industry. During the decade of the 1930s, the city suffered a much more severe decline in manufacturing jobs than the national figure of 6 percent. The value of goods produced went down 35 percent, compared to 11 percent nationally. The city ranked third in the United States in "unused labor supply," that is, in unemployed workers. Kansas City was too dependent on agriculture and without significant industry. But how was the problem to be solved?

Typically, J.C. Nichols took the positive, optimistic tack. He waxed eloquent about the boundless natural resources and raw materials in the central states: minerals, timber, gas, oil, coal, water. He was in the forefront of pointing out the abundance of agricultural by-products, formerly just farm waste, that could be processed into cellulose plastics, synthetic fabrics, and other new materials. He pointed out the geographical advantage of central location and the immense pool of labor, the farm boys and girls who were trained from youth to "fix it."

He began his efforts at home, working with the Kansas City Chamber of Commerce, the boards of directors of banks, and business and industrial executives. As Kansas was particularly hard hit by the farm depression, Nichols took the lead in getting a Kansas Industrial Association organized, with the aim of stimulating and assisting existing industry and attracting new companies. Foreseeing that aviation would be a frontier for new industry in the country and realizing that the wide open spaces of the central states were ideal for aviation purposes, Nichols pressed this idea hard with Kansas City bankers and with the leaders of towns in Kansas. To his frustration, he too often found them apathetic about industry.

Meanwhile in Europe, which seemed very far away at the time, Adolph Hitler had seized power in Germany and was building the largest military the world had ever seen. In 1936, he invaded the Rhineland; in 1938, Austria; in 1939, Czechoslovakia and Poland. Denmark, Norway, Belgium, the Netherlands, and France all fell to Hitler in rapid succession. Hitler's Luftwaffe was poised for the anticipated invasion of England.

In the United States, President Roosevelt, seeing that war was inevitable, and over opposition from appeasers and "America Firsters," had begun a massive defense effort that included extending aid to Great Britain. A National Defense Advisory Commission (NDAC) was set up, with members appointed by the president. Edward Stettinius, on leave from the presidency of U.S. Steel, was put in charge of the production of raw materials necessary for national defense. Manufacturing the raw materials into finished products was the responsibility of William J. Knudsen, on leave as head of General Motors.

By 1939, J.C. Nichols was no stranger to Washington, D.C. He was in his thirteenth year as a member of the key National Capital Planning Commission and was serving on the Advisory Council of the Department of Commerce. The federal establishment had expanded enormously during the New Deal with an "alphabet soup" of new agencies, and it was beginning to swell even more in response to the defense effort; new federal workers were arriving in the capital at the rate of 3,500 per month.

Nichols was also serving on the space control committee of the Department of the Budget to allocate new office space, as a consultant to the Public Buildings administration, on a committee to overhaul Washington's overloaded public transportation system, and on a decentralization committee to relocate agencies where possible to other cities with more office space and more adequate facilities (one result was the move of the Farm Credit Administration to Kansas City).

Nichols was known to President Roosevelt. On one occasion, he was invited to the White House to meet one-on-one with the president on the nation's housing problems. J.C. had prepared himself thoroughly for the Oval Office meeting, but he reported confidentially to his family afterward that the affable, charming Roosevelt had done almost all the talking and had scarcely permitted Nichols even to answer his questions. When the president's appointment secretary came in to announce the next visitor, Nichols felt let down.

From his Washington perspective, J.C. saw that the defense effort would lead to industrial expansion on an unimaginably massive scale, one that would set the pattern for decades to come. But in the infancy of this expansion, the entire middle belt of the United States was being ignored. As most existing manufacturing plants were either in the industrial East or the far West, it was easier and faster to give them the defense contracts. Large companies were reluctant to build new plants in an unknown area that, in the words of one eastern newspaper, was "only fitted to raise hogs, wheat and corn."

The urgency of the situation was not lost on a number of business and industrial leaders in the central states who realized that without large defense production, the area might forever be an "industrial wasteland." One powerful ally to them and to Nichols was Roy Roberts, the editor of the *Kansas City Star.* J.C. and Roy teamed up to convince the federal government that the central states were the ideal location for war-effort manufacturing.

Their great opportunity to make headway in this effort came unexpectedly in early 1940 with an invitation to J.C. to come to Washington and head up a major division of the National Defense Advisory Council.

Thus, the Great Depression had provided J.C. with the impetus to turn his energies to public service. The decade of the 1930s saw his influence on his fellow realtors and developers continue to grow significantly. His was a leadership role in the cultural and educational life of Kansas City. Now he was poised to provide great and lasting service regionally and nationally in the closing decade of his life.

Chapter 6

1940 - 1950

Just as the twenties had been J.C. Nichols' busiest decade as a real estate developer, the forties were in many ways his most productive, particularly on the national scene. He was able to turn his energies toward serving his city, his region, and his country, because during the period from 1930 to 1946 residential and commercial construction were largely suspended as the Great Depression was followed in turn by the diversion of construction materials during World War II.

Industry for the Central States

In early 1940, J.C. was in Washington, D.C., trying to get some defense production for Kansas. One day he was approached by an aviation executive who had been helping China in its war against Japan and had recently returned home. He told J.C. that, having had to move air bases every few days or weeks to avoid Japanese bombing, he was alarmed to see virtually the entire aircraft construction industry in America concentrated on the West Coast within range of naval guns and aerial bombs. Having hurried to Washington to warn defense production authorities of the danger he perceived and to persuade them to disperse aircraft production, he had met a blank wall.

J.C., together with Roy Roberts, was able to get an appointment with William Knudsen, head of manufacturing for the nation's defense production. After the China veteran expressed his alarm, the Kansas City men presented their case for locating defense industry in the central states. Knudsen agreed with the wisdom of the proposal.

J.C. asked him who might help them accomplish it.

Knudsen said, "Why don't you do it?"

"What do you mean?" stammered J.C. "How would I go about it?"

Knudsen said, "Come here to work for me at NDAC [National Defense Advisory Commission]. I need someone to head up the Miscellaneous Equipment Division. You could do that from nine to five, and the rest of the time you could work on getting more defense plants in the middle of the country."

Nichols replied that he would have to think about it but would reply as soon as possible.

When J.C. returned home, he immediately got in touch with state and city officials, business and industry leaders, chambers of commerce, university presidents, and other concerned leaders in the central states. He told each of them of his offer, but said, "I don't think I can accept."

They urged him to do so, of course, stressing the urgent need and the great opportunity he had. He would demur further, and as they grew more insistent, he would fix them with his gaze and ask, "Well . . . what will you do to help me?"

When J.C. got to Washington, D.C., in June 1940, he had only to call in these commitments and a steady steam of people flowed to Washington. Although he was working nine to five for NDAC, he met with the visiting delegations before and after, in the dawn hours and far into the night, planning strategy and suggesting approaches. Knudsen later declared that never in his life had he seen a man so willing to work so hard or able to accomplish so much. "One of the most able executives I have ever met," he commented.

The Miscellaneous Equipment Division was a tremendously important respon-sibility because of the wide range it covered: from shoe laces to overcoats, spoons to stoves, pills to power shovels, forceps to road sweepers, knives to wheelbarrows, horses and mules to power equipment, razor blades to parachutes, radios to helmets, aircraft warning to camouflage equipment, needles to saddles. The division helped handle procurement for every branch of the Army, Navy, Marine Corps, Coast Guard, and Air Corps.

Nichols' salary as director of the division was the same as that of Edward Stettinius, Knudsen, and the other executives of NDAC—$1.00 a year.

Back home, in a memo to J.C. Nichols Company employees, John Taylor emphasized that there was no company-connected reason for Nichols to accept

Gen. William Knudsen, as a dollar-a-year man, headed manufacturing at the NDAC and recruited J.C. to go to Washington, D.C.

Kansas City Star *editor Roy Roberts helped J.C. get war production plants located in the Plains states.*

the post: "Our company has no industrial property for sale and the only possible gain for our company by his activity is simply . . . the ultimate general benefit to the middle-west." When Nichols accepted Knudsen's invitation, he said in a company memo, "I am going to Washington, first to fight for the preservation of our country; and second, to try to get some recognition of the [central states]."

While awaiting his official appointment by President Roosevelt, Nichols stepped up his efforts to mobilize the leaders of Kansas City and the rest of the area to present the case for locating industry there—an effort that had been gathering momentum. Under the leadership of Kansas City mayor John B. Gage and the mayors of other towns in Kansas and western Missouri, a Mid-Central War Resources Board was formed with Lou Holland, head of a Kansas City engraving company, as chairman.[35] The Mid-Central Board collected data from some 15,000 area industries, large and small, and sent it to Nichols in Washington.

The Kansas City Real Estate Board made a detailed survey of industrial plant sites—square footage, heights of ceilings, floor loads, railroad trackage, power supply—which was sent to the military.

One obstacle that became apparent early was that the region's small manufacturers had no idea how to bid on government contracts. They feared the red tape involved and the other requirements in government work, and they were reluctant to have the government set wage standards. Nichols suggested that an industrial mobilization committee be formed to provide information on how to bid, to answer questions, and in general to help in obtaining contracts. Nichols, in turn, informed the committee about upcoming orders. The Kansas Industrial Commis-

sion, the Mid-Central War Resources Board, and various Chambers of Commerce ended up running "schools" and clinics on how to bid on contracts.

In addition, leaders of the Chambers of Commerce of the principal cities in the Midwest met in Kansas City to plan how to bring about the decentralization of defense industries. They called a nine-state conference of industrial leaders and other representatives from 200 communities, out of which grew the Midwest Defense Council. The former president of TWA and president of the Kansas Industrial Development Commission, Richard W. Robbins, was elected chairman of the council, which became an effective lobbying force for changes in defense industry policy to benefit the central states.

For example, a ruling from the Revolutionary War days required that bids on military contracts—from tents to tanks—had to be quoted FOB Philadelphia. That meant that a manufacturer in Kansas City wishing to make uniforms that would be used in Leavenworth, Kansas, had to quote prices based on delivery to Philadelphia. This naturally put all manufacturers outside the eastern seaboard at an unfair disadvantage. Nichols and Robbins got the regulations changed to permit military suppliers to quote prices FOB factory.

Similarly, they succeeded in effecting a policy change to permit "split orders," which meant that small Midwest plants would not have to compete directly with large eastern factories in bidding for orders too large for them to handle alone. Now they could bid on part of the total order.

In both these efforts (and particularly the latter), Nichols and Robbins were joined by Robert L. Mehorney, president of a Kansas City furniture company.[36] The three men pushed incessantly for decentralization of defense production, so that, rather than relying on a few large plants, small plants throughout the nation could do whatever they were best equipped to do. This policy was dubbed the "Kansas City Plan" after its proponents, who argued that it would greatly lessen risk of destruction of production capacity in the event of enemy attack. They also pointed out that it would "reduce dislocation of industry and redistribution of labor," and that this, in turn, would ease the demobilization of industry and labor after the war. After the United States entered the war and President Roosevelt called for all-out war production, the "Kansas City Plan" became government policy.

In his autobiographical comments, J.C. wrote of his NDAC experience in Washington:

> As soon as I arrived I was astounded to find that the proposed program of new defense plants included no . . . plants or air bases between the Mississippi River and the Rocky Mountains, except in the extreme south. (At that time there were more than 500 men leaving Kansas City each week for defense plants on the east and west coasts.) I immediately contacted the top officials in Washington, including President Roosevelt; Secretary of Navy Frank Knox; Secretary of War Stimson; Admiral Towers, head of the Navy Air Corps; and many others—not once, but many times. . . . I rallied support from industrialists, business officials and heads of chambers of commerce throughout the Middle West, getting large delegations to come from the [central] states.
>
> We finally changed the whole thinking in Washington and brought about the establishment of a reasonable number of defense plants through the Middle West.

The latter sentence was an understatement, according to Mary Katherine Goldsmith, whose thesis, "J.C. Nichols— City Builder," provides an excellent summary of the defense industry that came to Kansas City. A local garment industry provided uniforms for every branch of the service. Other area plants produced tents, parachutes, marine nets, bunk frames, radio transmitters and receivers, TNT cases, and a long list of other miscellaneous equipment. Steel made from Midwest scrap was fabricated into Navy landing craft that were floated down the Missouri and the Mississippi Rivers to the Gulf of Mexico. Local manufacturers of farm tanks and vending machines converted to manufacturing aerial bombs, mines, and other munitions. The Ford automotive assembly plant switched to assemblies for airplane engines manufactured by Pratt and Whitney in Kansas City. The machine shops of Black, Sivalls, and Bryson fabricated 6,000 tons of steel monthly into combat tanks. More gunstocks for infantry rifles were shipped from Kansas City than from any other area.

On September 27, 1940, Nichols announced a breakthrough that brought a major defense plant to Kansas City—a Remington Arms plant that would cost some $18 million, cover 4,000 acres, include more than 200 buildings, and provide jobs for thousands. Nichols received the credit for this plant, and also for an $87-million bomber plant in Fairfax, on the Kansas side, employing some 26,000 persons and bringing subcontracts to local machine shops and sheet metal works. He also had a part in locating the Sunflower Ordnance Plant at De Soto,

Kansas, the largest defense plant in the central states, authorized at $100 million.

The Tulsa (Oklahoma) *Tribune* reported that by the end of 1941 there were 24 defense plants between Mississippi and the Rockies, and that "probably more than any other one man, J.C. Nichols was responsible for the location of most of them." The Lincoln (Nebraska) *Evening State Journal* said, "Few men have done more in pleading the cause of the Central United States as a region of great industrial potentiality . . . than J.C. Nichols of Kansas City." Senator Capper characterized Nichols as "easily the first and most important citizen of the Great Midwest."

Perhaps the most impressive and touching tribute to Nichols' Washington service was the dinner tendered to him upon his departure from NDAC in July 1941, at the end of his 14 months of voluntary service. Among those who gathered were Vice-president Henry Wallace; Edward Stettinius, head of U.S. Steel and director of materials for defense production; Secretary of Agriculture Leon Henderson; Secretary of Commerce Claude Wickard; Assistant Secretary (later Secretary) of War Robert Patterson; Undersecretary (later Secretary) of the Navy James Forrestal; Sen. Harry S. Truman; and Nelson Rockefeller.

At the dinner, Nichols cashed his two government paychecks as a $1.00-a-Year-Man. One was for 90 cents, the other for 98 cents—after withholding tax and social security had been taken out.

The *Kansas City Star* said in a 1941 editorial: "With J.C. Nichols' understanding of the problems and his contacts, he is in a position to be of even greater service in the years ahead. . . . There is a vast field of unfilled needs and fresh opportunities. . . . No one man can do the job. But the west is fortunate in having the dynamic and intelligent leadership of J.C. Nichols to point the way."[37]

Nichols himself did not cease his efforts simply because he was no longer working full-time in Washington. By the end of the war, no less than 100 plants and military installations were located in the Midwest as a result of the decentralization program. The Kansas City area (including Jackson and Clay Counties, Missouri, and Wyandotte and Johnson Counties, Kansas) was turning out Mitchell bombers, ammunition, rocket powder, aircraft engines, landing craft, most of the ground equipment of the Army air communication service, and much other defense equipment. Some 332,000 workers were employed in these defense plants. One cent out of every dollar spent on war production was being spent in the Kansas City area. Many of the plants remained in the peacetime that followed, converted to nonmilitary use and providing an industrial base to balance the region's dependence upon agriculture.

The Family

Miller Nichols entered the decade of the 1940s with a low draft number. In April 1941, faced with an imminent draft call and induction into the armed services, he decided to make the best of the situation and establish temporary residency on the island of Oahu in Hawaii, there to await his draft notice.

Hearing of his plan, Red Callaway, an acquaintance from Kansas City, joined him. They rented an apartment on Waikiki and were given the use of a convertible Oldsmobile by Ted Bland, a salesman for the Nichols Company who was stationed at Scofield Barracks. Recalls Miller with a twinkle, "We proceeded to introduce ourselves to a few girls."

When their induction notices arrived, they reported and found that they were virtually the only Caucasians among many Japanese, Chinese, and Polynesians being called up. As Miller relates:

> The induction officer looked at us, checked our passports and said, "You shouldn't be here. You'll have to go back to your home draft board in Kansas City."
> I told him, "Well, I've moved here. Are you going to pay for my transportation back to Kansas City?" He said, "Come back tomorrow." The next day we were inducted into the Army.

At Scofield Barracks they were issued uniforms and told to fall into the chow line where lunch was being served from a big metal tub perched over a wood fire. Miller was assigned to a tent that he shared with three Japanese Americans: Mouki, Morimoto, and Yochita. "I could not have hoped to live in a tent with nicer, cleaner, or more delightful people. Miller further recalls:

Twenty-five years later, when Dave Jackson and I were researching ideas for the Alameda Plaza hotel, we took a trip to Hawaii to look at a new hotel, and I decided to take a side trip over to Kauai, where I hoped to be able to locate my Japanese friends. While Dave went to rent a car, I walked over to the airport information desk and said, "I'm looking for a man named Mouki, but I don't know the rest of his name."

To my surprise, the girl looked at me, smiled, and asked, "Are you Miller Nichols?"

"Yes," I stammered.

"I was with Mouki just last week," she said, "and he was telling me about some of his experiences with you."

We had dinner that evening with all three of my Japanese friends, who had fought in the Nisei Battalion and survived the North African campaign and the invasion of Italy, and their wives. It was amazing how things fell into place.

One day in boot camp, Miller was in his tent after lunch listening to the radio when he suddenly recognized the voice coming over the air. It was his father, J.C., giving a talk in Washington, D.C. It turned out that Lt. Gen. Walter Short, the Army commander in Hawaii, was listening to the broadcast as well. As a result, Private Nichols' first assignment was with the real estate division of the Quartermaster Corps. Told to wear civilian clothes, he was picked up by a driver each morning and taken to specified locations where he was to map out future gun sites.

But the story Miller most enjoys retell-

Drafted into the army in 1941 in Hawaii, Miller shared a tent with three Japanese-American recruits. They remained lifelong friends.

ing from that era is that of Roxie Brown, his former secretary at the Nichols Company. One day Roxie cabled that she was sailing over on the Lurline to marry a Navy lieutenant. Could Miller meet her, find her a job plus a place to live, and be best man at the wedding?

Coincidentally, the chief of Army personnel in Hawaii, Col. Russell Throckmorton, was also a former J.C. Nichols Company salesman. Miller and Red Callaway had purchased a sailboat, and Throckmorton, who loved to sail, frequently joined them. One afternoon, as they were skimming across the waves, he complained about how difficult it was to find a good secretary and how badly he needed one.

"Why, Russell," said Miller, "I think I can find you a good secretary."

"Who?" asked Russell. "Where? What's her name?"

"I'm not going to tell you," Miller replied. "You won't pay her enough, you'll start her off at the bottom of the Army scale." Russell continued to plead his case and Miller finally made him a conditional offer. "Okay, if you hire her, you can pay her anything you want for one month. After that, you'll have to either fire her or pay her the top allowable salary."

"I can't do that," protested Russell.

"Then you can't have her," Miller declared.

A week later, when they were again out sailing, Russell said to Miller, "I got General Short's approval to hire her."

So Roxie Brown went to work for Colonel Throckmorton. But not for long. A few weeks later, she was General Short's secretary!

Several months later, the Japanese attacked Pearl Harbor. During the investigation that followed into the reasons for the lack of preparedness, Roxie was the recording secretary. There were no electronic aids in those days, so she took all the testimony in shorthand. Roxie Brown may be the only person who knows the *full* story of Pearl Harbor. The ensuing Roberts Report resulted in both General Short and Admiral Husband F. Kimmel being relieved of their commands.

Today, Roxie is still married to her Navy man, now a retired captain in Norfolk, Virginia. Miller keeps in touch, most often through her sister Bonnie, who manages the Ward Parkway Garage for J.R. Sayre.

In September 1941, Congress passed a law exempting all servicemen over the age of 30 who had been drafted—Miller had recently turned 30. Watching for and then catching the news on the teletype that the president had just signed this bill, Miller moved quickly enough to become the only member of Army personnel to be released from the Hawaiian Department because, once alerted, General Short chose not to release any men from his command.

Following the outbreak of war, Miller applied to the Navy where he was commissioned a lieutenant, junior grade. His second draft notice and Navy approval arrived on the same day. Following a whirlwind courtship, he and Catherine (Katie) Caldwell were married at her family's home soon after Pearl Harbor. Miller and Katie spent the war years in Washington, D.C., and in San Francisco where he was with the Bureau of Yards and Docks, assigning equipment and recommending personnel for the famed Seabees.

Meanwhile Earl and Eleanor Allen and their two young daughters, Suzie and Mollie, moved to Arlington, Virginia, where Earl served in the Navy Department's Bureau of Architecture.

As a married man, Clyde, Jr., was exempt from the prewar draft but chose to do his bit in a defense industry. In 1940, he entered training for the Pratt and Whitney Engine Company in Hartford, Connecticut, a major manufacturer of engines for fighter aircraft. Clyde became manager of the inspection department.

J.C. commuted to and from Washington on a variety of assignments and so was able to keep in touch with all three offspring and their young families. Miller recalls lunching with J.C. at the famed Jockey Club, "a favorite choice of Washington's wartime elite. Dad walked through the restaurant to our table greeting most everyone in the room by name, and he was greeted by almost everyone who was seated after we were. Few could have been as well known in wartime Washington."

Probably the best known photograph of J.C. Nichols, one for which he posed on the roof of the J.C. Nichols Company offices gazing out over the Plaza with a rolled blueprint in his hand, was taken by Sally Ruddy.[38] Although her regular job was to photograph houses listed for sale and place prints of them in the salesmen's books, she was asked one day, on short notice, to take a publicity portrait of the company founder. Typically, J.C. took charge, suggesting they go up to the roof and taking along the roll of plans as a prop, even setting up the pose and camera angle. "He was so nice to me," Sally remembers. "I was nervous, so I was clumsy and slow, but Mr. Nichols tried to make me feel comfortable, joking with me to put me at ease. He offered to stand still for as long as it took." The resulting photo

was used in the *Kansas City Star*, on several magazine covers, and for the portrait that hangs in Miller's office.

Lindsay Hughes Cooper of the Nelson Art Museum won a scholarship from the Rockefeller Foundation to study Persian and Arabic art in New York City in the summer of 1941. She remembers that while she was there, she met with J.C. at Parris Watson's, a Persian and Arabic art dealer who was going out of business. Nichols was, of course, interested in picking up a bargain for the museum. Lindsay shares an anecdote:

J.C. said, "Lindsay, if you will have dinner with me and go to a show, I'll stay over in New York tonight." Mr. Nichols wanted to see a Broadway hit, "Helzapoppin." I guess that I would have loved it, but at the time I talked him into seeing "My Sister Eileen." He would have liked the other one.

We went to the Paramount roof for dinner and then to the show. He was having a wonderful time and asked, "Do you know any place else we could go?" I said, "We could go to Cafe Society Uptown," where Albert Ammons and Pete Johnson, two wonderful black boogie woogie piano players, were performing. I just loved boogie woogie but could see that Mr. Nichols wasn't having such a hot time. He looked kind of bored. I said, "Mr. Nichols, did you know that Pete Johnson is from Kansas City?"

He sat up straight, perked right up. "From Kansas City? Oh!" He looked around to make sure everybody was enjoying Johnson. J.C. wanted the whole New York audience to love this Kansas City musician. I think that

Perhaps the best-known picture of J.C. Nichols is this photograph taken in the early 1940s by Sally Ruddy on the roof of the company offices against a backdrop of the Plaza Medical Building tower.

attitude had a lot to do with everything he did.

When Betsy Dodge [Pearson], Marty Nichols' younger sister, went to New York City in 1943 as a KU graduate and got a job as an assistant art director at Lord & Taylor department store, J.C. sent her a congratulatory note, which was the beginning of a regular correspondence between the two.

> He had no reason to write to me. I was just a kid, but he made me feel he was really interested in me. Then one day I got a letter saying he would be in New York on a certain date, and could I arrange for Dorothy Shaver, President of Lord & Taylor, to have lunch with him?
>
> Well, I was able to set it up and he invited me along, and I can tell you, it was a thrill! It turned out to be a kind of historic luncheon because at that time Lord & Taylor did not have any suburban branches in shopping centers (nor did any other big New York department store, as far as I know); and Mr. Nichols didn't have any national name stores on the Country Club Plaza. And yet that's what they talked about at lunch. Here were these two remarkable people way ahead of their time, picking each other's brains.

National Capital Park and Planning Commission

When World War II began, Nichols and his fellow members of the National Capital Park and Planning Commission performed a herculean feat. Almost overnight, they were given the task of approving and locating each of the flood of office buildings that had to be erected,

from the "temps" to the permanent behemoths like the Pentagon. The city underwent a huge, almost overwhelming expansion from a sleepy southern town to a frenetic city of 1.2 million people—half of them single! For this flood of people, there was no housing, no hotels, no services—water, sewage, transportation, restaurants, laundries, all had to be provided. Quickly, 42,000 houses were thrown up, designed to be equally quickly dismantled after the armistice.

As the influx choked the city, Nichols pointed out that instead of the 3.5 families per acre that was normal for peacetime, dormitories could house 25 people per acre. So build dorms! And they did. He urged the decentralization of offices and their accompanying workers to outlying sections and even to other cities such as Philadelphia and New York.

After J.C. Nichols' resignation from the commission was reluctantly accepted by President Truman in 1948, J.C. wrote to the commission's staff his own summary of some of the accomplishments during his 22 years. He estimated he had made 150 trips to Washington, and that, counting travel time, this totaled two-and-a-half years of his life (without compensation).

"It is interesting to recall," he wrote, "that when I went on the [new] Commission, Constitution Avenue had seven different widths, with many narrow throats, and very inferior buildings on the north side. The whole group of buildings on the triangle had not been built. Lincoln Memorial, Jefferson Memorial, National Gallery, Pan American Building, Memorial Bridge, the drive to Mt. Vernon, the Supreme Court Building, the Library of Congress Annex—none of these were in existence, and their location all came before our Commission."

Over the years Nichols helped acquire

many playgrounds, swimming pools, parks, and trafficways. Streets were widened and access roads built. The commission built more than 95 percent of the 22-mile-long Fort-to-Fort drive, making possible a parkway drive on both sides of the Potomac all the way from Mt. Vernon to Great Falls. Most of today's zoning laws in Washington, D.C., originated during J.C.'s tenure. Slum clearance and greater segregation of industry were accomplished. A big stadium site was acquired.

Nichols wrote:

> One of the things I think has been most worthwhile has been bringing about the abandonment of the checkerboard street plan for Washington's rough topography in many undeveloped areas, and the substitution of subdivision plans adapted to the contours of the land.
>
> When I went there 22 years ago, there was no connection of Potomac Park with Rock Creek Park. Many of the present drives in Rock Creek Park were not yet built. . . . One of the things we also accomplished was to encourage the decentralization of some of the government buildings so as to relieve downtown traffic. I have always been strong for this.
>
> When I went to Washington, I felt it was the most lopsided city I had ever known. . . . There had been no houses built across the Anacostia River for years. It was a dead area.

Nichols took the lead in acquiring parks and playgrounds, building traffic arteries and boulevards, locating schools, and improving approaches across the river in order to bring that large area of vacant land into use and give a better balance to the city.

I have always felt that our capital should become the most beautiful and best planned capital in the world. It should be an example and inspiration to all American cities. As I look back, I see many things which have not been accomplished, but as a total we have gone a good ways. The great multitude of bad things we prevented, which no one realizes, is one of the results of an aggressive planning commission.

He concluded in 1948: "It is quite a wrench for me to give up this job because I've really loved it; but all my friends here, and particularly my family, have been insisting I do a bit more to conserve my strength. Believe me, the demands on me have been pretty strenuous the last few years."

The Urban Land Institute

As a founding member of the board of the Urban Land Institute, J.C. helped guide and nurture the fledgling organization in the early 1940s. The developers of planned residential communities had continued to meet informally and periodically to share experience in their own special field of interest—a field that J.C. felt was sure to burgeon following World War II. As early as 1942, he warned the ULI that it should start considering the consequences of the great migration to suburbs that he felt sure would occur.

Accordingly, in January 1944, the ULI organized the Community Builders' Council (CBC). Hugh Potter was president of the parent ULI at the time, and J.C. was elected chairman of the CBC. The objective of the council was to provide a medium of regular exchange and ongoing analysis of the real estate practices and knowledge of a small group of highly experienced and respected men, geographically distributed throughout the United States and Canada. It was a more structured extension of their informal meetings—but with a critically important addition, namely, the creation of a Community Builders' handbook. Despite a proliferation of books on housing, landscaping, and architecture, nothing authoritative had been written on community planning and developing.

"The real objective," Potter wrote Nichols, "is to crystallize now the experience and thinking of the small group of men in this country who have done worthwhile jobs in the field. This knowledge has heretofore been confined to small groups gathered in homes, offices and hotel rooms." Saying that he felt such a book would be one of the greatest contributions the ULI could make to the problems of city rebuilding and future housing that were sure to loom larger than ever before, he continued, "I shudder at the thought of you and Ed Bouton and Hugh Prather . . . and others passing on to whatever reward God has in store without getting down in some enduring form the advice which only you are able to give to those who will succeed you." Nichols accepted the challenge and the responsibility for producing such a book, and the *Community Builders' Handbook* was published in 1947.

The Community Builders' Council held its first national meeting in June 1944 in Columbus, Ohio. The outstanding developers who attended came up with a vigorous postwar program: to halt haphazard construction of small, isolated groups of houses and to promote, instead, well-balanced neighborhoods that would provide recreational facilities, churches, schools, attractive shopping centers, and a careful blending of dwellings in various price ranges. They set down eight criteria for such neighborhoods based on their own years of experience. For example, subdivisions should be based on analysis of the market rather than first purchasing acreage and then trying to find a use for it. Financing must be for the long haul. Developers should provide buffers against undesirable land use or unpleasant views. They must control land use and architectural design through covenants consistently enforced. Streets should be well engineered and of excellent construction. Although these points may have seemed revolutionary to the traditional sell-and-get-out subdivider, they were certainly familiar to any students of Nichols' work.

The CBC held two other "shake-down" meetings—in Washington, D.C., and Chicago—its first year and then continued a demanding schedule of meetings and forums, sometimes as part of ULI, sometimes in connection with the National Association of Home Builders' conventions, sometimes putting on meetings of its own. The best remembered, as well as the most useful and productive, of the CBC meetings under J.C.'s chairmanship were the "plan analysis" sessions. These generally lasted one or two days. Developers, for a modest fee, brought their subdivision or shopping center plans to be reviewed, analyzed, and critiqued by the expert members, who then provided valuable recommendations. At some meetings, Nichols arranged for what amounted to a laboratory course, visiting and critiquing housing developments in the city where they were convened. Chairman Nichols drove these plan-analysis sessions with his usual tireless energy, demanding two 12- to 14-hour days, back-to-back, during which from eight to fifteen cases were addressed. The participants moaned about

"Nichols' marathons" and went home exhausted.

It was from these sessions that ULI's first Technical Bulletins emerged, authored by J.C. Nichols and entitled "Mistakes We Have Made in Developing Residential Communities" and "Mistakes We Have Made in Developing Shopping Centers." These candid admissions allowed his peers to avoid making the same errors. But Nichols also had a canny grasp of psychology and thus undoubtedly realized that if he bragged about his successes, if he couched his remarks in the vein of "here's how smart we have been, fellows," he would have immediately turned off his audience. His fellow developers would have resisted the messages he was trying to convey. But when he presented the same points in the negative, as "mistakes we have made," he immediately had their sympathetic ear.

His approach proved most effective. The bulletins became classics in their field and the points covered in them are still part of the ULI literature. In the residential Technical Bulletin, J.C. stated that large carrying costs can undermine the most conscientious developer's effectiveness. He pointed out that overestimation of the market caused him to purchase too much land for several early subdivisions, resulting in substantial carrying charges on the remaining undeveloped property. Prior market analysis could have prevented this. In a statement aimed perhaps at real estate speculators lacking in civic conscience, he added, "Every community builder should avoid planning any unneeded subdivisions in his city."[39]

Nichols' talks to the council were unselfish endeavors to share the insights gleaned from hindsight and an effort to help others develop sufficient foresight to avoid similar pitfalls. He reminded them to communicate with the local board of education to assure the dedication of enough school sites in a large subdivision; to work with transportation companies in order to guarantee adequate transportation for the future; to find or create buffers (parks, golf clubs, rivers, even cemeteries) to protect a subdivision from encroachment; to arrange with utility companies for future needs, giving them adequate easement through the rear of lots.

J.C. elaborated on the importance of transportation: "Plan your main arteries of travel of sufficient width to carry increased traffic as the territory beyond your area is developed. Later street widening is very costly. Certainly in planning your whole street system you should always consider future extensions beyond your property and all future traffic needs of your city."

The builder's concluding words of advice to his fellow developers in ULI's Technical Bulletin No. 1 are a restatement of his vision and underlying philosophy:

> We have a great responsibility to make our residential developments fit into the plan of our cities and be a real asset to our cities, and so plan and control them as to make them desirable places in which to live through many generations with permanency of real home values. I admit this is a difficult task in present rapidly changing and drifting American cities, and challenges the best thought, foresight and effort of every developer in our land. Let us be sure we are not building future blighted or slum areas. To this end, the Community Builders' Council of the Urban Land Institute is devoting its efforts for the benefit of the whole nation.

In the Technical Bulletin on shopping centers, J.C. gladly set aside considerations of competitive advantage in order to spread his gospel to other planners, developers, builders, and realtors for the public good.

Nichols said he preferred short blocks in shopping centers, to provide more choice corner locations as well as a quicker trip for individuals who window-shopped around the block. He believed a congregation of stores, epitomized by the Plaza, to be preferable to a linear alignment as a design for a shopping area. One of J.C.'s most impressive areas of expertise, based on his 40 years' experience, was in street and sidewalk design. Narrow streets were a mistake, he believed. He recommended 70-foot widths for diagonal parking on both sides, 60-foot-width minimum for parallel parking, and the use of safety islands to help pedestrians negotiate the wide streets.

Changing his approach, he said, "We believe we have not made a mistake in giving harmonious architectural character to all buildings in any one center, using one distinctive type of architecture in each center. . . . Certain merchants desire their own distinctive 'fronts,' but we think this should be controlled within reasonable limits." More specifically, he said that money spent on distinctive architectural additions, such as towers and domes in the Plaza, helped give the center character and identity. "We believe we have *not* made a mistake in controlling all exterior signs in our shops built in recent years. We permit no projecting or roof signs—no garish signs of any character."

Nichols concluded his piece on shopping centers with a flood of practical advice on design and construction, parking and leasing. He repeated his familiar theme: "Do not underestimate the value of ample customer parking space!" He emphasized strongly that tenant leases should spell out hours a store must remain open and closed—uniformly throughout the center, if possible. Finally, he put in a strong plug for percentage leasing.

In conclusion, Nichols warned that developing outlying shopping centers "is a perilous adventure and must be planned and studied carefully." History has validated his wisdom. Where developers of commercal centers have taken advantage of Nichols' delineation of his "mistakes," the surrounding communities have greatly benefited. On the other hand, those who have opted for short-term profits with little concern for the quality and *permanence* of a project have added significantly to the blight of numerous suburban communities.

Meanwhile, under Nichols' direction, information was being gathered from council members and others for the Community Builders' handbook. Max Wehrly, former executive director of ULI, recalled, on the occasion of his retirement in 1968, "During 1946/47, a major portion of my time was involved in working with a small committee of the CBC headed by J.C. Nichols, pulling together the first draft of the *Handbook*. . . . The desire to pass on those experiences to others became almost a religion with J.C. in the last few years of his life."

The *Community Builders' Handbook,* as written by Nichols, was published in late 1947 and contained about 200 pages liberally illustrated with pertinent tables, diagrams, and photographs.

The *Handbook* created an immediate stir in the real estate and home builders' world and received excellent reviews in newspapers and magazines. Revised and enlarged periodically ever since, it now comprises five large volumes and runs thousands of pages. It remains the bible of the industry.

By the late 1940s, the ideas and philosophy that J.C. Nichols had been developing for nearly half a century had fully matured. Leading community and city planners throughout the United States sought his advice and consultation. His work on the National Park and Planning Commission brought him in contact with the leading city planners from abroad. His mature thinking found perhaps its best expression in the address "Planning and Permanence" made at the 41st annual convention of NAREB in New York City in November 1948. The oft-quoted part of that talk, which J.C. called the "essentials," summarized his views:

Here are the assurances we must give future generations:

That children can be reared and still live in the neighborhoods of their forefathers.

That the home, the most precious possession in life—the real heritage of a free people—will have permanent value, and desirable, healthful and inspiring surroundings for many generations.

That neighborhoods will have ample playgrounds; adequate park areas; quiet, carefully planned, curving residential streets designed to discourage through traffic; major highways; boulevards, parkways, and circumferential drives—all worked out to fit into a good municipal and regional pattern. This long-life home area, carefully restricted [against commercial incursion], must have elementary and high schools, libraries, shopping centers, churches with

community activities . . . all carefully located, well spaced, planned for essential expansion as the area grows.

Residential areas must provide sites for smaller homes as well as a larger ones, carefully located in respective areas. . . .

Buffers to protect home areas should be provided. . . .

Municipalities and public utilities should be able to plan and invest with assurance of long-time stability. . . . I am not one of those who predict an exodus from our large cities.

Roy P. Drachman, a pioneer real estate developer in Tucson, Arizona, who was still active in 1992 at the age of 85, tells of his first meeting with J.C.:

It was at my first NAREB Convention in November 1947. I attended a panel on shopping centers with about 25 people in the room, and Mr. Nichols was sitting in the back, which impressed me right away. A member had brought in his plans to be checked by the experts. They would discuss a specific point for a while, and then they would say, "J.C., what's the answer?" And he would tell them.

I introduced myself to him, and he seemed pleased to meet me. He immediately asked me, "Why not join ULI?" It cost $100 a year which was a lot of money to me in those days, but I joined anyway.

Although I saw J.C. at other real estate meetings meanwhile, I really got to know him well when he spent a couple of months in Tucson at the El Conquistador Hotel in the winter of 1949. His wife Jessie had been ill and the doctor had suggested she come to a warm, dry climate. J.C. contacted me and we spent considerable time together. He would call me up and say, "Let's take a ride," and I showed him the city.

Our firm was developing a small shopping center with Del Webb, so I asked J.C.'s advice. He immediately agreed to drive out and said, "Bring a pad and pencil and your plat of the property." Well, he told me to set the buildings back 135 feet, provide two double rows of parking, showed where to put in sidewalks, and made all kinds of helpful suggestions on the buildings.

When we were all through, I thanked him profusely and said, "If there's ever anything I can do, Mr. Nichols. . . ."

"Yes," he said, "you can do two things for me."

"Sure, Mr. Nichols, just name it."

"First," he said, "remain in the ULI as long as you are in the real estate business. Second, whatever you learn as a result, however you benefit from it, don't keep it to yourself. Pass it on."

I have kept my part of the bargain. As I went on to serve on the board of trustees and the executive committee of ULI, I constantly reminded them of J.C. Nichols' credo. I have also spread it to other real estate organizations I belong to.

(Roy Drachman returned to Kansas City in 1980 as the featured speaker at the celebration of the J.C Nichols Company's 75th Anniversary.)

Midwest Research Institute and Linda Hall Library

The seed that germinated in Kansas City and grew into the Midwest Research Institute was planted during the period when J.C. Nichols served in Washington, D.C., as a $1.00-a-Year-Man with the National Defense Advisory Commission. A key associate in this project was Robert L. Mehorney, a spokesman for the furniture industry and also from Kansas City, who headed the small business section of NDAC. Both men were in close touch with Kenneth A. Spencer, vice president of the Pittsburg and Midway Coal Company in Pittsburg, Kansas. Spencer, who was planning to develop a diversified chemical business based on coal and petroleum, was pursuing a chemical production defense contract.

While in Washington, Nichols, Mehorney, and Spencer became well acquainted with another Kansan and $1.00-a-Year-Man, Dr. Ernest W. Reid, an eminent scientist who had been director of research for Union Carbide Company and was now head of the chemistry division of the War Production Board. J.C. also formed a close friendship with Dr. Edward R. Weidlein, director of the Mellon Institute in Pittsburgh, Pennsylvania, and another transplanted Kansan. In his effort to procure "miscellaneous equipment," Nichols often found that a particular product or article was in short supply, and he would seek a suitable substitute, only to discover that it, too, was unobtainable. He found Ed Weidlein to be an invaluable resource in researching possible solutions to such problems. For example, England, under heavy bombardment from the air, had a severe shortage of fire hoses. Not only were there too many fires to cover with the hoses they had, but even these hoses were getting burnt up. So more durable fire hoses was an urgent Lend-Lease "miscellaneous equipment" item that Nichols had to supply. Ed Weidlein and the Mellon Institute helped him find what he needed.

In the course of such experiences, Nichols realized the central states sorely lacked a research facility similar to the Mellon Institute. In their efforts to get defense plants and defense contracts for the central states, the Kansans in Washington constantly ran up against prejudice on the part of the easterners, who denigrated the agricultural region as being devoid of technical competence.[40]

Nichols, Mehorney, Spencer, Reid, and Weidlein all foresaw that when the war was over, plant closures in the central states would be inevitable unless alternatives to defense production could be developed for the industries there. The region had two tremendous assets. The first was the vast wealth in raw materials, including oil, gas, and coal (sources of cheap energy as well); metals such as lead, zinc, and aluminum ore; helium, tungsten, gypsum, chalk, huge quantities of salt, silicates for glass, ammonium nitrates for plastics, phosphates for fertilizer, and many others. The second great asset was the region's agricultural wealth: corn, wheat and other cereals, soy beans, sugar beets, sorghum, peanuts, and livestock with all its by-products, including leather.

Ed Weidlein in particular had long conversations with J.C. Nichols about the potential of these materials for industry. America was on the brink of a new industrial revolution, he said, this time in plastics and synthetics from these very raw materials and agricultural products. So he believed the central states had a bright and exciting future, provided a research organization could be created to help retain what had been gained and to attract *new* industries that would use the resources of the region. J.C. listened and became fired up with a new cause.

These Washington conversations became the basis for the most famous talk J.C. made in his long career. Entitled "Central United States—A Sleeping Industrial Giant," it was first delivered before the Oklahoma City Chamber of Commerce in October 1941. Carefully researched and full of information, the speech was exciting and inspirational as well. For the first 15 or 20 minutes, Nichols reviewed the drainage of manpower, the plight of the farm-dependent central states, and his experiences in Washington, D.C., that had resulted in defense plants and contracts coming to the area. He then turned to the future. "Let us not be misled into thinking that the defense plants permanently solve our problems," he said. "We have violent headaches ahead unless we plan now for the post-emergency period."

Nichols called for "superhuman leadership," "stamina," and "cooperation" to "accept the gauntlet and build private industries to balance agriculture" and thus to "stem the tide of declining population." "As miraculous as it seems," he said, "synthetic chemistry today is outdoing nature in breaking down molecules and rearranging atoms into articles of daily use and necessity. This juggling of atoms spells future industrial growth for the Central United States."

The heart of the talk was a litany of the natural resources and agricultural products of the region, with descriptions of what could be made from them. Finally, J.C. spelled out the thinking that would lead eventually to the founding of the Midwest Research Institute. He spoke of the need for "red-blooded, two-fisted leadership to develop, *through scientific research,* new industrial uses for the products of our farms and mines; to build new industries based upon our natural resources; and to claim our share of the nation's industrial progress" (emphasis added).

"I propose," he declared, "that research authorities of institutions and private industries in Kansas, Nebraska, Oklahoma, Western Missouri . . . work out a coordinated plan of scientific research. . . ." He pointed to research facilities already being erected at the Universities of Kansas and Oklahoma. "Let us arrange a series of joint meetings of the best research men in our section [and] lay out a list of all our products, agricultural and mineral." After finding out what studies were already under way, he suggested sending "a committee of our best scientific men to travel from laboratory to laboratory to ascertain all research being done that relates to our products."

Delivered in J.C. Nichols' most forceful and inspirational style, the "Oklahoma City speech" apparently hit home. It created a considerable stir, with the Oklahoma City Chamber of Commerce reprinting thousands of copies that were distributed widely throughout the region. Over the next 18 months, Nichols was asked to repeat the speech in a number of other places. One occasion, naturally, was before the Kansas City Chamber of Commerce, which reprinted and distributed several thousand additional copies. On January 3, 1942, the *Kansas City Journal* carried the entire text of the talk, filling six full columns of the paper. It was headlined, "Nichols Calls for Daring Leadership to Realize Possibilities of Area," with the subhead, "Points Way to Amazing Developments."

In January 1943, Charles F. Kettering, head of research for General Motors, was scheduled to speak before the Kansas Industrial Association in Topeka and also to address students at the University of Kansas. Nichols had met Kettering through General Knudsen in Washington, so he immediately wrote him and arranged for an informal meeting in Topeka with leaders in research from around the area. On all three occasions, Kettering highly recommended the establishment of a research institute in the Midwest.

Although J.C. and Bob Mehorney were the sparkplugs of the research project, they were not acting alone. They consulted frequently with, among others, Dr. Roy Cross, whose input was invaluable as president of the Kansas City Testing Laboratory; C.J. Patterson, a chemist who was head of research for the Campbell-Taggart Baking Company; Charles T. Thompson, head of Thompson-Hayward Chemical Company; J.F. Stephens, a mechanical engineer and vice president of the Gustin-Bacon Manufacturing Company; Ralph Gray of the Sheffield Steel Company; Roy Roberts and George Longan, editors of the *Kansas City Star*; James and Crosby Kemper, bankers; John B. Gage, attorney; and key members of the Chamber of Commerce. These leaders were enthusiastic supporters of the concept.

Although they sometimes met in Nichols' Plaza office, they gathered more often informally at his home—in the evenings, on Saturday afternoons, and on Sundays. Both Miller and Clyde, Jr., recall these meetings on the big sun porch, where, they say, "the Midwest Research Institute was born." MRI may have incubated there, but it took a while to hatch. Other, more formal meetings were also held, to which business leaders of Kansas City and the surrounding area were invited.

Herbert F. Hall, grain merchant, had been one of Nichols' earliest and most important financial backers. Upon his death in 1942, he left his magnificent stone mansion plus $6 million (only a part of his estate) to establish a library in his wife's memory. The type of library was not specified, so that decision was left up to the trustees of the estate: Paul Bartlett, chairman, nephew of H.F. Hall and also a grain dealer; Frank Bartlett; Sigmund Stern; Timothy O'Sullivan; and George Harris. They were leaning toward a Shakespeare-oriented collection when J.C., sensing a tremendous opportunity, began lobbying them to make the library a scientific and technological one. Charles N. Kimball, later president of MRI, called this "a critical development toward beginning a research institute. Without this library, MRI could not have flourished as it has."

Initially, Nichols and Mehorney called on Paul Bartlett and the other Hall estate trustees a number of times to present the need for a technological resource in the central states and to press their case. Although the trustees favored the suggestion, they postponed their decision. In April 1943, J.C. invited Dr. Ernest W. Reid, who had become head of research for Corn Products Company, to Kansas City to speak to a group of business leaders on the need for a research facility. The meeting was held at the Nichols' home, and J.C. saw to it that the Hall trustees were present. Reid presented his strong feelings about the need for a science and technology library in Kansas City, citing the fact that the closest such library was in Chicago, and pointing out that some local scientists had to go as far as the Mellon Institute in Pittsburgh, Pennsylvania, to pursue their research.

Concurrently, J.C. wrote to the heads of universities in the area, asking them to write letters setting forth their opinions about the value of such a library. Their

The original Linda Hall Library, former home of Herbert F. and Linda Hall.

response was, of course, unanimously in favor. J.C. presented these letters to the Hall trustees.

In October 1944, they announced their decision to build the Linda S. Hall Library of Science and Technology on the site of the Hall mansion at 51st and Cherry, on the western edge of the University of Kansas City campus—two blocks from the eventual location of MRI. It has grown enormously in size and reputation in the ensuing years and is now recognized as one of the largest and most important science and technology libraries in the world.

Meanwhile, Nichols had taken steps to call a research conference, the idea he first aired in his Oklahoma City speech. He began by writing letters to a select group of Kansas City businessman and civic leaders, outlining his own ideas on the necessity of getting a research effort under way and asking if they would share prorata expenses of mounting a two-day research conference if he would do the organizing. Amazingly, they agreed without a dissenting voice.[41] These were the "sponsoring committee" of the research conference and later of the Midwest Research Institute itself.

From the states of Missouri, Kansas, Iowa, Nebraska, Oklahoma, and Arkansas, J.C. invited the state geologists, university presidents, and research department heads in chemistry and engineering, as well as other scientists. Of these invitees, about 40 accepted. The two-day conference was held June 7/8, 1943, at the Phillips Hotel, with Nichols presiding. Each participant was invited, if he wished, to present a short paper and/or to bring an exhibit to be displayed. The conference was an unqualified success with a high degree of interest and spirit. At the close of two days, more than 100 Kansas City

businessmen were invited to a banquet to meet the participants and hear their ideas.

At this point, there was no thought of developing an independent, freestanding institute. Instead, the conference called for the establishment of a Midwest Research Council, under the chairmanship of J.C. Nichols, as a permanent organization to coordinate research programs in chemistry, physics, biology, agronomy, and engineering—as requested by industry—to develop area resources. (As it turned out, "the idea suited the businessmen but not the universities," according to Kimball. "Inter-institutional rivalries created problems, and some university personnel were unwilling to pursue applied research aimed toward regional industrial conversion . . . [preferring] pure research.") Another result of the conference was preparation by each state of a resource map similar to the one Kansas had developed. These were combined into a single map that was used to attract industry.

Nichols had arranged for the entire research conference to be recorded—the talks, comments on the papers, and recommendations. The report filled 200 pages. Nichols felt strongly that every person in attendance and other interested parties should have a copy of the lengthy transcript, but was unable to find a letter shop willing to take on such a huge mimeographing job. Undaunted, J.C. simply gave the task to his secretary, Ethyl Treshadding, who, with some extra temporary help, did all the mimeographing, collating, binding, and distributing of the 200 copies from Nichols' office.

Dr. Ed Weidlein, Nichols' friend from his Washington service, may have been the first to suggest the establishment of an independent, freestanding research facility—out of his own experience at the Mellon Institute. Locally, it was Dr. Roy Cross who synthesized and championed the idea. Having made a success of his commercial laboratory in Kansas City, Dr. Cross knew about researching under contract, financing, bookkeeping, etc. And he promulgated the idea that such an institute should be self-supporting from the beginning.

Realizing by mid-summer that their university-based plan could not succeed, Nichols and Mehorney seized with great enthusiasm upon the suggestion of an independent facility. They prepared a report that Mehorney delivered as chairman of the industrial committee of the Chamber of Commerce. The Chamber adopted the report and in August passed a resolution calling for the creation of a scientific and industrial research institution to be located in Kansas City.

As a first step, Nichols, Mehorney, and others of the sponsoring committee, accompanied by Dr. Reid, visited the Mellon Institute, the Battelle Institute in Columbus, Ohio, and the Armour Research Foundation in Chicago. J.C. also wrote a number of letters to similar but lesser-known research institutes, seeking further information and advice. Nichols and Mehorney, with the crucial help of Cross, Patterson, and Spencer, then worked up a plan to develop an independent, not-for-profit research institute that would perform scientific research under contract from sponsors on a project-by-project basis. The institute would also serve as a clearinghouse for scientific information to be shared with the community and as a focal point of technical assistance to large and small industrial and agricultural operations.

The committee held a series of luncheon meetings for various groups of businessmen—for example, realtors at one luncheon, retailers at another, garment manufacturers at a third—until they felt they had covered the city. At each meeting, they outlined the need, set forth their plans, and asked for suggestions. Finally, they asked for their active help in raising $500,000 to get the institute started. The luncheon meetings succeeded in generating inspiration and enthusiasm that translated into action. All members of the sponsoring committee freely lent their names and influence to the cause. From their Washington experiences, Nichols knew a vast array of manufacturers and defense contractors and Mehorney had a comparable acquaintance among small businesses. Both of them used this leverage without hesitation in seeking contributions. The half-million dollars was raised in a surprisingly short time.

On December 7, 1943, nine men signed the request to the Jackson County Circuit Court for incorporation of the Midwest Research Institute. The first signatories were Nichols, Mehorney, Spencer, Cross, Patterson, and Paul Bartlett; the remaining three—Benjamin C. Adams, Charles T. Thompson, and J.F. Stephens—were officers of firms represented on the sponsoring committee. The charter, granted by the court on December 23, emphasized regional development through science, making the most of the region's natural resources.

All the central states were represented on the large board of trustees—educators, geologists, scientists, business and professional people—which was established to oversee the institute. J.C., on the basis of both his tireless efforts to bring the project to fruition and his commitment to its aims, was elected chairman of the 200-

person board. He held the position until his death six years later.

MRI took off with a bang. In 1944 and early 1945, projects came in faster than they could be researched. The first priority was to hire staff, and even sponsors had to be put on a waiting list. While some of the assignments came from local firms, many of them represented on the original sponsoring committee, there were also national sponsors such as Aerosol, Carnation, and Chicago Bridge & Iron. It had been estimated that it would take three to four years for the institute to break even; in actual fact, it was self-supporting within the first year.

MRI outgrew its original stone building in the Westport area almost immediately. The staff spilled into four nearby locations that were leased or rented: one was a single-story, shabby structure that looked as if it dated back to the days of the Santa Fe Trail; another had been an auto repair garage; two others were residential houses converted to commercial use. The result was that Nichols and Mehorney called their teams together again and raised an

Original location of the biology and chemistry staff of the Midwest Research Institute, formerly the Westport, Missouri, city hall and fire department. (Courtesy of Midwest Research Institute archives)

additional $250,000 to provide enlarged space and more equipment. Nichols' goal of having the central states recognized for expertise in science and technology was becoming a reality.

In 1947, J.C. negotiated purchase from the Nelson estate of a 10-acre plot of land at the end of the broad lawn sweeping down from the Nelson-Atkins Museum of Art. The land faced Volker Boulevard, was adjacent to the University of Kansas City campus, and was only two blocks from the Linda Hall Library of Science and Technology. For J.C., it was the fulfillment of his dream of a cultural-educational-scientific center near the Country Club District and the Country Club Plaza; for MRI, it was the ideal site for permanent headquarters.

Planning of a suitable building began, only to be temporarily set aside in 1948 when director Harold Vagtborg left to become president of Southwest Research Institute in San Antonio, Texas. After two years of management-by-committee (which was not successful), Charles N. Kimball was hired in June 1950 as director and president of MRI. He proved to be a fortuitous choice, leading the institute into an era of extraordinary growth and prominence.

The Company

In the four-year period between the end of the Depression in 1937 and the entry of the United States into World War II, the J.C. Nichols Company had begun five new subdivisions: Armour Fields, Sagamore Hills, Mission Woods, Fairway, and Prairie Village. But as building supplies for civilian use became unavailable, construction was put on hold. During the war years, however, the subdivisions' homes associations remained active, electing officers, setting budgets, and appointing committees, usually at their annual dinner meeting. During the war years of 1942, 1943, and 1944, some nineteen homes associations convened annual dinners, often with a guest speaker. On occasion Mr. Nichols was able to present a speaker of national note.

When construction resumed after World War II, the strategy of the J.C. Nichols Company took an important turn. J.C. foresaw the need for high-quality, modestly priced, single-family housing for white and blue collar employees. No doubt he was influenced by his observation of other midwestern communities such as Wichita and Tulsa and

also by sharing perceptions with his fellow community planners at the Urban Land Institute. In addition, he was aware of new building techniques, such as partially prefabricating house modules and erecting them at the building site.

A spectacular result of this emphasis was Prairie Village, where attractive, moderately priced, quality homes were snapped up by returning veterans as fast as they could be built. The home salesmen had only to sit at a table and take orders! Fred Gibson, then head of the land development and field construction department, recalls, "When we were going full steam ahead on Prairie Village, the Company was building and finishing houses at the

This overview of Prairie Village illustrates the growth of this single large development. No other contiguous development of this size had been built by one developer in the United States. The J.C. Nichols Company's first postwar subdivision marked an important turn in strategy, featuring quality, moderately priced, single-family houses for returning veterans and young families of the baby boom.

rate of one every two days! It was a fun time; the Company was small enough that everyone had a chance to do everything."

The company had also begun the Prairie Village Shopping Center, to which another stage was added later. (Today, the shopping center comprises 350,000 square feet of shops and services.)

A big push after the war was to raise commercial rents, which had been frozen. Weekly Saturday meetings were held with J.C., who encouraged success among those in the business properties department by awarding Christmas bonuses based on the dollar amount of the increases they succeeded in bringing in over the year.

Following World War II, company staff and departments were rebuilt, and commercial development, as well as residential building, was soon in high gear. On the Plaza, the first construction to get under way was the Plaza Time building (on the northwest corner of Wornall Road and Ward Parkway). The large Sears building was started as well. J.C. had agreed on the sale of the property and plans for the store with Gen. John S. Wood, chairman of Sears, during World War II; he was anxious for General Wood to build his first-ever suburban store on the Country Club Plaza rather than on the old Electric Park site at 47th and Paseo, which had been offered to him.[42]

"The J.C. Nichols Company has always been a team," says Fred Gibson. "We have always liked to say that we insist on doing things the JCN Company way. We have done it that way because we felt it was the right way. Much of the work we do in the Land Development Department is buried; no one would know for quite a while if we did shoddy work. But that has never been our style; we don't want to embarrass our own sales people down the line."

Gibson cites the deliberate engineering of curb design as an example of "doing things the JCN Company way." Nichols sent a memo to the land development department asking them to examine why it was so jarring to back an automobile out of a driveway in the Country Club District. Gibson and his fellow engineers immediately recognized that the problem lay in the traversal of the gutter at the base of the driveway. They measured the radius of a large sampling of tires, compared the results with the roll-back curve of their rounded cement gutters, and determined that the curve of the tire matched exactly the curve of the cement. When homeowners backed their cars onto the street, their rear tires would slip snugly into the gutter, causing the slight jarring motion noticed by J.C. The radius of the curve was then enlarged to alleviate the problem.

The thirties and forties were a time of labor unrest throughout the country, and in Kansas City, the AFL construction workers tried to unionize the J.C. Nichols Company. The company refused to knuckle under. The AFL imposed a strike that was long, drawn-out, and bitter. Ansel Mitchell, head of field construction at the time, was out at one of the remote construction shacks when a caravan of strikers pulled up, got out of their cars, and badly beat him up.

J.C. was furious. Union representatives had been trying to set up a meeting with him for quite a while, so now he invited them to his office. When they were seated, J.C. stood up and said, "That's the last time any of you will get away with something like that. I want you to know that if something like this ever happens again, I'll come after you with my shotgun and I'll kill you."

There was dead silence.

"You don't believe me, do you?"

"Yes, we do, Mr. Nichols," one of the men replied. "We sure do."

Ed Tanner's widow, Katherine Tanner, remembers J.C.'s heavy cigarette smoking habit (as many as three packs a day), which did not diminish despite wartime rationing. "During the war J.C. was having difficulty getting enough cigarettes. He used to drop by our house at dinner time, pretend to be concerned about some insignificant business matter, then hit Ed up for cigarettes. He continued the rounds to a number of friends' houses, until he had mooched enough cigarettes to tide him over." Clyde adds: "Dad was forever running out of cigarettes at work and when talking to an employee he would blurt out, 'Gimme a cigarette.' When proffered a pack, he'd take out a cigarette to smoke, plus several more which he would pocket."

When Miller Nichols returned from the Navy in 1945, he was named sales manager of the company. With platted lots in short supply because of the wartime hiatus in building, Miller recognized that there was an opportunity to sell off all of the odd-shaped lots that had accumulated in the company's inventory as the result of laying out curvilinear streets rather than rectangular blocks. These scattered vacant lots were not only a tax burden but were expensive to maintain with mowing, spraying, and tree trimming. So he challenged the company salesmen to get out and sell them "like blue plate specials, all of them." His concept was right, and they sold in short order, thus improving neighborhood appearance.

Before Miller departed for his military tours of duty, J.C. had reminded him to be on the lookout for high caliber young men who might join the organization after the war. While Miller was serving in the Navy's Bureau of Yards and Docks in Washington, D.C., his job was to recommend personnel for the Seabees who were then assigned by a fellow Yards and Docks officer, Davis K. "Dave" Jackson. By coincidence, both were subsequently reassigned to the same office in San Francisco. Miller suggested that Dave come and see him at the Nichols Company when the war was over.

Jackson did just that. Regarded as one of the most talented men to join the company in the postwar era, Jackson had graduated from the University of Missouri in 1933 with a B.S. degree in civil engineering. He held various engineering and public relations positions in the construction field before joining the Naval Reserve when World War II began. He joined the J.C. Nichols Company in 1946 in the business properties department; in 1973, he succeeded Miller as president.

Another outstanding individual who joined the company following the war was John J. Ruddy. A 1936 graduate of the University of Missouri's School of Law and a member of Beta Theta Pi, Ruddy had been in private practice for several years before joining the Army in 1942. He was discharged in 1945 as a captain, having served in the office of the Judge Advocate General. While stationed in Washington, D.C., Ruddy met Miller, who suggested that he apply for a job with the company after the war. In 1948, after serving as assistant counsel for Kansas City and as special assistant to the U.S. attorney general in the prosecution of war fraud cases, Ruddy approached Miller and was immediately hired.

On his return from military service in 1946, Bob O'Keefe joined the business properties division under George Tourtellot.[43] After thirteen years, he took over the department; a year later, he was made a vice-president and director. "J.C. took a *deep* interest in the merchants," declares Bob. "He attended their dinners with me. We would get there early, and my job was to prompt him on their names and other pertinent information as they came in. Then he would greet them, 'Hello there, Harry. Glad to see your flower business is going so well. How is Blanche?' When he was away from Kansas City, he would drop postcards to every tenant."

Randy Knight, who became a top residential salesman, was still another postwar recruit. When he moved to the Kansas City area in 1948, he purchased a home in the Country Club District. Having met Miller in the process, Knight asked him about employment. Miller brought the young man to his father's office, where J.C. offered Randy $200 a month. Uncharacteristically, he increased it to $300 when Knight balked at the first proposal. The condition attached to the higher figure was that Knight agree to apprentice in every division of the company before moving into sales. Randy agreed and thus found himself laboring on one of the Nichols Company building crews.

When the building trades union discovered that Knight was working without union membership, they called J.V. Walker (Nichols Company vice-president in charge of construction) and threatened to shut down the job. Walker, who had been with the company since 1915, went to J.C.'s office to discuss the situation, taking Knight along. Nichols listened and without batting an eye said, "Randy, you now have the title of Supervisor." Project supervisors didn't have to belong to the union.

Fred Gibson came into the Nichols Company as a surveyor in 1948. He says:

Mr. Nichols and Miller used to have reservations about engineers, because occasionally we would have to tell them that one of their ideas was not workable. Shortly after I came to work, I was told to locate a piece of statuary on an island in an intersection. Mr. Nichols, who was a stickler for detail and quality, said, "Stake it out, but let me know so I can look it over before you begin setting the pedestal." I used the transit and sighted it a number of times. Something about it was bothering me, but since it all checked out mathematically I told Mr. Nichols it was ready to be approved.

When he got to the site, he took one look, shook his head, and said, "That's not right." I told him that I'd felt the same thing but couldn't figure out what needed to be changed. He backed up about twenty paces, crouched down and waved me over to his side. "You see those trees," he said, pointing to the ridge of a distant hill. "You can see from here that the statue doesn't line up correctly with that backdrop. Move the pedestal a few feet to the right." Sure enough, it looked fine once we'd moved it.

That incident taught me a great lesson about land development. To this day, I insist that we take the time to back up a few steps and make sure whatever we're doing *looks* right. On many occasions we've ignored the transit and changed the layout of a road or whatever just to improve the aesthetics. That's the way Mr. Nichols did things, that's the way Miller did things, and that's the way it's still done.

The Nichols family gathered for a group photo at a reception in the 1930s. In the front, left to right, are Eleanor, Jessie, and Marty; in the rear, Miller, J.C., Clyde, and Earl Allen.

The Family

On the same day in October 1937, Eleanor and Earl Allen and Marty and Clyde Nichols had bought houses in the 6800 block on Cherry. The two families entered into a partnership on the purchase of a washing machine. "It was suppose to be a joint venture," Marty recalls. "We split the cost of the purchase price and agreed to locate the machine at Ellie's house, in exchange for which she would provide the detergent. After the war in 1946, when the Allens sold their house and were preparing to move, we sat down to figure out how to deal with our share of the machine. Ellie settled the problem by announcing that we had used up our half of the machine in detergent, water, and electricity."

Marty recalls that during these years Ellie diverted her high energy into domestic pursuits. "She did a great job with her kids. She was a master knitter, so skilled that she could, and did, knit while sitting in a dark movie theater! She used to knit beautiful outfits for Suzie and Mollie and tried to get me interested in knitting, but it simply didn't take. While I was pregnant with Jay, I started working on a baby sweater, but somehow I never finished it. When I got pregnant with Wayne, our next oldest, I started working on the sweater again. When Wayne was born and I still hadn't finished the darn sweater, I figured it was hopeless and threw it away."

During the war years when J.C. was away and Ellie and Earl and their daughters were living in Arlington, Virginia, Marty and Jessie became very close. "Marty spent a lot of time with Jessie," says Clyde, "enjoying her delightful sense of humor. One time, Marty came home and asked, 'How do you like my new fur jacket?' My mouth dropped open and I stammered, 'We can't afford that beaver jacket, why do you have that on?' She laughed and said, 'Granny bought it for me,' meaning my mother."

However, the friendship did not stop Jessie from speaking her mind. One afternoon, according to Clyde, "Marty, who was then about 24 years old, swung by mother and dad's house on her way down to the Plaza. Mother took one look at her and stated, 'You are not going to the Plaza dressed like that.'

"Marty asked, 'What do you mean?'

"Mother snipped, 'Ladies don't wear blue jeans to the Plaza. Marty, I bet when you are 40, you'll still be wearing blue jeans all over town.' She was right about that. Marty was, and so was the rest of the world. And what's more, she still wears them at 78!"

At the end of World War II, Clyde intended to return to the J.C. Nichols Company. He explains why he did not:

> I hadn't been able to get Dad to talk to me about my prospects with the company. One day in the fall of 1945, I managed to persuade him to drive out to our Stanley farm with me on some pretext. When we arrived, I told him, "I want to talk to you about a job, because the War will be over shortly." He got real restless and muttered, "Skeet, I have to hurry back to town."
>
> I said, "No, Dad, I've got the keys to the car and we aren't going anywhere until we talk about this."
>
> He was stubborn, didn't like being held hostage, and countered, "I'm going to get someone to come out and pick me up."
>
> I said, "Dad, this won't take long." I told him that I wanted to come back and work for the Nichols Company, handling advertising and public rela-

tions. I reminded him I had spent one year with the Blaker Advertising Agency in New York and had developed considerable expertise in that field.

He replied that I couldn't have that position because it would be unfair to an existing employee, Bessie Palmer. He offered me a job in business properties instead, leasing store space and working on commission.

Well, I had sold for four years and knew I hated selling. When the phone would ring at home, I'd shrink. "Arghh, it's got to be that customer wanting me to take him out and show some property or house. Oh God, let it be for somebody else." Saturdays, Sundays, nights and mornings, your life wasn't your own in that business.

I had been more interested in all the other things that I did. For instance, Betsy Dodge [Pearson], George Tourtellot and I put together a fabulous booklet presentation of Armour Hills Gardens, which wasn't selling well at the time. A competitor's subdivision, Leawood, didn't have gutters or sidewalks, so we emphasized the advantages of these features in our booklet. I came up with what I had thought was a great line, "Sidewalks are children's streets," which stressed the safety element. But, as I said, I was in sales. I wasn't even supposed to be messing with advertising.

Now I had a wife, three kids and a house, so I told Dad I couldn't make ends meet on the income I would make in business properties. In short, we could not make a deal.

During World War II, Clyde worked as a foreman at the new Pratt and Whitney plant in Kansas City. Gas was rationed and Clyde rode to work in a car pool with a young engineer from the University of Missouri, Dan Truog. Dan and Clyde both wondered what they were going to do after the war. Together they began examining ideas—for new products, new services. Immediately after V-J day, the firm of Dan Truog and Clyde Nichols was incorporated—in a 16-by-33-foot ex–hamburger stand rented for $25 a month at 63rd and Cherry Streets.

Meanwhile, when J.C. was notified by his rental department that the hamburger stand was occupied by Dan and Clyde, he summoned the young partners to his office. "What's going on here?" he demanded.

"We're going to run a home maintenance business," Clyde informed his father. "Anything you want done around the house, we'll do."

"I had just assumed," said J.C., "that you were coming back to the company." When Clyde reminded him they couldn't make a deal, J.C. said, "Well, we'll work something out. Have Dan come down and talk to Pitrat about getting into the maintenance end of the company."

Says Clyde, "Dan and I talked about it and Dan decided to talk to Pitrat. Dan was a very knowledgeable guy, a mechanical engineer, and a college graduate who had experience working for Johns Mansville and Pratt and Whitney. Like me, he also had a house, a wife and three kids. Pitrat was interested in Dan and asked him what kind of salary he would need to come to work for the Nichols Company. When Dan quoted him a figure, Pete nearly swallowed his pipe! That was the end of that conversation."

Randy Knight remembers Clyde, with a straight face, announcing to members of the company's sales staff, "The office simply isn't big enough for both my father and me, so I've decided to leave."

Says Clyde:

In the early years of the Truog-Nichols Company, Dan and I received a number of calls to solve the problem of basement flooding. We soon discovered that we could perform seeming miracles on those jobs. The advent of bulldozers had resulted in extra large excavations for foundation work. The dirt from the backfill acted like a sponge and drew moisture up against the foundation.

The first thing we did was to repair any cracked and broken gutter downspouts to carry water away from the foundation. We installed new elbows and cement pads for the runoff. Then we sloped the backfill away from the foundation and—voila!—no water in the basement.

What Dan and Clyde lacked in business experience, they made up for in energy and hard work. Clyde laughs at one early gaffe:

The first couple of months we were working like mad. We had a growing payroll and more and more customers. I pulled Dan aside one day and asked, "Why aren't those customers paying the bills you sent out?"

He looked at me kind of funny and said, "What bills that *I* sent out?" Hell, nobody had sent out the bills! Someone else had always done it at the Nichols Company, and I hadn't had to deal with it at Blaker in New York or at Pratt-Whitney either. Fortunately, Dad loaned us enough money to tide us over.

Dan and Clyde were already on their way. Later, they were to receive the good-

will of the elder Nichols. They shifted emphasis away from home maintenance to new products that were coming on the market: air conditioning, a folding door for home interiors, an upward-acting garage door with the optional attachment of an automatic opener, and meal-serving equipment for airlines and hospitals.

It was fortunate that Clyde's new enterprise received J.C.'s blessing. As they both had the same name, J.C. sometimes received phone calls from Truog-Nichols customers by mistake. They would tell him, "Nichols, I want you to fix my garage door." He would patiently take all the pertinent information, then have his secretary call Clyde's business.

In 1950, five years after starting business in the converted hamburger stand, Truog-Nichols had moved to larger quarters at 63rd and Troost and was grossing over a million dollars a year. This revenue statistic and Clyde's age (under 40) qualified him for membership in the Young Presidents' Organization, a prestigious national association of young, successful entrepreneurs.[44]

In all, six children were born to the young Clyde Nicholses and the Allens between 1937 and the mid 1940s. Ellie and Marty had been in the hospital together for their firstborn, who arrived only a few days apart. Clyde's second son, Wayne, and Ellie's second daughter, Mollie, were also very close in age. Relates Clyde:

Mother, of course, liked to come over on occasion to visit and to see the grandchildren. One day when she arrived, she said in a state of shock, "I need a scotch, fix me a scotch and water." Marty sat her down and asked, "What's wrong?" She replied, "I'll be alright, I'll be alright." Finally she explained that as she was driving up the street she saw four disreputable-looking children who were obviously trespassing in the neighborhood. "What are those children doing in this neighborhood?" she said to herself. "You would think people would keep them home where they belonged. They are dirty and a disgrace." When she got closer, she realized that the four urchins were her own grandchildren. She just came unglued.

Sally Ruddy has quite a different memory of the children. "I had been invited to a party at the elder Nichols home. Marty and Clyde were there with young Jay. He was a beautiful little boy, all dressed up in miniature uniform of 'army pinks.' Some of the adults were in uniform too, of course, and little Jay was saluting like mad."

Jessie did not have much patience with the rambunctious antics of her children or her grandchildren. Clyde recalls when he and his siblings or his children would get too loud, Jessie would recite, "Little son, little daughter, aren't you talkin' more than you oughter." And when her endurance reached its limits, his mother would show them outside with: "May joy go with you and peace remain!" Marty agrees that Jessie really did not have much patience with small children.

Though she was only six at the time of J.C.'s death, Miller's daughter, Kay Callison, remembers her grandparents and their home.

> He was a fairly stern person, very serious about his commitments. He wasn't what you would call a jovial grandfather, the kind that would hold you on his lap. There were always a lot of phone calls, and he was often off to meetings or conferences. He

had to prioritize his time, and probably grandchildren were pretty low on his list. He would tolerate us for about 15 minutes before announcing, "OK, it's time for you children to go outside." My grandmother Jessie took care of most things around their house because he was away so much. She was always soft spoken with the grandchildren, but she never laughed or played with us.

Kay remembers her grandparents' home as very grand and formal, with massive furniture, iron lamps with claw feet and heavy Edwardian chairs with fringe.

> I remember one vignette that describes the ambiance in my grandparents' home. My cousins and I were playing together when Walter, the butler, arrived carrying a handsome silver tray. When he bent down to serve us, all he was carrying on that tray was chewing gum with the outer jackets removed to reveal the inner foil wrapping!

Granddaughter Suzie Allen remembers that she and Mollie loved to come to their grandparents' to dinner:

> The food was always so good. We thought the little footed salt dishes and all the silver accoutrements on the table were great fun. We didn't like to remain at the table until grandmother dismissed everyone, but we were allowed to play under the table while the grownups lingered over their dinner conversation.

Suzie remembers climbing onto the wide sunroom windowsills to read, hide-and-seek games in the nooks and crannies of the house, playing in the large Spanish recreation room downstairs with Jay and

Shown here in the 1930s, J.C. and Jessie Nichols relaxing in their garden was a rare occurrence.

Wayne, and the huge yard the boys loved to run in. She remembers that after dinner, when grandfather J.C. took to his couch for a nap, she and Mollie often had fun running around the borders of the Oriental rug and then darting across in front of the couch to test if grandfather was really napping. Sometimes he would reach out and grab an ankle, sending them tumbling in giggles.

J.C. had, of course, always enjoyed driving the family about to look at new subdivisions and projects on Sunday afternoons. Now that his children had their own families and homes, not infrequently he would invite Suzie and Mollie or Jay and Wayne to take a Sunday afternoon drive. Suzie remembers how carefully he explained the different places and things the Nichols Company was doing, the particular buildings, shops, and neighborhoods. "On the way home there was always a stop at the drug store for some comic books."

Jay and Wayne took some of these drives, but Jay recalls that the times the boys enjoyed most with their grandfather were the hikes on the farm out in Stanley. On these Sunday walks the children could scamper about as they pleased and it was quite all right to interrupt their grandfather with a question. "It was our special time with him," Jay says.

J.C. Nichols was very close to his mother, and when in town he usually dropped by both morning and evening to see her. Away from home, he wrote her daily postcards. The Kane cousins chuckle over how during the 1940s the previous trading of Christmas visits came to be "every Christmas in Kansas City," because of J.C.'s fear that each Christmas would be Granny Nichols' last. She died in 1947.

A few months after her death, Jessie Nichols suffered a heart attack. Fortunately, her children were all in town and attentive to her while she recuperated.

Ellie had put Suzie and Mollie in Sunset Hill, her alma mater. She made all their clothes until they reached the age of resistance, saw to it that they had piano lessons, art lessons, music lessons, swimming lessons, tennis lessons. Looking back, Suzie recalls that it always meant a lot to her and Mollie that they came first with their parents.

Ellie enjoyed all kinds of gardening projects, whether designing or planting or simply pruning and nurturing, and the children learned early that gardening and yard work were a family project. They could play on Saturdays after they cleaned the birdbath and helped pull dandelions. Marty remembers one incident in which Ellie was coordinating an effort on the part of the Westport Garden Club to landscape the new Junior League Clubhouse. Upholding a longstanding Nichols tradition, Ellie promoted the project and then pressured her friends into becoming part of it. After a particularly taxing afternoon, one of Ellie's exhausted recruits looked up from her task and moaned, "This is crazy, I have a yard man at home doing this kind of work, while Ellie has me out here digging on my hands and knees!" During the postwar years, J.C. and Jessie Nichols had the delight of seeing their three offspring settled into handsome homes in Mission Hills, just a few blocks from their own. Eleanor and Earl were first, purchasing in early 1946 a red brick colonial on Drury Lane. Company scrapbooks contain charming pictures of the housewarming garden party Earl and Ellie hosted for the company's employees.

The following year, Miller and Katie bought an elegant Ed Tanner–designed house close-by just up the hill from the Verona Columns on Verona Road. The backyard was left in a natural state with a stand of pines in which their daughters loved to climb and build. Schoolground play equipment was brought in, along with a construction-site shed for a clubhouse. Miller insisted that children should be able to play outdoors in a safe environment, and he felt that a large sandbox was essential. The sandbox was placed next to the driveway, which was constantly strewn with sand.

Kay recalls that somehow the family came to an understanding that "Mother could have her flowers on the left side of the yard. The right side was for the kids, and it was always full of them." Unique to the rest of the Mission Hills neighborhood was a sidewalk Miller had built in front of the house so that the girls would have a place to roller skate.

In 1947, Clyde and Marty also bought their large Tudor home on Drury Lane, just three doors from Eleanor and Earl; they still live there today. The neighborhood was bustling with Nichols grandchildren, eleven in all; Clyde's backyard, dubbed Hell's Half Acre, was the center for numerous neighborhood projects.

During the decade of the 1940s, J.C. continued to serve as the senior university trustee at the Nelson-Atkins Museum of Art, advising and assisting Paul Gardner. Likewise, he continued to serve on the board of the philharmonic. On the education front, at Pembroke Country Day School, a major building campaign was launched in 1944, one that would establish the quadrangle concept proposed by J.C. Nichols fourteen years earlier. In 1946, Miller became the first president of the school's alumni association.

The End of an Era

By early 1949, it was evident to his family and close business associates that J.C. Nichols' health was declining. At first both he and they attributed this to his being over involved and under pressure. A business associate once said, "J.C.'s engine has only one gear: full speed ahead." Even though J.C. drove himself as hard as ever, that engine had begun to slow a bit.

While he did not discuss his health outside the immediate family, he must have felt some alarming symptoms. On October 6, 1949, he flew alone to the Mayo Clinic in Rochester, Minnesota. The following day, he called the Nichols Company to request that someone bring his Kansas City X-rays. Bob O'Keefe volunteered to get the films from St. Luke's Hospital and fly them up.

> I stayed with J.C. the next three days in a motel near the clinic. Then the call came to me from the surgeon, telling me that J.C. had inoperable lung cancer. He asked me if we should tell the patient that his condition was terminal. I rationalized that J.C. was a highly organized person with a hundred irons in the fire, and if I were in his shoes, I would want to know the facts, no matter how bad, so I could put my affairs in order. That's what I told the surgeon.
>
> We met with him at 4:00 P.M. that day. When he gave J.C. the bad news, J.C. never batted an eye. He persuaded the surgeon to tell him his estimate of how long he had to live. The surgeon said, "Ninety days." He lived exactly 89 days!

J.C. and Bob returned to Kansas City by plane. J.C. made notes en route on whom to call when he got back.

He asked that his extensive files be brought from the Plaza to his home and that his secretary work out of the house. He was still deeply involved with the Midwest Research Institute. He kept up at least a semblance of his old flood of correspondence: notes to associates, suggestions to the office staff, letters to key people who were part of his myriad interests. Dr. Clarence Decker, president of the University of Kansas City, said afterward, "Only a few weeks before his death, ill as he was, he sent me one of his typically thoughtful and congratulatory notes on a newspaper story concerning the progress of the university." J.C. virtually stopped eating. He would come into the first floor of the office, shoot the breeze briefly with a few associates, then lie down on a couch. At the office, only Miller, John Taylor, O'Keefe, and a very few others close to him knew how bad his condition really was.

The first weeks after his return from Mayo's were an ordeal for the Nichols family. Clyde, Jr., recalls that period:

When Dad knew he was going to die, he became just terrible, bemoaning his fate, going up to his favorite daybed, covering up with blankets and shutting out the world. John Kane [J.C.'s Beta roommate and brother-in-law] called from Bartlesville and asked Jessie, "How is Nick doing?"

"Terrible," she replied, and told him about it.

He said, "I'll be up there tomorrow."

When he arrived, he and J.C. went into the library and closed the door. After about 20 minutes, Kane came out and said to Mother, "He's

going to be all right." After that, Dad did a 180-degree turn! I remember he had Franklin Murphy, dean of the KU Medical School, over. He says, "Now, Franklin we've got to get this land for the Kansas City campus of the Med School protected. You've got to see about buying such-and-such a plot." He had different people around the city come over, had meetings about MRI and such.

Jessie called John Kane and reported, "He's changed, he's great. How did you do that?"

Kane replied, "Well, I just said, 'Nick, you've met a lot of challenges in your life and always have been an outstanding success in handling them.' I built him up on this theme for a while. We reminisced about the big road blocks in his life and how he whipped them all. Then I said, 'You're doing one miserable, poor job in dying. You're making a mess of it, and after all your success in meeting other challenges, are you going to fail at this?'

"Nick said to me, 'Well, I never thought of it that way. You're right, John, it is just another challenge.'

J.C. managed to remain active until a scant three weeks before death claimed him. Then, dreadfully ill, weakened, under heavy medication for the pain that wracked him, he became bedridden, needing constant nursing care. Members of the family took turns sitting with him. Finally, when the cancer reached his brain, he began hallucinating. He cried out orders to John Taylor and other earlier associates, orders that went back to the Bismark Place days. He insisted he had to get up and go to meet nonexistent people. He failed to recognize his children and relatives.

On February 16, 1950, at 3:15 P.M., Jesse Clyde Nichols died at his home with his family at his bedside, just six months shy of his 70th birthday. News stories of his death, editorials, lengthy obituaries, biographies, photographs, and tributes from local and national leaders filled the Kansas City papers. The story was carried on the national and international news wires; Betsy Dodge Pearson, sister of Marty Nichols, remembers hearing the news bulletin on the car radio as she was returning to New York from a skiing trip in Vermont.

Nearly 2,000 people filled and overflowed the Country Club Christian Church for J.C. Nichols' funeral. At the family's request, the only flowers were a blanket of red roses over the coffin, which was flanked by two baskets of red roses (one from the Nichols Company employees). In a moving eulogy, Dr. Warren Grafton, the pastor, sounded the theme of many other editorials, resolutions, and tributes to Nichols:

> The great architect, Sir Christopher Wren, along with his other immortal works, designed St. Paul's Cathedral in London, his masterpiece, and his remains lie buried beneath its floors. On a tablet is inscribed his epitaph— "Si monumentum requiris, circumspice"—"If you seek his monument, look about you." And I say to you now, if you want to see J.C. Nichols' monument, look about you as you go out the doors of this church. Never did so great a community owe so much to one man. We who live here and work here will be eternally indebted to him.

Tributes poured in from everywhere. Carl B. Rechner, president of the Kansas City Real Estate Board, said, "J.C. Nichols has been America's greatest realtor and developer for a generation. He was the Middle West's staunchest supporter. His creative genius, vision and ability have contributed to the enjoyment and happiness of thousands of families. He was a public benefactor."

President Truman wrote a letter of sympathy to Jessie Nichols, as did senators from Missouri and Kansas, directors of the National Capital Parks and Planning Commission, and presidents of national real estate organizations. At a February 21 concert of the Kansas City Philharmonic Orchestra, Dale M. Thompson, president, paid tribute to Nichols as a founding member of the board, and the audience stood as the orchestra played a Bach chorale in his memory.

At a convention of the National Association of Home Builders, fellow developer and friend David D. Bohannon, said:

> The consolation we have in our grief is that he lived and that his genius was lavished so generously on the profession which he loved and dignified. His devotion to the ideal of making life more worth living marked him as a great humanitarian. . . . As developer of the Country Club District in Kansas City, he set a pattern for the whole world in community planning and in the creation of *homes* instead of houses in which to live. . . . His integrity and ethics established in the public mind a confidence which in turn has reflected on the entire profession.

Jessie Miller Nichols survived her husband by only 14 months. The heart attack she suffered in 1947 repeated on Thursday evening, April 26, 1951, at home. Again the family gathered round a parental sickbed. Her sister Louise (Mrs. John H. Kane) hurried up from Bartlesville, Oklahoma. Two days later, Saturday, April 28, at 4:30 P.M., she passed away.

The following Monday, funeral services patterned after those for J.C. were held at the Country Club Christian Church with Dr. Grafton again officiating. Her obituary in the *Star* noted her close association with J.C.'s business and professional life:

> Mr. Nichols took home his problems and his dreams and lived them with his family. Jessie's opinions,

freely spoken, were as markedly independent as they were intelligent. She edited the Nichols speeches. While Mrs. Nichols never had an active part in the business, their partnership at home was classed by observers as quite as vital and real as the corporate ones at the office.

Mr. Nichols would say of an afternoon to expect two or three guests and then appear at the dinner hour with a dozen. . . . Naturally, there was much entertaining at the Nichols home, with many of national distinction among the guests. Even now the term "the Hoover china" refers to the

The Country Club Christian Church on Ward Parkway. J.C. Nichols was a founding member of this church, and both his and Jessie's funerals were held here.

particular set used when the former President had breakfast at their home.

The writer of the obituary quoted an earlier story about Jessie written in a 1926 edition of the *Star*: "Mrs. Nichols is a woman of singularly attractive personality. She is vivacious and an extensive reader. In any company her conversation is always interesting and often brilliant. . . . Many of the Italian marble fountains and garden decorations that adorn the Country Club District reflect her taste as well as that of Mr. Nichols."

Dr. Grafton in his eulogy made perhaps a more significant point when he said, "A community cannot be built by a man who has not first found goodness inside his own home. We find around us in Kansas City a projection of the spirit nurtured inside the Nichols home."

It was the end of an era. The *Kansas City Star*, editorializing about J.C.'s "vision and boundless energy," summed up his impact on the world:

> Nichols is best known for his Country Club District, a concept that changed the whole idea of residential development in America. Yet it was only one of many projects in a life of ceaseless action. High strung and overflowing with ideas, he rushed from one enterprise to another, taking time to give at least one-third of his time to public service. Few men have had the quality of driving power to such a degree. In him it was combined with a sense of mission and hard practical sense, a rare combination. . . . When he first started building in the Country Club District, the idea of orderly planning for cities was unknown. No city offered its people even the minimum zoning protection for their homes. J.C. Nichols, building for profit, visualized residential districts planned for beauty and protection for a century or longer against all encroachments that might destroy them.

On the day following J.C.'s death in February 1950, the Kansas City Star's *editorial page carried this S.J. Ray cartoon, which expresses the theme of many other tributes to Nichols: "If you would see his monument, look around you." This cartoon was later cast in a bronze bas-relief plaque and set in the sidewalk in front of the J.C. Nichols Company offices on the Country Club Plaza.*

"IF YOU WOULD SEE HIS MONUMENT, LOOK AROUND"

Ten years after Nichols' death, at the dedication of the heroic-sized J.C. Nichols Memorial Fountain at J.C. Nichols Parkway and 47th Street, Roy Roberts, president of the *Kansas City Star*, spoke these words:

> J.C. Nichols was one of those rare individuals, a dreamer with a capacity for making his dreams come true. He

dreamed, moreover, in terms of great practical benefit to the city. Few men can have so variously and profoundly influenced the development of any American community. Mr. Nichols not only revolutionized the planning of residential districts and shopping centers, but he did it *here*, on a scale that still excites national attention. Many of our major civic institutions and industrial expansions of today bear the mark of his extraordinary vision and driving force.

Chapter 7

1950 · 1959

I express the hope, without making it obligatory upon my Trustees, that they will cause the Company to carry out the purposes, ideals and principles which have guided and are now in effect in the development of the area . . . known as the Country Club District, and that this work shall be carried on as to be an example and an inspiration for this and other cities for better city building, for the stabilizing of property values and the protecting of home surroundings, as well as civic betterment in general.

—from Jesse Clyde Nichols'
Last Will and Testament

J.C. Nichols and John Taylor were ably assisted over their 45 years of building the company by long-tenured, loyal company officers: George Tourtellot, Ansel Mitchell, Dave Kennard, Frank Grant, Walter Basinger, Ed Tanner, Stanley McLane, Ray Jones, Bob O'Keefe, Charles Pitrat, and Max Stone, among others. These men provided Nichols with a hard-working, talented, and motivated management team as well as a closely knit group of friends. J.C. Nichols observed in his autobiographical comments:

Through the years, many [individuals] have become part of the organization and have remained to build a great

company and a great residential district. I am inordinately proud of the long association of these men, and wish to give them every possible credit for the splendid part they played in the final building of the Country Club District and all that it means to Kansas City. Without their loyal cooperation, hard work, and heartfelt interest and belief in the ultimate goal toward which we strove, it could never have been done.

Miller Nichols' Leadership

After the death of J.C. Nichols in 1950, the company never faltered, despite the enormity of the loss. Miller Nichols had been groomed all his life to succeed his father, and he remained faithful to J.C.'s wishes as expressed above. Heading an efficient managerial team already in place, Miller took over as president; John Taylor moved up to chairman of the board. Dave Jackson recalls: "In the early years following J.C.'s death, the officers of the company were quite senior in age and conservative in their thinking. Their choice was to simply manage the company's assets as they had been developed, but Miller said no. He saw new opportunities and he set out to pursue them."

The magnificent, heroic-sized J.C. Nichols Memorial Fountain, located in

Mill Creek Park just east of the Plaza, stands as a fitting memorial to, in *Kansas City Star* publisher Roy Roberts' words, "this man who did so much for a more beautiful city of gracious living."

Miller relates the fountain's history: "Shortly after Dad's death, some of his friends, wanting to do something in his memory, asked for my advice. I told them that a memorial to my father should be two things. It should include a fountain, hopefully with sculpture, and it should be gotten for a bargain price. They asked if I would help them locate such a piece. I agreed, and went straight to Mitchell Samuels, then head of French and Company in New York, to enlist his help. I told him that we needed a fountain with some statuary, lots of water and, in keeping with my father's nature, one that could be bought at a bargain price."

Samuels understood and was delighted when he located a magnificent but badly mutilated piece, the creation of French artist Henri Greber, on the Mackay Estate on Long Island. Mackay had been president of the Postal Telegraph Company. After he and his wife died, vandals had hacksawed heads, arms, and legs from the bronze fountain. Upon viewing the statues, Miller agreed with the choice, but realized they would need extensive re-sculpturing and restoration. He proposed that he, Clyde, and Ellie provide the piece and the committee raise the money to do the rest.

It was a challenge to find a skilled artisan who would agree to work on some-

Among the "old-timers" in the 1950s at this dinner in their honor are (at table in foreground, front row, left) Ray Jones, manager of the farm department, and his wife; (second row, right) architect Ed Tanner and wife, Catherine; (at rear table, front row, left, in profile) Miller Nichols and wife, Katie; (right end) Randy Knight, sales department.

one else's art. Miller finally found 80-year-old Kansas City sculptor Herman Frederick Simon, who agreed to resculpt the missing pieces if he could work at his own pace. At the end of two years he had finished the pieces in clay, which Miller then shipped to Florence, Italy, to be cast in bronze. Finally, Simon attached them so well that no seams are visible.

The resculpted masterpiece was formally dedicated as the J.C. Nichols Memorial Fountain on a Sunday afternoon, May 15, 1960. Since that time it has been featured in literally thousands of Plaza pictures. Each of the four heroic-sized bronze figures of the horses stands ten feet high and weighs one-and-a-half tons. Laurence Sickman, former director of the Nelson Gallery, studied the figures and offered a theory about their meaning: "I believe the equestrian figures are an allegory of rivers. Greber was interested in rivers which were the inspiration for a work in the French town of Beauvais where he was born."

Sickman went on to point out that one of the mounted figures is an American Indian battling an alligator under the hooves of his horse; this figure could represent the Mississippi River. Another figure depicts a horseman slaying a bear; the bear, traditional symbol of Russia, probably represents the Volga River. The other two riders are on horses rearing above human figures with scaly fish tails; Sickman suggested they represent the Rhine and the Seine. Spaced equally between them are smaller bronze figures of dolphins and cherubs. The eight statues rise from an 80-foot-diameter pool and are sprayed with high arcs of sparkling water.

Miller Nichols inherited his father's commitment to the long-term preservation of quality on the Country Club Plaza and in the Country Club District; he also in-

herited his appreciation of outdoor art. Says Miller, "My philosophy is that beauty and quality are not created solely with large figures. I've felt that we need smaller pieces too. One example is the little lion's head built into the side of the Hall's Building. In the warmer months it often has beautiful geraniums cascading from the planter. And many of the lovely antique well-heads are filled with trailing flowers as well. We look for neglected corners where we can tuck statuary or a small fountain and flowers."

Miller likes to tell how he came to purchase another of the Plaza's best-known art pieces, the Neptune Fountain. On a warm Saturday morning in July 1952, as Miller was working in his office, he received a call from Lou Galamba, a dealer in scrap metals. Galamba said, "I have a fountain with a lead statue that I really think you ought to see. If you will meet me down at my warehouse, I would like to show it to you." Miller gathered up Ed Tanner, Earl Allen, and Dave Jackson and drove down to see the fountain, which was housed at the very back of a large metal warehouse where the temperature was about 120 degrees. The sculpture was a large figure of Neptune holding his trident, astride three sea horses.

"Miller, if you have some place you could use this, I'll make you a very good price," said Lou.

Although Miller immediately wanted the piece, he replied, "I'd have to think about a place for it. What could you sell it to me for?"

"Well, Miller, I'd like you to have it and I'll sell it to you for the price of junk lead."

"What's that?"

"Twenty-two cents a pound."

"Sold," said Miller. "What can you tell me about the piece?"

"I can't tell you anything," Lou replied.

The Neptune Fountain was placed on 47th Street in front of what is today the Laura Ashley shop, then Cricket West. Miller's curiosity about its origin persisted, and he was delighted when the workmen installing it found a small inscription on the base designating the Bromsgrove Guild. "Of course I had no idea where the Bromsgrove Guild was," recalls Miller, "but I figured I had nothing to lose by simply writing to the Bromsgrove Guild, England. Sure enough my letter was delivered and I had a reply from a Mr. G.H. Whewell. He told me regretfully that due to the shortage of lead after World War II and bad economic conditions in Britain, the Guild was going out of business. He mentioned that they did have a few pieces left that could be purchased, however, and agreed to send pictures. I bought his entire stock." Familiar pieces from the Bromsgrove Guild now displayed on the Plaza are "The Boy and His Hound," on Ward Parkway facing the tennis courts; "The Boy Riding Dolphin"; "The Boy and Seahorse"; "Draped Eve," out in Red Bridge; and "The Boy & Fish Fountain." (Mr. Whewell later negotiated the purchase of the Bacchus Fountain in Chandler Court.)

A few years afterward, as Miller and his wife, Katie, were browsing for garden statuary on 3rd Avenue in New York City, Miller showed one of the shopkeepers the company's pictorial brochure on the Country Club Plaza. When the man spied the Neptune Fountain, he exclaimed, "Where did you ever get that?"

"I got it from a junk dealer and I really don't know where he got it," replied Miller. "He wouldn't tell me."

"Well, I think I can tell you," said the dealer. "I owned it and I sold it to a cemetery operator in Oklahoma who wanted to use it there. I shipped it out but before it was installed he died. His heirs didn't think it appropriate in the cemetery and refused to pay for it. Now I know what happened to it."

A final footnote occurred still later when Miller was in England with Fred James, who was painting sketches of Sulgrave Manor for the Sulgrave Apartments. He decided one afternoon to drive up to Bromsgrove in Worcestershire to see if he could locate Mr. Whewell, with whom he had continued to correspond. As he entered the village, he stopped at a filling station and asked if they possibly knew where he might find a Mr. Whewell. "Oh, yes," was the reply, and he was given directions.

Miller drove to the address and knocked on the door, which was answered by an elderly woman. He said, "I have come to see Mr. Whewell." The lady replied, "Oh, I am so sorry, but Mr. Whewell hasn't been well, and he isn't seeing any visitors." To which Miller responded, "I'm sorry. Here is my card, would you please give it to Mr. Whewell." She read the card and exclaimed, "Miller Nichols from Kansas City!" She then turned and called back over her shoulder, "Henry, it's Miller Nichols from Kansas City," and promptly showed him in. They visited for two hours during which Miller received a liberal education about the Bromsgrove Guild and the use of lead statuary in England during the eighteenth and nineteenth centuries.

Miller Nichols' legacy from his father included sharp business acumen, artistic sensibility, and unshakable commitment to the growth and beauty of Kansas City. But to these Miller added his most valuable character trait: persistence. He says, "My father did have the capacity to dream and see those dreams come true. I've had the opportunity to act on those dreams and expand upon them. I'm by nature a persistent person, and I drive hard in pursuing my goals. My parents didn't give me a middle name, but Mother Nature did—persistence." To emphasize this point, on the inside of Miller's business card is a quotation from President Calvin Coolidge:

> Nothing in the world can take the place of persistence. Talent will not; nothing is more common than unsuccessful men with talent. Genius will not; unrewarded genius is almost a proverb. Education alone will not; the world is full of educated derelicts. Persistence and determination alone are omnipotent.

During Miller's tenure, he pursued a diligent course of reclamation, buying back properties that had been sold during the Depression and World War II and purchasing adjacent properties. By so doing, he extended the original boundaries and tripled the company's holdings around the prestigious Country Club Plaza. J.C. Nichols' death in 1950 prevented him from witnessing one 18-month period in 1953/54 when new construction expanded the size of the Plaza by nearly 25 percent, requiring the addition of two multi-level and two surface-level parking areas. The Neptune Building, the present Plaza III restaurant and office building on Ward Parkway, and the Harzfeld's Building (now The Limited) on Nichols Road were completed. Harzfeld's Plaza store was the first suburban location for the well-known downtown women's apparel firm and the largest single leased area, to that date, on the Plaza, with four floors of merchandising. The retail/office building that houses Helzberg's was also completed. Slowly the transformation of the Plaza from neighborhood shops and services to upscale gift and fashion shopping was occurring.

For many years the Country Club Plaza security force consisted of three senior citizens, one a retired prison guard, one an ex-farmer, and the third a former postman. They were unarmed and untrained and their primary responsibility was parking control. In the late 1950s, Miller decided that the presence of a guard-dog on the Plaza would reassure tenants and shoppers alike that the company was committed to security. The task of finding one was given to Lee Fowler, recently retired vice-president of public relations and formerly in charge of security. Lee recalls, "I tried to pretend I didn't hear him in hopes that he would forget. I should have known better. About every five or six weeks, he'd ask me how I was progressing on the guard-dog research. I finally had no choice but to look into it."

Lee first advertised locally for an experienced dog handler, but had no replies. He tried regional ads; still no response. In desperation, he placed an ad in the *Wall Street Journal* and received one reply—from a young, newly discharged veteran named John Holcomb in West Virginia. The Nichols Company flew him in for an interview and hired him on the spot. He stood ramrod straight, had crewcut blond hair, and no sense of humor. Relates Lee:

> We sent him to Springfield, Missouri (on full salary), for six weeks of training with the dog we had purchased, an ugly runt of the litter named Erikan Von Schwartzbeck, alias Rex. Rex and John got along famously. When they returned to town, we had to give them a room at the Bartleson Apartments while we waited for a special-order uniform for John and a custom-made leather saddlebags affair for Rex, one which he only tolerated for a few days.

Frank Grant, who was Company treasurer at the time, was so tight it was said that he asked to see used pencils before we could put in for new ones. Needless to say, Mr. Grant was not pleased with the expenses of our canine security program. He was particularly displeased when I took him the bill for Rex's tonsillectomy.

In the winter, when the road crews salted the streets, John felt that Rex's feet might become irritated, so he had us order some custom-made doggy galoshes. It took several weeks for the booties to arrive, during which John and Rex logged some more hours at the Bartleson in front of their soaps, on full pay. At last the boots arrived. We took Rex out to the sidewalk in front of the Company offices and put on his new footwear. He looked down at the silly booties and was so humiliated that he refused to take a single step until they were removed. It was difficult to justify *that* expense to Mr. Grant!

Tony Sweeney continues: "Rex and his handler used to stop by our offices on the first floor. Bill McGugin and Lee Fowler were scared to death of the dog. Whenever Rex entered the office, Bill left! The dog would then swagger over to Fowler's area, put his forefeet up on the desk top and growl as he drooled over Lee's papers. The only person the dog ever attacked was Lee Fowler. It happened one time when John, with Rex at his side, came to collect his paycheck. As Lee handed John the check, Rex attached his jaws to Fowler's arm!" Lee is able to joke, "That was a case of literally biting the hand that feeds you."

Rex and John eventually became fixtures on the Plaza, until Rex began to growl and show his teeth at children when they approached him. Fowler finally convinced Miller to reconsider the guard-dog project. Rex was retired and sold to John for one dollar.

The J.C. Nichols Company moved ahead in the mid-1950s, buying and developing the limestone mine at 95th and Holmes in order to consolidate its extensive residential and field construction operations. Negotiations got under way for the establishment of The Landing shopping center at 63rd and Troost (opened in 1961), which was to be built around Macy's first suburban store. And in 1957, Plaza Insurers, another wholly owned subsidiary, was added to the company, one that would write full lines of commercial and personal insurance.

Residential Development

Working with John Ruddy, Miller initiated a good deal of land acquisition over the decade. One important acquisition was the Herb Woolf farm in Johnson County, 79th to 83rd and Mission Road to El Norte, the present site of Corinth Downs and Corinth Shopping Center.

At the close of the war, the Kansas City, Missouri, boundaries ended at 86th Street. The purchase of the Red Bridge properties in Jackson County outside the city limits was the first time the J.C. Nichols Company acquired property that was not contiguous to land it was developing residentially. This was a bold move on Miller's part, and he has regretfully acknowledged that he wishes he had been bolder in the immediate postwar years. "Remembrance of Dad's suffering early in the '30s depression left me with a conservative bent," he says.

During the decade of the 1950s, new adjacent residential subdivisions continued to be added: Prairie Fields, Prairie

197

Ridge, Prairie Hills, Corinth Hills, and Sagamore Hills. The Armour Fields Public Golf Course had been opened by the J.C. Nichols Company in the 1920s, initially east of Ward Parkway. As the Country Club District grew towards the south and Ward Parkway was extended south from Meyer Circle to Gregory in 1935, the course was moved west between Ward Parkway and State Line. As this area was developed residentially in the early postwar years, the golf course was again nudged to the west, sometimes just one hole at a time, to the area between State Line and Belinder, where it finally adjoined the Indian Hills Country Club course. The opening of Sagamore Hills west of State Line as an upscale residential neighborhood of luxury homes spelled doom for the popular public Armour Hills Golf Course. Sagamore Hills also filled the last "close in" tract of land for custom home sites in the Country Club District.

John Ruddy became director of residential sales for the Nichols Company in 1954; a year later, he was named a mem-

Postwar Prairie Village Shopping Center, early 1950s, when men wore wing-tipped shoes, women wore hats and platform shoes, and television sets in the store windows lured customers inside.

ber of the board. In 1960, John was elected vice-president and secretary.[45] Ruddy recalled that the tendency among northeast Johnson County subdivisions to become small, independent municipalities in the late fifties and early sixties created major headaches for Frank Grant, company vice-president and treasurer. One after another of the homes associations of subdivisions on the Kansas side of State Line—Westwood Hills, Mission Woods, Mission Hills, Fairway, Prairie Village, and others—opted to incorporate.

It was Ruddy's belief that territorial pride motivated this trend, with the resulting new municipalities becoming more jurisdictional about building codes and zoning ordinances, among other things. New sets of municipal boundaries were created by the process, as well as a plethora of bureaucracies with which the company had to contend. John stated that the newly incorporated entities were not difficult to deal with on an individual basis, but that their sheer numbers created logistical problems for Frank Grant, who had traditionally represented the company in all legislative matters concerning Johnson County, Kansas. As municipalities, they became less closely related to the J.C. Nichols Company, but loyalties to the homes associations remained.

Miller believes that what differentiates the Nichols Company from other developers is that "we create beauty and value, and make it pay. . . . We develop home areas, not house areas. Over a period of time, the characteristics of any neighborhood are determined by the people who live there, not by the houses. We merely set the stage and provide a reason for each resident's pride of ownership. This is motivation for an owner to maintain his property and protect his investment.

When pride of ownership deteriorates, the neighborhood will do likewise."

The residential home building department had been profitable for the J.C. Nichols Company during its first fifty years. In 1958, however, the company decided to remove itself from the home building business. The decision was dictated by two considerations: Independent builders who had less overhead (such as building crews on the payroll year round) provided stiff competition and Nichols sales personnel, as exclusive agents for new homes in the new company subdivisions, could be considered to have a conflict of interest when they showed houses elsewhere.

With the phasing out of the residential home building department, the planing mill, site of Miller's first job with the company as a teenager, was closed down. Although no more homes would be built by company crews, the company has continued to do the engineering and platting of all new subdivisions. Its field construction crews are still responsible for the installation of all improvements: grading, streets, sidewalks, sewers, utilities, and lighting.

The Cultural/Educational/Scientific Center

The Midwest Research Institute was J.C.'s last major undertaking before his death, and Miller took his father's place on the institute's board just as Dr. Charles N. Kimball was hired as director and president. Kimball grew up in Boston in a family of modest means, worked his way through Northwestern University, and received his masters degree and doctorate in electrical engineering from Harvard. After jobs with RCA and an aircraft company,

he became technical director of Bendix Aviation Research Laboratories in Detroit. It was from there that he was recruited to head MRI in 1951.

In 1952, MRI's board of trustees decided to go ahead with construction of a permanent headquarters building on the Volker Boulevard site. To do this, the trustees, with Miller leading the charge, raised $1 million in six months, a record for Kansas City at that time. Miller served as chairman of the construction committee, and ground was broken the following year for a large building that would face north up the mall, toward the Nelson-Atkins Museum of Art. This building, completed in 1955, was almost immediately outgrown. A west wing was added in 1958 and an east wing in 1970. (The facility was named the Charles N. Kimball Building when Kimball retired in 1975.)

Dr. Nicholas Pickard remembers that Miller was influential in saving the MRI headquarters building from later flood damage. Dr. Pickard states, "When they were building it, the engineers were unsure about the proper elevation. They strung balloons on the other side of Brush Creek and took sights on them through transits. When they had made their determination, Miller eyeballed the site and said, 'No, you need to have the building one foot higher because it's in the flood plain!' They deferred to his judgment, and he was right."

A remarkable feature of the headquarters building for the time was a 5,000-square-foot computer center, the only one in the Midwest and one of the first in the country. With the early coming of the space age, NASA contracted with MRI to adapt space innovations and technologies for use by industry.

Like his father, Miller also sought to

serve in those areas of community life that he felt were essential. In 1956, he chaired the United Way Campaign. In 1958 and 1959, he served as president of the crime commission, a group with which he has remained affiliated. Just as J.C. planned for churches and schools in his developments, Miller also saw their value to the community. In 1949, Bob Meneilly, the new minister of the United Presbyterian Church, located then at 47th and Roanoke, called Miller to tell him the church (originally a mission church) needed to move and expand. Meneilly asked Miller to find an appropriate piece of property. "Keep in mind that our

Kenneth Spencer, Miller Nichols, Harold Moreland, and Charles Kimball (left to right) looking at blueprints at the Midwest Research Institute site. (Courtesy of Midwest Research Institute archives)

denomination does not call for large facilities," he added, "because we like our congregations to be no more than 400 people."

Miller interested him in a company-owned parcel at 67th and Mission Road, adjacent to the newly developed Prairie Village and where they could share parking facilities with Prairie Elementary School. He also suggested that the church allow for future growth by making an offer on an adjoining lot, owned by a Mrs. Porter. The minister liked the price of the two parcels, but Mrs. Porter could not be persuaded to sell. Miller researched the legal descriptions of the two lots and discovered that the Porter home had inadvertently been partially built on Nichols Company property. Gently apprised of this fact, Mrs. Porter had a change of heart and was happy to make the sale. The Village Presbyterian Church (USA), established in 1949, has since grown beyond anyone's wildest expectations and is currently one of the three largest churches in its denomination with 7,700 members!

Miller and Katie's four daughters, Kay, Nancy, Ann, and Lynn, all had some school years at Sunset Hill School, their mother's alma mater. Miller was active in the school's behalf during these years as his father had been before him. Sunset Hill had become overcrowded by 1959, so the board planned to add two new classrooms to the middle school at an estimated cost of $75,000. Board treasurer Milton McGreevy approached Miller to head the school's first fund drive, a departure from the school's traditional dependence on "a few extremely generous friends."

Miller's first reply was that he wasn't needed if they only wanted to raise $75,000; the trustees could do that—they didn't need a fund drive. But he agreed to help them if they set a larger goal that would address broader needs, which they did. Determined to enlarge the base of support, Miller called a meeting of one father from each class, who would be responsible for raising funds from other class parents, introducing a practice that has been used by the school ever since. The result: The school set and exceeded a $250,000 goal, one that acknowledged substantial building, maintenance, and administrative needs.

Upon his father's death in 1950, Clyde was elected to the board of the Conservatory of Music, later serving as chairman. He recalls that the conservatory was still on Armour Boulevard in 1950. W.T. "Tom" Grant offered a matching grant of up to $150,000 for a suitable new campus building as part of the city's cultural center if the board could raise the same amount. The amount was raised, and the new building was named Grant Hall. Clyde remembers Tom Grant's dedication to the conservatory and his love of music. A violinist, he was playing in a musical program that was part of a quarterly trustees' meeting, with Henry Haskell, Jr., accompanying him on the piano. He had just completed a piece and was receiving a standing ovation when he collapsed with a sudden heart attack and died on the spot.

His son, William D. Grant, took his place on the board, serving for a number of years with Clyde, who credits him with being the moving force in negotiating a merger of the Conservatory of Music with the University of Kansas City (subsequently the University of Missouri at Kansas City). Miller's present wife, Jeannette Nichols, recalls much discussion at several Junior League Cultural Resource Panel programs she moderated concerning the proposition that the Conservatory of Music and the Art Institute become divisions of the university in order to eliminate duplication of faculty for degree programs.

The conservatory faculty was composed of music teachers and academic teachers. The latter had to travel up from the Central Missouri State College at Warrensburg, Missouri, to conduct their classes in Kansas City. Added to this, the conservatory was not accredited; its students could not earn degrees unless they went on to an accredited institution for one additional semester after completing four years at the Conservatory of Music. Hence, the merger with UKC, which occurred in 1959, was both a wise and necessary move.

Prior to World War II, cultural arts programs in Kansas City were kept alive largely by individual patrons. But with the coming of the graduated income tax during the war and its escalation afterward, this was no longer viable. The arts institutions to which J.C. Nichols had been dedicated now needed to broaden their bases of support through the initiation of support groups to provide the funds to survive and grow. The problem was that the institutions were reluctant to reveal how precarious their finances were or where they were now looking for funds. But the Junior League in Kansas City, through its Cultural Arts Panel, persevered until a dialogue was established. Once the needs were indentified, a variety of support groups emerged.

Eleanor with daughters Suzie and Mollie in the rock garden of their Drury Lane home.

The Family

Each of the three families of J.C. and Jessic Nichols' adult children had a particular focus in their family life during the decade of the 1950s. For Eleanor and Earl it was the striking contemporary home that he designed for his family, one that she surrounded with handsome landscaping and exquisite gardens beautifying a hillside that dropped down to Mission Drive. As early as the fall of 1953, before the roof was on the house, Ellie was busy establishing her rock gardens and roses; a *Kansas City Star* article advised those out for an afternoon drive not to miss the sight of this lovely emerging garden.

In the several years that followed, the Allen's garden was not only a frequent choice for garden tours but also was featured several times in the *Kansas City Star* Sunday garden section. One particularly charming set of pictures shows Suzie, Mollie, and their mother in different parts of the garden. Eleanor carried this enthusiasm into the activities of the Westport Garden Club and displayed them at the Art Institute Garden Club as well.

The Allen family traveled a lot together, particularly to Mexico. Ellie never lost her love for Spanish art, music, and dancing, which she had celebrated in the Spanish fiestas she helped introduce to the Plaza in the 1930s. The extended motoring and sightseeing vacations also produced lots of photographs, which were duly catalogued in voluminous family scrapbooks.

In the mid-1950s the Allens experienced marital difficulties, which led to a divorce in 1955. But, to the delight of family and friends, they remarried in 1957. After completing Sunset Hill, the talented and accomplished Allen daughters went off to Northwestern University.

A highlight for the Miller Nichols family were summer vacations at western dude ranches. After a couple of summers at the C Lazy U Ranch near Granby, Colorado, Miller and his friend Joe Gregg decided that it would be a good idea (and maybe cheaper) to buy a ranch for their families. They scouted ranches in Colorado, Wyoming, and Montana and in 1954 found a suitable one, reasonably accessible, near Basalt, Colorado, 200 miles west of Denver. It had a large working acreage that included some 3,200 acres, with improvements appropriate for two families. It wasn't available, but that winter the owner died, and the following summer Miller and Joe Gregg were able to buy it—complete.

As soon as financing was arranged with Jim Kemper at the Commerce Bank in Kansas City, the Gregg and Nichols families set off for the new ranch. This was not an easy trip at a time when there were no interstate highways and cars were not air-conditioned. Miller's eldest daughter, Kay, well remembers that first drive to the ranch. In the old blue family station wagon, packed full, Miller drove his three older daughters and their white cat Muffy on the two-and-a-half-day trip to Colorado (with Katie, baby Lynn, and Myrtle, their cook, to follow by train). By the time they reached the majestic Glenwood Canyon, says Kay, "it was a moonlit night, silent except for the howling of the coyotes. Dad kept us spellbound with ghost stories for the hour or more it took to navigate the spooky canyon."

The Cap-K Ranch was so named at the suggestion of Mr. Caldwell, Katie's father, to honor the ladies' partnership in the ranch ("Cap" for Cynthia Ann Pickering and "K" for Katie). Here there were horses to ride, the Frying Pan River to fish, and acres and acres of beautiful forested mountains to hike, picnic, camp, and explore. Thus began a 40-year love affair with Miller's "working ranch" that continues today. For Miller Nichols there is no greater relaxation than a long working day irrigating the hay fields, checking cattle. building sheds, or mending fences. Summer lunches and dinners are served in the former chicken house adjoining the stone patio that Miller laid with his own hands, complete with a fire to ward off the evening chill.

By the mid-1950s, Clyde and Marty had five children: two sons, Jay and Wayne, and three daughters, Blair, Jessie, and Dell.[46] As noted earlier, to accommodate their large family, the younger Nicholses had moved into a large Tudor home at 2401 Drury Lane in Mission Hills.

Here a desire to give their boys an unusual birthday gift led to a hobby for which Clyde became famous. He had learned that the Kansas City transit company was about to dispose of some retired city buses, so he called to inquire about buying one as a kind of playhouse for his sons. When a spokesperson for the transit company assured him he was welcome to a vehicle, Clyde said he would send a tow truck for it. "Oh, it runs," said the person on the phone. "Just come down and drive it away."

So Clyde did just that. As it turned out, he was a lot more excited than his sons about the new acquisition, so instead of deactivating it, he removed the seats and converted it into perhaps the world's first recreational vehicle. Since city buses are limited in speed to less than 35 miles per hour, he soon graduated to a converted school bus. This, in turn, gave way to a much larger and more elaborately refurbished overland bus, dubbed Pawhuska (the destination named on its rollover sign in front.) Probably the best-known of the Nichols' buses, this full-sized Greyhound contained a lounge area with electronic piano, a kitchen, a bath, and sleeping space for 18!—"if some of them are children, or if they're compatible." The extended Nichols family—"including in-laws and out-laws"—and friends toured in these buses from coast to coast and border to border, from Colorado ski trips to Florida beaches.

Chapter 8

1960 - 1977

As the J.C. Nichols Company entered the decade of the 1960s, the residential building boom was still in full flower. Prairie Village, Prairie Fields, Prairie Hills, Prairie Ridge, Corinth Hills—subdivisions to the south—as well as Indian Hills, were largely complete; and in 1961, Kenilworth, a 320-home development site on 160 acres to the south of Prairie Village, was opened. Verona Hills along State Line beyond 115th Street followed with sites for 800 homes on a 350-acre tract; and furthest to the southwest, Oak Park was opened in 1965. During these years, the last close-in section of fine homes, Sagamore Hills, from 67th to 70th and State Line to Belinder, was being developed.

Down on the Plaza in the executive offices of the J.C. Nichols Company, the reins of management had been largely picked up by younger postwar recruits to the company. On the board, Clyde had succeeded his father in 1950, followed by John Ruddy, Dave Jackson, and Bob O'Keefe, all noted earlier. In 1961, Fred Brady (son-in-law of John Taylor) came aboard, and in 1964, Lynn McCarthy joined the group. These men were eager and ready to follow Miller into new areas of real estate development.

In 1963, Miller succeeded John Taylor as chairman of the board; Taylor had joined J.C. Nichols in 1905 before the Country Club District was begun. This same year George Tourtellot retired as vice-president in charge of commercial properties, after 55 years with the company. In 1966, J.C.'s only nephew, Ansel Mitchell, retired as vice-president in charge of field construction, after forty years (not counting summers in his school years).

J.C.'s only nephew, Ansel Mitchell, was vice-president in charge of field construction. He began working summers for the company while still in school and retired in 1966 after forty years' service.

A Crime Commissioner Says: The Crooks Get All The Breaks
HOW TO TEACH THREE-YEAR-OLDS TO READ
Singer Connie Francis and A New Story By William Saroyan

POST
The Saturday Evening

Sept. 23, 1961

20¢

Country Club Plaza
KANSAS CITY, MO.

A measure of the national fame of the Country Club Plaza was its appearance on the cover of the September 23, 1961, issue of the Saturday Evening Post. In this painting by noted illustrator John Falter, the J.C. Nichols Memorial Fountain is in the foreground.

After his retirement, Ansel apparently concluded that J.C. Nichols Company stock was priced unrealistically low, and he sought to have the company registered with the SEC so that more public disclosure of its financial position would be required. He tried more than one plan and finally, according to company attorney John Ruddy, sold 355 shares to individual owners, which brought the number of stockholders above 500, thus requiring SEC registration. "Nobody but an engineer would have thought of such a scheme!" said Ruddy. The company went public in 1971, and full financial disclosure followed. But as Miller had contended, the fuller market appraisal of the stock did not bring a significant increase in its price.

During these years, Miller and his friend from Navy days, Davis K. Jackson, were a powerful and effective management team. Dave's focus since his arrival in 1946 had been in commercial proper-

Management succession at the J.C. Nichols Company from 1905 to the 1960s is captured here. Miller's friend from navy days, Dave Jackson (left), was recruited into the Nichols Company in 1946 and became president in 1973. Miller (right) became chairman of the board upon the retirement of John Taylor (left portrait), who, in turn, had succeeded J.C. Nichols (right portrait) upon his death in 1950. Under Miller and Dave's leadership, the 1960s and 1970s marked a period of dynamic growth for the company.

ties. He became a vice-president in 1956 and joined the board in 1958. Paul Wenske in a *Kansas City Times* article documents Jackson's impact on the company and on the city: "Jackson became an astute company president and civic leader who held many city posts, including the presidency of the Kansas City Board of Parks and Recreation Commissioners, the presidency of the Starlight Theater Association and the presidency of the Real Estate Board. Jackson was instrumental in helping to consolidate the day-to-day operation of the growing Nichols empire."

According to Clarence Roeder, recently retired vice-president and secretary of the company, "Miller's style of leadership could best be described as one with an open door policy, and one concerned with substance rather than form. Miller has always been accessible for personal visits or for phone calls, even unexpected calls if he can work them in. Unless in a meeting, he answers his own phone and his home is listed in the Kansas City directory.

Roeder continues: "As Chairman of the Board, Miller presided with patience and openness. While J.C. Nichols Company directors knew that he and his family controlled the large majority of stock, his style was to let everyone have their say, whether in agreement or not. His brother, Clyde, frequently had additions to the agenda. Dave Jackson was inclined to elaborate at length. Lynn McCarthy brought perceptive questions. But the Board meetings nevertheless almost always moved along efficiently and with consensus." One might say Miller expected this. Clyde frequently commented that major decisions had already been made in executive committee.

New Areas of Real Estate Development

During the decade of the 1960s, the company focused on three new areas of real estate development, all located on the south side of Brush Creek facing the Plaza. On both sides of Wornall Road, the land climbs steeply up bluffs, part of the site of the Civil War Battle of Westport. East of Wornall, the steep site had previously been thought too rugged for residential development, despite the existence of houses atop the rocky hillside and apartments below bordering the creek. Miller, however, concluded that this "found land" could be made suitable for upscale high-rise residential living. And so, in the mid-1950s, the company embarked on a joint venture with City Bond and Mortgage Company to build a cooperative high-rise apartment house (forerunner of today's high-rise condominiums) on the most accessible hillside location.

Bill McGugin, who joined the company in 1950, represented the Nichols Company in the new venture, called the Wornall Plaza. By 1960 Miller was eager to get on with the building of an adjacent high-rise residential apartment to be known as Regency House, a second joint venture that would be managed by the J.C. Nichols Company. Dave Jackson and his wife were among the first occupants, in April 1962. In less than five years, the company was ready to build a second high-rise luxury apartment next door, named the Sulgrave. (Sulgrave Manor in England was the ancestral home of George Washington's family.)

This second tier of high-rise residential living to the south of Brush Creek furthered J.C.'s vision of residential living encircling the Plaza. These handsome buildings were also designed to allow for more grass, trees, and landscaping, a point to which Miller gave increasing attention as the company moved into high-rise development. At the Sulgrave, a swimming pool was included.

Provided with ample parking, the new apartments were designed to attract executives and their families, upscale residents who became walk-in customers for the lovely shops and restaurants on the Plaza. "The more we can do to give merchants better business by bringing more people to their door," said Miller, "the better off they are going to be and con-sequently the better off *we* are going to be."[47]

The second new undertaking on the south side of Brush Creek was the Board of Trade Building, the Nichols Company's first venture into a mid-rise freestanding office building. Younger members of the Board of Trade had decided that they wanted to move south, out of downtown, and to have ownership in their headquarters/office building. They decided on a J.C. Nichols Company site on the corner of 48th and Main Streets, where an arrangement was made for a handsome building to be erected, with 51 percent

Construction of the Regency House and the Sulgrave Apartments added to the already existing residential units in the southeast quadrant of the Plaza.

owned by the Board of Trade, in partnership with the J.C. Nichols Company, which would oversee the construction and maintenance of the building.

A hue and cry arose at the Board of Trade's departure from downtown. This was probably the first time that the Nichols Company had been questioned about its Plaza development. The company was subjected to a good deal of pressure not to go through with this deal with the Board of Trade. One reason for the move was that the Board of Trade had offered to purchase the 10th and Main building where they were located, but the owners were unable to meet the agreed time schedule. Says Dave Jackson, "We took the position that it was a decision that the Board of Trade should make and that we shouldn't try to influence them but just present the facts and let them reach a conclusion."

Even greater resistance was met in the third new area of development for the J.C. Nichols Company, the Alameda Plaza Hotel, to be located across Brush Creek to the south. When J.C. Nichols was still alive, the possibility of constructing a hotel was discussed with the Frank Dean family, who owned and managed the downtown President Hotel. But with no site forthcoming, the idea was put on hold. By the early 1960s, Dave Jackson suggested that it would be a good investment for the company. "Fortunately Miller agreed with me," he says. "Some of the other Directors on the Board were not so certain, but this is not a Company that goes on popular vote."

The property to the west of Wornall Road and bordering Brush Creek seemed the logical site to Miller. Most of it was owned by Dr. E.D. Fear, who had bought up as many as 14 or 15 duplexes in the area. When Dr. Fear died, Miller and

Dave decided not to build the proposed hotel anywhere else until his estate was settled. John Taylor, the very able and also very conservative chairman of the board, still wasn't convinced that the company should purchase the land. Jackson remembers that he and Miller were standing with Taylor at the window of his office on the third floor, which had been J.C.'s before him, looking out at Fear's property. Also present were two Urban Land Institute friends of Taylor, one from Houston and the other from North Carolina. After listening to the discussion for awhile, they said, "John, you really ought to own that property." This support for the idea from two gentlemen whom he respected helped Taylor make up his mind.

Jackson adds a side note on John Taylor's conservative approach. Miller had decided almost a decade earlier, just after his father's death, that the company really should be acquiring the small houses in the old neighborhood atop the hillside, south of the site he had reclaimed for the Regency and the Sulgrave apartments. Taylor had demurred. Miller persisted, and Taylor finally agreed that Miller could go ahead and buy the houses for his own account. He did so, holding them for some 30 years, until the company took them over in the mid-1980s as part of its Kirkwood Circle Plan.

The purchase of the hotel property turned out to be a long and arduous process. The Nichols Company negotiated a contract with the estate, but since Fear didn't own one crucial parcel of the ground, Miller and Dave insisted on having time to acquire it before obligating themselves to the estate's holdings. The property also had to be rezoned, a process that took over four years and stands as one of the most notable zoning battles in Kansas City history.

Difficulties over the hotel marked the first time the J.C. Nichols Company had had a personal confrontation with a neighborhood constituency. As emotional and significant as the neighborhood resistance was, the legal battle was much more serious. In fact, the company lost in circuit court, but after two hearings before the Missouri Supreme Court, the zoning was unanimously approved.

"That decision could not have come at a more fortuitous time," Jackson declares. "We were in a position where we could not extend our option contract with Fear's estate. We were faced with either having to go ahead and buy the property for just under $1 million, a lot of money in those days, and take a big chance—or just let it go. Time was to run out for us in June of 1967. The Missouri Supreme Court handed down its ruling just two weeks before our deadline."

When the J.C. Nichols Company had announced its plans to build a hotel in 1963, Miller and Dave Jackson were approached by Jud Putsch (operator of Putsch's restaurants on the Plaza) and the Gilbert-Robinson Group, who proposed to make it a joint venture. The J.C. Nichols Company accepted. But due to the years of delay, under the final terms of the agreement, the company became the owner/landlord, with the Gilbert-Robinson Group as tenant; Mr. Putsch bowed out. Miller and Dave wanted a hotel professional to plan and oversee management of the new hotel. "We didn't want a 'chain' hotel; we preferred to have local management," says Jackson. The person everyone agreed on was Phil Pistilli who, at the time, was general manager of Kansas City's most prestigious hotel, the Muehlebach.

Says Jackson, "There are few individuals who would have been willing to devote the time to planning that Phil did with the Alameda Plaza. Most people are too busy to delve into that kind of detail. Neither Gilbert-Robinson nor the Nichols Company were big enough that decisions would get delegated to fifth-, sixth-, seventh-tier management people. Miller or I had to make those decisions. On the other hand, we didn't have to put up with any bureaucratic nonsense. We sat together through long meetings with the architects, the tenant, and others."

In 1966, Miller, Dave Jackson, and Kansas City architect Ralph Myers went to Spain to study architecture and to collect Spanish art, artifacts, and furniture for the hotel; they visited Seville, Cordoba, and Ronda. They also traveled to Hawaii to take a look at some of the new concepts being introduced in resort hotels there.

Because of his engineering background, Dave Jackson, working closely with Pistilli, was given responsibility for the myriad details on the Alameda project. Their compatibility was indicated by the fact that they operated from a simple page-and-a-half agreement, which simply outlined their respective responsibilities.

Pistilli says with a chuckle that he lost all his fights with Dave Jackson and the Nichols Company. He admits they had strong words on occasion, but attributes that to honesty in business:

> The Nichols Company has been called autocratic, tough, single-minded, but no one will disagree that it has always been dedicated to quality. Since the days of Mr. J.C. Nichols, whom I didn't know personally, the company has had a reputation of integrity.
>
> I wasn't stamped out of a yes-man mold and neither were Miller Nichols

or Dave Jackson. Miller is a much tougher guy than I am. He chooses to go through the strongest point of resistance. If he were an infantry commander, and I speak as an ex-infantry soldier, I wouldn't want to be under him. We'd win a lot of battles, but I might be dead! Also, the J.C. Nichols Company could never have developed the Alameda Plaza without Dave Jackson.

The construction of a hotel was a complete departure from anything the company had done up to that time. In 1968, when planning got under way, there weren't many hotels being built, so recent precedents were lacking. It was literally an adventure for all concerned. Architects did not play a very significant role. Instead, life-size models of the rooms were built in the company's underground shops, where every detail could be studied: how the lights would work and how the bathroom doors should swing.

The company set a budget for the Alameda Plaza and managed to live within it. The hotel was built to make money for the J.C. Nichols Company and for Gilbert-Robinson; there were no egos involved. Decisions and judgments were based on sound business criteria.

The Country Club Plaza, 1960–1970

While new J.C. Nichols Company residential subdivisions continued to mushroom to the south and southwest during the decade of the 1960s and while the Nichols Company embarked on new areas of real estate development (i.e., high-rise apartments, a mid-rise office building, and a hotel, all just to the south of Brush Creek overlooking the Plaza), significant

developments were taking place on the Country Club Plaza as well.

In the early 1960s, Joyce Hall decided to build a large retail store on the Plaza, one that would encompass a full square block between Ward Parkway and Nichols Road. For some time, Mr. Hall had been interested in retailing. His first venture had been to buy T.M. James china, downtown on Petticoat Lane, expanding it into a large new Halls store that featured china, silver, and decorative gifts. Now he was ready to expand even further, and the J.C. Nichols Company was delighted he had chosen a Plaza location.

One Saturday, Joyce Hall invited Miller and Dave Jackson to lunch, after which they walked around the Plaza together. According to Jackson, Mr. Hall made several suggestions. "He wanted the Plaza to be just the finest it could be," Jackson remembers. "Later, Miller and I agreed with some chagrin that he had come up with some things we hadn't thought about."

After the terms of the lease were agreed upon, Mr. Hall invited Miller and Dave down to the Hallmark offices. A table had been set up with a model on it that was covered by a draped cloth. Mr. Hall said, "Miller, I had Edward Durrell Stone draw up a proposed exterior design for our new store. I know that you have the right to accept or reject it, but I must tell you that if you can't accept this proposal I won't have anything more to do with the exterior design for the building."

Says Miller, "That was one of the hardest decisions I have ever had to make in more than 50 years of business. I very much respected Mr. Hall and I wanted to defer to his choice, but the contemporary design he presented did not complement the Spanish architecture of the Plaza. It just wasn't compatible with the Plaza im-

Miller Nichols (left) with Joyce Hall at the ground-breaking ceremonies for the construction of the future Halls retail store, July 23, 1964.

age. And so Ed Tanner designed the Halls store as we know it today."

While the Halls store was under construction, Miller received a call from Mrs. Chandler—the widow of Ed Chandler, the Plaza's earliest merchant, who had had a large florist shop with greenhouses on the site of the new Mark Shale store (formerly Swansons) and Chandler Court. She said she was ready to sell the property and retire from business and that she preferred not to sell to anyone else if the J.C. Nichols Company wanted this property. Miller immediately accepted her offer.

In the mid-1960s the company became concerned about some of their single-ownership principals who were getting on in years; they suggested to several that perhaps they should plan ahead for the future. One of these was Swansons, founded by Mrs. Walter Springey, who was no longer living, and run by her two nieces. Eventually the nieces called Dave Jackson to say that they would like to sell

their business and asked for a suggestion as to who might want to buy it. Their elegant small store featured couturier fashion and beautiful lingerie as well. Over time, a joint ownership group was formed that assured Swansons a larger and even finer store located on the former Chandler's site.

In discussing the design of the new building for Swansons, Miller requested two unique features of the architects, both of which reflected a sentimental touch. He requested that the building be beautified with a handsome patio courtyard along the north side, to be named Chandler Court in honor of the Chandlers. Clarence Chandler had been the superintendent of grounds at the St. Louis World's Fair in 1904. From 1905 to 1909, he served as the superintendent of Swope Park, after which he opened his own landscape company. In 1916, he moved to the 47th Street location, making Chandler's

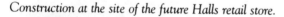

Construction at the site of the future Halls retail store.

the earliest retail operation on the Country Club Plaza, one that preceded its development by the J.C. Nichols Company.

For the Chandler courtyard, Miller took a recommendation from Mr. G.H. Whewell of the Bromsgrove Guild and purchased one of their major works, a large fountain, "The Nymphs of the Fields and Meadows, Waters, Winds and Flowers offering Homage to Pan."

Like his father, Miller loves towers, and he chose this opportunity to reproduce the grandest of them all, the Giralda Tower that stands beside the magnificent cathedral in Seville, Spain. J.C. had seen the tower on his travels; one time he sent a postcard of it to the office with the comment, "You know this is something we ought to do sometime on the Plaza." So great was his fascination that he purchased a multi-tile plaque of Seville's Orange Court and the Giralda Tower, by Spanish artist Ramas Rejano, which he placed on the upper wall of his office.[48] In early 1929, J.C. had plans drawn to incorporate the basic design of the Giralda Tower into the proposed Time Building. However, the drawings revealed that such a tower would be too tall for that particular site.

Miller envisioned that the Chandler Court would furnish an appropriate setting

Miller, his first wife Katie, and their daughter Kay stand in a square in Seville, Spain, with the original Giralda Tower behind them.

Miller erected a replica to scale on the Country Club Plaza, and Seville became a Sister City of Kansas City.

for the Giralda Tower. His challenge was to find the original drawings in Spain so that it could be built to scale. He succeeded, and working with Ralph Myers, he decided that one-half scale would be appropriate for the Plaza location. Seville's Giralda Tower features a large circular ramp up the center of the tower that enabled horsemen to ride to the top and post lookouts there. Atop the tower stands an heroic-size statue of Faith, believed to be a protector of the city. During the era of the Moorish conquest, the statue was positioned to face attacking armies. Accordingly, a seven-foot, 2,700-pound bronze replica of the original statue of Faith now sits atop the Kansas City tower.

Pleased with the concept of the Giralda Tower, Miller felt it should be embellished by having the handsome "Seville Light" reproduced just to the north of it and in the same relationship to the tower that it enjoys in Seville. As this was not an original work, there was considerable discussion by the Municipal Art Commission, but approval was finally forthcoming. Sculptor Bernard Zuckermann, whose studio was near Carrara, Italy, was hired to create the Seville Light according to the original design.

Ilus W. Davis was mayor of Kansas City in the 1960s. He liked the idea of establishing sister city relationships, and thought that Seville, Spain, was the logical choice for a first sister city. When he heard that Miller and Katie had planned a trip to Spain to visit their daughter Nancy, who was studying in Granada, Mayor Davis asked them to go to Seville and deliver the invitation to the Spanish city's officials.

Miller arrived on the first day of the bullfight season; the mayor, Felix Moreno de la Cova, was nowhere to be found. There was no official to receive him at the city hall, and he had to leave the invitation. The next morning, to Miller's chagrin, a cartoon making fun of the sister city concept with Kansas City appeared in the Seville paper. Fortunately, Mayor de la Cova heartily endorsed the concept, and the newspaper changed its tune.

Once the sister city relationship was agreed upon, Spanish dignitaries were invited to come to Kansas City in 1967 for the October dedication of the Giralda Tower and Seville Light. Seville sent a group of 25 prominent citizens, including their mayor. The group was put up at the Hilton Plaza Inn, then the only hotel near the Plaza. Miller arranged for a bus with an interpreter to pick up the honored guests. They were driven around the Nelson-Atkins Museum and through the UMKC campus. As they approached the Plaza from the east on 47th Street, the driver paused next to Winstead's and Miller stood to address the group. Before he could say anything, the Spaniards rose out of their seats and began to applaud.

"What are they applauding about?" Miller asked the interpreter. "I haven't told them anything yet."

The interpreter replied, "My friends are saying, 'More Spanish than Spain!'"

While the Giralda Tower is certainly one of Kansas City's most noted landmarks, another small but very popular Plaza work of art appeared in the 1960s. This is the Wild Boar, located on the north side of 47th Street. The original statue of the Wild Boar, carved in marble by the Greeks before the time of Christ, was lost with the sinking of the ship carrying it to Rome. Later, from memory, the Romans made a copy, which is now in the Uffizi Gallery in Florence. From the marble, a bronze reproduction was cast in 1857 by the Italian artist Benelli. Today, it stands at the entrance to the Florence Straw Market and is known as "The Wild Boar of Florence."

Miller purchased another casting of the Wild Boar in 1961 while on a tour of Europe. In Florence, he invited his oldest daughter, Kay, out for a late afternoon walk. They strolled along the Arno; near the Rialto Bridge, they came upon a gallery shop full of handsome sculpture. By then it was getting late and the store was closed, but they could see the bronze statue of a wild boar through the window. "You know, I would like to have that," Miller said to Kay, "but I don't have the slightest idea where I could put it. If we had it in Kansas City, I know we would figure out a way to use it someday, someplace."

The next morning Kay asked her father, "Dad, what would you be willing to pay for that bronze of the wild boar?" "I think I would pay $2,500 for it," he replied. Later in the day, the two again dropped by the gallery shop of sculptor Ferdinando Marinelli, where Miller pretended interest in some of the smaller pieces. Finally, he asked about the boar. Mr. Marinelli told him its unusual history, and then quoted a price of $2,500. "Having told Kay I would pay that, I could hardly refuse," says Miller.

The Wild Boar launched one of the Plaza projects that Miller has enjoyed most over many years. In April 1962, he installed the statue on 47th Street along with the suggestion to "drop in a coin, rub the boar's nose, and make a wish for your children and for the children of Mercy Hospital." All the coins collected at the Wild Boar, and subsequently in all the other Plaza fountains as well, go to benefit the children at Kansas City's Mercy Hospital. Miller confesses he got this idea from Florence, too; all coin donations there go to benefit a local Italian orphanage.

The project was so well received that Miller ordered a second Wild Boar, at a cost of $7,500, to be used in the same way at Kansas City's new international airport. He also gave a small reproduction to Mercy Hospital. Today, gift donations of between $6,000 and $7,500 are collected each year from the Plaza fountains.

In the late 1960s, Miller pursued the opportunity to add yet another handsome courtyard to the Plaza. One valuable site he sought to repurchase was the 8,400-square-foot Standard Oil station on the corner of Broadway and Ward Parkway. It had been sold by J.C. for $11,000 many years before, and although Standard Oil was more interested in selling gasoline than selling the site, Miller finally negotiated a three-for-one trade. The J.C. Nichols Company received the valuable Plaza property in exchange for Standard Oil's right to choose and lease three Nichols Company–owned sites for filling stations elsewhere.

Using approximately 5,000 square feet of this repurchased property to enlarge the Woolf Brothers store, Miller designated the remaining 3,400 square feet as an open patio. Others in the company questioned the courtyard idea, favoring a two-story extension of the building. But Miller rejected that notion because it would have disturbed the symmetry of the roof lines and ruined a unique opportunity to beautify this gateway to the Plaza.

Social and Security Problems

The racial tensions that flared in many cities in the late 1960s affected Kansas City as well. There were telephone threats to Plaza merchants, several broken windows in the shops, and the intimidation of shoppers by carloads of black youths shouting threats and obscenities. The National Guard was eventually called to the Plaza to help. Miller recalls that politicians, clergymen, and local leaders of the civil rights movement attempted to calm the small radical minority, but it wasn't until someone thought to enlist the aid of high school coaches from the predominantly black neighborhoods that the turbulence ceased.

Several of the Weathermen (a student faction associated with violence, vandalism, and bombings), along with other student leaders at the University of Missouri at Kansas City, demanded a meeting with Miller to discuss their objections to capitalistic society. To the shock and chagrin of some of his associates, Miller agreed to meet with them in the board room at the J.C. Nichols Company. He selected the time of 5:00 P.M., feeling that this would cause the least amount of disturbance in the office. When the student leaders and their associates arrived, there was considerable consternation among company officers; several remained in their offices after hours, both out of curiosity and out of concern for Miller.

The leaders of the 16 disgruntled college students opened the discussion with a torrent of profanity. Miller immediately admonished them. "If you swear one more time," he said, "you are not welcome here and I will walk out of this meeting. There is no reason why we can't speak without cursing. If you insist on talking that way, then the meeting is over." Miller's comment not only startled the students, but immediately changed the quality of their language; not another word of profanity was heard during the session, which lasted well over an hour. Later, one of the company officials commented, "Not too many

men of Miller's stature would have taken the time let alone subject themselves to that kind of unpleasant gathering."

Several pipe bombs were placed in and around the Country Club Plaza during these weeks, but fortunately there were no injuries or major explosions. Late one night a small pipe bomb was thrown through a window of the Nichols home in Mission Hills, but it caused only minor damage.

Although actual rioting in Kansas City in April of 1968 lasted only a few days, it resulted in the company's temporary closure of The Landing Shopping Center and indicated the need for a professional security staff on the Plaza. From inauspicious beginnings, the Plaza security force has grown into a current annual budget in excess of $1 million. The force employs a staff of 25 full-time officers (including dispatchers and office personnel) and 25 part-time, off-duty police officers. The Nichols Company provides all its security personnel with vehicles, firearms, uniforms, and radios.

The decision to establish Guardian Management, a wholly owned property maintenance subsidiary of the J.C. Nichols Company, in the late 1960s, has been an exceedingly popular one. Shopkeepers, doctors and dentists, office tenants in the new office buildings, residential tenants in high-rise apartments, garden apartments, and condominiums, all appreciate the fact that the J.C. Nichols Company has its own maintenance crews to look after them—crews that are on call to address building problems and to keep the exterior of their buildings looking shipshape as well. In the 1960s, to the south and west of previous J.C. Nichols Company subdivisions, the company constructed garden apartments and townhouses, reflecting new residential trends and tastes. Kenilworth garden apartments was followed by Villa Medici with its several ponds with swans and peacocks, and in turn by Georgetown, featuring garden townhouses. The residents of these types of communities especially appreciate the services of Guardian Management.

As new social attitudes emerged following World War II, the public began to question any decisions that related to them, particularly those that brought change. When the company proposed to build the Corinth Square shopping center in the sixties, the Prairie Village Homes Association vehemently protested. Residents of the southern Prairie Village subdivisions, in Lee Fowler's words, "liked the idea of being a bedroom community, protected by self-imposed zoning ordinances" and could not envision a need for another commercial center in their midst.

A public hearing was scheduled to be held in the basement of the Prairie Village Shopping Center. When more than 600 people showed up for the meeting, it was moved to the spacious and recently completed Shawnee Mission High School auditorium. The J.C. Nichols Company, in spite of much advance preparation for an anticipated uphill battle, was taken aback when an informal show of hands at

The Wild Boar added to the menacing atmosphere when 180 members of the 436th Signal Corps, a Kansas City National Guard unit, received orders for deployment throughout the Plaza in April 1968. (Courtesy of Kansas City Star)

the beginning of the hearing showed 594 citizens against the rezoning and only six in favor, all company employees!

Led by Mayor Robert F. Bennett, who later became a state senator and finally governor of Kansas, the town's elected officials cut through the emotional issue and discussed the importance of Corinth Square in terms of both city tax revenues and convenience for resident shoppers. They ignored the groundswell of negative public opinion and granted the zoning change. Obviously, Bennett's strong stand in favor of Corinth Square did not negatively affect his political career; 25 years later Corinth Square is an attractive and thriving neighborhood shopping center, much appreciated by its surrounding homeowners.

Education and Arts, 1960–1977

Miller shares his father's conviction that colleges and universities are vital to a city's cultural and business health. He foresaw that as local educational institutions grew, they would run out of space; at that point, they would be forced to move from the heart of the city to find room for expansion. "There is no metropolitan university in the United States that has an adequate campus," Miller declared in a *Kansas City Star* interview in March 1980. "A great university is dependent upon adequate land on which it can expand. In all likelihood there is nobody living in the properties around a campus who will be living there 25 years from now. The future needs of a university should come ahead of the individual's needs."

Miller's first opportunity to act on this opinion came in the early 1960s, on behalf of Rockhurst College. Viewing Rockhurst as part of the cultural/scientific/educational center envisioned by his fa-

ther, he looked at its 19-acre campus directly across Troost to the southeast of the University of Missouri at Kansas City campus and concluded it would not be adequate for the years ahead. When he was invited to be a member of the Rockhurst College Board of Regents, his first move was to persuade them to embark on a program of acquiring additional land, parcel by parcel, over a period of 50 years if necessary. Today, the Rockhurst campus and acquisition area encompass 35 acres.

Trustees of the Barstow School, a school for girls, kindergarten through 12th grade, located adjacent to the Midwest Research Institute and to the University of Kansas City, had expanded their campus in 1954 by acquiring the Shields mansion on some seven acres, two blocks to the south of the school on Cherry Street. This division of the school campus, coupled with a desire for a coed program, led Barstow in the early 1960s to move south to where could be built a modern school on a planned site, one that would allow for athletic facilities and would be more accessible to new residential neighborhoods. The Nichols Company had an appropriate site that Miller agreed to trade for their intown property.

The Barstow School move freed up property that adjoined the Midwest Research Institute. Says Miller, "Many of the MRI Trustees weren't anxious to buy this bargain land with its outmoded improvements, but fortunately Arthur Mag was." MRI bought the property, tore down the old dormitory, built the Mag Conference Center, and promptly filled the other school buildings with offices.

Miller became a trustee of the University of Kansas City in 1962; three years later he was elected chairman of its board. His greatest contribution to UKC, and subsequently to UMKC, was as chairman of the Real Estate Acquisition Committee, implementing the same philosophy he had introduced at Rockhurst. For nearly 20 years, he was, in fact, virtually a one-man acquisition committee, purchasing 52 parcels of land for the university trustees, mostly homes and lots and other small pieces for a total investment of $6,630,000. He continues to advise on the purchase of homes in the university's acquisition area. The original 40-acre campus is now up to 177 acres and is well on its way toward becoming an even larger campus.

Several UKC acquisitions were especially important: The Shields tract with its handsome Tudor home was first used to house the Law School and was more recently incorporated into the Henry Bloch School of Business. This tract also provided the site for the new Law School. And the more recently acquired Lynn Insurance Building on the east side of Oak Street is an imposing 90,000-square-foot building that now houses the administrative offices of the university.

"The Trustees turned me down when I suggested they purchase the Shields' property that formerly belonged to The Barstow School," recalls Miller. "But I made them an offer they couldn't turn down: the seven-acre tract with its large Tudor home for my cost in the raw land going to Barstow, financed for five years at one percent interest. Today this seven-acre site could accommodate still a third University school, as future needs demand."[49]

The Kansas City Philharmonic

After coming to Kansas City in the late 1940s, Hans Schwieger served for 23 years as musical director of the Kansas City Philharmonic. Over the years, Hans and Mary Schwieger became good friends of Miller and Katie Nichols. The Schwiegers took pleasure in showing the Nichols family some of their favorite places in Hans' native Germany—and in Austria in 1961 during the family's three-month European trip. Miller served on the Philharmonic board of trustees for more than a decade and was its president in 1963/64.

Recognizing the annual funding crisis the orchestra faced each year, he worked successfully to get the orchestra into the black and then promoted and secured the establishment of an endowment fund (which was relinquished in a later financial crisis). With Paul Willson, Miller made a gift of the handsome bronze Orpheus statue that has resided with the orchestra in its different homes ever since. Schwieger, who remains in touch with Miller, mentioned touchingly in a 1991 letter that Miller's term as Philharmonic president was the high point of his Kansas City experience.

At the time Miller was working with the orchestra, Marty Nichols served as chair of the Women's Committee of the Philharmonic Association and as such was a delegate to the national Women's Association of Symphony Orchestras; she subsequently served for six years on the executive committee of that organization.

Owing in part to disagreement over Hans Schwieger's retirement in 1971, the orchestra musicians and the trustees were in such disarray that it was decided to cease operations. As soon as the board made the announcement, Kansas City mayor Charles B. Wheeler and a number of Philharmonic musicians initiated a campaign to save the orchestra. They promptly raised $55,000 from business and individual contributions; this evidence of community support led to the formation of a new board of governors.

Heading the new board was Marty Nichols, the first woman president of a major orchestra. Through Marty's leadership, a new artistic director, Jorge Mester, music director of the Louisville Symphony and the Aspen Music Festival, was engaged. A $300,000 fund was initiated; miraculously, the Kansas City Philharmonic Orchestra opened its 39th consecutive season on November 9, 1971.

As the enthusiasm of the 1971/72 season continued to build, the orchestra reintroduced a chamber music series at the Nelson-Atkins Museum of Art to standing-room-only crowds, as well as a new series of concerts for young people. In 1976/77, an eastern tour that included performances in New York City's Carnegie Hall and Washington's Kennedy Center brought rave reviews from the *New York Times* music critic, who said that the orchestra "played with the kind of assurance and homogeneity that used to be found only in a few symphonic super groups."

Family, 1960–1970

Just as the Nichols family had entered the decade of the 1950s with the loss of J.C. and his wife, Jessie, so in the early 1960s they experienced another tragedy with the

Marty Nichols (second from left) served as president of the Kansas City Philharmonic—the country's first woman head of a symphony organization. She is shown here with husband Clyde (left), guest singer Roberta Peters, and conductor Jorge Mester in November 1978.

untimely deaths of Eleanor Nichols Allen and her husband Earl. The couple perished February 1961 in a fire at their home. Both of their daughters were attending Northwestern University at the time.

A memorial fountain to the Allens was placed on the Plaza on Nichols Road, a project of their daughters, Suzanne Allen Weber and Mollie Allen Kennedy, along with Eleanor's brothers, Miller and Clyde. Miller selected the fountain group of a seated mother looking down to talk with a child standing on the back of a small turtle in the basin below; three ducks grace the rim of the basin. S. Gemignani was the Florentine artist, and the bronze work was cast in the Marinelli studio and placed on its present site in 1962.

There were also prospering and happy times for the three families. Katie, busy with the activities of her four daughters, found time to pursue favorite hobbies that included gardening, her mah jongg foursome, and golfing with friends. Marty took up painting, horseback riding with daughter Dell, was ladies tennis champion at Mission Hills Country Club, and managed to serve concurrently on three school PTA boards. The 11 grandchildren of J.C. and Jessie Nichols were growing to maturity and enjoying their college years. Eleanor and Earl's two daughters were married in the early 1960s, as were Marty and Clyde's two sons. The four young couples embarked on raising families.

In the sixties, Miller frequently invited the J.C. Nichols Company board and other company colleagues to his Cap-K ranch in Colorado. The latter agree that it was indeed a "working ranch." The meetings were billed as "retreats" or even "vacations," but according to the participants, it was more like a term at a forced labor camp. "Miller worked harder than

anyone else," says Randy Knight. "He would never ask you to do something that he wouldn't do himself."

Bob Boeshaar, an avid fishing enthusiast, remembers devising a system to thwart Miller's fanatic workaholism during one trip to the Cap-K. Miller assigned Boeshaar the task of setting a new row of fence posts at one of the small outlying homesteads. Bob smuggled a fishing rod out to the job site so that he could relax at the edge of the Frying Pan River. When he heard the sound of Miller's pickup, he quickly hid the pole, grabbed the posthole digger, and pretended to be hard at work.

Bob O'Keefe remembers that the only instruction given, prior to board retreats at the ranch, was, "bring blue jeans and leather gloves." He describes a restful day at the Cap-K: "We'd get up at the crack of dawn, move the cattle, scrape manure out of the chicken house, fix the tack hangers,

The Earl and Eleanor Allen Memorial Fountain on the Plaza was a Nichols family gift to the city.

cut and burn brush, have cocktails followed by dinner, and finally sit down to a night meeting of the Board!"

Family and friends alike agree that Miller is never happier than when at the ranch with a daily choice of projects and chores. Fortunately, his wife and daughters also took to life on the Cap-K. There were picnics and camp-outs, the mountains to explore afoot and on horseback, friends to entertain, and lots of family projects.

The Company, 1970–1977

As the 1970s began, the J.C. Nichols Company was moving ahead in all of the new facets of real estate development introduced by Miller during the 1950s and 1960s. Members of the staff, as well as officers at the company, were involved in many levels of community service. Over the years, the company has enjoyed a strong presence in the community. Through the efforts of its employees, there are few civic projects and organizations that have not benefited.

During Dave Jackson's presidency of the company (1973 to 1980), there were almost weekly requests for someone from the J.C. Nichols Company to serve on a community organization board or to join a new civic project. Jackson and John Ruddy both served as president of the Kansas City, Missouri, Real Estate Board. Dave also served as a police commissioner, president of the Kansas City Board of Parks and Recreation, and president of the Starlight Theater Association.

Lynn McCarthy chaired committees for the United Way and served as chapter chairman for the Boys Scouts of America. Clarence Roeder twice chaired the board of Trinity Lutheran Hospital and succeeded Frank Summers on the advisory

board of the Salvation Army. Tony Sweeney, vice-president, long active in Junior Achievement, also served for some years as a governor of the American Royal Association. Mike Shields, assistant-vice-president, served on the board of Planned Parenthood, on the board of Kansas City Tomorrow for the Civic Council, and with the Main Street Development Corporation. Lee Fowler, vice-president, served on the board of Westport Tomorrow and the Coaches Council. Don Dixon, assistant-vice-president, served with Kansas City Consensus, Bill McGugin with the Chamber of Commerce, and Fred Gibson with the Junior Achievement and United Way. John Ruddy and Bob O'Keefe had numerous offices and committee chairs in all of the community real estate boards and organizations.

Over the years, officers and employees of the J.C. Nichols Company have also served on all the local chambers of commerce, the United Way, the American Cancer Society, the Urban Land Institute, numerous Rotary, Optimist, and Kiwanis clubs, the boards of St. Luke's Hospital, Research Medical Center, Shawnee Mission Medical Center, Trinity Lutheran Hospital, the Leukemia Society, and various events benefiting health and social service organizations.

Miller Nichols, invited into the honorary "Man of the Month Club" in the early 1960s, was a charter member of the Civic Council in 1964, a member of the board of regents at Rockhurst College, a director of the Chamber of Commerce, and recipient of its "Mr. Kansas City" award in 1969.[50] He had previously chaired the United Way, Crime Commission, and UMKC Trustees.

In 1970, Miller received the Chancellor's Medal from the University of

Missouri at Kansas City for his "distinguished contributions to the aesthetic, cultural, economic and educational development of the community." And in that year he was also elected "Kansas City Realtor of the Year" by the directors of the Kansas City Real Estate Board. He later served as regional vice-president for the National Institute of Real Estate Brokers. Active on the board of governors of the Midwest Research Institute for many years, he chaired its building committee and served as vice-chairman.

Like his father before him, Miller played a major role in assuring the success of the city's major bond drives in the late 1960s and early 1970s. These drives gave Kansas City its unique dual stadiums at the Truman sports complex and its equally unique international airport (KCI).

At the time of the campaign for the sports complex, Dutton Brookfield was president of the Chamber of Commerce. Dave Jackson was co-chairman of the committee appointed to come up with a bond program for Jackson County that would include the sports complex. In addition to passing a county vote, Mayor Ike Davis recognized the need for a full city endorsement, which he promptly issued. As finance chairmen, Dutton and Miller were very persuasive; George Powell, Sr., the overall chairman, was greatly respected across the community. The vote was close, but it passed.

In the case of KCI, Miller, as finance chairman, was charged with raising the funds to mount a campaign that would get the bonds passed. He worked with three women appointed by Mayor Davis: Anita Gorman, Jean Green, and Suzanne Statland. Davis credits Anita Gorman with the idea of bringing two passenger jet planes to Kansas City and putting them

out on the single air strip at the proposed site. Few people had flown in a passenger jet in the early 1970s. It was thought, optimistically, that perhaps 10,000 people would brave the frigid weather. Some 150,000 showed up, completely blocking all roads. The bond issue passed with a 96 percent majority, the highest in the city's history.

For a cause he considers legitimate, Miller has no qualms about making personal appeals for financial assistance. He has said, "When you ask people to contribute money, not for yourself but for the good of the community, you can ask for any amount and not worry that you will be criticized. You offer them the opportunity to participate."

Anita Gorman continues: "Miller always raised the money; that's where I learned about fund raising. He would get a group together, sit down, and say, 'Now here's what we have to do.' It was always very well organized and nobody ever turned him down. He would simply hand out 3x5 card assignments to those present, and you didn't mind this because everyone knew he had already done a lot more than he was asking of you. On new projects we came to take it for granted that Miller would be raising the money and everyone knew it would work."

Miller was instrumental in getting Davis, an extremely popular and effective mayor, to run for a second term in 1968. Davis, ready to depart for a European trip, told Miller he wasn't interested. "Ike," said Miller, "we really need you for another term. I'm willing to guarantee that if you'll run, you won't have to raise a cent. I'll take charge of fund-raising and you won't need to ask what's in the bank. Just spend whatever you think you should." On his return, Ike agreed to run. Taking Miller at his word, he never asked about funds; when the election was over, Miller still had $65,000 in campaign funds in the bank.

Residential Development, 1970–1977

During the decade of the 1970s, residential development continued apace. Verona Gardens, to the north of the new Barstow School campus, was opened in 1972; that year Corinth Downs was also established.

These luxury townhouse condominiums in a garden setting extended along Mission Road from 79th to 83rd Streets and introduced a new residential concept to Kansas City. The site was the old Herbert Woolf farm, which the J.C. Nichols Company had bought in 1955 after Mr. Woolf retired his racing colors and retired from horse breeding as well. (1955 was the year that Lawrin, Woolf's 1938 Kentucky Derby winner, died and was buried beside his sire, Insco, who had also sired a triple crown winner.) The Corinth shops had already been built on the site of Mr. Woolf's five furlong track. The new Corinth Downs condominiums came to occupy the farm site where, in the interim, the farm barn had served as a community theater and art gallery and the manager's home as a Montessori School.

Instead of laying out the new development with a traditional subdivision plan, Miller suggested the company should try something new. Most of his associates disagreed; John Ruddy, who was in charge of residential development, objected strenuously. The Woolf farm was a prime piece of real estate; the company had held it for twenty years waiting for the appropriate time to develop it. But Miller believed there was an untapped market for luxury garden townhouse condominium homes which individual owners could design within the framework of a master plan.

Miller thought this kind of residential neighborhood would create its own additional value over the single-family house arrangement, while incorporating a higher and hence more profitable density. The limited access in the plan introduced elements of security, while the full exterior maintenance freed the homeowner of cares when he wanted to be away. The company set out to try the concept.

Corinth Downs was laid out in four residential courts with several cul-de-sacs and just two entrances. Compton Court, the first, was an interior court built around a central terrace with swimming pool. Exterior architecture varied from one court to another. For each court there were several basic residential plans, and within these the owner could adapt the interior space and walled patio to suit a particular life-style. Guardian Management assumed responsibility for the care of the area—the landscaping, snow removal, and other services.

Compton Court, the first, was designed in Williamsburg-style and marketed by J.C. Nichols Company real estate salesmen. Despite Miller's enthusiasm, initial sales were very slow; only six sold in the first three years. In 1973, Miller decided that it would be a good idea for a single salesman to be responsible for marketing Corinth Downs, and he named Jim Nicholson. Nicholson says he spent a very quiet year-and-a-half showing the first 24 condominiums that had been built and listening to people's comments. Their main complaint was the fact that the middle units opened only to the east and west; only the two units on the end had a third exposure. The older clientele didn't like the lack of a downstairs bedroom; they wanted to live comfortably on the first floor, with the upstairs bedrooms available for guests and grandchildren.

Jim recommended these and other changes to the company, which went back to the drawing board and developed new floor plans for the remaining units around Compton Court as well as for the other courts to follow. Once it took off, Corinth Downs became one of the most successful projects the company had ever put together. In 1973, a lot was bringing $17,000 to $20,000 depending on location. Eleven years later, in 1984, the last lot was sold for a free-standing unit, at $170,000.

The Alameda Plaza Hotel

Construction of the Alameda Plaza Hotel was delayed by lengthy labor strikes. Miller felt that such costly interruptions were a real handicap to development in the city. He assigned Clarence Roeder to work to bring the Associated Builders and Contractors National Association to Kansas City. This was accomplished in 1971. The association was allowed by law to bid on jobs using a two-gate operation whereby the non-union contractors on a job would enter and exit by a second gate. While this was not a pleasant working arrangement, it provided that no one could be shut off from a job just because they were non-union. Miller hoped it would bring the construction unions into a more amicable working relationship.

In 1972, four years after construction had begun, the Alameda Plaza opened for business. During the delays, Gilbert-Robinson bowed out of the hotel business and the Nichols Company acquired ownership and management of both the Alameda Plaza and their Raphael Hotel in San Francisco. Phil Pistilli became president of the company's new hotel division.

Miller now turned his attention to the aesthetics of the hotel grounds. To grace the front of the hotel as viewed from the Plaza, he had in mind a waterfall fountain adorned by a group of sculptured figures such as the one made by the Bromsgrove Guild for Moreton Hall in Warwickshire. This fountain had been offered for sale in the 1950s. Through Mr. Whewell of Bromsgrove, Miller had tried unsuccessfully to negotiate for its purchase for nearly a decade. So, once more, he hired Bernard Zuckermann, this time to reproduce the "Diana" figures in a suitable arrangement for the waterfall fountain.

The resulting tableau has become another Plaza landmark. The popular fountain turns blue when the Kansas City Royals baseball team competes in a national championship and green on St. Patrick's Day. The surrounding flowers are changed seasonally as well.

To the west, next to the hotel, Miller selected "The Wagon Master," another popular piece of sculpture, which was formally dedicated in 1973. A sound system set into the boulders on which it stands dramatically recreates the historical adventure that it represents. "The Wagon Master" depicts a Santa Fe Trail wagon train leader on horseback, surrounded by pampas grasses. Standing ten feet tall, it pays tribute to the courageous settlers who journeyed west by prairie schooner.

The statue was originally intended for a location at 10th and Main Streets. Some downtown business people had talked to Miller about finding a piece for that location. He got in touch with L.E. "Gus" Shaffer, who gave him some ideas and made up a very small model for committee consideration. Members of the Chamber of Commerce and the Downtown Committee rejected his design, saying that they didn't want Western art. But Miller loved it.

He told Shaffer that the J.C. Nichols Company would be interested in the piece if he would do it again with the man and the horse facing to the right; the work was cast in Italy.

"We wanted the Alameda Plaza to be a profitable undertaking, but we also wanted it to be a warm, intimate hotel," says Dave Jackson. Operating results suggest that they succeeded. By the time the Re-

publican National Convention met in Kansas City in 1976, the Alameda Plaza had a nationwide reputation, acquired not with promotional dollars, but with attention to sound principles of innkeeping. The hotel has been awarded a Five Diamonds rating by the AAA for 13 consecutive years. In 1974, the operating income from the hotel constituted 40 percent of the J.C. Nichols Company's operating income.

According to Dave Jackson, one of the reasons for the hotel's success was that, in addition to attracting more upscale clientele to the Plaza, it catered to locals as

The construction and operation of a first-class luxury hotel on the Plaza was a complete departure for the J.C. Nichols Company, although J.C. had discussed the possibility at one time. Dave Jackson and Miller began planning the Alameda Plaza Hotel in 1968, and it was completed four years later. The Alameda became an immediate success and proved extremely profitable. Today it is the Ritz-Carlton.

The "Wagon Master" depicts a Santa Fe Trail wagon train leader heading west. This work of L.E. "Gus" Shaffer sits on Ward Parkway below the Ritz-Carlton Hotel where children can punch a button and hear about this historic adventure.

well. The Country Club Plaza's village atmosphere in an urban setting is one of
Kansas City's most important draws for
visitors. It is the number two tourist attraction in the state of Missouri. The
importance of the Plaza to Kansas City's
convention industry can't be overstated.
But also, the Alameda Plaza became the
preferred meeting place of Kansas City.

However, everything did not always go
as the J.C. Nichols Company wished. Jack
Fox, whose position in the commercial
properties division of the company gave
him responsibility for the Brookside Shopping Center in the 1970s, cites an instance when the J.C. Nichols Company
was forced to relinquish an objective.
Years before, the company had sold the
city an attractive, Tudor-styled building on
63rd Street east of Brookside Boulevard for
use as joint fire and police station. By the
1970s, the company had decided that the
Brookside shops needed more parking, and
since the building no longer served as a
station, they planned to buy it back, demolish it, and build a parking lot. The
public was united in its opposition to the
plan, one man going so far as to describe
the demolition of the building as "knocking the front teeth out of the area's
beautiful smile."

One snowy Christmas Eve morning Jack
received a phone call from Miller asking
him to round up a person from public
relations and meet him at his house to
discuss strategy. The three of them agreed
that a public relations campaign could
probably convince the public to support
their purchase of the building. But they
were wrong. In the end, the city retained
ownership of the structure, which presently houses a bank.

The Plaza post office is another case in
point. The post office needed to double its
size, but the Nichols Company had tenants on either side of its Ward Parkway
location and was unable to accommodate
the request. The postal service suggested
that they simply remove the other tenants,
but Miller declined, pointing out that
shops make the Plaza. Moreover, there was
no parking space for a large fleet of postal
vehicles. He agreed to give the post office
a new five-year lease during which time
they were asked to find an alternate location.

As the five-year period drew to a close,
with the post office no closer to seeking
out a new location, Miller took it upon
himself to find an alternate site. He did so,
a few blocks to the east on Oak, just south
of 47th Street. Postal officials were not
interested. And so, when it finally came
time to vacate the premises in 1978, there
was a large public outcry. A dozen articles
appeared in the *Kansas City Star and Times*
claiming that the Nichols Company had
taken away a basic service, the post office;
the paper simply chose not to print the
full account.[51]

As the Country Club Plaza grew and
evolved, more parking space was needed
for shops and offices. The large, partially
sunken, aesthetically designed open parking lots that were a distinctive feature of
the early Plaza gave way to more costly
multi-level parking structures. As Miller
put it, the company's real estate decisions
are often driven by parking considerations.
Bob Boeshaar emphasizes that the company has never balked at paying the
hundreds of thousands of dollars necessary
for preventive maintenance and safety of
parking facilities. "Although the funds
were sometimes earmarked for other
projects, Management realizes that the future of the Plaza depends on parking."

Fred Gibson likes to cite examples of
how ongoing research has helped form

specific design features for parking lots. For example, it was discovered over time that if the cross-slope of a lot exceeded 5 percent, it wasn't comfortable for a woman driver to open her uphill door. Accordingly, parking stall designs had to be changed. Also, certain drivers habitually park their cars either to the right side or the left side of a parking stall, resulting in annoying crowding and inconvenience for the adjacent car. So the company began separating stalls with a double line to provide a buffer zone. Many drivers tend to back straight out of a parking stall before turning their wheels (in contrast to those who turn while backing). So the company increased clearance between stall rows to 65 feet.

Gibson says, "I remember on several occasions talking to architects hired to work on one of our newer developments. They argued that architectural manuals prescribe only 55 feet between stall rows, to which we answered simply that the J.C. Nichols Company has its own set of standards."

Seville Square

Sears' Plaza store, its first suburban store, was redundant by the mid-1970s. Not only had Sears built three larger suburban stores on different sides of the city in the interim, but the Plaza's clientele had become increasingly upscale. Sears decided to sell. Upon learning this, Miller immediately set off for Dallas with Dave Jackson, a check in his pocket for the down payment. Sure enough, the deal was concluded before his return.

Considerable discussion followed as to the best use for the large structure. The concept finally adopted, to be known as Seville Square, was to put a four-story atrium up the center of the Sears building

and to surround this with a variety of small shops and a few specialty restaurants.

Ralph Myers, of Kivett and Myers, was the architect. The exterior would have a four-story glass enclosure with elevator at the southeast corner of the building. Architect for the interior was Norwood Oliver from New York. Myers and Oliver traveled to Mexico to select the appropriate Spanish-style architectural appointments. Special events were planned that would be celebrated seasonally throughout the year; in the spring of 1977, just a few months before the flood, Seville Square opened with a flourish; Plaza customers were delighted to have yet another new shopping concept on the Plaza.

The Family

Between 1960 and 1977, J.C. Nichols' grandchildren grew to adulthood. Their parents had remained in Kansas City, but in this next generation, eight of the eleven grandchildren scattered across the western half of the country. All are college graduates enjoying a wide spectrum of professions and avocations; eight of the eleven started families of their own during these years.

The year 1977 was a difficult one. In January 1977, Miller lost his wife of 35 years, Catherine Caldwell Nichols. The family rallied around Miller and his four daughters, including the Kanes of Bartlesville, the descendants of Jessie Miller Nichols' sister who had married J.C.'s college roommate, John Kane.

Miller established a memorial to Katie—a fund for the purchase of real estate as needed by the Sunset Hill School. The J.C. Nichols Company presented a lovely fountain, which was placed in a courtyard landscaped by the alumnae and named in her honor.

The 1977 Flood

The J.C. Nichols Company's greatest disaster occurred in the wake of what was termed a "500-year" flood. Torrential rains fell one September night, sending the waters of Brush Creek rampaging over its banks and damaging over half the Plaza's buildings. Water reached as high as six feet in the J.C. Nichols Company offices and flooded the lower tier of safety deposit boxes at the Commerce Plaza Bank. Many retail stores were a total loss. The cost to the Nichols Company to repair the buildings was approximately $10 million. Several hundred cars were swept away, and 25 people lost their lives.

The next morning, from the vantage point of a nearby hill, Miller surveyed the damage. "We just have to get to work and get things cleaned up and pumped out," he said. Bob Boeshaar says he felt sick to his stomach as he and Miller scanned the blocks of damaged shops and stores and watched as, suddenly, with a lurid eruption of flame, Eddy's Loaf and Stein restaurant caught fire, most likely from a gas leak.

The level of company commitment and employee loyalty during the cleanup effort was remarkable, Bob remembers. "People pitched in and company crews worked around the clock." Fred Gibson's crew had the herculean task of pumping out the vast underground parking areas. Barbara Barickman had the huge task of ordering

Torrential rains in September 1977 caused Brush Creek to overflow its banks and flood the Country Club Plaza with several feet of water. It was the greatest disaster in the J.C. Nichols Company's history—twenty-five people lost their lives and hundreds of cars were swept away. Company crews worked around the clock, the public pitched in, and many shops were back in business for the Christmas season. More extensive restoration and repairs were completed the following year.

650 Big Macs and distributing them to the volunteer citizenry on the Plaza. Company employees remember Miller in his shirt-sleeves, manning the pumps day and night at the Halls building. When asked how he could stand the night chill in only a shirt, he answered, "I've got my mind on something else!"

The tenants had faith, and the company didn't let them down. The response from the public was astounding. Contractors donated pumps and trucks. Ordinary citizens wanted so badly to help that they wouldn't leave the area. Miraculously, the outdoor mud and debris was sufficiently cleared away to enable the Plaza Art Fair to occur on schedule—only 10 days after the flood!

Plaza merchants were primarily Kansas City people who didn't have to check with corporate superiors to determine how to respond to the situation. In spite of the overwhelming amount of cleanup and inventory restocking necessitated by the flood, they decided, almost to a person, to keep their businesses on the Plaza. Showing invincible spirit and resilience, some tenants welcomed the opportunity to redesign their floor plans and merchandise displays, updating and upgrading their shops as they refurbished.

Despite finding an automobile halfway through the front show window of its beauty salon when the waters receded, Salon Klaus was the first to reopen, just a week after one Kansas City newspaper had prematurely printed the headline, "Plaza is Gone."

Work continued unabated through the fall months; many stores whose interiors had been ruined by silt and high water were back in business for the important

The Plaza lights are on!

232

Thanksgiving-to-Christmas shopping season. Major reconstruction requiring structural repair was concluded the following year. Miller recalls that just prior to the flood the company had purchased the Phillips family holdings at the southwest corner of the Plaza. Some of these marginal tenants did not rebuild, which gave the company an opportunity to bring some new shops to the Plaza. On Thanksgiving night, the Christmas lights came on with the traditional ceremony, then nearing its fiftieth year. For the more than 100,000 people gathered on the Plaza, it was truly a poignant moment.

Chapter 9

1978 - 1994

The year 1978 marked many new beginnings for Miller Nichols. The previous year, he had suffered the loss of his wife, Katie, followed by the disastrous September flood. Now, professionally, he began to direct the attention of the J.C. Nichols Company toward renewing the Country Club Plaza and to developing new opportunities for residential and commercial building.

On the evening of March 7, 1978, a special event took place. The setting was the Alameda Plaza Hotel. Arthur Mag of Stinson, Mag, and Fizzell, along with Bob Gaynor, regional head of AT&T, planned a surprise evening in honor of Miller. "'One man with courage makes a majority,'" said Mag in his opening remarks. "We think this quote by Andrew Jackson exemplifies Miller Nichols. We have brought together a group of mutual friends who agree that society should recognize a person who makes contributions both to the business world and to the community—consistently, persistently, without fanfare and with courage."

The list of friends at this gathering included Dutton Brookfield, Tom Deacy, Joe Gregg, Jim Kemper, Don Hall, Dave Jackson, James Olson, Charles Kimball, Bob Long, Milt McGreevy, Jack Morgan, George Powell, Dr. David Robinson, John Ruddy, Jerry Scott, Don Smith, Father Van Ackeran, and Ike Davis.

The year 1978 was also a time when Miller focused his energies on the national political scene. Like his father before him, he had had serious problems with local construction unions, particularly during the building of the Alameda Plaza Hotel. He regretted seeing many long-time downtown Kansas City businesses moving south into Johnson County during the 1970s. And he was keenly aware of the new firms being attracted to Kansas rather than to the core city or its industrial parks.

Miller concluded that lack of a "Right to Work" law was a significant factor. Kansas has a Right to Work law without mandatory union membership and attendant high scale union contracts. Working again with his dynamic sidekick Dutton Brookfield and Kansan Reed Larson, head of the National Right to Work Committee in Washington, D.C., Miller organized a state committee and worked tirelessly to fund its efforts, speaking on the subject before civic groups.

Many Missourians recognized the need for a Right to Work law. As polls began to show that voters favored it, the national unions undertook to fund opposition to the proposed law. In the last few weeks before the August 1978 vote, *Time* magazine noted this in an article describing Miller's role. The unions reportedly poured some $10 million into the Missouri effort, with union members posted outside grocery stores in all sections of the city and state, handing out literature and bumper stickers proclaiming "Right to Work is a Rip-Off," and "Right to Work Means Back to the Minimum Wage."

At this time, Miller was building a condominium home at the top of Corinth Downs. He was also courting Jeannette Deweese, a widow who lived next door to his brother, Clyde. (They were married in March 1979.) On those evenings when Miller wanted to stop by the house to see how construction was coming along, Jeannette wondered why they were always stopped by a policeman. Miller explained, "Well, we have had quite a bit of vandalism up here, so we need security." Some time later, Jeannette learned that there had been threats on Miller's life.

As hard as Miller and Dutton worked statewide, they could not raise money fast enough to counteract the media blitz of false information the unions were putting out. The Right to Work proposal for Missouri was soundly defeated. Undaunted, Miller looked for another type of enabling legislation that would make redevelopment within the core of Kansas City more attractive. He was also saddened by the loss of his long-time conservative activist cohort, Dutton Brookfield, in a tragic residential fire.

Miller's new pro-development cause became "tax increment financing"—a substitute for tax abatement in which the city does not lose the tax revenue it has been receiving before a redevelopment but receives increased new tax revenues on improvements and buildings beginning as soon as the cost of demolition and other site preparation has been recouped by the developer. Miller's associate in this endeavor was Mike White, a one-term Democratic County Executive and a senior partner in the law firm of Polsinelli,

White, Vardeman, & Shalton. It took the full decade of the 1980s before appropriate legislation and trial challenges in the courts made "tax increment financing" fully available.

During the 1980s, Miller spent considerable time in Washington, D.C., as J.C. had done, working for national causes. Much of his effort went to the Right to Work Committee, which was challenging in the courts the right of national unions to use individual compulsory dues to support the unions' political activity and choice of candidates. Miller endorsed and solicited aid for the committee, whose position was that a union's use of membership dues for political action denies a person's civil rights unless that member has voluntarily contributed the money. Analysts credit the public attention given this court battle with being a factor in the substantial decline of union membership over the decade.

A significant new addition to the national political scene at this time were the private PACs (political action committees), the counterparts of the PACs of the national labor unions. Miller believed that a private citizen, contributing voluntarily to these new PACs, could have a political voice similar to that with which the unions had established their political clout by charging compulsory membership dues. One private PAC with which he worked was the NCPAC (National Conservative Political Action Committee). Its goal in the 1980 campaign was to defeat those five senators who most often took positions and sponsored legislation harmful to the free-enterprise economy.

On one visit to Washington, Miller was asked to look at the NCPAC list and decide if he would be willing to raise the committee's budget to defeat one of them. Miller agreed and chose George

McGovern. To his surprise, he and Jeannette were then given the job of recruiting conservative South Dakota congressman Jim Abnor, whom they believed would be a strong challenger. Before Abnor would consider challenging McGovern, however, he requested that a poll be conducted that would compare his voting record on a dozen issues with that of McGovern, one that would show who best represented the views of the South Dakota constituency. At that time, George McGovern was a folk hero in South Dakota, the only native to have been nominated for the presidency, and local media had not portrayed him as a liberal. The poll would tell this story. Miller raised funds for the poll; when the results favored Abnor, he agreed to run. George McGovern was defeated.

Throughout the 1980s, Miller continued his involvement with Republican Senate and House support groups. Pete du Pont, former congressman and twice governor of Delaware, founded GOPAC (Grand

During the 1980s, Miller spent considerable time in Washington, D.C., working for national causes. Here he and Jeannette are guests of President Ronald Reagan at the White House.

Old Party's PAC) in the early 1980s. Du Pont was concerned that House of Representative members were not adequately representing their constituencies. Local polling had indicated a conservative viewpoint in many districts, a viewpoint voted at the presidential election level but not in the home congressional district. The reason, du Pont believed, was a lack of qualified conservative candidates. It was his thesis that the Republican Party must seek out, counsel, and help elect qualified candidates at the city, county, and state levels, thus in time qualifying them to run for Congress when Democratic congressmen retired or appeared vulnerable to challenge.

Also during the early 1980s, Miller became involved with the National Taxpayers' Union, headed by James Davidson, whose basic agenda had been to pass a balanced budget amendment to the Constitution. Miller and Jeannette became acquainted with Davidson when he came to Kansas City to work on passage of a Missouri resolution to this effect. After a year and a half of strenuous efforts, Missouri became the 32nd state to adopt the resolution. Thirty-four states are needed to require congressional action, and Miller has continued to support this effort.

The Nichols family trips to Washington often included several agendas. Jeannette Nichols, representing the state of Kansas, was appointed to the President's Advisory Council on the Arts at Kennedy Center in 1982 and served in this capacity until 1989. In 1985, she chaired a ten-day "Imagination Celebration," assisted by Kennedy Center staff, showcasing the arts programming available to Kansas City children and youth. Clyde Nichols, Jr., continued his national activity with the National Council on Economic Education, which he has sought to fund at the state and local level while continuing to serve on the national board. He spoke on this topic at the 1990 annual meeting of the Urban Land Institute.

The Charitable Trust

In the late 1970s, assessment was made of the company's civic commitments and it was decided to draw down the J.C. Nichols Company Charitable Trust in order to honor all company pledges and to continue ongoing support of community services. And with the breadth of company involvement in the community, this commands considerable company time as well as resources—from Fair Share participation in the United Way to support of Bryant School.

The involvement of the company, as well as its individual employees, in community affairs has been an important goal because the company relies so heavily on the community for its support. But it is more than that, says Miller: "We want to employ people who want to be a part of the community and we need to know a constant effort is being made to improve the community." He is quick to point out, "as the community goes, so goes the Nichols Company."

Evolving Management of the Company

In 1980, Dave Jackson retired as president of the J.C. Nichols Company. He was succeeded by Lynn McCarthy, who had been with the company since 1958. Lynn states:

> I agree with Miller's philosophy that those who work hard are a little better than those who don't. I worked with Miller on Saturdays and Sun-

days. We worked damn hard, probably too hard. He delegated responsibilities very generously, and expected and demanded performance.

> Although Miller was obviously interested in the whole company, he and Dave Jackson were involved primarily with the commercial end of the business, especially the Plaza. John Ruddy shepherded the Real Estate Sales Department and the rest of the responsibility for the company was on my desk. Everyone who has ever been involved with this company has known the value of hard work. Growth has happened because we had good people. I think that recent retirees and the guys my age who are looking back are proud and pleased with what they accomplished.

Miller's eldest daughter, Kay Callison, who worked for eight years in the company's apartment management division as assistant manager of the Georgetown Apartments and later as director of leasing for the Villa Medici Apartments, joined the board in 1982. Replacing retiring Bob O'Keefe, whose board service spanned 25 years, she is presently the only woman serving on the board of directors.

Kay's comments reveal that the independent streak of the Nichols family is alive and well: "Someone resigned from the board. Dad discussed the situation with the Executive Committee and asked me to take the vacant position. I told him, 'Dad, I need a day or two to think about this. I'll get back to you. It's a big commitment and I consider it a serious decision.' When I called him to accept, I cautioned him that I might have a viewpoint different from his and hoped that he could accept that. I don't know if he accepts it all the time, but I believe it's important to express our differences at the board level. I have to be free to ask questions and express my viewpoint. Why else am I there?"

Kay wants to see the company continue its activity in the volunteer sector of the community. She notes that her grandfather had, and her father has, a tremendous sense of community, which they successfully structured into each subdivision through the creation and support of the concept of homes associations. She cites the company's Christmas-in-August program of home renovation for the needy and its involvement as a "business partner in education" to the Bryant Elementary School as recent examples of its ongoing commitment to the volunteer sector. Hav-

ing "adopted" Bryant School at 57th and Wornall, the J.C. Nichols Company is very active in sharing ideas with the administrative staff and in supporting enrichment activities. "The company can't stay in the closet," Kay asserts. "This kind of involvement in the community is important for public relations."

Lynn McCarthy continues: "Although the Plaza became a primary focus of the company's evolutionary concept during the latter years of Miller's tenure, our residential developments have been and continue as a very important part of this city. We began as a planner and developer of residential communities. Providing those homes and neighborhoods has influenced more people's lives than the Plaza

Top management of the J.C. Nichols Company changed again in 1980, as Lynn McCarthy (right) succeeded retiring Dave Jackson. Miller (left) retired as chairman of the board in 1988, remaining a director and member of the executive committee but devoting much of his time to civic endeavors and other real estate interests.

ever will. Our company has developed over 9,000 acres at an average of three families per acre. We have put a lot of people into homes. J.C. always emphasized the stabilizing impact of home ownership upon society. The J.C. Nichols Company has made a significant contribution to Kansas City in this area."

Over the years, the J.C. Nichols Company has been criticized by individuals and groups interested in low-income housing, claiming that the company's focus on upscale neighborhoods has not benefited Kansas City's poor residents. McCarthy answers these critics by stating: "The laws of real estate suggest that when you add a unit of housing to the market, no matter how expensive, it frees up a unit some place else. Eventually it trickles down and affects the availability of lower income housing. Building a $500,000 home is just as important as constructing a $20,000 unit."

The Country Club Plaza

In the J.C. Nichols Company offices on the Country Club Plaza the immediate post-flood years of 1978 and 1979 were a time for reevaluation of the threat of future floods. Today there is much less open undeveloped land to absorb heavy deluges of rain, and hence there is faster and heavier run-off, leading to possible flooding. Following lengthy consultation with the Corps of Engineers, plans got under way to replace the Wornall Road Bridge, which had acted as a dam with a hole in it during the 1977 flood.[52]

As the Plaza was rebuilt, refurbished, and in some instances re-leased, increasing attention was focused on J.C. Nichols Company market studies as well as national forecasts of trends for retailing in the 1980s. From these, Miller, Dave Jackson, Tony Sweeney, Mike Shields, and others recognized an opportunity to bring to the Country Club Plaza nationally prominent specialty stores that had heretofore operated exclusively in one or a very few large cities.

In 1979 Saks Fifth Avenue announced that it would build a store on the Plaza. There had been local speculation about the possibility of Saks or Nieman Marcus coming to the Plaza one day. And, in point of fact, Nieman Marcus had the first option on the one site the company considered feasible for a sizable new store. However, other priorities caused them to allow the option to lapse.[53] It was recognized that Saks would not undertake the building of a major store without extensive demographic and economic analyses. Hence, when they chose the Plaza as a suitable location, other "national retailers had their eyes opened," Dave Jackson declared. "The arrival of Saks focused attention on the Plaza and generated a tremendous amount of broad retail interest."

As expected, Plaza customers were delighted and excited; however, there were also a few who didn't want to give up their 1950s Woolworth's dime store or the bowling alley. A similar response came from some when the J.C. Nichols Company announced its intention to move the adjacent full-line grocery store, George Muehlbach and Company. Grocer Robert J. Muehlbach was impressed, however, with the company's long-range planning. He was told five years before his lease expired that his grocery store would be relocated within the Plaza and that he should offer more gourmet foods. "The Nichols Company people know what is going to happen ten years down the road," says Muehlbach. "That's one reason why they are so successful."

A changing pattern of tenants was the retail story of the 1980s, not only on the Plaza, but in other Nichols' neighborhood centers as well. Crestwood, for example, largely moved away from neighborhood services into handsome specialty antique, gift, and interior decorating shops. Prairie Village added upscale specialty fashion boutiques, furs, a gourmet cheese shop, decorative gifts, and home accessories to its mix of grocery store, drug store, and expanded department store. It was also given a Colonial-style updating that features a brick clock tower. The Corinth and Red Bridge Shopping Centers were both expanded to add new specialty stores and specialty services as well, and a new group of shops reflected the residential move southwestward as Shannon Valley on College Boulevard was opened in the mid-1980s.

New retail trends were most noteworthy and observable on the Country Club Plaza. The company's market research indicated that premier nationally known stores, be they large or specialty boutiques, were going to move beyond New York, Chicago, and Los Angeles. The company knew that if it could convince them that Kansas City was a viable market, they would choose a Plaza location for their shop or store.

The J.C. Nichols Company was challenged, however, in recommending particular locations for these new shops because, unlike the new shopping malls, it could not build space to their requested requirements. Rather, the company had to convince these premier retailers to adapt to space that could be made available for them in the buildings presently on the Country Club Plaza. The company was remarkably successful.

Vice-president Mike Shields, who has overseen Plaza leasing for more than a decade, was largely responsible for shepherding this transition. "Having the ability to match some of the most exciting and successful retailers in the country with the most beautiful and original shopping center has been a very enjoyable as well as a challenging opportunity," says Mike.

In 1994, the list included Abercrombie & Fitch, Laura Ashley, Banana Republic, Barnes & Noble, Bennetton, The Body Shop, Brooks Brothers, Coach Stores, Crabtree & Evelyn, Eddie Bauer, F.A.O. Schwartz, First Issue, The Gap, Gucci, The Limited, Mark Shale, Mondi, The Nature Company, Overland Sheepskin, Polo/Ralph Lauren, Saks Fifth Avenue, Scandia Down, The Sharper Image, Ann Taylor, and Williams & Sonoma. But, as company men frequently point out, it is also the special and unique local shops and stores such as the Absolute Florist, Asiatica, Bennett Schneider, Catch Kansas City, Complements, Connoisseur, The Fireside, Function Junction, Grandeur Gardens, Hall's, Jack Henry, Kaplans, Maxims, Nicholas Luggage, Panache, St. Crispin Leather, Superlatives, Taum Sauk, Toscano, and Tivols—together with the art galleries and some thirty restaurants—that make shopping on the Plaza an enticing experience. These Kansas City merchants, most with a single store, create the Plaza's unique ambience.

In the early 1990s, significant updating was done by national retailers who, at considerable expense, gutted the interior of older Plaza buildings and completely redesigned the space. The Limited was the first to do so, converting the original Harzfeld's store into three handsome shops—The Limited, Limited Express, and The Body Works. The Gap similarly renovated the former Duvall space, Eddie Bauer completely overhauled the former Woolf Brothers store, and Mark Shale extensively redesigned the former Swansons building.

Barnes & Noble constructed a three-story atrium for its new bookstore in the former Dillards space. F.A.O. Schwartz's beautiful redesign of Hall's Plaza store delights local customers and out-of-town browsers as well. This architectural updating helps keep the Plaza abreast of the times and responsive to today's market.

Plaza Beautification

Coincidental with the decision to court nationally prominent specialty shops during the 1980s was increased attention to beautification. Miller felt that it was time for more professionalism in the planning for landscaping and flowers on the Plaza and time to develop an annual master plan for seasonal changes with the introduction of new plantings and color from year to year. He felt that someone should give the Plaza landscaping a weekly inspection, noting where shrubs needed to be pruned or replaced, where flowers required extra care, or where additional flowers could add color and charm.

Betty Goodwin, a talented horticulturist, was engaged for the task. Miller comments, "The increased flowering of the Plaza with changing seasonal patterns has not only heightened local appreciation and pleasure but has greatly diminished vandalism. It's the little touches that really make a difference."

A noteworthy example of planned flowering appeared with the new Wornall Road Bridge. The city had promptly recognized that the old bridge had contributed to the 1977 flood damage and announced that the bridge would be replaced. As this bridge is a gateway to the Plaza from the Country Club District's residential neighborhoods, Miller, with

board approval, proposed that the company act as partner with the city.

The company asked the city to allow it to hire an architect to draw up plans for a handsome rather than just a utilitarian bridge, a bridge that would complement and enhance the beauty of the Plaza. Miller suggested that the difference between this and the cost of a purely utilitarian bridge be paid for by the company, which the city cheerfully agreed to. It took some time for the Corps of Engineers to complete its study of the kind of bridge that should be designed, but in the early spring of 1980 construction got under way.

In the meantime, in May of 1979, Miller had made a gift to Kansas City of a heroic statue of Wampanoag Sacham (chief) Massasoit, the work of Cyrus Edwin Dallin who also sculpted the "Indian Scout" in Penn Valley Park. A duplicate casting of this heroic "Massasoit" stands at Plymouth Rock. The availability of this one was brought to Miller's attention by the Fenn Gallery in Santa Fe. Miller purchased it without a firm idea of where it might be placed. At the suggestion of former mayor Ike Davis's wife, Bea, he decided on a location on the southeast corner of 47th Street and J.C. Nichols Parkway. (Because of the Brush Creek flood control project, a new site will be selected.)

In the summer of 1980 with the construction of the bridge well along, the Nichols took a motoring trip north to Michigan to visit friends. They drove across southern Canada, before dropping down into Maine and Connecticut. When they crossed over the lovely flowering bridge at Petosky, Michigan, Miller was reminded of the flowering bridges he admired in Europe. "We've got to have flowers on that Wornall Road Bridge," he said to Jeannette. At a luncheon stop,

Miller called Kansas City and asked that company architects incorporate this feature into their plans.

Continuing across Canada, Miller admired the variety of bronze statuary placed in little parklets along the route, often the gift of local Rotary clubs who landscaped and maintained them. "If we are going to have a really handsome bridge, I think we should have a piece of sculpture," he declared. That evening he called Kansas City again.

In Connecticut a week or so later, Miller received new plans that showed how the bridge could be embellished with flowers and sculpture and how the southwest corner could be modified to accommodate a patio setting for a work of art. Having envisioned flowering boxes that would trail over the sides of the bridge, he was rather surprised at the new design, which featured enclosed flower boxes

along the walkways of the bridge, the better for pedestrians to enjoy.[54]

Back in Kansas City, Miller pondered what kind of sculpture would suit the site. One day while Miller's mouth was filled with cotton, his Plaza dentist, Dr. Joe Jacobs, asked, "What are you going to do with that patio on the bridge down there?" When Miller couldn't reply, the dentist proceeded to tell him of British sculptor Oscar Nemon, a long-time friend, whose studio was in St. James's Palace in London. Nemon dreamed of creating an heroic-sized sculpture of the only work that Winston Churchill himself had commissioned. Entitled "A Tribute to Married Love," it is a small, seated bronze portrait of himself and Lady Churchill created for Blenheim Palace. Nemon's dream was to have two heroic-sized castings made, one to be placed in the states and one to be placed in England, to commemorate

The handsome new Wornall Road Bridge, "gateway to the Plaza," displays lovely seasonal flowers.

Churchill's British-American heritage. "We ought to have the American work right here in Kansas City on the Wornall Road bridge," Jacobs said as he removed the cotton from Miller's mouth.

Oscar Nemon was invited to Kansas City as a guest of the Nichols. He was a small man, about five-feet-four-inches tall, slender and frail for one who turned out heroic-sized sculpture. After inspecting the Plaza and the proposed site, Nemon agreed to go ahead. Miller commissioned the work, then set about inviting friends to join him on the project.

Nemon's decision was based in part on the fact that Dwight Eisenhower and Winston Churchill, together with Joyce Hall, had selected Kansas City as the world headquarters for the new "People to People" organization. Nemon was familiar with Churchill's Iron Curtain speech, which had been delivered at Westminster College in central Missouri in 1946; he was also aware of Eisenhower's early roots in nearby Abilene, Kansas. In addition, Hallmark had reproduced many of Churchill's paintings in greeting card form. Thus Kansas City was a logical choice of location for a monument to the legendary prime minister.

Back in England, so many political obstacles were encountered in determining a location for the British casting of the work that Oscar Nemon abandoned that part of his dream. He went ahead with the American statue, finishing it in the spring of 1984. Laura Rollins Hockaday reported in the *Kansas City Star* on April 24, 1980:

The only sculpture Winston Churchill personally commissioned for Blenheim Palace was this heroic-sized work by British sculptor Oscar Nemon, "A Tribute to Married Love." It was dedicated in 1984 on the new Wornall Road Bridge, with the Duke of Marlborough, Ambassador and Mrs. Charles Price, Churchill's granddaughter Edwina Sandys, the sculptor, and Miller and Jeannette Nichols looking on (right to left).

British and American dignitaries will be in Kansas City for the unveiling on May 12 of a statue of Sir Winston Churchill and his wife, baroness Clementine Spencer-Churchill.

The work, titled 'Married Love,' is by Oscar Nemon, a British royal sculptor. He created the original, much smaller version for Blenheim Palace at the request of Sir Winston, who was Prime Minister of Great Britain during World War II.

The statue, made for the Plaza, which is about six-feet tall and twelve-feet wide, was commissioned by Miller Nichols, Board Chairman of the J.C. Nichols Company, and his wife, Jeannette, about three years ago.

Mrs. Nichols said British and American flags would fly behind [above] it. Flowers would be planted [behind it] and a push-button tape of famous orations by the British statesman would be installed.

The dedication was held on the bridge with Scottish bagpipers in tartans leading the procession of distinguished guests, driven down from the hotel in carriages to a viewing stand for the dedicatory remarks by Ambassador Charles H. Price II and the Duke of Marlborough.

Another beautification project of the early 1980s was the Court of the Penguins. For some 25 years this property had been the Sears batteries, tires, and accessories store. In the late 1970s it was reacquired by the company, and Miller challenged architect Bill Linscott to make this unique and unsightly space complement and beautify the Plaza image. "Why can't it be turned into a courtyard with boutique shops?" he wondered. Linscott came up with an appealing design that featured iron grillwork, red tile roofs, and a fountain courtyard. Miller was delighted, but, as with all new properties, the next question was what to call it: Segovia Court? Salamanca Court?

The answer came to Miller as he was examining three eight-inch bronze penguins on a coffee table at the Tom Deacys'. They were the work of Arthur Kraft, a brilliant young Kansas City artist and Yale graduate, who had died at an early age. Miller borrowed the little figures and took them to a J.C. Nichols Company board meeting. "How about a 'Court of the Penguins' featuring these three bronze penguins done in heroic size, about three-and-one-half to four-feet tall?" he asked. There was an embarrassed silence followed by a barrage of questions. "How do these penguins relate to the Plaza?" "Won't they look rather strange among all the lovely European art we have there? Certainly they are not Spanish in motif."

Miller countered with, "How many people know where the Esplanade building is? How many people can identify Pomona Court? *Everybody* would know the Court of the Penguins." Discussion continued and then a vote was called for: In favor, Miller's one vote; opposed, the remaining eleven directors. "Well," said Miller, "we are going to have a Court of the Penguins and we'll put a plaque in front of them commemorating Arthur Kraft."

So the courtyard with its charming boutique shops was completed, with Gucci moving into the striking corner space. Between two fountains, the trio of bronze penguins face one another in a semicircle. Children like to climb on them. Local merchants drape them in festive garb on holidays.

Shortly before the dedication of the Court of the Penguins, Dave Jackson sent Miller a birthday card depicting a pyramid of twelve penguins, eleven of which were frowning, but the top penguin showed a wide grin. Greatly amused, Miller had the illustration from the card reproduced in enamel on copper as a plaque, which he set into the courtyard bench. As a private joke, he put the directors' initials on the feet of the penguins on the lower tiers of the pyramid, with his own initials on the smiling bird at the top. If you look closely, you can see them there today.

Another aspect of beautification that captured Miller's attention during the decade of the 1980s was the alleyways behind some Plaza buildings. Cluttered with the paraphernalia of additional electric power, air-conditioning, and plumbing and heating support added over the years, these alleyways had become an eyesore.

One area of special concern was that behind the Commerce Bank, Gerhardts, and the Jenkins Music Company, where a plethora of pipes, wiring, and electrical boxes had created an unsightly mess. The adjacent old Plaza garage, no longer structurally sound, was being replaced with Plaza customer parking space. In the rebuilding process Miller envisioned adding a new tower to stand at the Plaza's northeast gateway.

The undertaking was difficult. The tower had to be built above an existing building that housed the Bridal Shop, Lou Charno, and Paul's Optical. These merchants lived patiently under a raft of scaffolding for several months while a second story and domed tower were added. The new second story restaurant, presently Figlio's, an Italian restaurant, was designed with balconies to offer outdoor dining overlooking Mill Creek Park and the J.C. Nichols Fountain.

Another unattractive alleyway became the entrance to the Mademoiselle Fitness Center. Cobbling the alleyway and adding banners and planters produced an attractive entrance that allowed rehabilitation of a block of unused space, once the backstage and dressing rooms for the Plaza Theater.

The reclamation that gave Miller the most pleasure involved the hodgepodge of older buildings behind Brooks Brothers and the Country Club Bank. After the area had been given a face lift, a striking bridge was added to connect the two buildings at the second floor. The bridge added a visually pleasing adornment while also providing access for a tenant to expand.

Miller wanted to dedicate another sculpture to Children's Mercy Hospital, one with provision for gifts larger than the coins tossed into Plaza fountains. He asked three sculptors to present drawings for a bronze eagle. From these, he chose a mother bird alighting on a nest to feed her

For Diana and Charles' royal wedding in London, the penguins were decked out for the celebration in Kansas City.

three small eaglets, the work of Lorenzo Ghiglieri, a Portland, Oregon, artist. A bronze mail box-type container was then to be attached to an adjacent brick column, with an invitation to make a gift to the children of Mercy Hospital.

Unable for many months to find the bronze box he wanted, he discovered exactly the right design in wood one day, next to the coat check at the Romeo Salta Restaurant in New York. He promptly took a picture of it, which he sent to his friend Raffaello Romanelli in Florence.

Friendship between the Romanelli family and the J.C. Nichols family dates back to Raffaello's grandfather and J.C. in the 1920s. The Romanelli Gardens subdivision was named for him, and many works from his studio grace the Country Club District. Favorites among these are "The Sleeping Child," in the median at 47th Street and Wornall Road; the "Young Michelangelo;" "Ruth," the lovely white marble statue that faces Mark Shale on Nichols Road; and "The Boy with the Thorn," in front of The Raphael Hotel.

When Raffaello Romanelli received Miller's request, he promptly replied that he would be happy to reproduce the letter box in bronze. Some months later it arrived with a note that it was a gift to Children's Mercy Hospital in remembrance of a daughter who had died at the age of three.

Horse-drawn carriages came to the Plaza in the 1980s. After learning that horses could be diapered and after convincing Plaza security that the carriages could move safely in automobile traffic, Miller concluded that such an amenity would have a nostalgic draw for visitors. Strollers and window shoppers today enjoy the variety of antique carriages that circle through the Plaza each evening.

Plaza Restaurants

Outdoor eating, long popular in Europe, highlighted Plaza restaurant development during the decade of the 1980s. Putsch's Sidewalk Cafe had been the Plaza's first outdoor eatery, followed by a deck added to Emile's Deli. The Classic Cup also added a handsome teakwood deck designed by J.C. Nichols Company architect Gordon Jarchow, which nearly doubled the restaurant's capacity. And some of the Plaza courtyards, formerly filling station sites, have been adapted for seasonal outdoor eating.

The largest new outdoor opportunity became Parkway 600. A Skelly gas station, last of nine Plaza service stations, stood on this site; as the date approached when Skelly had to renew its lease or lose the location, Miller held his breath. When Skelly failed to sign before the deadline, Miller claimed the site. He envisioned a domed restaurant with a courtyard. Attention was given to beautifying the location and selecting the kind of tree that would best shade its patio in summer. In Aspen, Miller located a charming fountain, a tall crane balancing on one foot on a flower pod from which water falls away in three directions. Two young Gilbert/Robinson alumnae, Forbes Jones and Michael Eastman, who were operating their own bistro in Waldo, were invited to run the new establishment; Parkway 600 opened in October 1988. It was the Plaza's first outdoor eatery with heat lamps, enabling customers to dine outdoors nearly year-round.

The Gilbert/Robinson restaurants became a significant part of the Plaza scene in the post-flood years. The Bristol, one of their most popular, is topped with a small tower and has an arcaded sidewalk in front. Patterned after an English seafood bar and grill, it has an embossed tin ceiling and old English artifacts. Miller particularly delighted in the use of the snug, so popular in Ireland, where parties of four to eight can pull the velvet drape for a private, intimate meal.

Annie's Santa Fe, with its colorful Mexican theme, is another Plaza original, which Gilbert/Robinson then took across the country. Known for its large painting of a reclining nude retrieved from a former downtown whore house, it was with some trepidation that Joe Gilbert called Miller down to look at the painting before hanging it; Miller thought it was dandy. Fred P. Ott's followed next door, featuring excellent hamburgers and fries, along with other barroom favorites. Self-service can

be enjoyed on its adjacent patio as well. The Cafe Fedora, with a Mediterranean choice of menu and the ambience of a trattoria, was also a highly successful concept that was carried to other cities.

Gilbert/Robinson's Plaza III, located on Ward Parkway, became a favorite traditional steak house. Dark paneling and crisp white tablecloths along with Western memorabilia and art make it reminiscent of the old Fred Harvey restaurants that once graced Santa Fe railroad stations from Chicago to the West Coast.

An out-of-town partnership presently serves the largest number of Plaza customers each day. Houstons, conceived and marketed by two young men from Nash-

Horse-drawn carriages are popular on the Plaza in all seasons—for proms, weddings, and special family celebrations.

ville and Atlanta, draws diners of all ages with its unique recipes. Another successful newcomer, the K.C. Masterpiece Barbecue & Grill, is the inspiration of Dr. Rich Davis and his sons. It occupies the former site of Mario's, which moved to the west side of the Plaza close to the popular La Bonne Bouche, the Granfaloon, the Gourmet Grocer, and the Better Cheddar. Starkers Private Reserve introduced a country French setting where gourmet menus are planned for private parties. Today the Plaza offers some thirty restaurant choices.

Lighting on the Plaza

Over the years, considerable attention has been given to lighting the Plaza towers. A variety of handsome wrought iron fixtures have distinguished different buildings, and special lighting is employed for courtyards, outdoor art, and fountains. Miller never hesitates to call an evening session to work on lighting when he has an idea. One particular interest has been street lights, and during the decade of the 1980s, he sometimes turned to lighting he had admired in his European travels.

In London, Miller spotted a wonderful old fixture with a sailing ship that he wanted to use on the Plaza. He learned that a family named Sugg, in Croyden, had been making lights for the city of London since the seventeenth century. He got in touch with Mr. Christopher Sugg, of the eleventh generation, who came to London with pictures of their work and the assurance that he had the molds for all the fixtures in the city of London. Miller ordered a pair of fixtures that today flank the entrance to Starkers Private Reserve.

On a rainy, misty afternoon in the fall of 1986, Miller and Jeannette stopped for tea on the plaza in Granada, Spain, where they admired at length the magnificent large candelabrum light fixtures. Miller managed to get a few pictures, and on their return to Kansas City he made inquiries about the lamps. He wrote a letter to the mayor of Granada, had it translated into Spanish, and sent it off. After several months, a reply arrived from a foundry in Seville, where the Granada light fixtures had been cast. Yes, they still had the mold and could cast a Granada light and ship it to the states.

Lengthy correspondence followed covering materials, cost, and arrangements for transporting the light to Kansas City. Translation was required for each message and reply. But the project came to fruition. Miller placed the Granada light on the extra wide sidewalk just west of Saks Fifth Avenue, where it can be seen from all four directions.

Since his World War II Navy days, Miller has admired the beautiful "Path of Gold" lighting fixtures along Market Street in San Francisco. With seven-foot high bases decorated with bas relief figures depicting westward migration, these splendid fixtures stand some 32 feet high and are topped with three handsome globe fixtures.

He mentioned his admiration to Nelson Emery of Emporia, Kansas, who reproduces old street lights. A few months later, Emery called to say that he had read in a trade journal that San Francisco had dismantled some of these handsome lights and that they would be for sale. With Emery and architect Gordon Jarchow, Miller flew to San Francisco to examine personally the various pieces and appendages of the lighting fixtures, which were strewn about a storage yard. Emery felt he could work from them. But back in Kansas City, Miller received a letter from San

Francisco authorities stating emphatically that the fixtures were to be sold only on an individual basis.

This, of course, only added to the challenge for Miller. He promptly asked Mayor Dick Berkley to contact the mayor of San Francisco and inquire further about the possibility of duplicating the lights for Kansas City. Mayor Art Agnos graciously responded in the affirmative.

So the process was begun. The wooden patterns needed repair and restoration. From the patterns, new molds were made in Fort Worth, Texas. The fixtures then had to be cast, some 93 pieces for each light, at the Morrow Foundry in Coffeyville, Kansas. Finally they went to Mr. Emery for buffing, painting, and assembly. Miller chose a dark green color for the Path of Gold lights, with gold-leaf framing

for the lanterns atop. The Kansas City Power & Light Company assisted in the preparation for their installation on 47th Street.

The location, like that of the Giralda Tower, allows the lights to be admired from some distance as one approaches the Plaza from the east. Situated between the magnificent J.C. Nichols Fountain and the Giralda Tower, they add a central focus. Miller presented the 17 lights in 1990 as a family gift to the city.

Office Buildings

As the J.C. Nichols Company was rebuilding the Plaza in the aftermath of the flood, the nation was entering an era (1978–1988) of unprecedented real estate growth. Recognizing this, the company

The 17 lights in the "Path of Gold Lights" lead into the Plaza from the east, framed by the handsome Giralda Tower and the sparkling J.C. Nichols Fountain.

determined to add mid-rise office buildings around the periphery of the Country Club Plaza. The buildings would not only identify the Plaza's perimeter but would also add population to patronize Plaza shops and restaurants.

The first of these new office buildings was One Ward Parkway to the southeast. The building's architectural concept was pure Miller Nichols—fanciful but doable—and the result is one of the most interesting buildings adjoining the Plaza. The entrance leads into an atrium whose landscaped garden has been designed around a 26-foot square marble and bronze fountain adorned with sculpted figures of some nine fish and animals that spray water into a pool. Acquired by Miller more than two decades earlier at the Mari-

nelli Foundry near Florence, the piece had sat in crates at the company storage facility ever since, awaiting a proper site.

During construction of the building and installation of the fountain, Miller took up the study of coi fish, a kind of large gold fish that can live for a hundred years or more. He read books, sought advice from coi owners, and finally determined to put some in the fountain pool. The coi did well enough for a couple of years with careful maintenance, feeding, and admonitions to the public not to throw coins into the pool. Maintenance of the quality of water eventually ended the fish project, but the fountain continues to make this office building a visual delight.

A second—the eight-story Park Plaza—was set on the west perimeter of the Plaza

The lush atrium garden and fountain of One Ward Parkway was completed in 1980 and joins the wings of the building.

at 47th Street and Roanoke Road, adjacent to the more recently located Richard and Annette Bloch Cancer Survivors' Park.[55] Here, again, clients could design space to their specifications. Next came the curved brick Gilbert/Robinson Building due east of the Plaza at the northeast corner of 47th Street and Main.

These were followed by 4900 Main, the tallest and most striking of the new office buildings, with its rounded curvilinear corners and landscaped garden with fountain between the building and its adjacent midrise parking. In front, Miller placed an enormous heroic bronze of a cowboy riding a steer by Bob Scriver. A third-story walkway connects 4900 Main to the Board of Trade just across the street to the north.[56]

By the late 1980s, office space in Kansas City had become over-built. Coupled with a change in federal real estate law eliminating the tax advantages for limited partnership participation in building projects and the growing problems of savings and loan associations, office building construction on the periphery of the Plaza came to an abrupt halt. The Plaza West building to the northwest developed by Kroh Brothers was foreclosed on when that company took bankruptcy. (The J.C. Nichols Company took over the leasing and management of Plaza West in 1988.)[57]

During these years, the company also added office buildings to its commercial developments in Corinth, Fairway, and Prairie Village. Space in the newer buildings, as well as the offices in various shopping centers, are maintained and managed by Guardian Management, a well-regarded subsidiary of the J.C. Nichols Company.

Mill Creek Park on the east along J.C. Nichols Parkway was another piece of the Plaza perimeter that caught Miller's attention during the 1980s. With no paths or facilities, it had become unkempt and overgrown, a place to be avoided rather than enjoyed. Miller felt something should be done. His logical partner was St. Luke's Hospital since it had the most extensive frontage on the park. Wouldn't a mile-long walking path with exercise stops prove helpful to St. Luke's Heart Institute and its Center for Health Enhancement?

Miller approached Dr. Ben McCallister of the Mid America Heart Institute, who agreed to help Miller solicit funds to improve the park. With the help of family and friends, Ben and Miller undertook the job of cutting back, digging up, raking, and cleaning out the accumulated debris and overgrowth that had snarled the east

Enhancing the corner of 4900 Main is this handsome curvilinear 12-story office building, joined by a walkway to the Kansas City Board of Trade.

hillside. The Park Department, for its part, did the hauling away.

Once the necessary funds had been raised, Frank Theis planned and advised on the landscaping. Volunteers planted trees, with professionals Joe Sweeney and Theis overseeing. Al Muehlberger put in the meandering circular mile path, eight feet wide, with a cushioning surface. The nurses at St. Luke's gave a handsome large spruce tree, which they decorate with lights each Christmas season. Funds solicited to meet the budget for the overall project include an endowment to provide for tree replacement, the addition of perennial plantings, fertilizing, and spraying for weeds. The park grows lovelier every year. Miller, Ben, and Frank Theis delight in counting the large number of people walking, jogging, or simply playing games in Mill Creek Park almost every day of the year. In 1991, Jim Stowers, chairman of Twentieth Century Investors, contributed money to light the path with 37 attractive street light fixtures; in 1992, the Mill Creek Park endowment stood at $220,000.

Residential Real Estate

The decade of the 1980s was also a very prosperous one for residential real estate development in the Kansas City area. At the top end of the scale for the J.C. Nichols company was the elegant Bradford Place, south on Mission Road. Sold out within an 18-month period, it featured lovely wooded lots on which several-million-dollar homes were built. This was followed by popular Waterford, two-thirds completed before the residential slow down began in 1989. To the east bordering both sides of State Line, Verona Hills and Verona Gardens continued to grow. Out in Overland Park, the company com-

pleted its 20-year development of Oak Park.

Meanwhile, Miller had embarked on his own building project, a free-standing condominium home in Corinth Downs, on the hilltop site of the old farmhouse. The project was vintage Miller. When his architects declared it was not feasible to restore the old farmhouse, he insisted that the cupola atop the original house must be saved. A crane was brought in. Design of the new house then had to accommodate the cupola.

Miller wanted a weathered stone facade, the kind of stone found in old fences. He located an abandoned stone fence and bought it. Several hundred paving bricks were delivered to the site, and he personally selected the ones for a fireplace wall. He tracked down a particular size of tree to be converted into living room paneling and sent it to Minnesota for match cutting. Instead of a patio, he opted for a large open porch with skylight and overhead fans where summer meals could be enjoyed.

Next he decided to enclose a small front garden with an old wrought-iron fence. He found what he wanted circling a condemned house in nearby St. Joseph, Missouri. One sweltering Saturday in mid-July, he drove to St. Joseph with a truck, a helper, and his son-in-law John Callison. Unfortunately, the iron fence posts were set in concrete, and to free them Miller had to rent a jackhammer.

There was more than enough fence not only to enclose the garden, but also to set off a small equestrian cemetery in the LeMans Court cul-de-sac in front of the house where Miller had moved the headstone for Insco, sire of a triple-crown winner, when the J.C. Nichols Company bought the Woolford Farm to build Corinth Downs. Next to Insco, he placed a headstone for Lawrin, the 1938 Kentucky Derby winner. Miller obtained old photos of these famous horses, Jeannette wrote up the history, and a display case was built to tell and illustrate the story. When Sally and John Ruddy found an old brass "Woolford Farm" sign at an auction and brought it to Miller, he was thrilled and placed it over the iron gate entrance. The project was completed, and the old Woolf farm properly commemorated. The cemetery attracts a surprising number of visitors, particularly during the Kentucky Derby.

Miller turned his attention to the cupola. He had a circular staircase built from the second floor to the attic, with a ship's ladder providing the means for the final ascent. After measuring the window openings, he slipped a wicker settee and a pair of swivel wicker chairs inside the cupola. The final job was to lift the cupola into place. Miller moved in on Thanksgiving weekend in 1988.

By then, Corinth Downs, with its luxury townhouse condominiums at 80th and Mission Road, was fully built out to 150 units. Jim Nicholson, himself not a native of Kansas City, recalls that many of those who were building condominium homes in Corinth Downs had grown up in the J.C. Nichols Country Club District, almost all having attended Southwest High School. Now in Corinth Downs they were enjoying friendships that extended back some 40 years.

Nicholson's experiences as the man in charge at Corinth Downs reveal some deep-seated social changes.

What surprised me most was that I worked largely with the wives. Previously, working with young couples buying their first house in the suburbs, the husband always played the prominent role, declaring what they wanted and did not want. Now, however, the wives almost invariably had a lifestyle in mind which they knew the two of them would enjoy. Accordingly, when putting the unit together, I didn't pay much attention to the man because she knew more about what he needed than he did. I must say, working with the wives was much easier.

But it was hard to get the builders to understand this. Chauvinism dies hard. If the builder had to call with a question about construction and the wife answered, he would always ask for her husband when he should have just asked her the question.

Across Mission Road from Corinth Downs was a tract of land owned by WDAF, on which the J.C. Nichols Company had a 99-year lease. Miller came up with the idea of building townhouses on this ground under a land-lease program. He proposed that the company put in the improvements and then let the interested parties build their own units, without having to buy the lot. Instead, they would lease the land under the unit for 45 years, at which time the condominiums and other improvements would all revert to the ownership of the J.C. Nichols Company.

Corinth Paddock, as this community was to be called, was a new concept for Kansas City, and the thinking within the company was that it would not be received very well. It turned out, however, that there was a market among people who no longer spent all of their time in Kansas City, but had family there. These people, when not away in the sun-belt or traveling, preferred a residence that did not require such a substantial investment but did have a prime location.

Across the street at Corinth Downs, condominiums started at $300,000, but in Corinth Paddock a condominium could be purchased for $90,000. Jim Nicholson noted that "a couple of residents in Corinth Downs sold their units for $300,000 and bought $90,000 units in Corinth Paddock, which enabled them to spend more time in the sun-belt. They were still close to their friends and their country clubs." In a year-and-a-half, Corinth Paddock was sold out, and Miller felt vindicated.

In the traditional Country Club District, home real estate values escalated rapidly during much of the 1980s decade, reaching prices several times higher than the original cost of the homes. There was a waiting list for houses in Mission Hills and Indian Hills that undergirded the premium prices. However, this escalation seemed modest to business executives moving in from either coast, which also helped to bid up real estate values. Thus, residential real estate became an increasingly profitable profession for top company sales people.

Continental Homes

During these years, the company also embarked on a new kind of residential construction, the result of a joint venture with the Marley Company. Marley owned a New England company, Continental Homes, that was developing a market for factory-built homes, units that could be assembled into homes from an assembly-line plant serving a 250-mile radius.

Marley approached the J.C. Nichols Company suggesting a joint venture in which they would build the module units for homes in a plant in eastern Kansas; the

Nichols Company would be responsible for selling the units and developing a regional market. The company agreed. Miller, Lynn McCarthy, and others looked over suggested communities, and their choice for the plant was Osage City, Kansas, situated on a north-south highway connecting Emporia and Topeka. With a Hallmark plant in the town, it enjoyed access to a work force from a number of smaller neighboring communities.

A 21,000-square-foot factory was built to construct house sections complete to windows, doors, closets, wall coverings, carpeting, plumbing, and lighting fixtures. Floor plans for apartment developments and for residential communities provided a choice of three or four models.

Quality was superior to the stick-built home—it had to be sturdier to withstand travel. The units were not exposed to weather during construction and quality control could be better maintained within a factory. The complex undertaking involved blending the technology developed by Continental Homes with the architectural, building, and marketing expertise of the J.C. Nichols Company. While the plant was being designed and built, Clarence Roeder and other company officers made frequent trips to Osage City. Other regional builders were brought in with the thought that this would be an excellent residential product for isolated lake, farm, and other recreational homes on sites that lacked close-by construction crews and services.

Two new J.C. Nichols communities were planned, Green Meadows near Stanley, Kansas, and Woodsonia just off Highway 7 near Bonner Springs. Both sought to meet the needs of specific local areas where attractive moderate-priced housing was thought to be in demand. But Continental Homes' ability to assemble the units in the field did not match its expertise in the factory. Getting the product properly assembled and finished for the market was a painfully slow process; as a result, the attractive residential communities of Green Meadows and Woodsonia developed only at a moderate pace.

Closer in, the factory-built units added 500 residences to the Coach House apartments in Red Bridge off 110th Street. This housing leased rapidly. The company also added shops and theaters to the Red Bridge Shopping Center.

Similarly, the company built the Corinth Place Apartments across from the Corinth Shopping Center, on the east side of Mission Road at 80th Street. These Continental Homes, prebuilt units in a two-story townhouse layout, offered a small pool, pleasant landscaping, and ample covered parking, and they found a ready market.

More upscale were the Corinth Villas, the last company project to use the new factory-built homes, built just east of the Corinth Place Apartments. Attractive townhouse condominiums, the Villas were designed for an upscale clientele seeking less space than in the Corinth Downs townhouses across the way.

The company also recognized the need for low-cost inner city housing; small factory-built units were offered to the Housing Authority of Kansas City, Missouri, for core redevelopment. Forty homes were built on a reclaimed site and were widely sought after. While the units were small in size, they were high in quality. Sadly, a change in the tax laws lengthening depreciation on this type of construction made it no longer profitable to the company nor affordable to the neighborhood.

As efficiency in the factory increased, more units were being turned out than

the J.C. Nichols Company could develop sites for or market in the adjacent 250-mile area. Inventory build-up was costly and production cut-backs could not be matched with a reduction in cost. Meanwhile the Marley Company had sold off its Continental Homes Division and wished to withdraw from the local project. As they had been unable to meet promised production and cost schedules, they concluded this was not an appropriate line of business for them.

The Nichols Company, in turn, decided to sell the plant to a group of factory employees. According to Clarence Roeder, the J.C. Nichols Company entry into modular housing was terminated by the devastating impact of the 1986 Tax Reform Act. Without the ten-year depreciation that made this investment economically feasible, financing for such projects simply disappeared from the marketplace.

Residential Living Bordering the Plaza

During the latter half of the 1980s, the company also undertook new residential projects both immediately north and south of the Plaza, locations that offered pleasant Plaza vistas and easy pedestrian access to the Plaza's amenities. These were the Neptune Apartments on the north and the Alameda Towers condominiums to the south on the Wornall Road hill just behind the Ritz Carlton Hotel.

It was not until 1987 that the last property bordering the Plaza on the north, 46th Street Terrace east of Broadway, was acquired by the company, some 23 years after Miller's first acquisition. Here the company built a four-story apartment building, naming it for the Neptune Fountain, which the apartments overlook.

Designed by Howard Nearing, the new balconied units also enabled the company to expand Plaza parking, both for the tenants and for Plaza customers. The concept of working, shopping, and living on the Plaza (and hence not needing to park there) is strongly advocated by Miller, and the Neptune Apartments expanded this opportunity.

The Spanish architecture of the Neptune Apartments, completed in 1988, complements the Plaza's ongoing design. Deciding there should be a work of art at the entrance symbolizing the name, Miller asked ceramicist Ron Taylor, a former instructor at the Art Institute, to draw up some sketches. From one of these he commissioned a five-by-eight-foot tile plaque in celedon bas relief of the Neptune Fountain.

The Alameda Towers

Overlooking the Plaza and the Ritz-Carlton Hotel, the first building of the Alameda Towers was completed in 1990. The Towers introduced a new architectural concept in residential construction, namely, access floors, sometimes called computer floors, which allow heating, cooling, fireplace flues, and plumbing to be installed in a plenum between each story. This enables the clientele to design their space to fit a particular life-style, disregarding the layout of the stories above or below.

Jim Nicholson, having overseen the completion of Corinth Downs, has been in charge of the project. He waxes enthusiastic as he explains: "It was hard to get the architects [Howard Needles Tammen & Bergendoff], and even the builder J.E. Dunn, to understand the necessity to design and build for this flexibility. For example, even with windows lining the exterior walls, the owner can have windows wherever he wants them; where he doesn't, he simply puts up a wall to cover them."

Jim traveled around the country visiting condominiums under construction or newly opened. He sat in the lobby of Trump Towers just to see how the building operated. He did the same in Dallas, in Houston, and in Los Angeles. It was in Dallas that he noticed that every few hours another well-groomed doorman would take over. Inquiring about this, he was told that a nearby seminary had the contract to supply doormen. Why couldn't the Alameda Towers use graduate students from UMKC and let them be responsible for the front door operation?

At the Alameda Towers, Nicholson planned many new amenities, in addition to security that allows owners to simply shut the door when leaving the city. A handsome flowering garden offers both a putting clock and croquet court adjoined by a garden room for entertaining. Arrangements with the adjoining Ritz-Carlton Hotel provide the option of membership in its health club and for hotel room service to the condominiums. The high-rise homes range in size from approximately 2,500 square feet to 6,000 square feet; most upper units allow vistas in three directions over the city. Among the first residents moving into the Towers in the spring of 1990 were the Miller Nichols.

Kirkwood Circle

As noted earlier, Miller was unable to convince John Taylor, then company chairman, to begin buying houses directly south of the Plaza, 49th to 50th Street and Wornall Road to Main Street. However, Taylor had not discouraged him from going ahead and buying them on his own. Thirty-five years later, in the mid-1980s, the company recognized the viability of developing this 11-acre tract. Buying houses only as they came onto the market, Miller had acquired a major part of the neighborhood, which the company now purchased from him. Moving ahead, although at a substantially higher cost, they bought up all but one parcel of the remainder for an investment of $600,000 per acre. An overall development plan was undertaken.

Miller chose the name Kirkwood Circle for the proposed development in memory of the Kirkwood family and his father's friendship with William Rockhill Nelson, father of Laura Kirkwood. (Kirkwood Hall at the Nelson Art Gallery was named for Laura and her husband.) Kirkwood Circle plans call for the removal of all the present streets, sewers, and utilities, along with the houses, and for a new plat design of buildings encircling a garden with underground parking beneath. The company's plat calls for a 450-to-600-unit upscale complex of mid- and high-rise apartments and condominiums circling a garden with underground parking beneath. Company architect Gordon Jarchow designed a pair of decorative wrought iron gates for its two entrances.

There was neighborhood opposition to the idea of mid- and high-rise residences, despite the existing high-rise apartments adjacent to the north and The Walnuts mid-rise apartments to the south. And so it took the company three years to navigate through the city's lengthy planning and approval procedures to secure the zoning for Kirkwood Circle. Miller anticipates that one day Kirkwood Circle will house several times the number of residents presently living in Mission Hills and Indian Hills combined, providing a much needed new tax base for Kansas City, Missouri.

During the zoning delays, the real estate market in Kansas City changed markedly. Those initially eager to participate acknowledged, with the company, that this project would have to be put on hold until the real estate recession has eased. But the company is pleased to have its largest single Kansas City, Missouri, residential development waiting in the wings, one that can help the city.

At the end of the decade the company also drew up plans for a joint venture to develop some 900 acres to the southwest in Johnson County. The new development, to be known as LionsGate, is comparable in size to the Oak Park development in Overland Park that took twenty years to build out. Lying between 135th Street and 151st Street, and Nall to Metcalf, it combines land owned by the company with adjoining farm land purchased from the Sutherland family. The new community is planned to include individual homes, townhouses, and apartments in a landscaped country club setting. This attractive development opportunity, too, awaits the resurgence of the real estate market. Like Kirkwood Circle, it reflects new trends in quality residential living.

In early 1990, the real estate sales division of the J.C. Nichols Company embarked on another type of joint venture. Jack Frost, a native Kansas Citian who had headed the Hardin-Stockton Company before it was bought by Coldwell Banker, had been made executive vice-president of this national company and located in California. Desiring to return to Kansas City, Jack discussed with Lynn Mc-

Carthy his concept for a large metropolitan residential real estate operation. Basically, he pointed out, the J.C. Nichols Company had served one quadrant of the city. Discussions followed with Moe Courville who headed residential sales for the company and, in turn, the board agreed that this was a viable new direction for the real estate sales division to go. In early 1990, a joint venture company was formed and named J.C. Nichols Real Estate. It is headed by Jack Frost, Larry Wallace, and Dave Cooper.

The J.C. Nichols Company Residential Real Estate Division had been composed of 110 agents; by the end of 1993, the new company included over 400 residential salespeople. During its first year of operation, J.C. Nichols Real Estate opened offices in Lee's Summit, on College Boulevard, and in Olathe, joining these with company offices on the Plaza, in Brookside, in Corinth, at Shannon Valley, in Red Bridge, and at Lakewood. The new company has enjoyed banner years, with sales that totaled $376 million in 1991, $564 million in 1992, and reached $831 million in 1993. New offices have been added in the Northland, in Paola, at 10203 Metcalfe, at 5000 West 95th Street, and in Belton.

The Ritz-Carlton

The J.C. Nichols Company venture into the hotel business in the early 1970s was terminated at the end of the 1980s. The early 1980s had been exceedingly prosperous for the Alameda Plaza and The Raphael Hotels, under Phil Pistilli, president of the company's hotel division, with profits peaking in 1984. No doubt because of this, the company was asked to take over management of the faltering Allis Plaza Hotel in downtown Kansas City and

did so in August 1987. Pistilli also became president of the American Hotel and Motel Association.

However, from the mid-1980s, hotel costs escalated rapidly, with insurance costs tripling and real estate taxes nearly quadrupling. Moreover, there was increasing competition from top quality hotel chains such as Marriott, Westin, and Hyatt, new arrivals on the Kansas City scene, whose sales people cover the nation scouting convention and other conference business. A small hotel company was hard pressed to compete. With this combination of factors to address, the high level of profitability for the hotel division declined.

Interestingly, it was at this time that the J.C. Nichols Company was approached by the Ritz-Carlton Company, seeking a hotel site on the Plaza. The sole remaining Plaza site was on 47th Street west of Broadway. But J.C. Nichols Company officials had to ask themselves what this would mean to the Alameda Plaza. Wouldn't it be difficult to retain stature as the city's premier hotel when competing with a Ritz-Carlton?

The upshot was that Lynn McCarthy, after many meetings and conversations, negotiated a joint venture in which the J.C. Nichols Company would provide the Alameda Plaza Hotel and its adjoining parking structure and the Ritz-Carlton would redesign and reconstruct the public areas and refurbish the hotel in the Ritz-Carlton style. The company viewed this opportunity as favorable, not only to the Country Club Plaza, but to the city as a whole. The Ritz-Carlton took a long-term lease on the hotel, with a noncancellable management contract, for which the Nichols Company was paid up front.

While some people in the community regretted losing the Alameda Plaza, the company realized the hotel was in need of updating. The Ritz-Carlton spent about $32 million redoing the hotel—more than its original cost. Since its opening in late 1989, ongoing meeting arrangements for companies, association groups, and others at the Ritz-Carlton have continued to bring new visitors to Kansas City and to the Country Club Plaza, and its occupancy rate has been the best in the city.

This decision focused attention on the other hotels owned and operated by the J.C. Nichols Company. Phil Pistilli expressed interest in continuing to manage the Allis Plaza Hotel and in purchasing The Raphael Hotels in Kansas City and Chicago. This was agreed to and the arrangements continue. Since the San Francisco Raphael was a lease arrangement, the company continues to carry this lease, with the Pistillis managing the hotel.

Communications and Public Relations

Top management at the J.C. Nichols Company tries to keep an open mind when controversy arises. Miller asserts: "It's good because it brings people's thoughts and feelings out into the open. The better informed we are, the better we can meet the changing needs of the marketplace." As related above by Jim Nicholson, after the very successful Corinth Downs project the company envisioned that a similar condominium development would be ideal to complete the residential development of Verona Hills. But when confronted with residents' objections to the required rezoning, the company backed off.

Lee Fowler, recently retired vice-president, points out that public complaint sometimes has its ironies. When the company proposed building the moderately priced Corinth Place apartment community described earlier, it designed the buildings to be largely prefabricated. As word got out, the company received phone calls from upset Country Club District residents who believed manufactured housing was beneath the lofty standards of the J.C. Nichols Company. The majority of the calls came from Prairie Village residents who were apparently unaware that many of their early homes were partially prefabricated!

On another occasion, the company had decided it needed to demolish several old apartment buildings located next to the Dillard's store on the Plaza. Maintenance costs for the old structures had become prohibitive, and they were potential eyesores. Realizing that the media would jump at the opportunity to report the "eviction of elderly tenants by the J.C. Nichols Company," the public relations department, in conjunction with commercial properties personnel, mounted an elaborate advance campaign to facilitate relocation of the tenants.

Wide-open communication was maintained. Company people informed the apartment dwellers of the manner in which events would unfold and discussed their options. Residents were charged no rent for the last months of their leases. Company employees continually provided them with updated information on available apartments in the area, some managed by the J.C. Nichols Company, others not. The newspapers, ready to pounce on the story, couldn't coax a negative word out of anyone. They were forced to settle for pieces praising the manner in which the relocation was accomplished. Lee Fowler states with understandable pride, "We didn't receive a single call from an angry tenant in the entire six months."

Communication and public relations pieces, such as eye-catching apartment resident handbooks and newsletters, are produced by the communications department to enhance tenant retention and help lease apartments. In-house, "The Fountain" newsletter keeps employees current on company happenings. Out in the community, newsletters such as "Coach to Coach," sent bimonthly to some 850 Coach House and Coach Lamp residents, help perpetuate the special feeling of a neighborhood community in J.C. Nichols Company developments. Special offers from the nearby Red Bridge Shopping Center are noted, as well as educational, musical, and sports activities available in the neighborhood. Barbara Barickman, a marketing specialist on the public relations staff, says:

> Hands on management style is still an important legacy to remember in 1994. Short-term mentality is prevalent in most developers today. It would be impossible to justify aesthetic projects, such as the Court of the Penguins, without a long-range perspective. People's deep concern for the Plaza and its art is revealed in a number of ways. In honor of Prince Charles' wedding, a merchant proudly decked out the penguins in bridal wear. The Girl Scouts celebrated their birthday by dressing them in Girl Scout uniforms, much to everyone's delight. On cold winter nights people have been known to tuck a blanket around the statue of the Sleeping Child or to slip a knit cap over her bare head.

Miller adds, "People show their concern in other ways as well. If one of our statues gets splattered with dirt, I rest assured that several people will call me personally and tell me about it. If vandalism occurs, we repair it immediately."

Lynn McCarthy's daughter, Kelly Sherman, joined the Nichols Company as executive marketing director in 1987, to formalize the coordination of marketing efforts for all company divisions. Her work has included advertising and public relations for both residential and commercial properties and partnerships, including the company's new joint venture, J.C. Nichols Real Estate, formed in 1990. She was made a vice-president in 1993 and joined the board the following year.

A pictorial brochure of the Plaza with a map locating shops and restaurants is kept updated by the Plaza Merchants' Association, which also offers Plaza gift bonds in striking packaging. During the 1980s, the association introduced "Music on the Plaza," first on summer evenings and then on Saturday and Sunday afternoons as well.

The traditional events, Easter bunnies and an Easter Parade, the Plaza Art Fair, and the turning on of the Christmas lights on Thanksgiving night continue, the latter drawing an ever-growing crowd described in 1991 as 250,000 people. During seasonable weather, the Plaza is often bustling on Sunday mornings with participants and support groups for the bikers, marathon runs, and community walks that today support many Kansas City charitable endeavors.

Since 1978, the J.C. Nichols Company has offered a "walking art tour" to schools in the greater Kansas City area. Each spring and fall, the Plaza is dotted with school groups seeking out the different works of art, doing rubbings of the historic plaques set in sidewalks, and identifying architectural features and fountains. The

The 60-year-old Plaza Art Fair held the third weekend of September draws artists from across the country and tens of thousands of patrons. This view looks east along Nichols Road in front of Halls Plaza.

plaques were another innovation of Miller's during the 1980s, and he particularly cherishes the one he set at the entrance to the company offices that celebrates his father's vision of the Plaza. An art teacher in the Blue Valley School District, Judi Stang, has developed a comprehensive work book on Plaza art for 5th grade students.

The Pembroke Hill School

At the Pembroke Country Day and Sunset Hill schools, during the 1970s, a coordinated high school curriculum was developed, built upon the faculty strengths in their respective schools. By 1980, there were a number of constituent families in the two schools encouraging them to merge and establish a fully coeducational program. The Pembroke trustees generally favored the move, while at Sunset Hill, flourishing as a girls' preparatory school, there was considerably more hesitancy. However, in the spring of 1983 the two schools signed a merger agreement. Jeannette Nichols served as president of the Sunset Hill Alumnae Association during this transition. With completion of the merger, the schools published their respective histories, designed for a common slipcase. The set was made available to students, parents, and alumnae/alumni.

The new headmaster of the merged school was John A. Bird. Along with the administrative offices, the preschool, primary school, and lower school were placed on the old Sunset Hill school campus on Wornall Road. The middle school and high school settled in at the former Pembroke Country Day campus on Ward Parkway, with its more extensive sports facilities. Thus, while the combined school accommodates a thousand students,

the boys and girls go to school on campuses of the same size as before.

In the late 1980s, the new Pembroke Hill School embarked on a capital funds campaign. Knowing that Miller would be making a gift, Clyde suggested that he designate the funds for economics education. As far back as 1958, Clyde had become concerned about the failure of public and private elementary schools to teach adequate understanding of how America's private capital, open-market system functions. In 1966, he almost single-handedly raised enough funding to launch the Missouri Council on Economic Education and convinced the University of Missouri to house the council. The MCEE became one of the most exemplary programs in the nation, and Clyde was asked to serve on the board of trustees of the Joint Council on Economic Education, the national body.

Miller agreed with Clyde's suggestion, and feeling that economics education should start in kindergarten, he designated that the income from his gift be used to support this program. In 1992/93 the Pembroke Hill Wornall Campus grades made the Plaza their laboratory for economics education. Classes studied the demographics of its use, as well as operation of the shops, restaurants, and professions located there. Plaza architecture and art and the construction of its bridges and fountains were researched, along with how the area is maintained. A miniature Country Club Plaza operated for a day in the school's fieldhouse, complete with tower, restaurant, book, art, and candy shops and vendors, bridges, and fountains.

In September 1993, Pembroke Hill honored Miller with the Distinguished Alumni Award.

University of Missouri at Kansas City

During the early 1980s, UMKC began to reap the benefits from Miller Nichols' 25 years of buying real estate in its behalf. He had finally purchased enough houses so that the income generated by them provided ongoing funds for the purchase of additional houses as they come on the market. The trustees and the University of Missouri curators had designated 225 acres as land needed for future campus expansion, and by the end of the decade nearly 80 percent had been acquired.

Under Chancellor George Russell, major additions were made, using this land. New schools and graduate schools were added during the 1980s, significantly enhancing the attractiveness of the campus. In late 1991, the university administration and the curators approved Miller's proposal to start acquiring an additional 29 acres to the south, from 55th to 59th Streets, for possible addition of a sports stadium, should the university choose to build one in the future. Miller's most recent UMKC project focuses on purchasing land for student housing. Working with a national developer who proposes to build the housing on university land with a lease arrangement, once the cost of the buildings has been recouped, ownership will revert to the university.

In 1989, Miller was awarded an honorary doctorate of business administration from the University of Missouri, and in October 1991, the Miller Nichols Library was dedicated on the UMKC campus. The occasion brought together some 350 friends who honored him with an 80th birthday gift, one providing for the purchase of the Le Corbusier Archives, a 32-volume set of architectural drawings; a collection on crime and justice in American history; and a collection relating to the Bill of Rights and American legal history. When the naming of the library was announced at the annual dinner meeting of the trustees two years earlier, Chancellor Russell had commented, "None of these honors can ever express the depth of our abiding respect for this man."

Real Estate Development outside Kansas City

During the mid-1980s, the J.C. Nichols Company embarked on two real estate ventures outside of Kansas City, their first. The company's experiences in Des Moines, Iowa, and St. Petersburg, Florida, could hardly be more contrasting, but they typify the changing real estate scene over the decade of the 1980s.

In 1982, the company was invited to participate in developing new properties in the Des Moines area. Three potential real estate transactions were proposed. The first was 56 acres of ground in West Des Moines, which was zoned for an office park. The second was a joint venture with Pioneer Seed Company to develop an apartment project in Johnston, Iowa, immediately north of Des Moines. The third proposed project was in an industrial development for the construction of a 100,000-square-foot warehouse (later expanded to 150,000 square feet) for the Lenox Corporation. The company decided to participate in all three of these projects. Prior to his retirement in 1990, Bill McGugin was the company's liaison in Des Moines, commuting regularly for more than five years.

The office building project is known as Three Fountains Office Park. The J.C. Nichols Company has continued to build out this park, with Dan Rupprecht increasing his share of participation in each new building. There are now seven office buildings, with available land for three more. Miller shipped one of artist Chapel's lovely crane fountains (another casting of the one placed at Parkway 600) from Aspen to Des Moines, to be used in the landscaping of the Three Fountains complex.

Next, the J.C. Nichols Company was invited to participate on the Terrace Place Building, west of downtown Des Moines and adjacent to the governor's mansion. Most recently the company has joined Dan Rupprecht on what Lynn McCarthy terms a "classic package," the Country Club Office Plaza. This development contains 165 acres in two separate parcels. In the east 100 acres, an area has been designated for an office park with a smaller acreage set aside for commercial development. The west 65 acres are reserved for a future office campus and possible additional retail development. Norwest Credit Card Services has leased a building there to house its credit card services. This building with approximately 275,000 square feet plus adjacent land is capable of accommodating an additional 300,000 square feet for office expansion.

"All of these ventures in metropolitan Des Moines have been quite successful, thanks to the encouragement and cooperation of the various local government authorities, which has speeded up and facilitated the projects," reports Tony Sweeney, vice-president, who serves as Des Moines liaison for the company.

In 1985, the city of Phoenix, Arizona, announced its desire to have a sports complex adjacent to downtown Phoenix and the state capital. To create a proposal, Robert Kaufman, Phoenix attorney, and Michael Van Butsel, Phoenix architect, assembled a team of professionals, including sports figures, developers, and architects. Neil Elsey of the Elcor Companies in Phoenix contacted the J.C. Nichols Company to be part of a team that proposed an $170-million sports complex. Ultimately and ironically it was the Kroh Brothers of Kansas City who were awarded the job. Soon afterward, they encountered difficulties and took bankruptcy. To date nothing has been built.

Simultaneously, the city of St. Petersburg, Florida, was embarking on ambitious plans to redevelop its downtown area and was seeking a developer who could create an upscale waterfront retail center. Familiar with the proposed project in Phoenix, they contacted Neil Elsey and, through him, the J.C. Nichols Company. The latter, joined by the Phoenix Elcor Companies, formed the Bay Plaza Companies and drew up plans. In 1986, the city, eager to have the J.C. Nichols Company involved, officially selected the Bay Plaza Companies.

The city of St. Petersburg, with a major domed sports stadium already under construction, was rebuilding its Bay Pier to be developed with retail shops and restaurants; the city was also refurbishing a handsome performing arts theater adjacent to its bay-side sports arena. This phase was turned over to Bay Plaza to lease and manage, and both of these waterfront projects have fared well.

After the city and Bay Plaza executed a redevelopment agreement in 1987, much careful planning and structuring went into the Bay Plaza Development Plan. Construction was initiated in late July 1989 for the first new space for shops and offices, plus extensive garage parking. However, the timing for the St. Petersburg downtown waterfront development was unfortunate. Again, the 1986 Tax Reform Act had dried up real estate development financing, and major retailers across the country were taking bankruptcy. These included such major retail operations as Allied Stores and Federated Department Stores, the latter the parent of Maas Brothers, the only major retailer present in downtown St. Petersburg. Bonwit Teller, Bloomingdale's, and Burdines, prominent national stores that Bay Plaza had been negotiating to bring as anchors to the waterfront development, were also owned by these national retailers. Without them, other prospects fell away. In early 1994, the large, speculative South Core building was still not leased up, but, in May 1994, the Bay Plaza Companies announced that a 24-screen theater, the largest in the country, would be leased by AMC in a new Phase II building. This new Mid-Core building will also include restaurants and shops, according to Bob Jackson, president of the Bay Plaza Companies, now solely owned by the J.C. Nichols Company.

The Bay Plaza Companies have continued to buy up land in the designated redevelopment area and have demolished several blocks of older inferior buildings, including the Sereno Hotel. Ten blocks west of downtown is the stadium, now in operation and reasonably well-booked despite the fact that St. Petersburg has four times been the disappointed finalist seeking to acquire the franchise for a major league baseball team. By court order, St. Petersburg is now number one on the list for an expansion franchise.

The Bay Plaza Companies, now solely owned by the J.C. Nichols Company, has been a costly and discouraging property to the company as well as for the city of St. Petersburg. Since the J.C. Nichols Company arrived, the political scene has changed with an all new city council. While the demographics define it as a natural site for redevelopment, at present no one is forecasting just how long St. Petersburg will be in a holding pattern.

Civic Involvement and Beautification

Continuing his concern with city beautification, in the 1980s Miller initiated a landscaping program for the I-70 freeway that cuts east to west on the south side of downtown. Increasingly, it bothered him that freeways in other cities were attractively landscaped while Kansas City's were not. Putting in the first $1,000, he appealed to the civic pride of downtown business friends and raised funds to plant trees, one section at a time as money permitted. Miller personally selected the kinds of trees, staked out where he wanted them planted, and checked weekly to see that they were watered. After some time and replanting, the trees along most of the freeway approaches into downtown have now matured nicely.

The death of Miller's good friend, Dutton Brookfield, in a tragic fire in 1979, was a real loss to Kansas City. He had headed the Board of Police Commissioners, chaired the Stadium Organizing Committee that spearheaded the bond drive, and had been a candidate for mayor. And along with Miller, Dutton had worked long and hard for the Right to Work cause. Miller felt strongly that he should be honored with a civic memorial. Discussing the options with Dutton's widow, Betty, he suggested an heroic piece of western sculpture. Dutton, at six-foot-seven-inches, was a dynamic, rugged man.

An ad hoc committee consisting of Miller, Lyman Field, and Doyle Patterson decided on Remington's Bronco Buster, a world renowned sculpture presented to Theodore Roosevelt by his former band of Rough Riders. However, it had never been reproduced in heroic size. The Remington Museum in New York gave permission, and sculptor Ken Clark, assisted by his wife Becky, was chosen to reproduce the piece. A downtown site at Barney Allis Plaza was selected. "Dutton was a downtown man," says Miller. "This work needs to be downtown and this park needs some beautification. It faces on 12th Street, just a block from the Brookfield Building." The proposal then had to work its way through the Kansas City Art Commission, a group not particularly friendly to western art, after which it received approval from the city council. A new stumbling block appeared when plans were announced to redesign and refurbish the park. Dutton's friends, who were making the statue a gift to the city, were patient.

The striking new Barney Allis park was to be set off with a large fountain, and Miller was consulted. He suggested that a company called WET be engaged; they created an elaborate computerized fountain that programs a variety of aesthetic water displays with colorful night lighting. The Bronco Buster found his home in the handsome new plaza and was dedicated to Dutton on April 6, 1985.

Miller Nichols in Retirement

Since Miller retired as chairman of the board of the J.C. Nichols Company in 1988, he has remained a director, a member of the executive committee, and an unpaid adviser to management. He maintains regular hours in his office at the company while dividing his time between civic endeavors, his own redevelopment plan, Plaza projects, and other real estate and company interests.[58]

In 1989, Miller had a call from his long-time friend, Lyman Field, pointing out that the 200th anniversary of the Bill of Rights was soon to be observed. Lyman felt Kansas City should have some sort of memorial to commemorate the occasion. Miller agreed, and Lyman contacted Mayor Richard Berkley, who appointed a committee on which both were to serve.

The majority of committee members were thinking of a bronze tablet. Miller felt the concept had much more potential. "Why not relate it to Independence Hall?" he asked. "We could make a replica of the top of the Hall."

Not sensing much enthusiasm, he asked approval to research the idea. He consulted the engineering firm of Burns and McDonald concerning the feasibility of reproducing the tower of the Hall. He conceived placing the tower as a town hall in the grassy plot on the southeast quadrant of Barney Allis Plaza. After examining the archival drawings for Independence Hall, he learned that the tower was 32 feet square, ideal for his town hall setting. Even more surprising, he found this dimension to be exactly the same size as the square concrete trellised area in the northwest corner of the park, which offered a structural base already in place.

In an effort to avoid misunderstandings with city hall, Miller brought members of the city council one by one to his office and showed them the drawings and received their encouragement for his plan. He spoke to Bill Dunn of J.E. Dunn Construction about the possibility that different Kansas City firms might donate materials and services to the project. Dunn estimated an overall cost of around $800,000, which sounded reasonable for the nation's first monument to the Bill of Rights that would surely draw many visitors.

Miller's plan envisioned rows of old-fashioned benches inside the town hall where groups of school children could sit and learn about the historical significance of the Bill of Rights. He would make a gift of a replica of the Liberty Bell and planned to install busts of the eight men who drew up the document. Outside on the village green, there would be larger-than-life bronze statues of the same men. One of the sculptures would be Benjamin Franklin sitting on a park bench, a work by George Lundeen that he had seen pictured at the Pam Driscol Gallery in Aspen.

Enthused by the response to all the homework they had done, Miller and Lyman reported back to the committee. To their dismay, the committee demurred; they were simply not interested in undertaking such an ambitious project. Miller was philosophical. "Twenty years ago," he said to Lyman, "I'd have tackled this on my own. I guess we'll just have to have Benjamin Franklin come to the Plaza by himself to celebrate the 200th birthday of the Bill of Rights."

Today, Ben Franklin sits in a little parklet to the west of The Gap. He shares his bench with many Plaza visitors who enjoy

The Benjamin Franklin bench, the work of George Lundeen, sits just to the west of The Gap. Ben is celebrating the 200th anniversary of the Bill of Rights. Miller had envisioned a larger grouping and the reproduction of the tower atop Independence Hall in Philadelphia set as a small town hall in one corner of Barney Allis Park as a major memorial to this historic occasion.

having their pictures taken with him as he sits quietly reading the preamble to the Constitution of the United States.

It was Lyman Field who gave Miller the nickname "White Heat." "He has a way of turning up the heat if you have to work with him," says Lyman. "It's like having a blowtorch turned on you! For a cause he considers legitimate, Miller has no qualms about making personal appeals for financial assistance. He points out that when you ask people to contribute money for the good of the community, you can ask any amount without worrying you will be criticized. You offer them the *opportunity* to participate."

Like his father before him, Miller continues to stroll the Plaza almost daily with his little black notebook, jotting down merchants he wants to call, names he wants to consult about an idea. In his pocket is a small cassette recorder into which he dictates memos for secretary Nancy Sweeney, who keeps tabs on and is a favorite with the family. Many of these memos address needs for maintenance; others, new ideas for the Plaza. When he sees a tree that requires trimming, he arranges to supervise it. When he sees trash on the street or sidewalk, he picks it up. He is often kidded by friends about this habit. His response: "It sets a good example."

He delights these days in what he terms "fine tuning with art." One example was his gift of the "Path of Gold" lighting on 47th Street. Another is the new clock tower that he commissioned for a triangle site on 47th Street across from Abercrombie & Fitch and Houston's restaurant.[59] From its ground floor space, Plaza information and other services are offered to visitors.

Equally important to the Plaza image and ambience, Miller feels, are smaller adornments. One of these is "April," the small lead figure of a little girl with her watering can and a bouquet of flowers, which Miller spotted at the Fenn Galleries in Santa Fe. Located on the west side of The Limited, "April" is surrounded by a low oval wrought iron fence designed by Gordon Jarchow and planted with a bed of ivy.

Particularly popular have been his benches. During a family clan trip to western Colorado in 1987, Miller spied a charming old iron bench in Silverton that was identified to him as an award-winning bench at the World's Fair of 1898. He bought the bench and arranged for the redesign of its medallion back with reproductions of art work found on the Plaza. He had a dozen of these benches cast with a gold bronze patina suitable for outdoor use and chose a dozen sites along Plaza sidewalks and tucked into courtyards. They are a popular choice for a little winter sunning, enjoyment of a shopping respite, or sometimes for a picnic lunch. To embellish the statue of Sir Winston and Lady Churchill, he had molds made to reproduce the bronze benches found along the Thames in London.

During the 1980s, Miller twice had the Plaza trash containers redesigned, and he continues to collect new ideas for these in his travels. The proliferation of news vending machines on Plaza corners is a particular source of aggravation for him; four to eight machines grouped together are an eyesore. However, he has not been successful in getting the city to address this situation. He attempted to do so on his own by building a handsome, four-sided, copper-domed news kiosk on the north side of 47th Street near Houston's restaurant, but the offer of kiosks didn't satisfy most of the media.

A sculpture—"The Organ Grinder," by Mark Lundeen—also from the Pam Driscoll Gallery in Aspen, reminded Miller of the days when the Plaza had an organ grinder and monkey. Although the city later forbade organ grinders with live monkeys, the statue evokes a bit of nostalgia. Miller chose a small garden site along the walk that leads into Pomona Courtyard and invited Bryant School children down for the dedication.

Just east of the Jayne Gallery on 47th Street is a corner that Miller long felt needed some decoration. Prowling about in the company storage caves, he came upon two small lead figures of a shepherd boy and girl that seemed to fill the need. He asked company architect Gordon Jarchow to plan a siting for them which would include a small fountain. The Shepherds Fountain was set in place in the summer of 1991.

On Columbus Day, October 12, 1991, the Miller Nichols family made a gift to Kansas City of a replica model in copper and wrought iron of the Santa Maria, Christopher Columbus' ship. The gift was in anticipation of the 1992 quincentennial celebration of Columbus' discovery of America.

Like many of Miller's gifts this one has a story. In Venice, Italy, the previous summer, he got lost while walking the twisting streets. All he could remember was a model of the Santa Maria that extended from the wall above a restaurant near his hotel. Nearly two hours beyond his intended return, he finally located this landmark. By the next day he was determined to find a way to bring this model back to Kansas City to commemorate the upcoming quincentennial. His Italian search was in vain, but back in the states he located the ship's plans at the Smithsonian. He found a model boat builder

in Connecticut and then an ironsmith who could fabricate the design that company architect Gordon Jarchow made from the plans.

Forty-two inches in length, the model sits in a two-branch wrought iron candelabra along with a legend that tells of Columbus' voyage, in Spanish on one side, and English on the other. The candelabra is mounted on a "Path of Gold" pole topped with a single lamp. Located at the edge of the Court of the Penguins, the Santa Maria was dedicated to the third-grade school children of Greater Kansas City.

Westport Today

In 1990 Miller embarked upon a new venture, "Westport Today." For some 30 years, he had been buying houses north of the Plaza that he felt were properly valued, to assemble a sizeable tract for redevelopment. He defines the tract as the area between 46th Street and Westport Road, bounded on the east by St. Luke's Hospital and on the west by Southwest Trafficway.

Miller explains: "I feel that this land, comprising some fifty acres, could and should be redeveloped some time in the future for mid- and high-rise moderately priced residential apartments and condominiums in order to satisfy the continually growing demand for housing in Kansas City. There are no large tracts of land left in Kansas City, Missouri, south of the river, so if we are going to provide homes for those who want to live close-in in Missouri, this can only be done through redevelopment, by identifying a tract of land and buying the houses one at a time when owners want to sell."

Working with others, Miller hopes to develop tax increment financing for the area; this would ensure the total redevelopment as an entity. Westport Today now owns more than 100 houses and needs to purchase some 250 more before the full acreage will be ready.

In platting for redevelopment, streets will be realigned to provide adequate entrance onto and off of Southwest Trafficway, the main artery between the Plaza and downtown. The plat will also clearly specify the new neighborhood as a moderate-priced residential apartment complex with architectural detail and landscaping. When completed, it will offer attractive residential living less than fifteen minutes from the center of downtown and less than five minutes from the Plaza.

The Family

In March 1979, Miller married Jeannette Terrell Deweese, widow of John Edward Deweese and daughter of Frank Hixson and Lorette Chapman Terrell. The mother of two children, Jennifer and John, she is a graduate of Sunset Hill, Vassar College, and the University of Kansas. Before her first marriage she had a career as a researcher with the Federal Reserve Bank of Kansas City and on the editorial staff of *Fortune* magazine in New York. Since 1980, J.C. Nichols' legacy of family has grown as well. By 1994, J.C. and Jessie Nichols' descendants numbered 36. Despite the scattered grandchildren and great-grandchildren, Kansas City remains the base for celebrating family holidays, with Miller's and Clyde's wives taking turns hosting gatherings at Christmas and Suzie Weber hosting the family for lunch on Memorial Day. With buckets of coral carnations, white daisies, and blue cornflowers, the family treks to ancestral gravesites in the Olathe Cemetery where

Nichols, Jackson, Miller, and Phenicie ancestors are buried. Occasionally they drive by J.C. Nichols' boyhood home. The custom is repeated at the Forest Hill Cemetery in Kansas City, Missouri, to decorate the Nichols family graves there.

There are also larger clan gatherings to which all descendants of the Miller sisters and their husbands, John Kane and J.C. Nichols, are invited. The role of convener has been traded between the two families annually for two decades. At the 1991 gathering, Miller and Jeannette distributed copies of the family history they had just published, *Ancestors and Descendants of Jesse Clyde and Jessie (Miller) Nichols*. It was the work of genealogist Joan F. Curran.

At the gathering, stories of the University of Kansas Beta chapter were exchanged. No less than 13 men of the family lived there as undergraduates! (Miller, Clyde, and Dick Kane all returned for their 50th reunions.) In 1978, Dick Kane was awarded the Distinguished Service Citation from the University of Kansas; in 1979, his cousin, Miller Nichols, was so honored.

In the years from 1978 on, the daughters of Eleanor and Earl, Suzie and Mollie, saw their children through teenage and college years and into marriages and careers. For Suzie, the focus has been family, school, and community. Like her grandfather J.C., she served as a trustee of Sunset Hill School and the merged Pembroke Hill. She followed Clyde into challenging years for Planned Parenthood, serving as president of its Kansas City board and on the national board as well. She also serves on the board of the Truman Medical Center and chairs the advisory committee for the Carolyn Benton Cookefair chair at UMKC.

Planning for her married children and

grandchildren, Suzie built a condominium second home in one of Susan and Wayne Nichols' developments in Santa Fe, New Mexico. There Suzie's daughter Deborah and husband Wayne White delight in joining her with their twins, David Allen and Kathleen Suzanne. Daughter Laura and husband Michael Lutz had their first child, Abigail Kathleen, in May 1994. These are J.C. and Jessie Nichols' first great-great-grandchildren.

Mollie Allen Chapman's home is in Portland, Oregon, where she and Manson Kennedy raised a family of three, Melina, Raud, and Magen. A theater arts devotee, she has enjoyed starring roles with the Columbia Repertory Theater company, which she helped found. In 1986, she married Harry Chapman and now gives priority to the horse show life, dividing her time between the lovely home they built in Portland and the horse farm where they train thoroughbred Grand Prix jumpers. Melina is married and living in England. Raud is a writer; Magen, a pianist and composer. Both live in Boston.

Miller and Katie Nichols' progeny are scattered, too. Kay Callison, the eldest, and her husband John bought Miller's home in Corinth Downs when the Nichols moved to the Alameda Towers. Condominium living enables them, with their children Mark and Elizabeth, to spend much of their weekend time at John's farm north of Kansas City that his family homesteaded in 1837.

Kay's life focuses around the children and community endeavors, particularly those with a historical emphasis. Historic Kansas City, the Wildlife Outdoor Education Center, and the Alvin Ailey American Dance Theater have been of special importance to her. Kay and John enjoy arts events and travel and vacations at the Cap-K Ranch. Son Mark in 1994 is a

freshman in college, and Liz is a freshman at Shawnee Mission East High School.

Nance Lopez, Miller's second daughter, a Stanford graduate, and her husband, Ramon, live in Santa Fe, where they are raising a family of four—teenagers Leon and Lilly, and twins Miller and Bo. Ramon was the designer-craftsman for their adobe hillside home. Both Ramon and Nance are artists. His focus is on the Spanish Colonial arts. Working in silver, carving and painting altar screens, and creating furniture, Ramon has work in the collections of the Smithsonian in Washington, D.C., and the Herd Museum in Phoenix, as well as in the Taos and Santa Fe museums. Nance's specialty is treasure necklaces, which she sells through gallery shops from California to Connecticut. A nationwide clientele collects her work. All four children are already pursuing artistic endeavors.

Ann Nichols has been the family's careerist. Her home in Seattle, Washington, is a corner 29th floor condominium overlooking the lakes and harbor. Down some 70 steps, it is a short walk to the pier-side office where a dozen accountants assisted her with purchasing for the Port of Seattle. A tireless worker, Ann has found Seattle an exciting city. For health reasons, Ann retired in the spring of 1994. Two of her closest Seattle friends are native Kansas Citians: Carolyn Davis, a lawyer who is the daughter of former Mayor Ike Davis; and Marty Dodge, daughter of the late physician Mark Dodge, brother of Marty Nichols.

Lynn Nichols and her husband Jim Gilchrest live on the Cap-K Ranch, where Lynn, a landscape architect, keeps the ranch abloom. Until recently, she served as librarian for the Aspen Community School. Their first son, Carson, was born in January 1994. Jim, an ardent fisherman and a technical mountain climber, teaches at the Aspen Community School.

For Miller and Jeannette the Cap-K has been a place to gather friends over the past 15 years. After restoring the Luchsinger homestead cabin, he built a clubhouse/bunkhouse for the grandchildren, made additions to former hay-hand houses across the road, fixed up a carpenter shop, expanded the machine shops, and has even added some ranch lakes. Miller insists on doing the driving on the 800-mile Kansas City-to-Cap-K trips.

Jeannette enjoys working in her patio gardens where summer meals are served. Housekeeper Lillie Isaiah, godmother to Lilly Lopez, "makes it all work." They are often joined by the Holton family—Jeannette's daughter Jennifer, husband Jim and sons Jonathan and Jason. The Holtons live on 40 acres overlooking Lake Reudi, six miles up the valley from the Cap-K; the boys attend the Aspen Community School. Jeannette's son John, having lived in scattered parts of the world studying esoteric cultures, now lives in Boulder where he is recording songs he has composed for his poems.

Back in Kansas City, Jeannette's interests have focused on the arts and education—Accessible Arts, arts programming for handicapped youth, for which she was the founding president; Arts Partners, a K-12 curriculum-based arts education program; and projects for the several performing arts boards on which she has served. She chaired the task force that recommended policy and programming for the new Cultural Education Center at the Johnson County Community College.

The Clyde Nichols continue to live in their lovely and extremely busy Mission Hills home. They not only believe in celebrating family and social occasions, but make their home available for countless committee meetings, political gatherings, and pre-parties to benefit one of the many civic endeavors they support. They travel widely—usually annually with the World Presidents Organization (the senior group to the YPO), which holds its meetings in foreign settings, most recently in Thailand. And they frequently join friends, family, or KU alumni on trips abroad. They drive regularly to their second home in Santa Fe. Built by their son, Wayne, in his first passive-solar home development, it has become a favorite family rendezvous.

Marty has been called a true Renaissance woman of uniquely diverse talents. A talented and commercially successful artist, she paints several times a week in a studio she shares with other artists; she rides weekends with the Mission Valley Hunt; she has taken on the leadership of major civic institutions, particularly when they were in crisis, as mentioned earlier. She has the capacity to come up with creative ideas for new projects and the tremendous energy to see them through.

Clyde and Marty have nine grandchildren, all boys. Jay Nichols, their older son and the only one living in Kansas City, now heads Nichols Industries, whose dominant company, Crimsco, manufactures hot-and-cold food serving carts for hospitals and penal institutions. Jay and Patsy Darnaby Nichols have two grown sons. Ben, a graduate of Chapman University with an interest in theater and films, is building film sets for a company in San Francisco; his younger brother Peter is finishing college and working in film.

In 1989, Jay married Loretta Lombardo, who heads her own typesetting and graphic design business, L&J Graphic Arts. Their leisure time is claimed by Jasen, their merry and energetic three-year old.

Wayne Nichols and his wife Susan have raised three sons, with Santa Fe their family home for the past 22 years. They were pioneers in passive-solar home building and during the 1970s and early 1980s were frequently invited to give seminars at architects and builders meetings across the country; their work was once featured as a centerfold by *Life* magazine. Wayne sites their residential projects, buys the land, and works out the financing. Susan, as the president of their company, oversees the design and construction of their houses, as well as the interior design. Wayne then takes over as the marketer of the products. Their most recent project introduced a concept that Wayne felt was timely for Santa Fe—condominium buildings whose units provide space for a work shop or studio on the first floor with residential space above, aimed at artists and artisans. It has been highly successful.

Wayne has expanded his business into Nichols Real Estate, adding residential salespeople. Representing the business perspective of New Mexico, he serves on the Small Business Advisory Council for the 10th Federal Reserve District, with headquarters in Kansas City.

Wayne and Susan's three sons are scattered: Eliot, a University of Colorado graduate, has a landscaping business in Santa Fe; Chris, a Stanford graduate who has worked in remote environments, is presently earning his Ph.D. in anthropology at Tulane University; Sebi (Sebastian), who skied in Junior Olympics competition in high school, attended the University of Vermont for a semester and seeks now to study at a university with summer/fall semesters to enable him to compete in downhill.

Blair, the eldest of three daughters of Marty and Clyde, is a graduate of Columbia University; having received her master's degree from Columbia Teachers College, she is working on a Ph.D. in counseling. Blair has worked in several Christian ministries and is now a certified counselor practicing in Phoenix. Her son, Jesse Lawrence, has completed his sophomore year at Rollins College.

Daughter Jessie Nichols, who, like her parents, practices meditation, has worked in numerous endeavors related to Maharishi University in Fairfield, Iowa. She has studied and taught meditation in different parts of Europe as well as in Thailand, India, and Russia.

Dell Nichols Richardson, youngest of the Nichols brood, lives in Tucson, Arizona, with her husband Joe and two sons, Jacob and Wade. Both Dell and Joe have masters degrees. Dell teaches a computer class and together they run a refinishing business.

Epilogue

In 1994, there were no longer any members of the Nichols family employed by the J.C. Nichols Company, although Miller and his daughter, Kay Callison, serve on the board of directors. Controlling ownership of the company was removed from the family to company management and employees through an Employee Stock Ownership Plan (ESOP) established in 1987. Approximately 25 percent of J.C. Nichols Company stock remains in the family and with other minority stockholders. The ESOP was established for the exclusive benefit of eligible company employees and their beneficiaries. The plan is designed to reward job productivity and to provide retirement benefits funded by contributions from the company. These are paid into the J.C. Nichols Company employees' stock ownership trust, which has three trustees: Tony Sweeney, Dave Cody, and Walter Janes, treasurer of the company.

The background of the establishment of the ESOP goes back to the mid-1980s. At that time the market quote for J.C. Nichols Company stock had risen above $600, but it paid a very low rate of return as company policy has always been to plow earnings back into the company for growth and expansion. Some Nichols family members were interested in having a larger voice in the running of the company and in seeing a change in this policy.

Having set the structure to pursue long-range plans, this did not seem viable to Miller and he said so. He agreed that those who had an investment in the company were certainly entitled to receive their fair share, but he believed it was better to build capital gains value into the stock and avoid carrying debt rather than to pay more earnings out in dividends. The company had an agreement with family members to buy any stock they wished to offer at any time at the current market quotation.

Lynn and Miller subsequently concluded that the thing to do for the ever more scattered family members was to have an appraisal made of the company's assets and to offer stockholders the opportunity to sell their stock at the value appraised. This stock, in turn, could be redistributed through an ESOP so that employees would be rewarded for their contributions and service to the company. At the end of 1991, some 9,000 shares had accrued to an employee ownership fund through the plan.

The almost yearly changes in tax and other regulatory requirements of an ESOP have made it complicated for the company. The basic procedure in setting up the plan was to borrow the money for the ESOP stock and pay stockholders for their shares at $735 per share, with the company in turn repaying the loan to the ESOP.

A retrospective look at Jesse Clyde Nichols' services to his city and his country reveals that they have survived and are still bearing fruit 40 years after his death.

The elements of the cultural/educational/scientific center are all there, and better than ever. The magnificent Nelson-Atkins Museum of Art enjoys a national reputation. The Kansas City Art Institute and School of Design turns out top-flight professionals.

The Midwest Research Institute and the Linda Hall Science Library are among the finest institutions of their kind in the country. The University of Missouri at Kansas City, thanks in part to Miller Nichols' leadership and contributions, is a distinguished center of learning with the second largest campus of any metropolitan university in the United States.

The performance of classical music in Kansas City has had a roller-coaster history since J.C.'s death, but his family has helped it survive and grow. The Kansas City Symphony plays to an ever larger audience each season, and the newer Cammerata, a chamber orchestra, has received wide acclaim for its fall and spring seasons at the Unity Temple on the Plaza.

The National Association of Real Estate Boards, with headquarters in the Wrigley Building on Michigan Avenue in Chicago, is today still the largest and most influential professional organization in the field. The Urban Land Institute, with headquarters in Washington, D.C., which had 700 members when it started, now has 14,000, and as many as 4,000 attend its conventions. The Community Builders' Council no longer exists under that name, but its objectives and services are carried on by a range of more specialized ULI councils that have succeeded it.

With the objective of perpetuating J.C. Nichols' ideals, a number of his friends in the Urban Land Institute established a J.C. Nichols Foundation in 1950. Its funds were used to give grants-in-aid for studies and theses in city planning and thus "to encourage able young college men at graduate level to enter fields of endeavor related to improvement of community development in the United States," an objective successfully met in succeeding years.

Twenty-three years after J.C.'s death, the J.C. Nichols Foundation was folded into the newer and broader Urban Land Research Foundation. The latter conducts seminars and courses, sponsors a program at the Harvard Business School, and carries on other activities closely akin to J.C.'s interests. One of the summer interns it sponsors is designated the J.C. Nichols intern. In agreeing with this move, Miller Nichols, as chairman of the board of the Nichols Company, said he "was already convinced that this was the proper way of handling these funds." He continued, "My family and my business associates have taken considerable pride in the activities of this [J.C. Nichols] Foundation and we are pleased to have been able to support it financially and are appreciative that so many of my father's friends have done likewise."

In November 1993, the Urban Land Institute, at its annual meeting, granted a Heritage Award to Kansas City's Country Club Plaza. The citation reads:

As the oldest shopping center in the United States—and one of the most consistently successful—the Country Club Plaza has been emulated both nationally and internationally for seventy-one years. A combination of innovative site planning, rich architecture, careful maintenance, and creative marketing has enabled the center to enrich the lives of residents, employees and tourists alike.

The National Capital Planning Commission (its name since 1952) still exists. But with the relinquishing of federal management of Washington, D.C., in favor of "home rule," its function is now to review and recommend, without legal authority to enforce, except in connection with federal property. With the politics inherent in home rule, national concerns have often been pushed into the background in favor of the concerns of local constituencies. Washington is all but drowning in the same problems that beset most large American cities, but are somehow exacerbated here. It is fortunate, perhaps, that J.C. Nichols did not live to see, in the words of the *Readers Digest*, "our nation's capital" become "our national shame." But let history record that the part of the capital that today attracts busloads upon busloads, indeed thousands upon thousands of eager, uplifted, and open-mouthed children with their teachers and parents each year—the magnificent public buildings and monuments, the grounds and parks, the trees and flowers, the broad avenues and boulevards, the very workability of the city—owes much to J.C. Nichols from Kansas City and his fellow commissioners in those demanding and creative years from 1926 to 1948.

Annually, in late October, employees of the J.C. Nichols Company attend an afternoon meeting at which the chairman reviews the year and describes new goals and projects for the year ahead. In the evening, with a spouse or friend, they

This Plaza Christmas scene called attention to the Heritage Award presented by the Urban Land Institute to the J.C. Nichols Company's Country Club Plaza at its annual meeting in Atlanta in November 1993. J.C. Nichols was one of the founders of the Urban Land Institute. (Courtesy of Roy Inman)

December 1993 $5.00

URBAN LAND

ULI

L. A. Markets
Contaminated Sites
ULI Awards for Excellence

gather for a company dinner at the Ritz-Carlton Hotel. Past officers and directors of the company are invited, along with members of the Nichols family. It is a time of camaraderie, for reminiscing, and a time to celebrate friendships built during years of service with the J.C. Nichols Company.

To honor years of service in five-year increments, pictures of each honoree are projected on a large screen while Barbara Barickman, from public relations, describes each person's background with the company and their personal interests. Lynn McCarthy presents a gift from the company, and all join in the congratulations. Anniversaries of 10, 15, 20, 25, 30, and 35 years are recognized. Even a 45-year veteran is not unusual. Along with the nostalgia and humor that such an occasion evokes, there is also obvious pride in remembering earlier years and the multitude of things large and small that the J.C. Nichols Company has contributed to the quality of life in Kansas City.

Anniversaries of the company's founding have also been celebrated with dinners and commemorative publications. In 1980, on the company's 75th anniversary, former chairman of the Urban Land Institute Roy Drachman, an early friend of J.C. and later of Miller and Clyde, was the guest speaker. On Miller's 50th anniversary with the company, the Plaza Merchants' Association honored him with a surprise gala at the Alameda Plaza Hotel, for which his four daughters slipped into town to celebrate with him.

Chairman Lynn McCarthy analyzes the company's position in the 1990s thus: "Our company is somewhat of an anachronism in today's economy, with the new emphasis on short-term profits. Because of this orientation, it's much more difficult to find long-term investors. Coupled with tax law inconsistencies, it makes for a harrowing time to be managing a real estate firm. Even if it's difficult to swallow, management must succeed in adapting the J.C. Nichols Company to the prevalent political and economic climate. We're attempting to do just that."

The spirit of J.C. lives on, McCarthy says. "We're interested in tomorrow as well as today. We are going to vigorously resist inappropriate developments, incompetent developers and certainly inadequate parking and traffic provisions; there are those who want to take advantage of what we've done over the last 85 years, what we've worked so diligently to create."

He concludes: "We must not forget that while J.C. Nichols had the vision to plan the Country Club District and for its shopping centers as well as for the Plaza, it is Miller who has structured and built the company. When I came here in 1958, company assets were less than $20 million. Today they exceed $500 million. It is Miller that structured the company and captained the team that made this possible. It has been a remarkable stewardship to the community that both men have honored."

Today, on a sultry summer evening when an elderly couple sits on a bench beside the cool fountain adjacent to the Verona Columns in Mission Hills; or when out-of-state visitors to the Country Club Plaza stand transfixed beside a fountain gazing up at Donatello Gabrielli's bronze masterpiece of the goddess Pomona; when a small child begs his father for a penny, rubs the Bronze Boar's shiny nose, closes his eyes, and makes a wish as he drops his coin; when a class of ninth-grade students stop in front of the Spanish bullfight mural on their walking art tour and learn that the colorful tiles were glazed and fired using a process that hasn't changed in over one thousand years; when a Kansas Citian feels a swelling of civic pride as he admires the Plaza's impressive Giralda Tower, with its seven-foot, 2,500-pound bronze statue of Faith—in all these moments it is apparent that the money and efforts put forth by Miller and by his father before him to beautify the Plaza, the Country Club District, and the city have not gone unappreciated.

Text Notes

1. The beautification of the view was achieved in the 1920s; the cultural center later became a reality farther south on Brush Creek Boulevard, and the civic center was eventually developed downtown.

2. Lindsay Cooper remembers calling on Nichols in his penthouse office, where she marveled at the quantities of papers that covered the huge table which served as his desk. They were not strewn haphazardly but were in neat piles, one pile for each of his myriad projects and activities.

3. Two more sons were born after the Civil War: Oslin, in Iowa; and Ed, in Kansas.

4. Jesse T. later bought out the rest of his family's interest in the home farm and continued to operate it until his death in 1916.

5. In 1909, partly through Nichols' urging, Kansas City extended its city limits from 49th Street to 77th Street, annexing Waldo. In 1947, the city limits were stretched out to 85th Street; and in 1963, to the Cass County line.

6. Chancellor Snow wrote Clyde afterward, "You have been more of a support to the University, have accomplished more for your school, than any other student."

7. Jarvis and Conklin went into receivership in 1894, and the English syndicate sold out to Bouton and a local Baltimore syndicate, at a profit, in 1903.

8. In 1917, the Taylors moved to 5625 Pembroke Lane, where they resided until relocating to 2725 Verona Terrace in 1938.

9. The second generations of both families have continued the friendship, as well as business and civic associations. When Miller retired from the Business Men's Assurance Company board in 1985, he and his father had served continuously for over 70 years.

10. Later, during World War I, Crowell was appointed by President Woodrow Wilson to enforce the Wheat Guarantee Act, and he served his country in administering the distribution of grain in foreign relief, for which he was decorated by several nations. Besides his grain business, Crowell helped organize and was a director of the Southwest National Bank, which was absorbed into the Commerce Trust; he was also a director of BMA, having backed W.T. Grant in its formation. Upon his death, Frank Crowell left more than $2 million to the University of Kansas Endowment Fund and another large bequest to St. Luke's Hospital.

11. After H.F. Hall's death, he bequeathed his home and grounds, together with a large endowment, to become the Linda S. Hall Library of Science, in memory of his wife.

12. The relationship thrived in spite of J.C.'s initial faux pas. Upon Nelson's death in 1915, J.C. Nichols became one of three trustees administering the former's $11-million bequest to acquire a collection of art for what was to become the William Rockhill Nelson Gallery of Art. (By the time of the gallery's opening, the name had been changed to the William Rockhill Nelson Gallery and Mary Atkins Museum, to reflect the latter's generosity.) He and Jessie continued a lifelong friendship with Nelson's widow, Mary McAfee Nelson, and their daughter, Laura (Mrs. Irwin Kirkwood). Also following Nelson's death, George Longan, his successor as one of the owners of the *Star,* became a staunch supporter who recognized the contribution that J.C.'s work made to the quality of life in Kansas City. George and Ann Longan were two of J.C. and Jessie's closest lifelong friends.

13. Over time, the Commerce Trust Company extended to the J.C. Nichols Company a line of credit enabling them to borrow up to $800,000 without collateral, which "gave us great moral and financial support," according to J.C. in his memoirs. It also proved an extremely profitable arrangement for the bank. J.C.'s ownership of Commerce Bank stock proved equally profitable.

14. The latter plan ran into a snag because the city limits stopped at 49th Street. However, Nichols and his associates had already been campaigning to get the city limits extended to 79th Street. It took

until 1911 for the matter to be finally approved by the Missouri Court of Appeals.

15. Both of J.C.'s sons, Miller and Clyde, Jr., have indelible memories of summer jobs in their youth with the Nichols Company's road-maintenance crews, which taught them that street building included laying down the heavy stones, further breaking them up with a napping hammer, and enduring the suffocating asphalt fumes as they spread the macadam top.

16. The Hares also laid out the Country Club Plaza shopping center in 1921. Herb Hare went on to become nationally recognized in his profession, serving as planning consultant to a number of other cities. His association with J.C. continued almost until the latter's death.

17. Some years after the repeal of national prohibition, Kansas passed a state law declaring that "the saloon is forever abolished" but permitting drinks to be served in private clubs. In 1954, the magnificent present clubhouse was built in the center of the golf course at a cost of $950,000. The abandoned clubhouse, with swimming pool and tennis courts, was bought by Lewis Kitchen and Paul Willson, who formed the Carriage Club.

18. Expanding to meet the needs of new home construction, the water company eventually had over 4,000 customers. The Nichols Company divested itself of the water company in 1985.

19. This block-long esplanade was so-named because it was planned to be lined with Colonial-style homes. However, when the Depression came along, in order to sell the expensive lots at all, it was necessary to allow the buyers to build homes that, though large and handsome, were more eclectic in style.

20. Today, Mission Hills landscaping is serenely spectacular and its stately homes, breathtaking. The area abounds with parklets and islands at intersections adorned with classic statuary and figurines. Seven pink Carrara marble fluted columns imported from Verona, Italy, stand at the corner of Mission Drive and Overhill Road, with a reflecting pool and a statuary fountain in the foreground. In the late 1980s, two Mission Hills mansions were purchased and demolished so the new owner could use the site for an even more magnificent residence—an impressive measure of the value of a Mission Hills homesite. There are no vacant lots left for a family intent on living in Mission Hills in a newly built home.

21. Nichols and Taylor discovered that the developers of the Riverside subdivision outside of Chicago had included several basic restrictions with their deeds, including a mandatory 30-foot, open yard set-back from the street and a minimum construction cost of $3,000. They adopted these restrictions for Bismark Place. They studied the restrictions covering other subdivisions in which Frederick Law Olmsted had been involved. In Cushing Island, Maine, these included advance approval of the location of the house on the lot and banning of stores, saloons, and hotels. In Brookline Hills, Massachusetts, the developers limited the community to single-family dwellings, established set-backs, set height limits for residences, and forbade privies and cesspools. Other subdivisions mandated home design in the "rural" style, limited the height of fences, and provided that property owners be assessed for maintenance of roads. Many of these restrictions were applied or adapted in the Country Club District.

22. The contests were discontinued with the onset of the Depression in 1930. An extension of this idea was the annual flower show, beginning in the spring of 1921. The entries were publicly displayed in the Brookside Community Hall, with awards and cash prizes given by category. This event became a high point of the year for many home gardeners. An ancillary benefit, of course, was the beautification of the district through more flower gardens. The company also sponsored a dandelion-pulling contest among the schoolchildren of the district. The children from each school were to pull all the dandelions they could and bring them to school in a large gunny-sack. The contestants from the winning school were photographed for the newspaper, standing behind piles of dandelions.

23. Another early figure whose name was synonymous with the company was George W. Tourtellot. After attending both the University of Kansas and the University of Michigan, he joined the Nichols Company in 1909. Like his bosses, he worked as a laborer on district improvements in the morning then changed his clothes to sell real estate in the afternoon and evening. Reflecting on those early days, he relates: "Mr. Nichols kept a milking cow near his home. But the weeds grew so high, the cow was forever getting lost. We soon learned not to visit him too close to milking time, or we would face a long jaunt through the weeds, hunting for that darned cow!" Several years after Tourtellot joined the company, J.C. assigned him the daunting task of assembling the land needed for the proposed Country Club Plaza, which was still a dark secret. It took Tourtellot nearly a decade to track down more than 100 absentee owners and persuade them to sell. During this time, in 1918, Tourtellot was named head of the newly formed business properties department.

Also during this process, one of Tourtellot's more nerve-wracking experiences occurred, which became a company legend. He was visiting the home of a woman who had indicated she was willing to sell her house. As they were sitting in her living room discussing the possible terms, she suddenly jumped up and exclaimed, "Quick, out the back door! Here comes my husband; he can't find you here!" Startled, Tourtellot blindly obeyed. He raced out the back door, scaring the cook in the kitchen, only to find himself in an enclosed back yard. He frantically scaled a seven-foot-high solid wood fence and ran all the way to the streetcar stop. He later found out that the husband had not been keen on selling the house and had sworn he would throw out any realtor who dared show his face. The postscript was that Tourtellot persevered and eventually made the purchase.

George Tourtellot retired in 1963 after 55 years of service with the J.C. Nichols Company. He died six years later at the age of 84.

Kansas University graduate Charles S. "Pete" Pitrat, maintenance supervisor of the company, assisted Tourtellot in the management and development of business and apartment properties. Charlie Pitrat's view was: "If I have a decision to make regarding an expenditure, I ask myself, 'If this were my money, would I spend it?'"

Frank Grant, having graduated from KU two years earlier, came aboard in 1909 for a salary of $50 per month. Grant served as treasurer of the company beginning in 1914. He was an organizer, a master of detail and policy, and a student of taxation and municipal affairs. His watchful eye over company finances and Missouri politics were among his contributions. He reputedly knew more about the inner workings of the company than anyone except J.C. himself.

John Ruddy recalls that Grant kept a watchful eye on the neighborhood homes associations in an effort to ensure that they didn't make funds or mailing lists available for partisan political interests or other "wrong purposes." He underscores Grant's notorious frugality: "Mr. Grant watched his pennies so carefully that he used to write notes and memos on paper he had retrieved from the waste basket."

Frank had a generous side as well, which children on the Plaza were quick to recognize. He kept a coat pocket full of roasted peanuts in the shell and would offer them to any child who held out a hand. Grant habitually walked through the Plaza after closing time each evening, checking to make sure all the shops were locked up properly. In ac-

knowledgement of this quirk, company employees gave him a key ring for Christmas one year.

Fred Gibson claims, "Frank Grant kept the office in line. All work orders and invoices passed across his desk and underwent his close scrutiny. I remember getting called into his office one afternoon. He held up an invoice, looked me in the eye, and asked, 'Are these your initials?' Fully expecting to be called on the carpet about some inaccuracy, I admitted that they were mine. He simply said, 'Just wanted to make sure they were your initials.' Ironically, invoices now have to pass across my desk. I do my best to examine them as carefully as Frank used to."

David M. Kennard joined the company in 1910 as a salesman, and Walter G. Basinger began in the same capacity three years later. Both men rose together through the sales organization, Kennard becoming sales manager and then director of sales. In the latter capacity, he was responsible for platting the properties, determining prices, and establishing the all-important restrictive covenants, among other duties. He was also entrusted with approval of house designs, color, placement on the lot, etc., in consultation with the architecture department. Basinger was first made manager of the Mission Hills subdivision, which became the company showcase, and later sales manager with a regiment of salesmen reporting to him. Both men eventually became corporate officers and members of the board of directors.

Edward W. Tanner, chief architect for the J.C. Nichols Company and therefore one of the most influential of the early team, became affiliated with the company in 1919, following graduation from the University of Kansas (which awarded him its Distinguished Alumnus Award in 1950).

J.C. stated that versatility was Ed Tanner's number one attribute. Gordon Jarchow, present head of Tanner-Linscott and Associates, describes him: "He was a Man-of-the-Year type of individual; very high profile. Although eventually he was not particularly involved with the day-to-day operations of the architecture department, he did offer suggestions, always in the most tactful manner."

Due to prevailing laws that made it illegal for architects to work in the employ of a developer, Tanner set up his own ostensibly independent firm, Edward W. Tanner Associates (later Tanner-Linscott and Associates, Inc.), which effectively functioned as the Nichols Company's in-house architecture department.

Tanner Associates (or the architecture department as it was known within the Nichols Company) was a division of John Taylor's building department. Ed and his group of up to 10 associate architects designed virtually all of the homes built by the company—from tiny cost-efficient bungalows to mansions costing hundreds of thousands of dollars, as well as all the commercial structures in the Nichols shopping centers.

A company publication noted: "On the issue of good architecture versus bad, [Tanner] is a stickler. One monstrosity can seriously affect a block or a whole neighborhood. . . . Architectural plans of independent builders in the Nichols districts are submitted to the Tanner organization for approval. He is an architect who is also a city builder." Ed's creative design in the 1920s for the Plaza Theater earned him local, national, and even international acclaim; voyages to Spain and Italy provided him with inspiration. Tanner's son, Ned, recalls that his father and mother acquired an abundance of Spanish tile in Mexico City during a visit. The tile, some of which is still in storage for future use, decorates the theater and many other Plaza projects.

Other Edward W. Tanner and Associates projects in the Kansas City area include the Linda Hall Library, the Kansas City Public Library, the Kansas City Life Insurance Company addition, Wornall Plaza, and Regency House Apartments.

Ed's abilities in architecture came naturally. His mother, Harriet Tanner, an architect in Lawrence, Kansas, where Ed was raised, had designed and sold many fine homes in that area. After Tanner's plans were accepted for the Danforth Chapel at KU, a project of which he was justifiably proud, he insisted that his name not appear on the final structure. It was instead dedicated to his mother. Ed's group was also responsible for designing KU's Hoch Auditorium.

Ed Tanner was made a director of the Nichols Company in 1938; he became a vice-president upon J.C.'s death in 1950. In addition to his work ethic and dedication within the company, Tanner held many responsible positions in the community.

Max Stone, who joined the Nichols Company as a salesman in 1907, also pitched in with manual labor assisting J.C. and John Taylor with the early Bismark Place "improvements." Eventually, and for the better part of his 30-year tenure, he served as corporate secretary, playing "a very active part in the upbuilding of the company." His ability to work with the bureaucracies at city hall made him invaluable to J.C. Through his regular attendance at city council meetings, company interests were represented and the company was able to maintain a sharp focus on city politics.

24. The burden of Nichols' increasing responsibilities, among them the chairmanship of the university trustees of the Nelson Gallery of Art (with the responsibility of assembling its collection as well as overseeing construction and operation of its building) and his work in Washington, D.C., as a member of the National Capital Park and Planning Commission, forced him to resign from the Board of Education in 1926. Although he stepped down with nearly four years remaining on his term, J.C. had served with distinction for eight-and-a-half years. Later, in recognition of his contributions to the Board of Education and to the city as a whole, an elementary school at 69th and Oak Streets in Nichols' Armour Hills subdivision was named the J.C. Nichols School.

25. Completion of the Liberty Memorial project was to drag on until 1934. After the dedication of the column, it took another three-and-a-half years to build the rest of the memorial structure. Beautification of the grounds was delayed until the city voted more bonds to grade the approaches and finish the landscaping. By then, George Kessler had left Kansas City, and the firm of Hare & Hare was hired to carry out the work Kessler had begun. Particularly significant was the generosity of R.A. Long, who by 1928 had given one-twentieth of the total money, had volunteered to pay one-twelfth of the cost of carving the vast frieze on the north face, and had offered to pay one-sixth of the maintenance cost of the entire project for five years.

26. The mayor of Kansas City, in a "state of the city" address delivered in 1933, said:

A few days ago came the announcement of the early coming of barge transportation. . . . New impetus should be given by this to the industry of our city and a new life to the agriculture of the Missouri River Valley. For more than fifty years, the community has sought this river transportation for the utilization of one of the longest and greatest rivers in the world. The Federal Government at this very hour is in the process of spending some seventy million dollars . . . to give us a nine-foot channel . . . placing us on a par with Minneapolis and St. Paul; with Chicago on the Illinois River and the Chicago Drainage Canal; as well as the Ohio River cities; with St. Louis, Memphis, and New Orleans on the lower Mississippi—giving us an outlet to the sea. No city in the world has become great in size that did not have waterway transportation. . . . The adverse competition of the Panama Canal which has had such a disastrous effect on the industry and agriculture of the landlocked territory in the Midwest will at last be overcome. Kansas City will be enjoying its God-given right of reasonable competition in freight rates for all heavy commodities which can be moved at less cost on the river. This should bring about a greater prosperity of the Middle West in which the railroads should [also] benefit.

27. According to a study by Dr. Richard Coleman of the University of Chicago, in 1975, after the company had greatly expanded its developments, of the more than 2,000 families who constituted upper-class circles, an amazing 83 percent lived in Nichols subdivisions. And nearly 20 percent were in the city of Mission Hills.

28. Many years later, J.C. was to become involved again in the issue when Macy's bought the department store at the corner of Petticoat Lane and Main Street in 1949. At his own expense he researched the possibilities for providing off-street parking and even went to New York to talk to the top executives at Macy's. Although years had passed since J.C.'s first effort to develop free downtown parking and much more was known about the use of the personal automobile for shopping, Macy's did not provide even one stall of off-street parking. This, in spite of the fact that they had spent $7 million buying, redesigning, and enlarging the store.

29. Mill Creek Parkway was renamed the J.C. Nichols Parkway at the time of Nichols' death.

30. The Indian Hills air strip was later chosen as a landing site for the U.S. Postal Service's maiden airmail flight.

31. Even today, Wolferman's English muffins and other specialty items are sold by mail-order across the country.

32. Sam Pasternak owned several bakery/deli shops each named The Cake Box. He remembers opening one in 1948 in a J.C. Nichols Company shopping center, on which the minimum rent was $150 a month against 5 percent of sales. "The idea of percentage rental was new to us then," he relates, "and our store did so well that before long we were paying $500 a month. Every single month I got a letter from J.C. Nichols personally, praising our sales record, complimenting my management ability and emphasizing that the Nichols Company was behind us. . . . Some of the other tenants resented having to pay higher rents as their sales went up, but I didn't—mostly because of those notes from Mr. Nichols."

33. Today, it takes a crew four months to hang and subsequently dismantle over 50 miles of lights, containing 156,000 individual multi-colored bulbs, all of which are placed every year. Adding to the festive scene are 100 eight-foot red metal candles for roof and sidewalk use, 80 large fiberglass bells swinging from light poles, and huge electric star clusters on the skyline.

34. He was said to have bragged that he could make a local haberdasher named Harry Truman a U.S. senator—and did so! In the process, he also made a great president.

35. Holland was later to go to Washington, D.C., himself as deputy chairman of the War Production Board (which succeeded the NDAC after Pearl Harbor) and was the first chairman of the Smaller War Plants Corporation. Meanwhile, he became an invaluable member of the Nichols team.

36. Mehorney was to go to Washington, D.C., in November 1940 to head the small business section of the NDAC, where he was able to help Nichols in his efforts to obtain defense industry for the Midwest.

37. Nichols was equally diligent and equally successful in bringing defense industry to other parts of Kansas—though this was a harder task because Kansas was perceived to be strictly a farm state with only farm labor available, lacking trained technicians. J.C. tried to turn the rural nature of Kansas into an asset, stressing the advantages of decentralization of defense production scattered in hundreds of small plants in small towns, rather than concentrated in big plants in big cities, with all the attendant problems.

Soon after he arrived in Washington, D.C., Nichols met with the Kansas delegation in Congress to line up their cooperation. Also, he, Roy Roberts, and Willard Breidenthal, a banker and civic leader from Kansas City, Kansas, called on the officials of the National Defense Council to present their case. After this warm-up, the governors of Kansas, Nebraska, and Oklahoma were brought to Washington; along with Nichols and Sen. Arthur Capper of Kansas, they met with Secretary of War Stimson, Secretary of the Navy Knox, coordinator of defense purchasing Donald Nelson, and other high-ranking officials. Governor Ratner of Kansas said on his return, "Everywhere we went, we found that Mr. Nichols and Senator Capper . . . had done excellent spade work. . . . Now we should be able to get some results."

Nichols became a member of the government committee working on including "negotiated contracts" along with bids, with the aim of distributing war production more widely over the country. This was a tremendous help, of course, in bringing more defense industry to the central states. The eventual payoff of all this effort is described in Goldsmith's thesis:

> [In addition to the Naval Air Base at Olathe and the Sunflower Ordnance Plant at De Soto, mentioned above,] the Phillips Refinery at Kansas City, Kansas, converted to high octane gas for the military; the Jayhawk Ordnance Plant in the Pittsburg–Baxter Springs area; a shell loading plant at Parsons; the American Aviation Bomber plant in Fairfax; a bomber base near Topeka; the Smoky Hill Air Base at Salina, the third largest in the nation; a Cessna glider plant at Hutchinson; helium plants at Cunningham and Otis; the Naval Air Base at Hutchinson with satellite fields at six other Kansas towns; an alcohol plant at Atchison, using Kansas grains; the airplane manufacturing center in Wichita, one of the most important aircraft production centers in the country; and others. [The] few Kansas counties [that] did not [have] defense contracts [were] agricultural suppliers to the government. . . . Altogether, the total cost of military installations in Kansas was over $206 million. Industrial facilities in the state cost over $341,000,000. The defense contracts totaled, in round numbers, three *billion* dollars.

38. Sally Ruddy is the widow of company vice-president and attorney John Ruddy and earlier the widow of George W. Tourtellot IV, son of the early vice-president of business properties. She became a part-time employee of the Nichols Company in the fall of 1941.

39. J.C. was drawing from his own experience. In 1905, he had purchased large acreage across the Missouri River from Kansas City, in Clay County. Not sure at that time which way the city was going to grow, north or south, he hedged his bet on his Bismark Place subdivision to the south by purchasing a 230-acre farm to the north—followed by two or three other farms in the area. Although the Clay County land was only two or three miles from downtown Kansas City, it was accessible only by ferry boat. Rumors that a bridge was going to be built prompted Nichols' land purchase, but it actually took six more years and the combined resources of the Armour and Swift meatpacking companies and the Burlington Railroad to complete the bridge. The A-S-B bridge opened in 1911. But by then, partly through Nichols' own efforts, city growth had turned toward the south. So, after paying taxes and carrying costs for years, J.C. finally sold the acreage. "It was much wiser," he wrote later, "to concentrate our efforts on the Country Club District and adjacent lands."

40. Spencer encountered just this kind of obstacle when he made a presentation to the site committee of the NDAC to obtain the chemical production contract he sought. An eastern businessman commented, "Your proposal is all very well except for one thing; you don't have the technical know-how in the West."

Spencer looked around the room and realized that every scientist there—including Ernest Reid and Ed Weidlein—were Kansans. He turned to the businessman and said, "All the technical talent in this room happens to come from Kansas. That leaves only you and me to be accounted for, and I don't know where you come from, but I'm from Kansas."

Spencer got his contract.

41. These enlightened and supportive leaders, in addition to those named earlier, were W.T. Grant, president, Business Men's Assurance Company; C.W. Allendoerfer, president, First National Bank; A.W. Zimmer, manager, North Kansas City Development Company; Guy E. Stanley, executive assistant, Union Pacific Railroad; Grant Stauffer, president, Sinclair Coal Company; Lynwood Smith, president, American Dairies; T.J. Strickler, general manager, Kansas City Gas Company; Chester Smith, president, Kansas City Power & Light Company; M.J. Stooker, general manager, Western Missouri–Kansas Telephone Company; R.L. Gray, president, Sheffield Steel Corporation; George Breon, president, George A. Breon & Company; and A.L. Gustin, president, Gustin-Bacon Manufacturing Company.

42. Although the sale of the Sears building property at the west border of the Plaza was considered a plum at the time, Miller later worked hard to repurchase it, along with the location across the street to the south on which Sears had built their

tires, batteries, and accessories store with an accompanying garage.

43. O'Keefe had been in the sales department when he enlisted in the army in 1942. He served overseas as a lieutenant in an anti-aircraft automatic weapons battalion, where he received a bronze star for bravery.

44. Clyde subsequently became international president of the Young Presidents' Organization (YPO) in 1961 and has remained active in it and affiliated organizations ever since.

45. John Ruddy died in 1991.

46. Ironically, Clyde later became a dedicated advocate of population control and a national director of Planned Parenthood.

47. The company later purchased City Bond and Mortgage's half interest in these buildings.

48. In 1989 Miller had this tile plaque copied on a large scale to decorate the Wornall Road side of the Williams & Sonoma shop.

49. Edwin W. Shields was one of the grain men who were early backers of J.C. Nichols. Along with Herbert F. Hall, Shields had bought 50 acres of land between 51st and 55th Streets, Oak to Holmes, land that adjoined J.C.'s original 1905 property. Each had reserved substantial acreage upon which they built two of the finest mansions in Kansas City. The remaining property was turned over to J.C. Nichols for his Country Club District. The addition of the Shields property to the UKC campus was another example of Miller seizing the opportunity to further his father's dream of a cultural/educational center.

50. Miller was a member of the chamber's Prime Time Steering Committee and Task Force, its Economic Development Committee, and its Presidents' Club, of which he is a lifetime member.

51. A small post office facility was placed in the lower level of the Plaza public library, but a larger facility has yet to be built.

52. The company also began a decade-long study of how to control future flooding. In 1993 a $43-million engineering project was undertaken that should not only prevent future flooding but also beautify the Country Club Plaza and the cultural/educational center to the east.

53. Some years later, Stanley Marcus confessed personally to Miller, when the two met at Nancy Lopez's home in Santa Fe, his regret that Nieman Marcus had missed this opportunity.

54. Fearing that budget cuts might one day eliminate flowers on the bridge, Miller raised enough money to endow the bridge with a fund for this and placed it with the Greater Kansas City Community Foundation.

55. At the dedication of the Cancer Survivors' Park, Anita Gorman, president of the Park Board, announced that in accordance with Miller Nichols' recommendation, gifts for park land would no longer be accepted unless their maintenance was endowed. "And, Miller," she said, "endowment for this park is already in the bank earning interest."

56. The design of 4900 Main calls for the eventual addition of a second office tower to the south.

57. No date has yet been set for the second high-rise office building which would complete this project.

58. At the May 7, 1978, salute to Miller, tributes included the following: Dutton Brookfield, who frequently referred to Miller as "White Heat": "I respect you because you haven't tried to be all things to all people. You are careful to limit your involvement to things you believe in. And when you make up your mind to do something, there isn't anything you can't do."

Jim Kemper, chairman of Commerce Bancshares and on whose board Miller had served for nearly 30 years: "Our relationship goes back to my grandfather and your father. We have also shared similar problems, being in businesses where our forbearers were well-known.

"I think one of your greatest characteristics is having a point of view and sticking to it. You may not always be right, but you are always there and you are going to be heard. You are a very persistent and determined man—a fighter who won't give up. And you don't ask other people to do something you are not willing to do. You put your effort where your mouth is. In serving on our board of directors, your definite point of view in community affairs has encouraged us to get into other banking endeavors. You are a skilled businessman, a master at negotiating.

"You epitomize cultural good taste and you have been willing to put sweat and blood into it. Equally important, you are a *maintainer*. If you have built something, you want it to be maintained, to endure. Somehow everyone feels like they should give you advice."

Don Hall, president of Hallmark: "Miller, you are practical and direct, a real pragmatist. You don't get caught up in niceties and side issues of a question. Instead, you get to the crucial point. You're impatient for an answer, action, results. Once convinced of a cause and a course, you are Kansas City's most courageous and tireless worker."

Dave Jackson of the J.C. Nichols Company: "You have always had a keen understanding of the contribution of the Nichols Company to this community in the way of orderly, sound development of residential and commercial property, that they may serve as a standard for others. Your leadership has resulted in an organization that can be counted on to carry out your philosophies in the years ahead."

Don Smith, regional head of Southwestern Bell: "There is a single word that describes the unique quality you have which has benefited Kansas City in so many ways over the years. Perspicacity."

In the early 1980s, Miller Nichols received the University of Kansas Distinguished Service Cita-tion, the William Booth Award for Humanitarian Service from the Salvation Army, and the William F. Yates Medallion for Distinguished Service from William Jewell College, while serving on the Executive Committee of the Civic Council and the Board of Trustees of the Midwest Research Institute.

59. The clock tower was Miller's gift to the Plaza in 1992.

Source Notes

As this book is intended to be a popularly written chronicle rather than a scholarly history, not all information is documented in detail. It is not a primary research source. However, everything in it came from somewhere; so, for those who wish to dig deeper, we have attempted to cite sources by subject and information in the pages. For more detailed information on the citations, including the location of the sources, see the Bibliography.

We are especially indebted to those who wrote dissertations on J.C. Nichols, his work, and his influence: William Worley, Mary Katherine Goldsmith, Gary Molyneaux, and Kristie Wolferman. The 70 large volumes of company scrapbooks are, like most people's scrapbooks, a rather random, unorganized collection of clippings from newspapers, company bulletins, etc. They are readily available in the company archives, but specific references to individual items in their pages would be tedious, difficult, and impractical.

Prologue

p. xiii	Opening paragraph: interview with Nichols, Jr.
p. xiii	Bantering with barber: ibid.
pp. xiii–xiv	Evelyn Fisher story: ibid.
p. xv	Quotes from visitors to J.C. Nichols' developments and from NAREB secretary: Goldsmith, "J.C. Nichols," p. 140.
p. xv	R.A. Long story: interview with Clyde Nichols, Jr.
p. xv	Oklahoma City visitors story: ibid.
p. xvi	The lasting impact on the nation's capital by the Planning Commission: Gutheim, *Worthy of the Nation.*
p. xvii	Quote on Nichols' impact on Kansas City: Haskell and Fowler, *City of the Future,* p. 119

Chapter 1: Before 1880

pp. 1–6	For this entire section, the primary sources are the Genealogy and Fannie (Oslin) Jackson's journal; J.C. Nichols' memoirs, pp. 1–6; Connelly, *A Standard History of Kansas and Kansans,* pp. 2279–80.
pp. 6–9	For the background of this section and information on Llewellyn Park, Lake Forest, and Riverside: Worley, *J.C. Nichols,* chap. 1; Goldsmith, "J.C. Nichols," chap. 5.
p. 9	1803–1838: "History of Metropolitan Kansas City"; Worley, *J.C. Nichols,* p. 50.

p. 9	Story of "One-Eyed Ellis": *Kansas City Star* clipping, Missouri Valley Room, Kansas City Public Library.
pp. 9–10	Dr. David Waldo, John B. Warnall, and the Battle of Westport: J.C. Nichols Company paper on "History and Development of the Country Club District
pp. 10–12	Figures on Kansas City in 1854; story of Kersey Coates; rest of chapter: Worley, *J.C. Nichols*, pp. 51–58.

Chapter 2: 1880–1905

pp. 13–22	Primary source for entire section: J.C. Nichols' memoirs, except for quotes credited in the text.
pp. 22–25	Ibid. J.C.'s Reed Brothers experience through hiring of John Taylor: Goldsmith, "J.C. Nichols," chap. 1.
p. 25	Figures on the city as "Gateway to the West": "History of Metropolitan Kansas City."
pp. 25–26	Information on city leaders: interview with Jeannette Nichols; also, newspaper clippings, Missouri Valley Room, Kansas City Public Library.
pp. 26–28	Rebuilding the first Convention Hall; Parks and Boulevard Movement: Goldsmith, "J.C. Nichols," pp. 18ff.
pp. 28–31	Transportation, Hyde Park, Rockhill: Worley, *J.C. Nichols*, pp. 59–73.
p. 31	City Beautiful Movement and other influences on William Rockhill Nelson and Mary Atkins: Goldsmith, "J.C. Nichols," p. 159; Wolferman, "Creation of the Nelson-Atkins Museum," pp. 20–33.
pp. 31–33	Roland Park: Goldsmith, "J.C. Nichols," p. 49; Worley, *J.C. Nichols*, pp. 40–44.

Chapter 3: 1905–1920

pp. 34–56	The sources for this entire section, except where otherwise credited in the text, are: J.C. Nichols memoirs; Goldsmith, "J.C. Nichols," pp. 27–78; Worley, *J.C. Nichols*, pp. 74–198.
pp. 56–63	Worley, *J.C. Nichols*, pp. 86–88; Goldsmith, "J.C. Nichols," pp. 79–92.
p. 64	J.C. Nichols memoirs.
p. 64	J.C. Nichols Company Fact Book, biographies of officers, pp. 27–38, and interviews with Bob Boeshaar, John Ruddy, Fred Gibson, Gordon Jarchow. Other references are credited in the text.
pp. 65–67	Worley, *J.C. Nichols*, pp. 252–257; Goldsmith, "J.C. Nichols," p. 116.
p. 67	Conservatory of Music: Goldsmith, "J.C. Nichols," pp. 171–172.
p. 67	Kansas City Art Institute: Goldsmith, "J.C. Nichols," pp. 170–171.
p. 67	Union Station beautification: Goldsmith, "J.C. Nichols," pp. 159–162.
pp. 68–70	J.C. Nichols Company Scrapbooks.
pp. 69–70	NAREB 1925 speech: NAR Archives.
pp. 70–72	City planning: Goldsmith, "J.C. Nichols," pp. 141–147.
pp. 72–75	Primary sources for this section: *History of Pembroke–Country Day School for Boys; History of Sunset Hill School.*
p. 75	Goldsmith, "J.C. Nichols," pp. 173–174.
pp. 75–77	The primary sources for this section: interviews with Miller and Jeannette Nichols; Marty and Clyde Nichols, Jr.

Chapter 4: 1920–1929

p. 78	Small committee: Goldsmith, "J.C. Nichols," p. 162.
pp. 78–79	First board minutes; J.C. and naming of monument: Aber, "Architectural History of the Liberty Memorial"; Liberty Memorial Archives.
pp. 78–79	Results of fund drive; report of meeting to celebrate: clippings in J.C. Nichols Company Scrapbooks.
p. 79	Location committee; selection of site: Aber, "Architectural History of the Liberty Memorial."
p. 79	Mazda Realty Company; acquisition of land: Haskell and Fowler, *City of the Future*, pp. 120–121.
p. 79	Site dedication: Goldsmith "J.C. Nichols," pp. 162–164; Aber, "Architectural History of the Liberty Memorial."
p. 81	Description of planned memorial: ibid.
p. 81	Dedication of column completion: Goldsmith, "J.C. Nichols," p. 164; personal memory of author.
p. 81	Completion of project: Aber, "Architectural History of the Liberty Memorial."
pp. 81–82	J.C. Nichols memoirs, pp. 47–48.
p. 81	Goldsmith, "J.C. Nichols," pp. 175–176.
pp. 82–84	Goldsmith, "J.C. Nichols," pp. 177–180.
pp. 82–84	J.C. Nichols memoirs, pp. 51–52.
pp. 85–86	Stanley McLane and the company nursery: J.C. Nichols Company Fact Book, p. 5; Goldsmith, "J.C. Nichols," pp. 101–102.
p. 86	Farm department; Ray D. Jones: Goldsmith, "J.C. Nichols," p. 81; J.C. Nichols Company Scrapbooks.
p. 280n23	Ed Tanner: J.C. Nichols Company Fact Book, pp. 31–32; Worley, *J.C. Nichols*, p. 199; Goldsmith, "J.C. Nichols," pp. 99–100; J.C. Nichols Company Scrapbooks.
p. 86	Ansel Mitchell: J.C. Nichols Company Fact Book, pp. 35–36; Goldsmith, "J.C. Nichols," pp. 106–107; J.C. Nichols Company Scrapbooks.
pp. 86–87	Kansas City Country Club; Loose Park: Worley, *J.C. Nichols*, pp. 126, 288.
p. 87	Southwest High School: ibid., pp. 295–296.
p. 89	Model Boat Regattas: ibid., p. 305.
pp. 89–90	Christmas caroling party: ibid., p. 306.
pp. 90	Homeowners associations: ibid., p. 192.
pp. 90–91	City planning and zoning: Goldsmith, "J.C. Nichols," pp. 141–148.
pp. 90–91	John Taylor's retirement talk remarks on zoning: J.C. Nichols Company Scrapbooks.
p. 91	Restrictions: Worley, *J.C. Nichols*, p. 146.
p. 91	Attraction of wealthy and influential people to Country Club District: ibid., pp. 94–95.
pp. 91–94	Primary sources for this section: Worley, *J.C. Nichols*, pp. 254–281; Goldsmith, "J.C. Nichols," pp. 109–133, see other citations noted in text. J.C.N.'s travel experience on Liberty Bond drives and vision of importance of the automobile: interview with Clyde Nichols, Jr.
p. 94	John Taylor's retirement talk: J.C. Nichols Company Scrapbooks.
p. 94	Story of Macy's failure to provide off-street parking downtown: interview with Clyde Nichols, Jr.
pp. 95–96	Anecdote of Tourtellot and Taylor's plane adventure: J.C. Nichols Company Scrapbooks.

Chapter 5: 1930–1939

p. 140   *History of Pembroke–Country Day School for Boys.*

p. 140   UKC opening: Western Historical Manuscript Collection, UMKC.

pp. 140–141   Liberty Memorial and Civic Center: Goldsmith, "J.C. Nichols," pp. 164–166.

pp. 141–149   Family: interviews with Clyde Nichols, Jr., Miller Nichols, and Lyman Field; and J.C. Nichols Company files.

p. 149   Eskew and MacDonald, *Of Land and Men.*

pp. 150–152   Primary source: Goldsmith, "J.C. Nichols," pp. 183–193.

Chapter 6: 1940–1950

pp. 153–155   Opening account of J.C.'s meeting with William Knudsen and lining up home support: interview with Clyde Nichols, Jr.; and Goldsmith, "J.C. Nichols," p. 198.

p. 154   Knudsen quote: Eskew and MacDonald, *Of Land and Men.*

pp. 154–155   John Taylor's 1940 memo: J.C. Nichols Company files.

p. 160   J.C. Nichols' rooftop photo session: notes from Sally Ruddy.

pp. 162–163   Primary source: Goldsmith, "J.C. Nichols," pp. 151–156.

pp. 163–168   Primary sources: Eskew and MacDonald, *Of Land and Men;* "Urban Land," publication of ULI; ULI News Service, December 1968 issue; Community Builders' Handbook.

p. 284n39   Nichols' investment north of the Missouri River: J.C. Nichols memoirs.

pp. 168–174   Primary sources: J.C. Nichols memoirs; Ethyl Treshadding's epilogue to memoirs; J.C. Nichols speech, "A Sleeping Industrial Giant," *Kansas City Journal,* Jan. 3, 1942; Kimball, *Midwest Research Institute;* Goldsmith, "J.C. Nichols," pp. 215–222.

pp. 174–178   Primary sources: J.C. Nichols Company files; interviews with company executives; interviews with Miller Nichols and Clyde Nichols, Jr., as noted in the text.

pp. 180–186   Primary sources: interviews with Marty and Clyde Nichols, Jr., Kay Nichols Callison, Suzie Allen.

p. 186   Bob O'Keefe quote: interview with Bob O'Keefe.

pp. 188–191   Details of funeral and tributes from obituary and accompanying articles: *Kansas City Star,* Feb. 17, 1950.

Chapter 7: 1950–1959

pp. 192–199   Sources indicated in the text.

p. 199   Midwest Research Institute: Kimball, *Midwest Research Institute.*

p. 199   Nicholas Pickard story: interview with Nicholas Pickard.

p. 201   Sunset Hill: *History of Sunset Hill School.*

pp. 201–202   Jeannette Nichols' recollections: interview with Jeannette Nichols.

pp. 201–202   Conservatory of Music: interview with Clyde Nichols, Jr.

pp. 203–204   Family interviews as indicated in text.

Chapter 8: 1960–1977

Chapter 9: 1978–1994

Selected Bibliography

Books

Community Builders' Handbook. Washington, D.C.:
Urban Land Institute, 1947.

Connelly, William E. *A Standard History of Kansas
and Kansans.* Chicago and New York: Lewis Pub-
lishing Company, 1918. See especially volume 5,
pages 2279–81.

Curran, Joan F. *Ancestors and Descendants of Jesse
Clyde Nichols and Jessie (Miller) Nichols.* Baltimore, Md.: Gateway Press, 1991.

Eskew, Garnett L., and John R. MacDonald. *Of
Land and Men.* Washington, D.C.: Urban Land
Institute, 1959.

Gutheim, Frederick. *Worthy of the Nation: The His-
tory of Planning for the National Capital.*
Washington, D.C.: Smithsonian Institution
Press, 1989.

Haskell, Henry C., and Richard B. Fowler. *City of
the Future: A Narrative History of Kansas City,
1850–1950.* Kansas City, Mo.: Frank Glenn Pub-
lishing Company.

Jackson, Fannie (Oslin). *On Both Sides of the Line.*
Journal edited by Joan F. Curran and Rudina K.
Mallory for Miller and Jeannette Nichols. Bal-
timore, Md.: Gateway Press. 1991.

Jackson, Kenneth T. *Crabgrass Frontier: The Suburbanization of the United States.* New York: Oxford
University Press, 1985.

Kimball, Charles N. *Midwest Research Institute,
1945–1975.* Kansas City, Mo.: Midwest Research
Institute, 1985.

Scofield, Carlton F. *A History of the University of
Kansas City.* Kansas City, Mo.: The Lowell Press,
1976.

Articles and Unpublished Works

Aber, Sarajane Sandusky. "An Architectural History of the Liberty Memorial, 1918–1935."
Master's thesis, UMKC.

Eckels, Mary, and Rosalee Ennis. "Listen to the
Echoes Ring: A History of the Sunset Hill
School." Smith-Grieves, Kansas City, Mo.: 1985.

Goldsmith, Mary Katherine. "J.C. Nichols—City
Builder." Ph.D. dissertation.

"A History of Metropolitan Kansas City." Prepared
by the Public Relations Department of the J.C.
Nichols Company.

"The J.C. Nichols Number." Special issue of *National Real Estate Journal* (February 1939).

Longstreth, Richard. "J.C. Nichols, the Country
Club Plaza, and Notions of Modernity." *Harvard
Architectural Review* (date unknown); copy in
Western Historical Manuscript Collection,
UMKC.

Molyneaux, Gary O.A. "Planned Use Change in an Urban Setting: The J.C. Nichols Company and the Country Club District of Kansas City." Ph.D. dissertation, University of Illinois, 1979.

Schulkin, Carl. "In Pursuit of Greatness: A History of Pembroke–Country Day School." Smith-Grieves, Kansas City, Mo.: 1985.

"The Story of the Country Club Plaza" and "History and Development of the Country Club District." Prepared by the Public Relations Department of the J.C. Nichols Company.

Wenske, Paul. "The J.C. Nichols Co.—A Family's Vision Helps Shape a City." Profile section of the *Kansas City Times*, November 22, 1964.

Wolferman, Kristie C. "The Creation of the Nelson-Atkins Museum of Art, 1911–1933." Master's thesis, UMKC, 1970. (Subsequently published as a book by University of Missouri Press, 1993.)

Worley, William S. *J.C. Nichols and the Origins of the Planned Residential Community in the United States, 1903–1930*. Ph.D. dissertation, University of Kansas, 1986. Ann Arbor, Mich.: University Microfilms International, 1988. (Later published as *J.C. Nichols and the Shaping of Kansas City*. Columbia: University of Missouri Press, 1990.)

Public Records and Other Sources

J.C. Nichols. "Autobiography" (herein referred to, by request of his family, as his memoirs). Written in 1949/50 just prior to his death; with epilogue by Ethel V. Treshadding. Manuscript. J.C. Nichols Company Archives.

———. Letters and papers. Western Historical Manuscript Collection, UMKC.

J.C. Nichols Company. Fact Book. Prepared by the Public Relations Department of the J.C. Nichols Company.

———. Scrapbooks (70 volumes). J.C. Nichols Company Archives. Microfilmed copies available in the Western Historical Manuscript Collection, UMKC.

Liberty Memorial. Archives. Kansas City, Mo.

National Association of Realtors (formerly NAREB). Archives. 430 North Michigan Ave., Chicago, Ill.

National Capital Parks and Planning Commission, 1926–1946. Minutes. National Archives, Washington, D.C.

"Published Articles about J.C. Nichols, Speeches about J.C. Nichols, and Speeches by J.C. Nichols." Looseleaf bound. J.C. Nichols Company Archives.

Urban Land Institute (ULI). Archives. 1090 Vermont Avenue N.W., Washington, D.C.

Authors' Interviews

Miller and Jeannette Nichols; Clyde, Jr., and Marty Nichols. Also, former and present personnel of J.C. Nichols Company, including Dave Jackson, Lynn McCarthy, Robert O'Keefe, Fred Gibson, Gordon Jarchow, Marian Pitrat, Katherine Tanner, Helen Harvey, Barbara Barickman, Randy Knight, Helen Mitchell (Thorne), John Ruddy, Kay Nichols Callison, Lee Fowler, Bob Boeshaar, Moe Courville, Marsha Goldman. Also, Howard Turtle, Phil Pistilli, Kristie Wolferman, Lindsay Hughes Cooper, Nicholas Pickard. Also, for views on J.C. and Miller: Lyman Field, Cliff Jones, George C. Dillon, Mayor Ike Davis, Dr. Dave Robinson, Michael White. Tapes and transcriptions are kept in the files of Robert Pearson Associates Writing Services, 17 Jones Park, Riverside, Connecticut 06878.

Index